1971

This b[illegible]

THE WAY OUR PEOPLE LIVED

W. E. WOODWARD

has also written

BUNK

LOTTERY

BREAD AND CIRCUSES

GEORGE WASHINGTON—The Image and the Man

MEET GENERAL GRANT

MONEY FOR TOMORROW

EVELYN PRENTICE

A NEW AMERICAN HISTORY

LAFAYETTE

(*The Bettmann Archive*)

A COVERED WAGON AND TEAM THAT CROSSED THE PLAINS.

American frontiersman and his family. (Painting school of Darley.)

THE WAY OUR PEOPLE LIVED

AN INTIMATE AMERICAN HISTORY

☆ ☆ ☆ ☆ ☆

by WILLIAM E. WOODWARD

☆ ☆ ☆

With Illustrations Showing the Habits, Manners and Customs of Different Periods in American Life.

LIVERIGHT PUBLISHING CORPORATION
New York

Library of Congress Catalog Card No. 63-8714

PRINTED IN THE UNITED STATES OF AMERICA

To My Friend

DR. HENRY E. MARKS

CONTENTS

LIST OF ILLUSTRATIONS

INTRODUCTION

MOST AMERICANS know the history of the United States in terms of battles and victories, of great sweeps like the Gold Rush, but few Americans know how their ancestors lived every day from breakfast to lunch, to supper, to going to bed weekdays and Sundays. Consider the Gold Rush. We all have visions of the covered wagon, the sailing ships landing in San Francisco Bay, the horses, but—what did they eat, when did they sleep, how many brought women or children, how did they talk? A dozen such questions arise and are answered in this book.

But there is a question that rides over all these—how does this affect our living today? It is almost astounding how the story of the past ties in both with our political and our international life today.

To know what people did in the past makes emergencies today easier to solve. It also makes easier to understand the character of our people and the inner reasons for our fabulous growth.

For instance, "A Country Store in the Times of our Grandfathers," a "general store" sold all kinds of things. We grew away from that to separate stores for groceries, meat and clothes. But what is happening today? We are going right back to that general store idea, only we call it a supermarket.

The modern "general store" started out, perhaps, as a grocery. Now it sells TV sets, cameras, clothing, shrubs, plants or what you will. It seems to be reaching the point where it will fill our every need. Well, the country store filled every need in days gone by. To be sure, it was probably not quite so neat and clean as markets today, but the reason for their being is the same.

Let us look at the illustration "The Country Peddler." Most of the people lived on farms or in villages, and the general store could not fill all their needs, so that for them the coming of the peddler was a great event. He had a real standing in the old days because he was badly needed since the roads were bad and the horses busy. Later, the need declined and his position declined with it until he became of rather shady repute and almost disappeared. But now the need for his service has risen again because of crowded roads and busy mothers. So the "country peddler" is back, only we call him the "Shopmobile."

Or, look at "Husking Bee in New England." Sometimes we are apt to think that the talk of decay in morals is something new. But it's just a matter of "olden days are here again." Our ancestors had that problem, too.

The picture "Interior of the First Pullman Car" reminds us, as we rest comfortably in a plane flying from coast-to-coast, that this primitive pullman, not suitable for ladies, was a giant step on the way to modern travel. But the little things, for instance the cuspidors, that vanished from the scene, were replaced with little antiseptic bags, and it is important to know that this development in travel, so much of it born in the United States, grew out of the everyday needs of the everyday people of the country, of the vast spaces that had to be covered. It came, too, as we see in reading the day-to-day story of these, our people, in the past because when a man had an idea that would make things better, he went ahead, showed it, got a patent and took his reward in royalties. And that goes on today on any Saturday, as we can see while glancing through the news of patents in *The New York Times*.

It is because of vast spaces and big farms that Cyrus McCormick invented his highly effective mechanized reaper. Of course, Russia had vast spaces too and needed these great railways and this reaper as much as we did, but they lived under a tyranny under which a man had to get approval from a whole series of "higher-ups" before he could make an improvement, so he was likely to say "I can't go through all that red tape" and made the best of what he had.

"Making the best of it" has not been the philosophy of the people of the United States. Not only in the glorious days of our history, but in the simple story of work and pleasure of our people, what is known by historians as mores, can we understand what is happening today and make a judgment on what may be coming next.

It took an historian with William E. Woodward's perceptive interest in people as individuals to see the humanity behind the history and to reveal it in stories as full of romance, adventure, tragedy and comedy as these lively true stories of American families out of our rich past. Each chapter, indeed, is a short story in itself, vivid with suspense, motivation, conflict and character—each set against a background of local color, real and true. In fact, for all its entertaining warmth and liveliness, "The Way Our People Lived" is so meticulously accurate as history that other historians consult it for reference and research. One of them, for instance, Henry Bamford Parkes, Professor of History at New York University, says, "Mr. Woodward has had the novel idea of describing the customs, ideas and daily lives of typical Americans at different periods and places. 'The Way Our People Lived' holds the attention of the reader from start to finish, is filled with unusual and interesting information and sheds more light on the evolution of American civilization than do most formal histories."

To this may we add a hearty Amen!

HELEN WOODWARD

October, 1962

Chapter I

BOSTON THREE HUNDRED YEARS AGO

I

ONE MORNING in October of the year 1652 a man was walking slowly along a street in Boston, staring uncertainly at the houses, and stopping now and then to look around. He seemed to be lost in the maze of crooked streets and narrow, winding alleys. Boston was, in that time of long ago, a village of about two thousand inhabitants. Though it was a small place, anyone not familiar with the town might lose his way while looking for a particular house. Few streets had names and the numbering of houses was an unknown device.

The clothing and countrified appearance of the bewildered stranger showed him to be a laborer or farm hand. He wore knee breeches of soiled leather, woolen stockings, and shoes made of deer hide and shaped like Indian moccasins without heels or hard soles. They were laced with leather thongs. His soft-brown leather coat had large pockets; it was roomy and long, reaching halfway to his knees. The buttons on it were made of wood, and were clumsy and large. His shirt was of coarse gray cloth and he wore a cap of rabbit skin with the fur still on it.

After a while he spoke timidly to a shopkeeper, who was standing in the street before his shop, and inquired the way to Master Doolittle's house. "Ye want to go to Doolittle's? It's not far from here," said the shopkeeper, looking at the man. "Follow your nose to the next corner, then turn to the right. Ye hear me?"

"Aye, sir," the man said.

"Turn to the right and when ye come to the Ship's Tavern, then turn to the left." He swept his arm around to show how the turn should be made. "Walk straight ahead then and Doolittle's is the third house beyond the church."

"Thankee, sir," said the stranger and started on his way.

The street on which he was walking, like all other streets in Boston, was unpaved and rough. It was simply a country road, with houses on both sides, and its surface was speckled with holes and humps. There was nothing unusual about that, for even the streets of London in that era had been left as nature made them.

Nearly all the houses in the town were built of wood.[1] Only a few of them were painted, and those were called "colored" houses and were looked upon as curiosities. The lack of paint gave the streets a brownish, drab appearance which was relieved a little by the gaily colored signs that swung out from the fronts of shops and taverns.

There were no log houses in Boston, nor anywhere else in the English colonies at that time. This fact will be, no doubt, somewhat disappointing to numerous modern illustrators who have drawn fanciful pictures of scenes in Plymouth and Boston with rows of log houses in the background. The typical middle-class house in New England towns throughout the seventeenth century resembled from the outside the houses that one sees today in factory towns—a two story, bare-looking, boxlike structure, without a porch.[2]

The man in the leather coat, following directions, reached the Ship's Tavern and had turned the corner when the thought occurred to him that there was no need of haste, rushing around and running his head off. Why not go into the tavern for awhile and drink some beer? There were a few pennies in his pocket. He decided that they could not be spent in a better fashion and after some little hesitation he pushed open the door and entered the tavern's long room. His movements were almost furtive and catlike; he was not sure that he would be welcome in the fine and prosperous-looking tavern. He was an indentured servant, sold to a master whom he had to serve for a term of years, and his social status revealed itself in his

[1] At that time there were brickyards in the colony of Massachusetts but the bricks were used almost wholly for chimneys and fireplaces and for the construction of baking ovens in the back yards. The first brick house in Boston was built in 1638, but it was many years before brick supplanted timber as a building material.

[2] The early English settlers had never seen a log house nor had even heard of one. Timber was too valuable in England to be wasted in such a fashion. But not so in Sweden, where most of the country was covered by forests. The first log houses in America were probably built by the Swedes who settled on the Delaware River. Eventually some were put up in New England, but the log cabin never attained much popularity on the Atlantic seaboard.

dress and manner. He slipped quietly along the dark-paneled wall of the room and seated himself in a corner on a bench before which stood a solid oak table.

The other men in the room gave him a mere glance and in a moment a red-faced fat man, wearing an apron, came over to the table. He thought that he would be ordered to sit in another room, but the fat man merely asked him what he wanted. He said he wanted a quart of beer and the man went off to fetch it. There was no doubt that he was welcome, and taken as a matter of course. He was surprised and pleased.

The long room had a low ceiling. The windows were small and the light came through diamond-shaped panes. On a shelf that ran all around the room, a little higher than a man's head, there stood a row of drinking vessels. Some of them were of pewter, but most of them were made of wood or leather. Opposite the windows there was a large brick chimney and fireplace. The hearth was so wide that a seven-foot log could be laid on it and the big-throated chimney was almost as deep as a small room. On this pleasant October day only a tiny fire—a nest of embers and hot coals—was burning in the center of the capacious hearth. Close to the chimney a door opened on a little room—or bar—where the liquors were stored and served.

The humble stranger did not inquire the price of his quart of beer, for he knew that it would cost twopence. That was the rate established by law, so when the aproned man brought the beer to him in a great leather flagon he laid his two pennies on the table.

The inns and taverns—usually called "ordinaries"—were permitted to sell beer and cider and a few varieties of light wine at regulated prices, but they were forbidden to sell sack, which was a strong and heady drink. Yet almost every vessel that came from Europe brought many casks of sack, which were sold to individuals who kept them in their cellars. Sack was a customary beverage at family festivals and convivial parties.

Even the sale of beer in the ordinaries was restricted to some extent. They were permitted to sell only one quart to each customer between meals, and as much as he wanted at meals. That meant the drinker could have one quart in the morning, one in the afternoon, and one in the evening, besides a quart at each meal from breakfast on. It would seem to be enough to satisfy even the most capacious beer drinkers, though evidently it was not, or the restriction would have been unnecessary.

Besides the indentured servant in the tavern's long room there were several other customers. Most of them were seafaring men, captains or mates of vessels in the harbor. The townsmen were too busily at work during the daytime to frequent the ordinaries, though they were there in numbers during the evening. As he drank his beer and listened to the sailors' breezy talk the servant kept looking anxiously around. He was afraid of being taken up as an idler because he was sitting in a tavern doing nothing. But he had an explanation at his tongue's end. He would say that he was Captain Brewer's servant and that he had been sent to town on the captain's business.

The law against idleness was severe; it was, indeed, one of the most drastic in the Puritan code. Anyone might be convicted of this offense and fined two and a half shillings if he passed more than an hour drinking in a public house during working hours. The punishment for inveterate idleness was a whipping on the bare back. For the third offense the lazy man was whipped to the boundaries of the township, and turned over there to the authorities of the next town, who whipped him through that township, and so on. The law does not say where the whipping stopped; presumably it kept on until the shirker decided to go to work.

2

When the farm hand had finished his quart of beer he rose, wiped his mouth with the back of his hand, and went out to continue his journey to Mr. Doolittle's house. A little way from the tavern he saw Doolittle's sign on a pole before a house and garden. The name "William Doolittle," painted in heavy black letters on the sign meant nothing to him, as he had never learned to read, but he understood pictures and the gaudy but crudely painted picture beneath the name told him that he had reached his destination. It showed a man standing by a cupboard with his hand on it.

The door of the shop opened on the street. The man entered, removed his cap and stood waiting. Several men and boys were at work in the place, hammering nails and planing boards. Sawdust lay on the floor. Scattered about the shop there was a number of cabinets, chests and tables. The bright sunshine fell on their gleaming surfaces.

William Doolittle, a tall, jolly looking man, whose hair was turning gray, came forward. His clothes were made of fine dark cloth; his coat had silver buttons on it and his broad, starched neckcloth or collar was folded over so that it reached to his shoulders. These were his best clothes, hardly ever worn except on Sundays or for ceremonial occasions. Ordinarily he wore the garments of a workman, but he had planned to call on some important people and he wanted to look his best.

Turning his smiling eyes on the man before him he said, "Looking for me?"

"Be ye Master Doolittle?" the man inquired, nervously turning his cap in his hands.

"Aye, that's my name."

"I be sent here by Captain Brewer, my master," said the servant. "He sent me here, sir, into Boston to bring back the chest of drawers you made for him."

"Oh, ho!" exclaimed William Doolittle with a sigh. "It is not finished. Not till Saturday. Tell Captain Brewer—" He broke off suddenly and asked, "How did you expect to take it to him? Did you bring a pair of oxen? Captain Brewer lives ten miles in the country."

"I have a boat, sir," the man replied. "I will put it in the boat and take it up the river, but somebody'll have to help me lug it to the boat."

"I see. But it is not ready yet. Tell Captain Brewer that we are at odds and ends here right now. My daughter is to be married tomorrow—bu—but he knows that. There will not be much done tomorrow—Wednesday—and Thursday is lecture day and the shop will be closed. Tell him he can get it on Saturday, sure and certain. Wait, I shall put it in writing."

While Doolittle sat at a desk and wrote the note Brewer's servant stood looking at the work going on. Timidly he reached out his hand and rubbed the lid of a chest. "I wanted to see if the paint is dry," he said apologetically to the whole room at large. Nobody paid any attention to him.

Early colonial furniture was ordinarily left unpainted, though the wood was thoroughly smoothed and polished. Painted furniture was an innovation on William Doolittle's part. He began it in imitation of the furniture he had seen in wealthy homes in England.

When Doolittle had written the note on a single sheet of rather stiff paper he folded the sheet and sealed it with a blob of yellow wax, melted at the flame of a candle. All this took some time. An apprentice boy had to light the candle at a fire burning in an iron pot; the sealing wax had to be found; and then the wax was melted and applied to the paper.[3]

Handing the letter to the servant he said, "It's noon time, and you have a journey before you. Go into the kitchen and get your dinner. Come this way." With the man following him he went to the back of the shop and threw open a door. Instantly the rich smell of roasting meats and spicy cakes, mingled with wisps of smoke, floated into the shop. A couple of maids scurried about the kitchen, preparing for tomorrow's wedding feast. "Give this man something to eat," said the master as Captain Brewer's servant went past him.

3

William Doolittle was born in England, like nearly all the men and women past the age of twenty who were then living in Boston. In his youth he had served an apprenticeship in the shop of a joiner, or cabinetmaker, in the English town of Northampton. He became an expert workman, skilled in the art and mystery of making handsome and durable furniture, but he had never been able to earn more than a journeyman's meager wages until he came to the New World across the sea.

Both he and his wife had been brought up as Non-Conformists, or Puritans, and had accepted the Puritan system of theology and civil government as a matter of course. Doolittle never thought much about such matters. He was a kindly,

[3] It is an astonishing fact—or so it seems to one who has great respect for human inventiveness—that envelopes for letters did not come into use until 1839. The envelope is such a simple contrivance that the idea might have occurred to anybody, one would think. Our forefathers folded their letters both ways, sealed them with wax and wrote the address on the back.

good-natured person, little given to introspection and moral doubts. He had some difficulty in keeping awake in church during the long sermons—especially on pleasant summer Sundays—yet he thought the sermons excellent and the preachers splendid.

When he arrived in Boston in 1631 he was thirty years old. He had left his wife and children in England, to remain until he could afford to send for them. Before he had been three months in the colony his little, one-man cabinetmaker's shop was swamped with orders. Without much forethought or design he had run into good fortune.

Furniture was too bulky to be brought over in quantity on the crowded little vessels, and many of the settlers' homes were almost as bare as an empty house. Occasionally a ship with a cargo of furniture—tables, chairs, chests of drawers, beds and other articles for house-furnishing—arrived in port, but the imported furniture was usually too high in price to have a ready sale. Doolittle and the other cabinetmakers of the colony (Longfellow's John Alden was one of them) could make a cupboard or a bed of native materials and sell it at a profit for much less than the cost of a similar article made in England and shipped across the sea.

Small as it was, Boston at that time—in the 1650's—was the largest community in the English colonies, and its seaport was the busiest. During the summer months there were often as many as a dozen ships in the harbor, and seamen were a familiar sight in the streets and taverns. Whenever a ship was seen to be coming in the town crier, beating his drum, went all over town announcing the news. Then people—men, women and children—hurried to the waterside and stood there talking, laughing and running around in high spirits while the boats from the ship were rowed ashore. The captain and the crew usually brought foreign goods to sell as a private speculation of their own and it was generally believed that excellent bargains could be picked up from these traders on the beach.[4]

[4] Boston and other Massachusetts towns were shipbuilding centers. This industry developed early in colonial history. The *Blessing of the Bay,* a thirty-ton sloop, built for Governor John Winthrop, was launched in August, 1631. At one time forty ships were being built simultaneously in Boston shipyards. These vessels were quite small compared to modern standards. Most of them were under

The ships brought cargoes of fabrics, household implements and tools, glass windowpanes, blankets, looking glasses, writing paper, pewter dishes and various kinds of liquor and rare foodstuffs, such as oranges, nutmegs and ginger. When they sailed for home they carried barrel staves, dried fish, beaver skins and other colonial products. But the ships usually remained in port for weeks. Everything in the nature of commerce was conducted in a leisurely manner. The transocean voyage took from five to ten weeks, so the shipmasters were inclined to look upon an extra week's stay in port as a matter of small importance. After a ship was ready to sail it was sometimes held for days while the governor of the colony got ready his packet of letters to England, or while some colonial man of affairs made his preparations to take passage in the vessel.

William Doolittle prospered in his trade. He sent to England for his wife and three children. His wife came—with one child, Robert, then four years of age. A little girl had died in England before his wife sailed, and another died on shipboard. Since she came twenty years ago, Mrs. Doolittle had given birth to eight more children, of whom four had died.

Soon after the arrival of his family the town authorities made Doolittle a grant of two acres of land in the town of Boston. His dwelling house and shop were built on land thus acquired.[5]

---

two hundred tons, but it may be remembered that the *Mayflower* was a vessel of one hundred and eighty tons, yet it brought one hundred Pilgrims safely across the Atlantic. On account of the cheapness of lumber ships of all kinds could be built in New England for about one-half of the cost of a similar vessel in England.

[5] The system of land ownership in early Massachusetts was somewhat peculiar. All the land belonged originally to the Massachusetts Bay Company, the English Puritan corporation that planned the settlement of the colony. The corporation's title came from the king. The land was not sold to the settlers, but given to them. Grants were made to groups of settlers who agreed to establish a new township. Dedham was granted to nineteen proprietors; Hadley to fifty-nine. These proprietors thus became the actual owners of the soil. They disposed of the land which they did not actually need. Reputable persons who desired to live and work in the township were usually given (or granted) parcels of land, for which they paid nothing except the legal recording fees. Sometimes, however, the township authorities sold tracts of land. Before the end of the seventeenth century this system was abandoned and the land was sold by auction. This led to an orgy of land speculation.

4

As soon as Captain Brewer's servant, whose name was John Nottey, entered the kitchen he lost his tongue-tied shyness and made himself at home. Seated at a table with roast meat, hot bread just from the oven, succotash, a pie and a leather flagon of homemade beer before him, he told the girls startling stories of his life. They became so interested in these tales that they paused in their work and stood listening.

One of his hair-raising adventures had happened one day last week, he said. According to his account he and the Captain went out in the woods hunting a large and fierce bear that had been frightening everybody for miles around. They tracked the brute down after much patient work, but he turned in his tracks and started toward them. Captain Brewer fired at him and missed. Then the Captain with the bear coming straight at him, turned and tried to climb a tree. At the same time he called out "John, help me, help me! Shoot him!" But it seems that John had already leveled his musket at the bear, and taking good aim, put a bullet through his heart. "We've had a lot of fine roast bear meat since then and still have some left," said John Nottey.

The tale was strictly true with only one exception, where John got a little mixed. He was the one who tried to climb the tree, and it was he who called out to the Captain, "Save me, save me!" And then the Captain shot the bear.

Its recital made a great impression on the girls in the kitchen, and they were sorry when he had to leave. They did not know that the lifelong guiding motto of John Nottey was "Tell 'em whatever they like to hear." Sometimes it got him into trouble, especially when he was dealing with men, but on the whole it made life more pleasant all around.

Although Doolittle had no difficulty in selling the products of his shop he encountered other difficulties which had seemed, at times to be insurmountable. There were only a few men in the colony who had been trained as cabinetmakers and all of them were employed. As his trade grew he needed assistants; in the end he found that he would have to teach them himself. In 1652 he had two assistants in his shop, also two apprentices and an indentured servant who was neither cabinetmaker nor apprentice, but a laborer. The indentured servant was working off a debt which represented the cost of his transportation as an emigrant from Europe.

These workmen were paid the wages established by law. The Puritan sense of discipline and detail always alert, had led the lawgivers into the regulation of all commercial transactions, and the question of wages had not been neglected. Skilled workers were paid two shillings a day, and unskilled workers one and a half shillings. The skilled worker's wages were reduced to fourteen pence a day if he lived with his master's family and had no board to pay.

The regulations concerning apprentices varied according to the trade and the locality. In the Massachusetts colony boys usually began their apprenticeship around the age of fourteen, and they served seven years without pay, but the law required a master to feed and clothe his apprentices and to teach them his trade. He was not obliged to give them any money at all during their term of service, but most of the employers did give the lads a little spending money now and then. At the end of his seven years the apprentice was usually given a suit of clothing and a small sum of money.

Another one of Doolittle's difficulties lay in the chaotic state of the colonial currency system. It was against the law in Great Britain to send English money to the colonies. The theory was that the colonials should always be paid for their exports in English goods. Nevertheless, some gold sovereigns and silver shillings and copper pence did trickle in from the British Isles, though not nearly enough to carry on the daily transactions of a busy town.

Various standard commodities took the place of money; most of them were of doubtful, fluctuating value. Financial transactions went on in a fog of uncertainties. Business was a speculation that often ran into unforeseen results. On one occasion Doolittle sold a settle for a package of beaver skins. He sent the skins to a friend in England to be sold there, and learned to his pleased astonishment that the skins were worth twenty times the price of his settle. Their former owner might have purchased a roomful of furniture with them.

Most of the surprises, however, were unpleasant. At another time he accepted some Dutch cheeses in payment and found that they were rotten. A farmer brought in a hog and exchanged it for a stool. The hog had some infectious disease; it died in three days, after spreading the malady to the rest of his pigs.

Indian wampum—which was colored beads made from sea shells—also passed as money. Another form of currency consisted of musket balls. Each bullet was worth a farthing, but no one was compelled to take more than twelve of them at a time.

New England trade with the West Indies added still another factor to the currency situation. Spanish silver money was brought back from the islands by the New England traders, and it circulated in Boston and elsewhere. The doubloon, a Spanish gold coin, was worth about thirty-five shillings, and the Spanish silver dollar was considered equal to four English shillings.

William Doolittle usually paid his workmen in Spanish money, though they sometimes received their wages in English coins. He disposed of most of the farm produce that he had to accept in payment for his wares to the commissary department of the British troops that were quartered in the harbor forts. These officials always paid the bills of the garrison in English pounds and shillings. By means of this roundabout money-changing, strengthened by an instinct for economy, Doolittle had accumulated a sum of more than five hundred pounds in English coin which he kept hidden in a secret place in his house. (This safe deposit box was a hole inside the brick chimney where it ran through the attic.) There were no banks in Boston or anywhere else in the colonies at that time, or for many years thereafter. Every man was his own banker.

But in the fall of 1652 William Doolittle went around smiling, with a handful of new silver coins in his pocket. In June of that year the General Court of Massachusetts—which was the legislative body and lawmaker of the colony—had decided to create a silver coinage of its own. John Hull, a Boston silversmith, was appointed mint master of the colony. From the mint thus established came the famous Pine Tree shilling, the first money coined by an English colony in America. All the merchants were highly pleased, and so was nearly everyone else. The coins were a rarity for only a few weeks; after that everyone had them . . . if not Pine Tree Shillings, they had Pine Tree pence. As he handled these coins Doolittle felt a great relief at not having to take any longer, as payment for his goods, a strange variety of articles which ranged from buckets of honey and Spanish dollars to barrels of tar and beaver skins.[6]

To gain a clear view of the daily life of that period we must get some idea of the value of things as measured by the medium of exchange. Money was scarce and it went a long way when expended on merchandise or food. Two shillings a day as wages for a skilled workman seems small, but in the Boston of the seventeenth century it had about as much purchasing power as three dollars today.[7]

The prices of food were so low as to seem almost incredible. A fresh codfish, weighing a dozen pounds, was usually sold for twopence. For a quarter of venison one paid ninepence and it supplied enough meat for a week, even if the family was large. Small turkeys could be bought for a shilling, and a large one—weighing as much as forty pounds—for two shillings. Beer and cider, ordered at taverns cost twopence a quart but cider purchased direct from the farmers who made it could be had at the price of a quart for a penny. The rent of a two-room cottage amounted to only a few shillings a month. Every one—including day laborers—had a garden where he raised vegetables and kept a pig and a few chickens. A cartload of firewood cost as much as two shillings. The chief difficulty con-

[6] The arrangement with John Hull—his contract was to run for thirty-five years, or until 1686—provided that the silver for coinage be furnished him, and that for his services he was to be paid fifteen pence for every twenty shillings coined at his mint. It works out as a 6 per cent fee, which was outrageously high. Several years later the General Court endeavored to buy him off, or to have the fee reduced, or to set aside the contract. Hull refused to be bought off, or to reduce the fee, so the government was held to its bargain. When Hull died he left a large estate. Judge Sewall, who wrote the well-known diary that bears his name, married his daughter. Her father gave her, as a wedding present, her weight in Pine Tree shillings.

[7] My readers will understand, I am sure, that this is only an estimate. To determine the purchasing power of money in past centuries is a difficult problem, complicated by the personal habits and tastes of the people who lived in those eras. The rates charged by inns and hotels are usually typical of the prevailing cost of living. In the 1650's at the Ship's Tavern, of Boston, board and lodging were only three shillings a day. The board included wine at dinner and beer between meals.

nected with this commodity was in getting it to town, as there were only a few roads, and even the best of them would be considered intolerably bad in this motorcar era.

Candles were rather high in price, owing to a lack of tallow to make them. Poor people did not use them—or did very rarely. Instead of candles, they lighted their houses with fat splinters of pine. These substitutes for candles made a fierce, spluttering light and burned quickly, meanwhile dripping tar over the floor. Rush lights provided another form of illumination. They were made at home by soaking dried reeds in melted fat. The light given by the rushes was poor and extremely smoky.

Clothes were also expensive but they were made to last for years. Every home had a spinning wheel and a hand loom, and the women spent hours, every day, spinning and weaving.

The workman's two shillings a day were just about enough to keep him and his family well fed and poorly clothed. In those days there were no amusements that cost money, no newspapers to buy and read, no busses or streetcars, and fashions in clothes changed so slowly that a woman might wear the same dress for the greater part of her life.

The law regulating wages was breaking down and becoming a dead letter in 1652. That was managed by employers' making gifts to useful and valued workers. Doolittle gave Nicholas Bowen, one of his journeymen, three or four shillings a week in addition to his legal pay, and to the others employed by him a shilling now and then. There was no law against making gifts.

By the standards of prosperity current in that age Doolittle was well-to-do. Besides his secret store of coin he owned two farms and a sawmill which produced far more lumber than he required in making furniture. He sold all that he did not need to carpenters who used it in building houses.

The Massachusetts colony was not democratic in any sense. There were sharp class distinctions among the people. John Cotton, one of the Puritan leaders, set forth the basic principle of its government when he wrote in 1636 that "Democracy I do not conceive that ever God did ordain as a fit government either for church or commonwealth. If the people be governor who shall be governed? As for monarchy and aristocracy, they are both of them clearly approved and directed in Scripture." The idea that the people might govern themselves does not appear to have entered his mind.

Members of the "aristocracy" were known as freemen. They alone had the right to vote, and they had other rights which were not enjoyed by the common herd. To qualify as a freeman a citizen had to show—first, that he was a member of the Puritan Church, in good standing; second, that he was an industrious and law-abiding person; third, that he was worth, in property or money, at least two hundred pounds, or that he had an income which an invested two hundred pounds would bring to him. A man might be as pious as any of the Puritan martyrs, but if he did not possess two hundred pounds he had no voice in the conduct of public affairs.

The revised Charter of 1691 made some changes in these qualifications. The religious clause was dropped, and the right to vote was made dependent on the ownership of property which had a value of forty pounds sterling.

A freeman had the title of "Mister" while a common person without the franchise was called "Goodman" and his wife was known as "Goodwife," or "Goody" in ordinary speech. Those who could qualify as freemen were comparatively few. In 1670, when the population of Massachusetts was around 25,000, there were only 1100 who were classed as having the right to vote. The Charter of 1691, with its mere property provisions, increased the number of voters to about one-fifth of the adult male population.

Freemen only, and their wives, were permitted to wear costly garments or ornaments. One of the ordinances prohibited the common people from wearing woolen, silk or linen garments if they had silver, gold or lace thread on them. In 1651 the General Court again expressed its detestation "that men and women of meane conditions, education and calling, should take upon [them] the garbe of gentlemen by wearing gold or silver lace, or buttons or points at their knees, or walke in great boots, or women of the same rank to wear silke hoods or scarfs."

William Doolittle qualified as a freeman after he had lived in Boston a little more than two years. He was a good citizen, loyal and law-abiding, but not quite good enough to be elected to public office. His fault, in the eyes of the Puritan elders, was his jovial good humor and his tendency to overlook the failings of other people.

5

Early colonial furniture was rough, heavy and crudely fashioned. Most of it had been made by the settlers for themselves until the growing prosperity of New England attracted artisans from the mother country. A farmer and his sons would cut down trees, split the logs into rough planks, then plane them down until they were fairly smooth and of nearly the same thickness. From this material they made stools, chests, the frames of beds, and boards for the trestle tables which were set up for each meal and taken down afterward.[8] They also made trenchers out of thick boards. The trenchers were used as plates at the table. Larger ones, hollowed out more deeply, served as platters for bringing in the food. A trencher, as you may know, was a wooden dish. The early settlers had no chinaware, and only the well-to-do possessed pewter dishes and drinking cups. The beds were plain wooden frames with tall posts at the four corners. They were usually so high above the floor that feeble old people had to use steps to get into them. The trundle beds on which the young children slept were slipped under the high beds in the daytime. The beds had no springs; cords or ropes were stretched across them in a sort of network and a hay-filled mattress was laid over the cords. Thick curtains were used, not for privacy, but to keep out the drafts which swept through all New England houses at that time.

William Doolittle made all kinds of furniture of that period in his Boston shop, but he specialized in chests of drawers, cupboards, settles and high-backed chairs. The colonials of that era had no piece of furniture which was quite like the modern bureau with its mirrors and little drawers. Clothes

[8] The trestle table consisted of bare planks laid on trestles, which resembled the familiar sawhorses used by carpenters today. After the meal the trestles were moved into a corner of the room and the boards were set against the wall. The first houses were so small and so crowded with beds, kitchen utensils and the members of the family that there was hardly room for a large table to remain permanently in place.

and household linens were kept in chests. Every room in the house had one or more of these receptacles. In the "common" room—we call it a living room—of the better class there were usually several chests placed against the wall. With cushions on them they were used as seats. Chairs, strangely enough, were not in general use, though every Puritan home had one chair with a high back which was reserved for the head of the family. No one else dared to sit in it, even when the husband and father was not at home. A chair of this kind was rather stately; it gave a sort of pontifical look to its occupant. The rest of the family, including the wife and mother, sat on stools, or on the ever-present settle which invariably stood before the fire. This piece of furniture was simply a bench with a high back and sides. None of the furniture in a Puritan home would meet our definition of comfort. It was all hard, clumsy and heavy.

Doolittle's furniture had no great distinction, and is not to be found in museums, for it was made for use rather than for show. All of it was well-built, and durable. The cupboards and chests that came from his shop had drawers that did not stick and doors and lids that closed neatly. His favorite wood for cabinetmaking was oak, which does not shrink or get out of shape. But oak was expensive, and a large part of his product was made of pine to suit the purchasing power of his customers. Many could not afford to buy anything that cost more than a few shillings. All the chest drawers made by him were lined with cedar, no matter what kind of wood—oak, pine, maple or ash—was used for the body of the piece.

One of the products of his shop was called a "cistern." It looked like our modern water cooler, though it had no tap or faucet, and sometimes it was actually used to keep a supply of water, but its ordinary purpose was to hold beer or cider, which were customary household beverages. Water was regarded with deep suspicion, both in England and the colonies, and probably with just reason. Our forefathers knew nothing of sanitation in the modern sense, and the water of wells and springs must have been swarming with germs. Beer and cider were given even to small children with their meals—and between meals whenever they were thirsty. Nevertheless water, as a beverage, was being tried out timidly during the early

Puritan period. The Reverend Mr. Higginson, a minister of the time, wrote, "Whereas my stomach could only digest and did require such drink as was both strong and stale, I can and oftimes do drink New England water very well." There was a rumor that Governor Winthrop drank water daily and by preference but the rumor was not generally believed.

Many cisterns came from Doolittle's shop, and some of them were expensive because of the carving on them and their silver hoops. He and other cabinetmakers also sold mirrors with carved frames to hang on the wall. But in his seventeen years of experience in Boston he had made only three picture frames, and those were intended for oil paintings that had been brought from England. The ordinary colonial home in the seventeenth century had no pictures of any kind for the reason that pictures did not exist except in the form of paintings and these were too costly to be purchased—or even desired—by the average household. The walls of the rooms were usually bare, though sometimes pieces of inexpensive tapestry were hung up here and there in homes of the better class.

6

The building that housed the Doolittle family and the shop was in the form of the capital letter L. The shop, with its door on the street, may be compared to the short arm of the letter; the long arm was the dwelling place. In calling on the family one did not have to go through the shop; there was a gate on the street front, and a gravel walk, passing through a pleasant little flower garden, led up to the house.

The house had eight rooms, not counting the large room which the shop occupied. It was considered a large house. On the ground floor there was the wide, spacious kitchen next to the shop. Then came the common room, and beyond that a bedroom used by William Doolittle and his wife. The house had two chimneys and four fireplaces. One of the chimneys was built between the shop and the kitchen and the other between the common room and the adjoining bedroom. The chimneys were poorly planned, as they were everywhere in Boston and, as a matter of fact, in all the colonies. They were so wide and deep that, looked down upon from above, they would have seemed to be large square holes in the roof. Anyone standing inside the chimney and staring upward could see a large patch of blue sky. As a result of faulty construction most of the heat from the great log fire on the hearth went straight up the chimney instead of warming the room and, in return, wintry blasts came down these huge openings, driving the smoke before it. To get any of the warmth of the fire in cold weather one had to sit very close to it, and even then one's back would almost freeze while his face was hot.

On the second floor the house had five small rooms, but no fireplaces or any other method of heating. All the rooms upstairs were used for sleeping. The two apprentices occupied one room, and three rooms belonged to the five Doolittle children. There was also a spare room, to be slept in by occasional guests. Thomas Mackey, the indentured servant—a rough, surly fellow—slept in the barn, where he had a mattress on the floor. One of the maids had a bed in the kitchen; the other one went home at night.

In winter the bedrooms were as cold as iceboxes. The younger children undressed before the fire downstairs and dashed up to bed, with lighted candles in their hands. Robert, the oldest son of the family, and his sister Humility, a lass of eighteen, went up more sedately with a candle in one hand and a copper warming pan in the other. The warming pan was at the end of a long handle. It was inserted between the sheet to take the icy temperature out of the bedclothes. To keep it from setting the sheets ablaze its perforated lid was tightly closed after hot coals had been placed in the pan.

At mealtimes the family and servants ate together at a long table in the kitchen. Midway down the length of the table there was a handsome, brightly polished bowl of silver, standing on three legs and containing salt. It was known as "the standing salt," and it indicated a rigid social distinction between those who sat above the salt and those who sat below it.

Those who sat below the salt were the servants and others of inferior degree. The younger children of the family also were below the salt, as a rule, though in some families the children ate at a little table of their own. Indians were sometimes guests for a meal at a Puritan home. On such occasions the chief sat above the salt, and his followers below it. There

(*Paramount, 1937—N.Y. Public Library Collection*)

CAVALIER OF VIRGINIA IN THE 1690's.

was no difference in the quality of the food—or the amount of it—served to those at the two ends of the table. But the servants and inferiors who were below the salt were forbidden by custom from making remarks to those who sat above it, though when asked a question they replied to it. As soon as they had finished eating they were expected to rise silently and leave the room.

7

On the particular afternoon William Doolittle left the shop early and went into the house. His daughter Humility was to be married on the morrow. It was to be a joyous occasion, a festival of meats and puddings and warming liquors, with the singing of songs and the telling of jokes and strange stories. Doolittle thought, as he walked across the garden, that he ought to feel gay and lighthearted, but his mood was one of sadness. His family was to be broken up, he reflected, and in the Puritan way of life the family was a single unit of intense cohesiveness. After a moment he put the distressing notion out of his mind. Humility was a young woman; she needed a husband; and she was not leaving forever, never to be seen again; her new home was near by. Don't be an old fool, he said to himself.

The sun was shining brightly when he went over to the sundial in the garden. The shadow on the dial was between three and four; he thought it showed the time as about a quarter to four.[9] He loitered about the garden for awhile, looking at the plants. Most of the flowers were dead—it was the month of October—and he cared nothing whatever for them, but his wife liked them, and he commented now and then on the flower garden just to please her.

Then he stopped for a moment to look at his cows. He had two of them and a calf, kept in an enclosed yard and cowshed behind the house. Every morning apprentices drove them to the Common and then back again early in the afternoon. Doolittle liked the cows—liked to look at them and rub his hands over their soft, smooth hair. But he often wondered why he

[9] There were only a few clocks in the colonies. In 1652 they were almost nonexistent. People went by sundials which were, of course, useless in cloudy weather. In Boston there was a clock in the meetinghouse; it struck the hours and its great booming tones were heard all over the town.

had undertaken the trouble and expense of keeping them. Very few people of that era cared to drink milk, for there was a general impression that it caused various diseases, and maybe it did, as it was handled in a most unsanitary manner.

Though the head of the house liked milk, and drank it daily, the rest of the Doolittle family—including the servants and the apprentices—cared little for it, and the butter was used only in cooking. Milk was peddled from house to house in those days, and sold from open buckets at a penny a quart.[10]

When Doolittle entered the house his daughter was in the common room, rearranging some pieces of furniture. A few chairs and about a dozen stools, borrowed from the shop, stood against one wall of the room. Some ornaments, such as colored sea shells, which were usually kept in the attic, stood on the shelves of a cupboard. Humility, lithe and slender, wore a simple pale-gray dress. Her curls of dark hair fell to her shoulders. "We've got everything nearly ready, father," she said.

Her father sat down heavily in one of the chairs and she took a seat on a stool beside him. "I'm going to lose you, maidikin," he muttered, "and it grieves me to the heart."

"But you're not losing me, dear," the daughter said. "I shall be living near—over there"—she pointed to a window where the roof of a cottage showed itself under the elms, "and every day I shall be here."

"Aye, I know," he agreed. "I'm a foolish old man. I know you'll be happy and that's the great thing."

"Father, I've picked out my text for the sermon," Humility said, leaping nimbly to her feet.[11] She went over to a shelf on which a *Bible* stood, brought it back and sat on the stool, turning the pages.

"Oh, you have," said the father. "Read it to me."

[10] The first cows were brought to the American colonies in 1634 by Governor Winthrop. Twenty years later there were a great many of them in the Massachusetts colony. They were valued chiefly on account of their hides and for breeding oxen. Until the nineteenth century the ox was always the chief working animal on an American farm.

[11] When young people were married the parson usually preached a sermon on the following Sunday from a text selected by the bride. Just before the sermon began the bride and groom rose in their pew and turned around slowly several times so that everyone in the church might see them.

She read slowly the eleventh and twelfth verses of the Eighty-sixth Psalm:

> Teach me thy way, O Lord; I will walk in thy Truth; unite my heart to fear thy name.
>
> I will praise thee, O Lord my God, with all my heart; and I will glorify thy name for evermore.

"Very good," was her father's comment. He reached over and patted her head. "Did you take it to the parson?"

"I did, and he said it was worthy."

"It is," William Doolittle remarked, "but rather hard to live up to."

"While I was there Mistress Fletcher brought out some wine and cakes, and I drank with them."

Humility was to marry a youth of twenty-two whose name was Hezekiah Pittman, commonly called "Kiah" by his friends. Before courting Humility he came to her father, as required by Puritan law, and formally requested permission to pay his addresses to the daughter, and permission was granted.

Hezekiah was a son of Oliver Pittman, a master ropemaker who had a busy shop near the end of the Long Wharf. With so many ships building in the colony the trade of ropemaker was a good one, and the elder Pittman was quite well off in this world's goods—measured, of course, by early colonial standards.

Pittman was a suspicious, grasping person with very few friends. After the young couple had plighted their troth there was a long-smoldering quarrel between him and Doolittle over the marriage settlement, and Pittman's indignation caused the engagement to be broken off for a brief period. Pittman had agreed to contribute the cottage in which the young couple were to live and Doolittle had agreed to furnish it completely and also to give his daughter one hundred pounds in English money. Pittman thought that was not enough; he argued that the girl should bring two hundred pounds to her husband. The dispute was finally settled by Doolittle's contributing one hundred and fifty pounds besides the furniture in the cottage. Pittman, on his part, agreed to raise his son's wages and give him a small interest in the ropemaking business.

Humility had replaced the *Bible* and had just left the room when her mother came in. She was a bustling, active woman of forty-four who kept an eye on everything and was never satisfied with anything. When she entered the room her face was red and she was fanning herself with her apron. The two servants, she informed her husband, were as lazy as usual—even lazier, if that were possible. Here it was, she said, late in the day before the wedding and still some of the roasting had not been done. But she was resigned to trouble, and could stand any amount of affliction, so she said. Her husband did not seem to hear her, but after awhile he arose and said he would take a look at the doings in the kitchen, so they went in together.

The kitchen was so large that even the long table running down its length did not seem out of place. At the huge fireplace one of the maids was turning a roasting turkey on a spit. The other maid was at a smaller table, putting freshly baked little cakes into jars. Doolittle took one of the cakes and ate it, saying that it was very good. He looked around the room and saw the rows of rich, juicy cooked food—baked venison, turkeys, dishes made of fish and corn, plum cakes and deep-fish pies. Then he smiled at the two servants and walked out, leaving his wife in the kitchen.

When he got back in the common room he hardly knew what to do with himself. After picking up various small articles and putting them down again without being conscious of his action he went over to a small bookshelf on the wall, and stared at the few volumes that stood on it.

The Doolittle library consisted of five books, and a dozen almanacs in pamphlet form. The *Holy Bible* was at the head of the list; then came the *Bay Psalm Book.*[12]

Besides these two he possessed a crabbed theological work entitled *A Blaste at Satan* that somebody had brought from London. There were also a *Book of Discipline* and a small volume of maxims for the guidance of young people. William Doolittle had looked into all these five books at various times,

[12] The *Bay Psalm Book* was the first book that was printed and bound in New England. In 1639 a printer named Stephen Day came over from England and, with the aid and encouragement of the Massachusetts Bay government, set up a printing shop at Cambridge. The *Bay Psalm Book* was one of its products.

but had wearily laid them down after glancing at a few pages. He could read rapidly and well, but he was not interested in literary works. Their subject matter seemed too remote. All his life he had been concerned with the Here and Now. A defective cupboard, sent out to a customer of his shop and returned because of its imperfections, would seem to him a more disastrous event than the fall of Rome.

Occasionally he would read a chapter of the *Bible*—from beginning to end—without missing a word. Whenever he or his family had a stroke of ill fortune, such as a death in the family, he would read a chapter every day for a week or more.

Of the Doolittle's eleven children six had died—two in one day of an ailment known then as "throat distemper," but which is now called diphtheria. The true nature of most illnesses was unknown and the remedies were fantastic. For "throat distemper" the children had poultices laid on their necks. These poultices were made of pepper, mustard and bark of the elder tree, all pounded together in a paste. In addition to this treatment the children were given copious draughts of "snail water," which was made by pounding snails and earthworms in a mortar. This mixture was then boiled in ale, together with a collection of garden herbs. It was one of the most widely used preparations in the whole range of colonial *materia medica*.

But these remedies failed to cure Penitent, the little boy, who was eight years old; and Nancy, a child of five. After their death their father read through the whole of *Leviticus*, though it took him nearly a month to do it, a chapter a day.

In gazing around the room and wondering how to spend his time Doolittle's attention was attracted to the shelf of almanacs. The *New England Almanack* had been brought out annually for twelve years and he owned a copy of each issue. These almanacs were pamphlets, cheaply printed. They were his literary treasures, his sole reading matter. He had read, over and over, every word of all of them. They contained sound advice, pithily stated; anecdotes; weather predictions, which were usually wrong; directions for farmers in the matter of treating sick cattle and growing crops; and little humorous stories interspersed among the serious topics.

He went over to the bookshelf and took down all of them.

Placing them on the settle beside him he spent two hours in silent reading.

8

The wedding day was clear and bright, with a tang of October chill in the air. The shop was closed at noon, so the journeymen and apprentices had a half holiday. This gave them time to brush up and put on their best clothes, for they were expected to attend the wedding.

The marriage ceremony took place late in the afternoon—at the hour of dusk—not in the church, but at the Doolittle home. In early colonial times in New England ministers were forbidden by law to perform the marriage rites, but the young people might be married by almost any officer of the law, or even by a captain of militia.[13] There was nothing, however, to prevent a minister of the church from being present as a guest at a wedding, and on the occasion of the Pittman-Doolittle nuptials the Reverend Mr. Fletcher and his wife were on hand.

The craving of the Puritans to simplify everything had an effect on wedding customs. No one was expected to dress in extravagant finery on such occasions, nor were there banks of flowers or rows of glittering candles. Humility and her mother wore simple but charming dresses of pale-blue woolen cloth. On her head Humility had a starched white cap, like those worn by hospital nurses today. William Doolittle and his grown son Robert, and the Pittmans, father and son, wore dark-gray coats and knee breeches, tied with ribbons at the knees.

About forty people, including servants and workmen, attended the ceremony. The common room was not large enough to hold them all, and the wedding took place outdoors, under a wide-spreading elm. The sky, seen through its bare branches, was a fretwork of darkening blue, for the sun was setting and the dusk of evening was coming on. Hezekiah and his bride wore gloves, but just before the ceremony, while they were standing before Judge Haskell, who was to marry them, each

[13] The reason for the act which prohibited Puritan clergymen from officiating at marriages is not exactly clear, but it was probably a part of the Puritan revolt against the gorgeous flummery of the Established Church in England.

held the right hand behind the back and the best man and the bridesmaid went up behind them and removed the gloves. They were kept thereafter by the best man and bridesmaid as cherished possessions.

Parson Fletcher prayed before the wedding ceremony began, a long and loud appeal to the Lord to protect this God-fearing couple. While the prayer was going on all the guests knelt on the bare ground. Then Judge Haskell, an impressive and solemn magistrate, said the few words that made Hezekiah and Humility man and wife.

There were only a few presents, for the relatives of the marrying couple were the only persons supposed to give them, and the presents consisted almost entirely of linen for the new household. Humility's aunt gave her a rag rug which she had made herself. All kinds of floor coverings were rare; in most of the early colonial homes the floors had nothing on them, and the new rug as a wedding present was much admired.

Immediately after the ceremony William Doolittle and his wife and the Pittmans—man and wife—kissed the bride and the whole company suddenly took on an air of jollity and fun. The bride's father stood on a stone, so he could be seen and heard, and he invited everyone into the house to partake of the wedding feast.

The rooms were so crowded that it was difficult to move around. The dignitaries and older folks sat with the bride and groom in the common room at a large table—it had been taken from the shop for the occasion—and the young men and women were at the long table in the kitchen. Even so, there was not room enough for all, and the inferior people perched themselves on chests of drawers or sat in corners of the wide chimney.

Before the eating began everyone had a glass of wine and the Reverend Mr. Fletcher prayed again for the blessings of the Most High. In the course of the evening, while the hilarity was not yet at its height, he and his wife silently departed. He knew that the fun would grow somewhat boisterous and he did not think it becoming for a minister of the gospel to be present and participating on such occasions.

The servants, and others who wanted to help, brought the

food out in great heaping trenchers. Everyone was furnished with a smaller trencher of his own, and with a knife and spoon. Forks had not yet come into general use.

There was a great variety in the food served, and a prodigious quantity of it. Imagine a dinner where there is roast venison, roast turkey, fricassee of chicken, beef hash, boiled fish, stuffed cod, pigeons, boiled eels, Indian pudding (made of corn), succotash, roast goose stuffed with chestnuts, pumpkin pies, apple tarts, besides many kinds of vegetables. The meal was not served in courses. Each one ate whatever appealed to his fancy; a guest might begin his dinner with a pie and end it with a baked codfish.

The drinks had a variety equal to that of the food. And it must be said that our forefathers did not mind mixing drinks. Beer, cider, claret, flip (which was made of beer, rum and molasses and stirred with a hot poker), sillabub, brandy and sack posset were all passed around indiscriminately. But sack posset was the most popular of the drinks. In making it they first mixed ale and sack, which was a heavy white sherry, then put in eggs and cream, sufficient in amount to thicken the mixture a bit. This mixture was seasoned with nutmeg and boiled for an hour or two. Then it was allowed to cool before serving. To the modern taste, it has the flavor of eggnog, and a little of it would go a long way.

Now and then the company sang songs, varied occasionally by hymns. There was much conversation about food, and the various ways of preparing it. Some of the older men told stories, humorous mainly, which could be heard only by those close around the narrator. William Doolittle told one about an Indian. There was an Indian, he said, who was a great drunkard. He hung around the settlements in the hope of getting brandy. One day he was asked, for a joke, what brandy was made of, and he replied that brandy was made of hearts and tongues. "Why do you say that?" somebody asked. "This is how I know," said the Indian, "when I drink much brandy my heart swells and I am strong as a hundred men, and my tongue talks louder and faster."

It was after ten o'clock when the company, full of meat and drink, all rose to escort the newly married couple to their new home, which was about a quarter of a mile from the house of the Doolittles. Curfew had sounded, as usual, at nine o'clock and everyone after that hour was expected to be at home and in bed, but William Doolittle had obtained special permission from the authorities for the movements of those in the bridal party.

The streets were not lighted at night, except here and there a public-minded householder, of his own volition, kept a lantern with a candle in it above his door. Those at the wedding did not care, they had planned a torchlight procession, so between ten and eleven a citizen who lived on the route might have seen thirty or forty persons, men and women, moving along the street in orderly procession, two by two, each holding a lighted piece of pine firewood in his or her hand.

They had hardly entered the little cottage—as many as could get in—when an alarm arose.

The bride had disappeared!

Stealing the bride was a practical joke, carried on with much laughter at Puritan weddings. The bridegroom was supposed to dash out and look for her. Hezekiah Pittman came out of the house and pushed through the crowd. He pretended to be bewildered and grief-stricken, and he went about wildly, looking behind trees and out in the lanes. In a short while he found her, somewhat disheveled, hiding behind a tree, with a man and another woman. She was brought back in triumph.

Then the wedding party dispersed. Some of the torches were alight, but most of them had expired. The guests went stumbling through the dark streets toward their own homes. Whenever they were stopped by a sharp-eyed watchman who demanded to know their excuse for being out so late they said simply "Hezekiah Pittman's wedding," and were allowed to pass without further inquiry.

Chapter II

A PURITAN VILLAGE IN 1680

I

WAITSTILL WALLING had lived in Sudbury all his life. He claimed, in his expansive moments, that he was the first white child born in that community. Some of the older people disputed that claim; they said that Patience Harden, a girl of low degree, who had run off with a sea captain when she was only fourteen, was the first Sudbury baby. Most of Walling's fellow-citizens took no stock in the Patience Harden story, and the honor of being the first child—whatever that honor may have been—belonged in their opinion to Waitstill Walling.

In 1680 Walling, then forty-five years old, was one of Sudbury's leading citizens, popular with everyone from the minister down to the farm hands. There were good reasons for this. He was a kindly, honest man, and always willing to do a favor for anyone in need.

During King Philip's War Walling served as captain of the local defense company and, in 1676, had saved the village from total destruction during an Indian raid. Under his direction the meetinghouse (the Puritan name for a church) had been turned into a fort. It had thick walls, small windows and a belfry that made an excellent firing place for a squad of musketeers. As soon as the alarm was sounded he sent all the women and children into the meetinghouse together with enough men to defend it. The rest of the armed force proceeded, under his command, to attack the Indians from the rear. They fled without taking any prisoners, but before their flight they burned several houses. Among them was the home of the Walling family, which had been built by Waitstill's father back in the 1640's. It was a ramshackle dwelling that had begun its existence as a one-room cabin. As the family increased in size the house had grown, rooms being added here and there without any definite plan. It had one crude, clay-and-stick chimney, a thatched roof which leaked, and a dim interior, as the sunlight came through windows of oiled paper. The ceilings of all the rooms were so low that a tall man was in danger of striking the cross beams with his head. The house had an attic, but to reach it one had to go outdoors and climb a ladder.

When Captain Walling looked over the smoldering ruins he felt an inward and unexpressed pleasure. "The old wigwam has gone up in smoke," he reflected, "and I'm glad to see the last of it." To his wife, Rebecca, who stood at his side with tears running down her cheeks, he offered consolation. "Aye, Rebecca," he said gloomily, " 'tis a sad loss."

"It is indeed," Rebecca sighed, "now we have no home, no place to lay our heads."

"A hard fate," her husband agreed, "but God willing, we shall have another house and, it may be, a better one."

She looked up at him and her face was a picture of despair. "It will never be the same," she wept. "For the better part of my life I have lived here, and all my children were born" —without completing the sentence she motioned toward the blackened ruins.

Waitstill Walling hardly heard what she said. His mind was already at work, planning the house he intended to build.

The new dwelling was of the salt-box type, and all the Wallings, including the tearful Rebecca, were very proud of it. The salt-box house was a typical New England creation; few, if any, such houses were ever built in the other colonies. The word "salt-box" was used to describe them because they were shaped like the salt receptacles in New England kitchens.

In the seventeenth century the salt-box house was considered a sign of prosperity. In that sense it had something of the significance of the beautiful Georgian houses of the Revolutionary period.

To form a mental picture of a salt-box house just imagine a square or oblong box with a cover that is not flat but runs up to a peak. The cover of the box—or the roof of the house —therefore slants down from the peak on both sides, but on the front side of the house the slanting roof is short and steep. At the rear the slant is more gradual. The house has two stories in front and only one in the back. There are no porches, piazzas or ornate doorways.[1]

The Walling house had nine rooms—four on the ground floor, five on the second floor—and there was also an attic. For that period it was considered a very large house, for most of the colonial families lived in cabins that consisted of one room with a loft overhead that could be reached only by climbing a ladder.

All the rooms of the new Walling home were small; indeed, they were tiny as compared to the rooms in modern dwellings. The five bedrooms on the second floor were mere cubbyholes. This was not looked upon as a defect, for in those days people used bedrooms only for sleeping.

There were no bathrooms in the house, but they were not missed, for no one in that era ever took a bath. The fanciful medical lore of the seventeenth century ascribed many human ailments to contact with water. Consequently, washing with water was limited to the hands and face. As was mentioned before, this prejudice extended to the drinking of water, and people in general avoided water as a beverage. On hot summer days even the farm hands, perspiring at their work in the fields, drank cider instead of water. Babies were given beer and cider as soon as they were old enough to toddle.

The front door on the ground floor opened on a short entrance hall. On the right of the entrance was the common room; on the left the combined kitchen and dining room. The Wallings, who were neither poor nor rich, but well-to-do according to the standards of the time, might have had a dining room apart from the kitchen, but they and their friends looked upon such devices as marks of vanity and hateful pride. The general principle was that if the kitchen was a suitable place for preparing food it was also a suitable place for eating it, so they ate their meals with the smells and smoke of cooking floating around them—and liked it.

These ideas and habits were in thorough accord with the prevailing Puritan belief in humility as a godly force. This

[1] A number of salt-box houses are still standing. One of the better-known is the Boardman house at Saugus, Massachusetts, which was built in 1651. Another excellent example of this type of architecture is the John Howard Payne home at East Hampton, Long Island. The author of *Home, Sweet Home* was born in it; hence the name.

belief was, generally speaking, a mere form of speech. The Puritans were far from humble in dealing with the Indians, or with the other colonies, or with the English authorities across the sea, or with one another in the practical transactions of daily life. But humility is a good word, and sounds well. The Wallings practiced humility as one practices a card game, getting familiar with all the fine points and sometimes inventing new and original methods of being humble.

Wooden pegs instead of nails were used in building the Walling salt-box house. This was a common practice in all the colonies until near the close of the eighteenth century. Machines that make nails by the thousands were not yet invented, and each nail had to be fashioned by hand. Nail-making was one of the secondary occupations of the blacksmiths. Their product was expensive and was sold at prices that would put a modern carpenter in a state of stunned bewilderment.[2]

Because of their high prices nails were carefully hoarded, and were often used in place of currency. Hence the expression "tenpenny nail," which is in use today. The nails to which it applies sold in early colonial times at tenpence a dozen.

There were no locks on any of the doors in the Walling house. The locks made at that time were so unwieldy, and the keys so heavy, that their use was limited chiefly to public buildings, such as churches and jails.

The doors of early colonial houses were usually fastened by a latch. Just above the latch a hole was made in the door panel and the latchstring was passed through it, so the string dangled outside. To enter the house a visitor had only to pull the string and give the door a slight push. At bedtime, or whenever the family did not care to receive callers, the latchstring was pulled inside. "For you the latchstring is always out" was an old-time form of cordial invitation extended only to intimate friends.

Waitstill Walling's latchstring was always out to a lot of

[2] Nevertheless, nails were used to some extent in house building despite their cost. In some of the colonies it was customary for the owners of abandoned buildings to burn them down in order to recover the nails. To discourage this practice the colonial authorities of Virginia offered, in 1645, to pay the owner of such a building the cost of the nails if he would refrain from burning it down.

A nail-cutting and heading machine was invented and patented by G. Chandlee in 1796, greatly reducing their price.

people, for besides managing his farm of many acres, he was engaged in public affairs. He was the captain of the local militia company, the magistrate of the village, and a deacon. At times he had been called to Boston as an adviser to the Governor, and in the years past he had served two terms as a member of the General Court, which was the name of the colonial legislature. He was greatly pleased at his own local importance, though his reverence for the spirit of humility would never permit him to acknowledge such a piece of vanity. Instead, he constantly deplored, in conversation, the duties and the honors that had come his way, or "have been thrust upon me," as he termed it, and he said repeatedly that he hoped to turn some of them, at least, or perhaps all of them, over to someone else. However, the prospect of doing this was slight, so he bore up courageously in his fairly exalted position.

He was familiar with Puritan law, and was probably the only man in that part of Massachusetts who knew all the crabbed provisions of the colonial code which, unlike the laws of today, attempted to regulate every detail of personal conduct.

Most of those who came to see him wanted advice, and Walling was always ready to give it. He had prescribed remedies for sick oxen, tonics for puny children and charms that would keep witches at a distance. He had advised quarrelsome couples about their domestic affairs and had sentenced many a scolding woman or a liquorish man to the stocks. In household affairs, he knew the best way to cook fish and to make cider.

Some of his callers came every day. Samuel Gaylord, the head man on the Walling place, appeared every morning an hour after sunrise to report on the affairs of the farm; and the next visitor was usually James Lawson, the village constable, who was a walking newspaper of local happenings.

2

On a bright, sunny morning in April of the year 1680 a young man waited patiently on a bench in the Walling garden for the constable to come out of the house and depart. The young man, whose name was Oliver Hillman, wanted to see Captain Walling on a very personal matter, and he much preferred to have no listeners to his conversation. Young Mr. Hillman was plainly nervous; he kept twisting about on the bench, and now and then he would rise and take a short walk around the garden.

But Constable Lawson remained with the Captain a long time. Besides his daily batch of news he had some problems. "Now there's Ben Hooper," he said bitterly. "I've warned him time and again that it is against the law for a man to wear long hair like a woman. But he pays me not the slightest heed. Says the men in the *Holy Bible* had long hair, and what was good enough for David and Solomon is good enough for him. Should I bring him into court, sir?"

Captain Walling thought a moment and then said, "No. Let him wear his hair long. He's just a fool."

"You are right, sir. I know he's a stubborn, turtle-headed fool, but don't fools have to obey the law?"

"Aye, James, they do," said the Captain, "but the law against men wearing their hair long is a dead ordinance. Years ago, when it was first enacted, nearly every man wore long hair. Now you seldom see one, so if long hair's his pleasure let him have it."

"Very well, sir. I'll say no more to him."

"His long hair, reaching below his shoulders," the Captain continued, "makes him look silly. Suppose I send him to the stocks for wearing hair as long as a woman's—well, that will not make him look any more foolish than he looks now." The Captain laughed and the grinning constable then broke out in a loud haw-haw. The young man sitting in the flower garden heard the laughter and he was pleased to learn that Captain Walling was in good humor.

"In such matters," said the Captain to his subordinate, "you cannot always go by rule. All of us break the law every day in some manner. If we put all the lawbreakers in jail or in the stocks we wouldn't have enough people left to carry on the work. You're breaking a law right now, if you'd like to know."

"Me!" said the constable in astonishment. He looked

quickly around the room, as if the broken law might be found lying in a corner. "What have I done, sir?"

"You have a silver buckle on your hat. You're not a freeman, and only freemen are allowed by law to use silver for ornaments."

"Oh, I didn't know." The man picked up his wide-brimmed felt hat and looked at it ruefully. "I'll take it off, sir."

Captain Walling smiled. "Aye, James, you'd better take it off some day when you have the time. There's no harm in wearing it, but as you're a constable I suppose you should be careful to keep all the ordinances." [3]

"I do try to observe all the laws," the constable responded, "but there's some I don't know."

"Very well. Anything else new?"

"I fear, sir, that you may have to deal soon with Jeremiah Sheldon and his wife."

"That so? Why? Quarreling again?"

"They are, Captain. Quarreling like cat and dog. Everybody is talking about it. It's the same story all over. Mistress Sheldon says Jerry won't work, and she has to do everything. She declares that she works her hands to the bone, milking the cows, making butter and cheese, brewing the beer, cooking, washing and taking care of the children while he won't turn his hand to a thing."

"Is that true?"

"Pretty nearly, I think, sir. I've been watching 'em."

"Have you spoken to Jeremiah about his idleness?"

"Nay, sir, I have not. I thought that might better come from you."

"Why don't they hire a maid to help out?"

"She says he won't let her. Wants the money himself to buy rum and gamble away on shovelboard. She declares he won't even cut wood for the fire. Just lies around drinking rum and playing the jew's-harp." [4]

[3] Many of the sumptuary laws of the Puritan colonies were never repealed. Their enforcement came to an end through the general public disregard of them.

[4] The humble jew's-harp, now owned and played usually by boys, was a favorite musical instrument for men in Puritan times. Almost every grown man of common status owned a jew's-harp and could play tunes on it.

"They have a man for the farm, I believe," said the Captain. "Is that so?"

"It is, sir. A man named Brown. He seems to do all the work on the place. Jerry Sheldon, when he's in the tavern and in his cups, boasts that he's retired."

"He does, eh? Well, I'll retire him in a way he will not relish. Give him a summons to appear before me in court next Monday. I'll write it now"—his goose-quill pen scratched over a sheet of paper—"and if he cannot show that he works every day and all day I'll send him to a place where he'll be busy."

Lawson folded the paper carefully and put it in his pocket. The Captain, on the other side of the table, watched with impatience the constable's slow, deliberate motions, and said suddenly, "Anything else?"

"I don't know, sir," the constable replied. "Maybe we ought to get Joe Lovell for swearing and cursing. A woodchuck bit him on the hand and he said 'Curse the woodchuck.' Is that swearing? If it is, we have a good case. There are four witnesses."

The Captain shook his head. "No, James," he said. "It is not swearing. To swear you must use the Lord's name. If Lovell had said 'God damn the woodchuck' he would have been breaking the law."

The constable rose to depart. While brushing off his hat with his sleeve an item of news occurred to him. He turned to Captain Walling and said, "Did ye hear, sir, that Goody Drake is sick—very sick it seems, in bed?"

"No, I haven't heard. What's the matter with her."

"I don't know, for some say one thing and some say another. She's got a fever, they say, and is lying in bed with spots breaking out all over her, so they say——"

Walling leaped up. "Spots! Did you say she has spots on her skin? It may be smallpox. Why wasn't I told of this before?"

"I just heard it myself this morning. It ain't smallpox, sir. Goody Tompkins—you know her—she's nursed almost every sick person around here for twenty years and she says Goody Drake has the measles. She's up there, now, nursing. She told me it's the measles this morning and she's keeping the Drake woman covered up and sweating under blankets and is givin' her a cup of Venice treacle every hour." [5]

"That stuff's a child's remedy—that Venice treacle," said Captain Walling. "It's for children with the whooping cough. When you leave here, James, go at once to the minister, to Mr. Goodwin, and tell him just what you've told me about this case of sickness. Ask him in my name to go to see Goody Drake, and find out what's the matter. Mr. Goodwin has studied medicine, off and on, for years."

"Aye, sir, I'll go to Mr. Goodwin. But I am sure it's not smallpox. There's nobody to catch it from. There ain't been any pox here for several years."

"Strangers coming through might have it," said the Captain, "and give it to our people. I've seen it kill folks by the hundred and I dread it." He passed his hand reflectively over his own pockmarked face. "Go along now; go at once to Mr. Goodwin, but don't speak to anybody else about it until we're sure. Let us be careful not to alarm people without good cause."

"Very well, sir," the constable said. "I'll attend to it right now." As he went on his errand he felt somewhat mystified by the Captain's show of anxiety over a simple case of measles.

The constable had hardly left the house when Oliver Hillman, who had been absent-mindedly picking a flower to pieces, got up from his bench in the garden. As he entered the common room Captain Walling smiled and extended his hand.

"Oliver, you've become a stranger," he said with a laugh. "Harvard seems to have kept you busy."

"Aye, Captain, it did in fact," the young man said. "What with the studies and duties a man has little time for much else."

"You're a graduate student, I think. Is that so?"

"It is, sir. I graduated last year, and since then I've been helping out with the teaching. But that is over now, and I'm back home again."

[5] Venice treacle was a repulsive compound made by boiling the pounded bodies of snakes with white wine and a mixture of twenty herbs. To this concoction a small amount of opium was added. The liquid was then drained off and put in jars. It was usually given to children for any illness that afflicted them.

Walling was well acquainted with young Hillman's father, who owned one of the few paper mills in the colonies. This mill was on a stream of clear, fresh water a few miles from Sudbury.

"Are you going to help your father in his mill?"

"That is our intention, sir. I know a deal about paper-making already, and I shall go more deeply into it." This was said stiffly as the young man sat upright in his chair. There was then a pause for a moment.

When the silence had become rather thick Captain Walling said, "Is there something that you wish to speak to me about?"

"There is, sir," said young Hillman. "Your daughter Harriet. May I call on her and be her—I mean be friendly with her?" This was uttered with blushing and hesitation.

Captain Walling was pleased, but he kept a solemn countenance. Young Hillman would be an excellent suitor for his daughter, and a most desirable son-in-law. After some reflection he said, "Have you spoken to Harriet?"

"I have, sir," the young man replied. "Yesterday, at Mistress Faulkner's. She said she had no objections, and then she said I must ask you or her mother—as I expected to do."

"Very well, Oliver, I consent, and I speak, too, for her mother."

"Thank you, sir."

Oliver Hillman had known Harriet Walling all his life. As children they had played together. But she was now seventeen and he was nineteen. Not only Puritan etiquette but also Puritan law required that he seek the consent of Harriet's parents before he became her beau.

Walling rose and shook hands with Oliver. "Come in any evening, my lad, whenever you please," he said gravely. "We shall always be glad to see you. If you want to talk to Harriet now you will find her in the leanter.[6] She is either spinning or weaving today."

Young women in the Puritan colonies did not accept the

[6] The word "leanter" is a corrupted form of "leanto." The leanto was the rear part of a salt-box house, only one story in height. It was usually given up to household industries, such as spinning, weaving, candle-molding and cheese-making.

attentions of a number of beaux, but this does not mean that the girls were kept in a state of nunlike seclusion. They went to parties, to dinners and to other social occasions and met the young men of the neighborhood. For steady company, however, the gallant swain had to obtain the consent of the girl's parents. Otherwise he was likely to be brought up before a magistrate for "inveigling" the young woman's affections.

The term "inveigling" appears to have had rather wide implications. There were cases in which the young man charged with this offense had done nothing more than to walk with the girl on a country road. Young women who consented to advances from the men were also looked upon with legal disfavor. For instance: In New Haven, in 1660, Jacob Minline and Sarah Tuttle were charged in court with "sinful dalliance." The evidence of witnesses showed that Jacob and Sarah were addicted to what we, in these modern times, would call petting parties. "They sat down together," said one witness, "his arm about her, and her arm upon his shoulder or about his neck; and hee kissed her, and shee kissed him, or they kissed one another, continuing in this posture for about half an hour." Sarah was asked in court if Jacob had inveigled her affections, and she said no. Thereupon she was fined and characterized by the court as a "bold virgin" who had better mend her ways. She said meekly that she would. Jacob was not fined, but was set free and told to shun such virgins as Sarah.

It was, indeed, a man's world. This extract from the Governor Winthrop's *Journal* (Vol. II, p. 265), is a clear indication of the prevailing masculine opinion of intellectual women:

> Mr. Hopkins, the governor of Hartford upon Connecticut, came to Boston and brought with him his wife, a godly young woman, and of special parts, who has fallen into a sad infirmity, the loss of her understanding and reason, which had been growing on her diverse years, by occasion of giving herself wholly to reading and writing, and had written many books. . . . For if she had attended her household affairs, and such things as belong to women, and not gone out of her way to meddle with such things as are proper for men, whose minds are stronger, she had kept her wits, and might have improved them usefully and honorably in the place God had set for her.

After Oliver Hillman had departed Captain Walling stood

musing for a moment. The young man's desire to keep company with Harriet had not surprised him: he had noticed Oliver's bashful, sheepish expression whenever he was in the girl's presence. The Captain hoped it would turn out well, and he thought it might if young Hillman could ever overcome his bashfulness to the point of asking her to marry him.

Harriet was seventeen, he reflected, and it was about time to think of marrying. In the Puritan scheme of things there was no place for old maids or bachelors. Waitstill Walling's niece Prudence had never married, and now at the age of twenty-eight she was for all time on the shelf. She had no home of her own, but lived with various relatives, taking care of the children and helping with the housework.

In Sudbury there was one man classified as a bachelor, Enoch Frale, who had reached the age of thirty without marrying. Under the law he had to report to the local magistrate—who was Captain Walling—from time to time to give an account of his doing. Walling permitted him to live as a boarder with Jonathan Bradbury and his family, and the Bradburys had to keep Magistrate Walling informed of his goings and comings and various activities.

On one occasion Walling, with the best of intentions, tried to arrange a match between this foot-loose male and his niece Prudence. His efforts came to nothing. Enoch appeared to be a woman-hater. He said emphatically that he never intended to marry. Prudence merely turned up her nose and sniffed disdainfully when the matter was brought to her attention.[7]

Walling then thought of his pretty and charming daughter. No, he reflected, she will never be an old maid, and I hope Oliver Hillman will be my son-in-law. Then he said, "Tut, tut, no sense in counting sheep so far ahead."

[7] In the Connecticut annals there is a story of a confirmed bachelor who, at the age of forty, abandoned his career of single blessedness and married the termagant of the community. This elderly spinster—she was thirty-two—had acquired a widespread reputation for bad temper and a quarrelsome disposition. When his friends asked the bridegroom why he had married her, when he could have made a much better match, he replied that he did it as a penance; that he had had too good a time as a bachelor, and he was afraid he might not get to heaven unless he suffered here on earth. The gossips carried this to the bride. She flew into a rage and declared that she was not going to be a packhorse to carry any man to heaven, and if he expected her to afflict him he was mistaken. Thereupon she became one of the most pleasant and dutiful of wives.

Sometimes Walling rode around the farm, but on this clear, sunlit day he decided to walk, so he started out afoot. He was a tall man with broad shoulders and a ruddy complexion. His costume was that of a prosperous colonial of the period—knee breeches and boots which came up to the knees, a waistcoat of scarlet velvet, and a dark-brown coat of fustian with silver buttons. He did not wear a belt or suspenders; his knee breeches were tied to the lining of his waistcoat by points, which were pieces of tape made usually of silk. His shirt was of white linen, to which there was attached a linen collar with "falling bands." The bands took the place of a necktie. On his head he wore a felt hat with a wide brim and a high crown. His scarlet vest, or waistcoat, was very long; it reached nearly to his knees.

Captain Walling crossed the barnyard and the vegetable garden that lay just beyond it. A large and tattered scarecrow stood in the garden, but it was ineffectual in warding off the flocks of black-coated birds. In the spring and early summer, until the corn and the vegetables were well-grown, Walling had to keep one of the farm hands as a watcher over the crop. This man was armed with a musket which he fired into the air now and then.

Plowing and corn planting were going on and Captain Walling, as he looked across the fields, could see several plow gangs at work. Colonial farming was crude, inefficient and slovenly. The farmers of that day knew nothing of crop rotation, and their tendency was to work the soil to exhaustion. They threw away their stable manure instead of using it to enrich the soil. They let their hogs run wild in the woods on the theory that a diligent pig could pick up enough acorns, or one thing or another, to sustain himself. The pigs did keep alive, but when they were rounded up for slaughter there was seldom enough pork on one of them to furnish more than three or four meals for a farmer's hearty family. Expert meat producers today never let a porker leave his pen; his sole business in life is to eat all he can hold.

The colonial plow was a primitive, awkward implement, crude in design and ill-adapted to the work at hand. It was made of wood shod with iron, which means that a thin strip of iron formed its cutting edge.

The purpose of a plow is not only to cut a furrow in the soil but also to turn upside down the earth that comes from this operation and lay it on each side of the furrow. The turning over exposes the furrow to the weather, which is an essential element in the technique of efficient crop production. The plow used by colonials was neither a good soil-cutter nor a good soil-turner. Its moldboard—meaning the wooden body of the plow—was so poorly shaped that it did not turn over the earth properly and a great deal fell back into the furrow. Two men, or a man and a woman, were usually required to run one of these antiquated plows—one to drive the oxen and plow the furrow, and the other to follow the plow with a spade and turn the soil which the plowing should have done. The cutting edge of the plow, called the plowshare, was such a defective cutting device that four, and sometimes six, oxen were needed to pull it through the soil.

The agricultural methods of the seventeenth century were almost precisely the same as those of the seventh century. For a thousand years—or, better say, two thousand years—there had been no improvement of any importance in the cultivation of the soil. The modern plow, the use of fertilizer, the reaper, the mechanical thresher, the cotton gin—all these originated in the nineteenth century.

Corn was the chief food crop for many years in the New England colonies. Indigenous to America, corn was unknown in Europe. The Indians taught the settlers how to plant it, harvest it, and turn it into food. The Indian method of planting corn was to dig a series of shallow holes, drop into each hole several grains of corn and two or three dead fish as fertilizer. Then the earth was replaced in the hole and smoothed over. The only change the colonials made in this procedure was to plow a furrow instead of digging the holes with a spade.

It is an interesting and curious fact that the North American continent lacked so many fruits and vegetables that are now grown in profusion. Corn was American, but wheat and oats were unknown until brought by settlers from Europe. Grapes grew wild and in great profusion, but there were no apples or peaches or pears until the seed was brought across the ocean and planted on American soil. Apples were not eaten, however, in large quantities; most of the crop was used to make cider, which was an immensely popular beverage in the seventeenth and eighteenth centuries. Persimmons, cherries and strawberries were well known to the Indians.

There is also some confusion over the origin of potatoes, caused probably by the use of the word "potato" to include white and sweet potatoes under the same classification. These two varieties of vegetable belong to quite different species. The white potato's botanical name is *solanum tuberosum;* the sweet potato is *ipomea batatas.*

The white potato evidently came originally from Peru, and was taken to Spain about 1560 and grown there. But it has been claimed that Drake and Hawkins carried it from the West Indies direct to England. There is reason to believe that the plant they carried to England was the sweet potato.

The most convincing evidence seems to be that the sweet potato appears to have been brought to the American continent from the West Indies some time in the 1700's. The white potato was taken to the British Isles—coming probably from Spain—early in the seventeenth century and was brought to America around 1720 by Irish colonists who settled in New Hampshire. In some sections of the country this prolific tuber is still known as an "Irish potato."

Rice came from Madagascar. In 1671 Dr. Henry Woodward, one of the founders of South Carolina, was given a small bag of rice by a sea captain who had come from some port of East Africa. Dr. Woodward planted the rice in his garden and it grew mightily, but neither he nor anyone else in the colony knew how to clean it for use, and for several years it was merely a garden plant. When the South Carolinians eventually learned how to get rid of the husks and prepare the rice for eating it became the principal crop of South Carolina until cotton displaced it in the 1800's.

Waitstill Walling was an incompetent farmer, and he knew it. That is why he left everything to Samuel Gaylord, his head man. His daily inspection of the farm and its operations was merely a piece of perfunctory routine. When he walked over the fields he had the air of a visitor who was simply looking on. He made a point of speaking politely, though with distant condescension, to each of the farm hands—even to Momacko, an Indian slave who had fought against the whites in King Philip's war and had been sold into slavery after the Indian defeat.

The basic principles of human conduct in the Puritan civilization were Work and Piety, but they were inseparable and had to be practiced together. If you had been a Puritan of the seventeenth century you might have been possibly one of the most willing, industrious and capable workers in the colony. But if you had lacked Piety, if you had neglected the church, if you had played games on Sunday, if you had observed Christmas as a holiday and a time of merrymaking, the heavy hand of authority would have fallen on you and most of your holidays would have been spent in the stocks. If your disregard of Piety could not have been cured by the stocks and whippings, if you had still remained unregenerate, there can be no doubt that you would have been expelled from the colony. Your refuge in that case would have been Rhode Island, where public opinion and the colonial government tolerated all forms of personal belief and religious practice.

But on the other hand, let us suppose that you were as pious as Cotton Mather, that you never failed to pray and to attend church, to read the *Bible* and to keep the holy commandments; but, let us suppose further, that you never got out of bed until ten in the morning, that you never did a stroke of work and scorned industry of all kinds. In that case, though your Piety would have been commendable you would have found yourself in the stocks, side by side with the atheist who made work his religion.

The Walling family combined Work and Piety in such sound proportions that the two parts fitted together perfectly.

Every member of the family—except the very young children—had some kind of work to do. Even little daughter Patience, who was only eight, had been taught to embroider samplers and to hem table napkins.

Henry, the oldest son—he was twenty-two—was employed

by his uncle in Boston. This relative owned a number of vessels that made trading voyages to the West Indies. Young Henry did not expect to remain permanently in the shipping trade. His father wanted him to pass a few years in that occupation, and to make voyages in the ships so that he might learn something of the world at first hand. After his experience in business and travel he was to come home and give his time to the Walling farm and other properties.

The second son, who had the Puritan name of Feargod, worked on the farm under Samuel Gaylord. He was not a laborer but a kind of student, learning what he could. Feargod Walling cherished a deep and rankling discontent which broke out occasionally in tantrums, or fits of temper. He did not want to be a farmer; he had no interest in the soil, in agriculture, in stock breeding, yet he was bound to these occupations, probably for life. If he lived today he would be called an intellectual. In seventeenth-century New England the only pursuits open to an intellectual were the ministry and schoolteaching, Feargod, although a faithful Puritan, was not sufficiently theological in temperament to pass his life preaching on Biblical texts. As to schoolteaching—that was impossible. In all colonial communities the schoolteacher stood low in the social scale, and usually with good reason. He was often a drunkard, or ne'er-do-well, and his pay was so small that he had to live in a state of perpetual shabbiness. No, Feargod Walling did not want to be a schoolmaster.

There were a few lawyers in the colonies, but the lawyer was a social pariah until far along in the eighteenth century. The colonial statutes classed lawyers with drunkards and keepers of bawdy houses. The law, with its finely spun logic and clever subterfuges, would have appealed to Feargod Walling as a desirable profession if it had been considered respectable. What he wanted was an occupation that was both intellectual and honorable, and he had begun to realize that he was living in an age, and in a community, where such a career was impossible.

Harriet, the Wallings' oldest daughter, had been taught to do everything that belonged to the duties of a Puritan housewife. Part of each day she spent in the spinning and weaving room in the leanto, where she spun flax and wool and wove them into cloth. Among her occupations was the accumulation of linen for her own hope chest. She had already twelve pairs of linen sheets. Four pairs of them were spun and woven by her and eight pairs were hollands,[8] which she had cut out, stitched and hemmed. She had also twenty-one towels and forty-six table napkins.

The large number of napkins was due to the fact that forks had not come into use as table implements. Food was picked up on the flat end of a knife, or in a spoon, or with the bare hands. Whenever bones were encountered, as in a turkey or a piece of pork, both hands were used. In the course of an ordinary meal the hands became soiled several times. Before each person at the table stood a small ewer of water in which he would dip his hands and wipe them with a napkin. As a result many napkins were used at each meal.

Forks were not unknown; they had been brought to England from Italy during the reign of Queen Elizabeth. But for some reason that is still obscure the use of forks was considered an affectation, so that humble appliance was generally scorned, and colonial folks went to a good deal of trouble to avoid using it. Expert knife-users who could balance a slippery piece of food on their knives were paid the respect that is usually given in our time to parlor magicians.

As it was hard to pick up peas on a knife blade, honey was sometimes smeared over the peas so they would stick to the knife. An old rhyme runs in this fashion:

> I eat my peas with honey;
> I've done it all my life.
> It makes the peas taste funny,
> But it keeps them on my knife.

Nevertheless, the Wallings possessed two silver forks which were kept in a leather case and shown now and then to callers. They were used at table only on important occasions, such as the time when Judge Samuel Sewall was an overnight guest. At dinner that day Judge Sewall ate his meal with one of the forks, and the other one was used by Captain Walling.

Waitstill's wife Rebecca, a plump and blooming matron,

[8] The term "holland" applied to a fabric of any kind meant that it was imported, not necessarily, however, from Holland.

was busy every day from morning to night with household tasks. Besides her grown daughter she had two maids to help her, and all of them had as much as they could do. Cooking stoves did not exist—nobody had ever heard of such a thing—and the huge meals were cooked on an open fire. In the yard back of the kitchen there was a brick oven for baking bread and roasting venison. All the water used in the house had to be brought by hand from a well in the barnyard.

In addition to the ordinary household activities there were others which are entirely unknown to the modern housekeeper, such as candle molding, soap making, weaving and dyeing, the making of brooms and the brewing of beer for the household.

Another of her jobs was the compounding of household remedies. Every girl, before her marriage, was trained to make palsy drops, mithridate, Venice treacle, snail water and pokeberry plaster, besides a long list of other salves and potions. There were no physicians in Sudbury and the nearest apothecary was in Boston, so the housewife had to be prepared to meet sickness in the family with remedies from her own medicine closet.

The Wallings, like most families in New England, had four meals a day, beginning with a breakfast of suppawn, or porridge, sausage and pudding shortly after sunrise. Suppawn is an Indian name meaning a dish of corn meal and milk boiled in molasses. Samp was another breakfast food, often eaten instead of suppawn. This dish was made of pounded corn and butter with milk poured over it.

Corn was the staple cereal on the Puritan bill of fare. Some of the dishes made of corn have remained popular to this day. There is succotash, for instance, made of corn and beans; and corn pone, which was called at first by its Indian name of "appone." In colonial times corn pone was often made with huckleberries, and sweetened, like a fruit cake. In this form it was called Indian pudding.

The famous early New England johnny cake consisted simply of corn meal and milk, baked hard so that it might be carried as sustenance on long trips. Its real name was "journey cake." The hungry traveler usually dipped it into cider to soften its hard crust and to give it a flavor.

Meat was plentiful—so abundant, indeed, that hunters would often take the hide of a slain deer and leave the carcass lying on the ground, as it was not worth the trouble to take it home. There was no effective way to keep meat from spoiling in the summer, and it did often spoil in colonial kitchens before it could be consumed.

Fish and oysters were highly esteemed but for some reason there was a widespread prejudice against shad. In the seventeenth century this delicious fish was never served to guests, yet there is ample evidence that large numbers of shad were actually caught and eaten. It seems that people were ashamed of eating shad, and that if a dish of it were on the table it would be whisked out of sight if visitors were seen to be approaching.

3

On his return from his morning walk about the farm on this April morning, Captain Walling was met by his little daughter Comfort who gleefully held up a gaudily dressed doll for him to see. Comfort was not yet seven years old and dolls were as important in her life as a sense of law and order was in the life of her father. But Comfort did not call them dolls, nor did her parents; they were called "Bartholomew babies." These little images were sold in quantities at St. Bartholomew's Fair in London; hence the name.[9]

"See, Father," the child called out, "what Auntie Temperance has sent to me from Boston."

Captain Walling took the doll and looked it over in his grave manner. It represented a grown lady, dressed elaborately in the latest fashion. These small figurines were used sometimes by dressmakers in Europe to convey fashion news, just as photographs and illustrations are used today.

"It's very pretty," said the Captain. "How did your Aunt Temperance send it?"

[9] The origin of the word "doll" is obscure. Some etymologists think it comes from *daul,* a Norse word meaning "woman," but this derivation is not proven, and is a mere supposition. The word "Doll," as a contraction of the name Dorothy was in use in England long before it was applied to a girl's toy. In Shakespeare's *King Henry IV,* there is a Doll Tearsheet. Whatever its origin may be the word "doll" was not used in its modern sense until well along in the eighteenth century. Until 1750 dolls were called Bartholomew's babies or Flanders babies.

"By Mr. Howland's son. He got here this morning, and brought a letter, too. A letter for Mother. Now I have three babies."

"Three? I thought it was two, with this one," he said, handing the doll back to her.

"Nay, Father, I have three. This fine one and the little old one and the Indian baby."

"Oh, true enough. I didn't think of the little Indian. Do you know where your sister Harriet is?"

"She's in her room, sir. It will be lecture day tomorrow. May I carry this new baby with me?"

"I cannot say. You must ask your mother."

Captain Walling went briskly up the narrow, uncarpeted stairs. He wanted to speak to Harriet a moment and tell her that he had given young Oliver Hillman permission to be her steady company.

That young lady was sitting alone in her narrow little room engaged in a secret operation. She was bending over a baking dish of pottery that contained milk in which she had poured a half a cupful of vinegar and the juice of a number of pears. With this device she was trying to remedy what she considered a serious defect of her complexion. She was a healthy, buoyant girl with rosy cheeks and a sun-tanned appearance. In some way she had learned that fine ladies were always pale, and that in Boston some of them wore masks when they went out of the house so the sun would not ruin their complexions. This was long before cosmetics and their use had become a fine art, otherwise Harriet might have given her cheeks an unhealthy pallor at the cost of only a few pence. Besides, any device which was contrived to change a complexion given by God would have been sternly frowned upon by the Puritan elders. If she had used as much as a single dab of face powder, or a touch of eyebrow blackever, they would have had her up in meeting, weeping before the congregation and confessing to the sin of vanity.

One of the girls in the village had told her that a pale complexion could be accomplished by giving the face, several times a day, a bath of a mixture of fresh milk, vinegar and the juice of pears. For a week or two Harriet had been doing this and it seemed to her, when she looked in her tiny mirror, that she really was a little paler, so she kept on with the treatment.

When her father knocked at her door she hastily put the pan of milk under the bed, and stood up to receive him. He did not sit down but stood smiling and said rather gallantly, "I have a prince for my young princess." Harriet said gravely, "What do you mean, Father?" just as if Oliver Hillman had not already told her of his interview. Her father replied that he had consented to the young man's request, but he would not have done so if he had not thought it would please her. "I do not want to force you to do anything," he assured her.

Harriet stood, as if in quiet reflection, for a moment and then said sedately, "It's all right, Father. If it pleases you I shall be satisfied. He seems to be a devout and serious young man. I hope I may grow to care for him." She might have added that she had been meeting him quietly and secretly for a month or more in various out-of-the-way places, but she said nothing, because she concluded, after a brief consideration, that such a statement would not add to her father's good humor.

4

Next day was a Thursday, and every Thursday in Puritan Massachusetts was known as Lecture Day. On that day all work, except what was absolutely necessary, was suspended and the people, after listening to an edifying lecture, or sermon, in the morning, turned to the enjoyment of sports, games and gossip for the rest of the day.

Most of these activities took place on the village green, where the stocks, pillory and whipping post were also placed. This conjunction of pleasure and punishment had a benign purpose. People who became too boisterous, or who were drinking too much, or who were attempting to inveigle a maiden, or who were spreading scandalous stories about their neighbors, had only to turn their eyes toward the southern end of the village green and there they would see, sitting miserably in the stocks, those who had failed to behave with piety and decorum or some previous occasion.

The Puritan temperament was deeply tinctured with an inclination toward needless self-torture. Their ministers seldom preached of the joys of heaven; the emphasis in the sermons was laid on the tortures and terrors of hell. Jonathan Edwards, the most famous of colonial divines, declared that God takes delight in the sufferings of poor lost sinners. Henry Bamford Parkes, in his *Jonathan Edwards*—a biography of most unusual merit—says that Edwards believed:

> The world was a drama, a picture, a melody, the most beautiful which God could have made; and men were puppets whom God elected, as He thought best, for goodness or wickedness.

In short, wickedness is not a matter of choice, or free will—nor is goodness—according to Jonathan Edwards. Parkes says further in elucidating the opinions of this eminent preacher—

> Those elected for goodness, having fought in this world against evil, would in the next be lifted up to an infinite happiness; and, looking down out of heaven, they would realize their own ecstasy by contrasting it with the infinite misery of the sinners in the flames of hell.

What a shocking thought! How cruel and sadistic—the conception of the souls in heaven looking down upon those in hell and their own ecstasy being sustained by the sight of the damned and tortured.

In his *Freedom of the Will* Edwards declared that it is not unjust that a man "should be made to fry in hell to all eternity for those things which he had no power to avoid, and was under a fatal, unfrustable, invincible necessity of doing."

Harshness was a characteristic of the Puritan mind, and the harshness had a sadistic streak. Therefore, it was natural and quite in keeping with the essential order of things, according to the Puritan way of thinking, that the stocks should stand on the village green, to remind the pleasure-seekers that all is not beer and skittles in this world of sin and temptation. The Puritan meetinghouses were unheated, and as cold as ice in the winter season, when they might just as well have had chimneys and fireplaces. But a warm and comfortable church would have seemed to make religion too easy.[10]

[10] Many of those who attended churches on cold days carried "foot-warmers." These were metal boxes with holes in their lids. Before leaving home the churchgoer would fill this device with red-hot coals imbedded in ashes. On arriving at the church it was placed on the floor of the pew and furnished a warm resting place for one's feet.

To the Puritan mind there was a touch of evil in almost every human activity that happened to be pleasant. One of the colony's statutes, for instance, forbade a man to kiss his wife in public. The chronicles of the time record the case of a Boston sea captain who had been away for a year on a long voyage. One day the town crier went around with his drum to announce that this seafarer's ship was coming into the bay. The captain's wife went down to the water's edge to welcome her husband. As soon as he came ashore he took her in his arms and kissed her, with many people looking on. For that serious piece of misbehavior he was taken before a magistrate and sentenced to two hours in the pillory on his first afternoon on land.

Curiously enough, these harsh restrictions on perfectly natural and human pleasures did not apply to liquor drinking. People who got drunk were, of course, taken up and fined or set in the stocks; and the taverns had to close at the curfew hour and also on the Sabbath, but otherwise there was no curb at all on drinking. As a matter of fact, everyone drank liquor, or beer or cider—and that really means everybody from ministers and magistrates down to nursemaids and two-year-old babies.

If a prohibitionist had appeared anywhere in the colonies he would have been considered a crackpot. In Massachusetts there can be no doubt that the Puritan authorities would have handled a prohibition movement in their forthright fashion. The leaders of the crusade against the demon rum would have been expelled from the colony as dangerous agitators, and their followers would have been warned to behave and drop their absurd notions.[11]

The ordination of a new minister always meant a tremendous drinking bout. When Reverend Edwin Jackson was ordained at Woburn, the itemized list of expenses on that occasion show that the congregation drank six and a half barrels of cider, twenty-five gallons of wine, two gallons of brandy and four gallons of rum.

[11] The first temperance movement in the United States began in the late 1820's, but as early as 1774 a book decrying the use of liquor was published in Philadelphia. Its author was Anthony Benezet, and the title of his book is *The Mighty Destroyer Displayed, In Some Account of the Dreadful Havock Made by the Mistaken Use as well as the Abuse of Distilled Spirituous Liquors.*

At the ordination of Reverend Joseph McKeen in Beverly the drinkables consumed on that occasion were thirty bowls of wine. At dinner after the meeting they drank forty-four bowls of punch, eighteen bottles of wine and eight bowls of brandy.

In Northampton in 1737 a new meetinghouse was built. Sixty men worked on it a week. During that week they consumed sixty-nine gallons of rum and thirty-six pounds of sugar, besides several barrels of beer and cider.

Mistress Rebecca Walling seldom paid any attention to lecture day, but Captain Walling felt that, as a man of public importance in the community, it was his duty to appear. So, fairly early in the morning he left his house, accompanied by his daughters, Harriet and Comfort, and proceeded gravely along the wide street to the village green. Harriet endeavored to look as pale as she could, but without much success. Before leaving home she studied her face in the mirror, and was disappointed when she saw that she still had the ruddy, red-cheeked complexion of a hearty milkmaid. Maybe the milk, vinegar and pear treatment was not much good, she reflected. Nevertheless, she intended to keep on with it.

There was nothing to prevent her, she thought, from adopting the manners of a fine lady even if she did not look like one. She could pretend to be bored with nearly everything, and to say now and then that she felt faint, and to look at people in a cold and distant manner. She had heard that fine ladies behaved in that fashion.

Anyway, Oliver Hillman liked her just as she was, and that was a pleasant thought. She felt certain that she would see him on the green, and maybe she had better invite him to come back with them for dinner. Her father would like that, she was sure.

Six-year-old Comfort carried her Bartholomew baby and showed it proudly to other little girls whom she happened to meet. She told them that the baby's name was Caroline, that her Aunt Temperance in Boston had taken Caroline off a ship that had "come from far, far away." Also that Caroline's dress was made in London, and that Caroline had been weeping because she was homesick, and had been seasick, too.

(The Bettmann Archive)

Waitstill Walling's own thoughts had nothing in common with those of his two daughters. As he and they walked slowly toward the meetinghouse he was wondering what he would say when called upon to speak. He seldom spoke on these occasions, for the minister was supposed to do all the talking, but the subject of today's lecture, or sermon, was *Moses as a Lawgiver,* and Mr. Goodwin had told him that he would be called on to say something, as the town's magistrate, after the lecture.

What could he say? He realized his own shortcomings; he was not a philosopher, or a deep thinker; he was a doer. He did things while other people were thinking about the whys and wherefores.

But he would have to say something. The Puritan code was based on the Mosaic Law. There were only twelve offenses punishable by death in Massachusetts, just the same as in the laws of Moses, while at that very time there were two hundred or more offenses that called for the death penalty in England. That is worth talking about, he reflected. "They say we're harsh," he said to himself silently, "but we're not. Over in England they can hang a maid servant for stealing a shilling, but not here. No, we are not vindictive or cruel." With these ideas flowing through his head Walling decided to make his talk on the differences between the English legal code and the Puritan code.

It occurred to him that there were many differences. The jury system, to mention only one. In England they had juries to listen to all important cases and decide on a verdict. Not so in the Puritan colonies. The judges, or magistrates, heard the evidence and made the decisions. Why are there no juries? "That's something I'll explain. Moses said nothing about juries, and we follow that great lawgiver."

Before they had reached the meetinghouse the substance of his forthcoming talk was in his mind, all arranged and in order.

He did not like lecture days, and he would have started a movement against them if he had thought, for a moment, that such a protest would be even halfway effective. Lecture day, to his way of thinking, was just a waste of time. The Sabbath was a workless day—a day of rest—and one day a week was enough, he thought. With no work done on either the Sabbath or lecture day, the Puritans had a five-day work week, and Captain Walling thought this pampering of the working class had gone too far.

There were other reasons why he did not care for lecture days, though he attended them from a sense of duty. On these occasions he was usually surrounded by people of inferior grade who asked him countless questions, and pretended to be impressed by his answers. That they were trying to curry favor with him was disgustingly apparent, or so he thought.

The blacksmith—whose name was Hamp Carson—always came out of his shop, smiles all over his broad face, when he saw Captain Walling. Before greeting the Captain he would wipe his hands elaborately on a corner of his apron. And there was Harry Blow, the jolly innkeeper. As soon as Captain Walling entered the inn Harry Blow would come leaping forward, and would wave to everybody to keep silent. The cooper and coffin maker, Ebenezer Buford, always seemed honored by the Captain's presence and drifted invariably into a discussion of lofty world affairs, when all Captain Walling wanted to know from him was the state of his trade and what he thought of the condition of things in Sudbury.

It never occurred to the Captain that these people really admired him, that they were not pretending, and that they asked his advice simply because his judgment was sound. In other words, he had a rather low opinion of his own abilities and he thought everybody shared it—which was not the case.

Walling's cousin John Passmore lived about a mile from the village. He was the black sheep of the family, a lazy, dissolute ne'er-do-well who was almost always in trouble of one kind or another. He never failed to attend on lecture days. On the village green his voice would be heard in raucous disputes and vain boastings of his own prowess. On one occasion the Captain, as magistrate, had to sentence this shiftless cousin to the stocks for six hours because of a remark he had made concerning Major Randall's house. He had been over the house, making some repairs, for he was by trade a carpenter. At the tavern next day he told an audience of drinkers that "Major Randall's house is not fit to live in. It will fall down some day and kill everybody that's in it."

For that remark he was brought up in court and Captain Walling sent him to the stocks. John Passmore was not a freeman and therefore had no right, under the law, to criticize the belongings of his superiors. If he had been on the same social level as Major Randall there would have been no legal offense, and no penalty, attached to his derogatory comment on the Major's house.

After sentencing him Captain Walling told him that he had hated to do it, but had to carry out the law. Thereupon John waved to him in a jolly way and called out, "It's all right. It's all in the family, you know." Whenever John saw the Captain, and he usually did see him on lecture day, he would call out cheerily, "Hi there, Cousin Wait!"

After the lectures and the Captain's talk in the meeting-house Harriet and Comfort went walking around the green, while the Captain accompanied the minister into the tavern, where they expected to drink a bowl of punch together and to have some conversation with any of the townsmen who were present.

Harriet, with a calculated sedateness, strolled slowly under the trees, speaking to some acquaintances and bowing to others. She was soon joined by Oliver Hillman. They looked first at the three men in the stocks. One of them had a card which said "Blasphemer" across his breast. The second man was a Quaker who had been sentenced to spend the day in the stocks, then be whipped on his bare back and expelled from the colony. Although there was an official watcher, a constable standing near by to keep watch over the prisoners, small boys in the crowd of onlookers picked up pieces of sod and threw them at the Quaker. He tried to dodge missiles by ducking his head, but he had not dodged them all for his hair and clothes were covered with dirt. Whenever a clod hit him in the face there was a roar of laughter from the crowd. The third man in the stocks had no ears; they had been cut off long ago, evidently, as the scars had healed. In the middle of his forehead the letter "P" was burned. It stood for "perjurer." He looked wretched and old and tired.

Harriet turned her head sadly and said to Oliver Hillman, "Oh, it is awful. I feel faint." Young Mr. Hillman took her arm at once to lead her away, and they went along slowly, with Comfort following them. They stopped now and then to see the games—the boys playing scotch-hoppers (the ancestor of hop-scotch); tip-cat, which was a sort of blindman's buff; leapfrog; and stool-ball. The games of the little girls were not so strenuous and were generally of the ring-around-rosy order.

On the far side of the green a dozen men or more were shooting at a target. Their old-fashioned heavy muskets made a terrific uproar. Comfort said she was frightened and began to cry.

In the meantime Harriet had invited her friend Oliver to come home with them and have dinner. "But you must take pot-luck," she said. "We have nothing special." In reply he remarked that her company was enough for him, and better than any dinner. After this exchange of amenities they made their way across the green to seek Captain Walling at the inn.

Harriet and her little sister waited in the entry of the tavern while Oliver Hillman went inside to tell Captain Walling that his daughters were outside. Young women, in those days, did not patronize houses of public entertainment except occasionally while traveling. In such cases, women who stayed overnight at inns did not ordinarily take their meals in the public room.

Captain Walling, young Hillman discovered, was listening intently to a stranger who had come overland from New York, and was on his way to Boston. This dusty and road-splashed traveler was telling his audience of the actions of Governor Andros in the New York colony, of the quarrel between New York and Connecticut, of the slightly disguised pirates who made the port of New York their headquarters. Harriet waited many minutes before her father appeared.

The importance of the colonial tavern as a news center can hardly be grasped in our generation of cables, telegrams, radios and printing presses. In 1680 there was not even one newspaper in the colonies. The village tavern, or inn, had the place that is now occupied by the newspaper, the radio and the newsreel. Much of the information that one obtained in such circumstances was ridiculously false, of course, and most of the news, even if true, was vague and uncertain.

5

In those days no one traveled for pleasure and only a few, except mariners, made business trips that were longer than fifty miles. The average man and his family stayed at home, winter and summer, and their personal interests lay within the borders of the township. Long journeys were simply out of consideration for most people on account of the time and expense involved, to say nothing of the bad roads, delays, uncomfortable inns, poor food and constant danger of accidents.

In 1704 a trip from Boston to New York took Madam Sarah Knight seven days. This lady, a gentlewoman, was called Madam on account of her occupation of schoolteaching. Today one may take a train at Boston around noon, have lunch in the dining car, and reach New York in time for dinner. Madam Knight—accompanied by various guides—traveled on horseback, for the road was too rough for carriages. She wrote an interesting diary of her journey. It has been printed and is to be found in many libraries.

On her famous trip Madam Knight wore "a little round cap of Lincoln green, a petticoat of green drugget cloth with puffed and ruffled sleeves, high-heeled leather shoes with green ribbon bows, and a riding mask of black velvet."

Note the riding mask. She wore that to protect her face from the rays of the sun, so that her skin would keep its fashionable pallor.

With her guide, who happened, in this instance, to be a post rider who carried the mails between New York and Boston, Madam Knight appeared late one night at the home of a Mrs. Billings and asked for a night's lodging. Mrs. Billings, who lived somewhere in Connecticut, was scared out of her wits and kept Madam Sarah at the door for some time before she could make up her mind. She exclaimed that she had never heard of a woman being out so late, and seemed to think that her caller was a witch. But the way-worn traveler, with the help of the post rider, finally convinced Mrs. Billings that she was merely seeking shelter for the night.

At one of the inns on the road she could not eat the food; it was unclean and greasy and badly cooked. Supperless and weary, she decided to go to bed, and said so to the maid. Then—

> Little Miss went to scratch up my kennel which rustled as if she'd been in the barn amongst the husks and suppose such was the contents of the ticking. Nevertheless, being exceedingly weary, down I laid my poor carkess (never more tired) and found my covering so scanty as my bed was hard. Anon I heard another rustling noise in ye room, called to know the matter. Little Miss said she was making a bed for the men; who, when they were in bed, complained their legs lay out of it by reason of its shortness. My poor bones complained bitterly, not being used to such lodgings, and so did the man who was with us; and poor I made but one grone which was from the time I went to bed to the time I riss, which was about three in the morning, sitting up by the fire till light.

In that era men and women—strangers to one another—often slept in the same room at inns. They did not undress, except so far as to take off their shoes, hats and coats.

Coming to a stream where there was no bridge, Madam Knight had to cross in a canoe. She wrote:

> The canoo was very small and shallow, which greatly terrify'd me and caused me to be very circumspect, sitting with my hands fast on each side, my eyes steady, not daring to lodge my tongue a hair's breadth more on one side of my mouth than t'other. A very thought would have oversett our wherry.

She witnessed much drinking and quarreling among the guests of the inns and overheard stories which, as a modest woman, she does not relate in her book for, she wrote, "they are not proper to be related by a female pen."

Perhaps the lack of news and the circumscribed, narrow lives of the people were the inspiration of many a hair-raising, incredible yarn, for many such tales were in circulation.

One of the most prolific tellers of queer yarns was Captain Lemuel Gulliver, of Milton, Massachusetts. This redoubtable captain was a native of Ireland. He took delight in astonishing his listeners with accounts of the monsters he had seen and his hairbreadth escapes. His friends did not take him seriously, but humorously, and he was called on to talk at numerous drinking parties.

In 1723 Captain Gulliver returned to Ireland. He met Jonathan Swift in Dublin and told him stories of frogs so large that they reached to a man's knees and had musical voices that sounded like guitars; and of mosquitoes with bills as long as darning needles; and of grass that grew as high as a house and was so tough that it could not be cut.

It is believed that his tales inspired Swift to write *Gulliver's Travels,* which was published in 1726.

Chapter III

A DAY IN A VIRGINIA PLANTER'S LIFE

(April 1713)

I

IN THE midst of a dream Edward Swain awoke, and for a time he hardly knew that he had been dreaming. It seemed very real, a scene from life, yet it was misty in spots, as dreams are. Parts of it were funny too, but at first he could not remember exactly why. Oh yes. He had been captured by a war party of the Tuscarora Indians who took him to their camp. After awhile they brought him out to where they were all sitting around a fire, and from their malicious looks he knew that they intended to make cruel sport of him.

Then he stood up and began to talk to them. All of a sudden he knew their language—or so he dreamed—and he made a jolly speech, and told some jokes. He was surprised at himself; he had no idea that he could speak so well. The Indians roared with laughter. When he had finished his talk they clapped their hands and begged him to keep on.

So then he brought out more funny stories, and the Indians sat spellbound. One of the stories was about a dog that had learned to talk. He wished that he could recall just what the dog had said—but no, the dream was confused at that point. But he remembered that in imitating the dog he spoke out of one side of his mouth and made queer sounds. It amused the Indians so much that they did not harm him at all, to his astonishment, but freed him and sent him home with gifts.

After his thoughts about the dream had drifted away Swain was still only half awake, so drowsy indeed that he did not realize where he was. He turned over on the soft feather bed and was about to drop into a doze, when he heard the hall clock downstairs strike six. It had a loud, dull, hammer-and-anvil note that quivered in the air, and was very different from the thin, silvery sound of his own clock at Belmore plantation. All at once he knew that he was in the home of his friend Henry Randall, near Williamsburg, where he stayed as a guest whenever he attended the meetings of the House of Burgesses. The dark curtains of the bed were drawn close together in the fashion of those days, when people were mortally afraid of night air, so he did not know the sun had risen.

But he was wide awake at once and before the last quivering sound of the clock had died on the air he was getting up. It was his custom to rise at six every morning; it was also the custom of everybody else in colonial Virginia except a few lazy sluggards. He went to a bedroom window and looked upon the awakening day. The sun was just above the horizon. Its long, level rays gilded the tops of the pine trees and ran across the brown fields. The April green of the new leaves on the trees made intricate patterns against the bleached whiteness of the sky. Behind the house, in full view from his room, were the slaves' quarters—tiny log cabins with white smoke coming from their clay chimneys. Near them were the stables, the kitchen garden and the sprawling blank-faced barns. Slow-moving white and black servants went about their tasks with the sedate and dignified reluctance of unpaid labor. A negro girl came from the cow-shed with a wooden pail full of milk. At the border of an adjoining field a white man of servile condition was hitching a horse to the harness of a plow. He wore a cap of raccoon skin with the tail hanging down his back, and knee-length leather breeches. From the knees down his legs were bare. He wore no coat; his shirt was of gray cloth. His blond hair was long and kept falling down on his face. Now and then he would sweep it back with his hand. As he worked over the buckles of the harness he glanced furtively, with the quickness of a sly animal, toward the windows of the house.

As Edward Swain looked leisurely over this sunlit and peaceful scene he thought *it is wonderful to be alive*. But this pleasant idea had hardly entered his mind before it was slashed to pieces by unfriendly memories that came like armed men prepared to ravage and destroy.

In some way, Edward recalled, he had offended Governor Spotswood. If he only knew what he had done he might make amends, but the Governor—when asked point-blank by Harry Randall—said that Mr. Swain had not offended him in any way. Nevertheless, on that same day, he withdrew Edward Swain's proposed appointment as deputy treasurer of the colony. There had been a good deal of gossip about the relations of the Governor and his housekeeper, Mrs. Katherine Russell, who was said to be his niece. Swain had heard a lot of it, but he had never repeated a word. No, not a word—unless, of course, he had said something when he had drunk too much. Rum and talk. Wine and loose speech. It was a mystery; maybe somebody had lied to the Governor about him.

And that was not all. At this session of the House of Burgesses—he sat down on the bed to calculate the number of days on his fingertips—at this session of twenty days he had lost more than fifty pounds sterling at cards and dice. It was more than he could afford. *Thank God, the session is now over,* he mused, *and I am going home today.*

Too much pleasant company, and too much card playing and drinking, and not enough work. Last evening, to mention one occasion he had drunk sillabub and French wine at dinner; afterward there was rum punch, eggnog and flip. Besides cards. He remembered that he had won at piquet but lost all his winnings and more at dice. These thoughts were disquieting.

Then there was the disturbing memory of his first attempt last Tuesday to make a speech in the House of Burgesses.

What a fool he had made of himself!

Before the House there was a bill for increasing the import duty on slaves. It was already twenty shillings for every negro brought into the colony, regardless of age or sex, and now they were trying to raise the duty to twenty-five shillings. Just think of it. Tobacco down to twopence a pound and everything else rising in price. An adult slave was worth from thirty to forty pounds, but after one had been brought into the colony it was a long time before he could be trained to farm work, and many died in the first year or two. The proposal to raise the import duty was a destructive measure. Of this Edward Swain had no doubt whatever, and he had resolved to deliver a speech against the bill. He spent much time in thinking over the ideas that he intended to bring out. He proposed to put sparkle and sting into his first oration on the floor of the

House. As a matter of fact, it was the first speech he had ever made anywhere, in the House or out of it.

When he got up on his feet and every face was turned expectantly toward him he felt very foolish. He forgot what he intended to say and started off with a rambling talk on good will and righteousness. In a few minutes he realized that he was making a mess of his speech, so he stopped altogether and tried to think of a more eloquent approach to the subject. When he resumed his discourse he got so tangled in words that he couldn't continue. Red-faced and stammering, he came to a stop. Some of his friends called out encouragingly, "Go on, Ned. Tell 'em what's what," while others not so friendly snickered and made derisive noises. The wag of the House, Shirley Archer of Henrico, called out, in his bellowing voice, "the orator of the occasion was Edward Swain, of New Kent County."

It had been humiliating. The pleasant spring morning had lost its charm when it appeared against the background of that speech. He took off his nightcap and went over to the pewter basin on a stand in the corner and soberly washed his face and hands. *Isn't it a pity,* he thought, *that dreams cannot come to life.* Consider that speech before the Indians. In the Tuscarora language, too. Although he had lived in Virginia all of his thirty-five years he had never learned more than half a dozen Indian words, and had no desire to learn any more. But in the dream he was speaking Tuscarora, telling funny stories, imitating a talking dog, and all the Indians were rocking with laughter.

From downstairs came the clatter of voices, the high treble of children, the soft tones of feminine speech and the deep, chuckling voice of Harry Randall. *The family is up and ready for breakfast,* Swain thought, *and I ought to be there.* By the time he was dressed it was six-thirty, and he was about to leave the room when he realized that he had not said his morning prayer. So he knelt down quickly by the side of the bed and muttered his prayer with such speed that it sounded like one long word, beginning with, "Ourfatherwhoartinheaven . . ." and ending with "praisebetothealmightygodamen." Though the prayer was a mere spatter of syllables he felt better after he had said it. On his way downstairs he began to whistle.

2

All the Randall family except Lucy, the eldest daughter, was at the breakfast table when Swain joined them. Lucy had gone to a dance with Mrs. Harrison, who was also a guest of the Randalls, and they had not got home until after one o'clock. Mrs. Randall thought they needed sleep more than they needed breakfast, and they were still in bed.

"I'm surprised that you didn't hear them, Ned, when they came home," Harry Randall remarked.

"Why? Did they make so much noise?"

"They did not, but those negroes did. As the coach turned in the gate the lines got tangled up with the horse's legs in some way. You could have heard Tim, the coachman, and Zeb—he walked ahead with the torch—talking about it for half a mile while they were trying to straighten it out."

At Swain's elbow stood a white maid in a dark-gray dress with a yellow apron. She put before him a bowl of hominy and milk which had been heated and then sweetened with molasses. Smiling, she said: "Eggs this morning, sir?"

"Yes, Minnie," he replied. "A dish of battered eggs." (Battered eggs were what we call scrambled eggs today.)

In the early eighteenth century negroes were seldom used as house servants in Virginia. All able-bodied slaves, both men and women, were needed for work in the tobacco fields. Another reason perhaps for their exclusion from household employment was that most of the slaves were still too barbaric to be acceptable as servants. They had not learned household manners. The Randalls had only three negro servants in the house. One was an old, white-haired, kindly darky who met visitors at the door and sometimes helped in serving dinner when there were many guests. Another was a bright boy—or young man—who took care of Mr. Swain's clothes and looked after his saddle horse. The third black house servant was a harum-scarum, careless girl named Betty who washed dishes and scrubbed the floors. The white maids were either indentured servants or the daughters of poor farmers.

As soon as he was through with the hominy and molasses Swain turned to the various platters on the table. His battered eggs were to be cooked and served hot, but there were many cold dishes. He selected a slice of baked ham and a piece of broiled partridge. There were two kinds of bread on the table—corn hoecake and wheat biscuits, both cooked that morning and served hot. He took a biscuit, cut it open and spread butter on it. From a shining silver pitcher he poured himself a tankard of cider. The tankard was made of wood with silver hoops around it.

Tea and coffee had not come into use in Virginia in 1713. It is true that a few wealthy families drank tea or coffee occasionally, but these beverages were almost unknown to the colonials in general.[12]

"I'm sorry to hear that you're leaving us today," said Mrs. Randall, a thin, sallow woman in her early forties. At breakfast she wore a silk dress, or gown, of bright colors laid down in an intricate pattern on the cloth. This robe was open at the neck and she had a white handkerchief as a neckpiece. The sleeves of the dress were wide, like those of a kimono. Her cap was of yellow silk.

Mrs. Randall seldom smiled or laughed on account of her teeth. They were black with decay and many of them were missing.[13]

"Yes, Mary, I have to be on my way," said Mr. Swain. "The House has adjourned until fall, as you know, and I have much to do at Belmore. I am thankful to you—to all of you—for your many kindnesses and hospitality."

"Don't mention it," said Mrs. Randall. "It was a pleasure. We've enjoyed your visit and whenever you come to Williamsburg I hope you will make this house your home."

[12] Both coffee and tea came into use in England around the middle of the seventeenth century. There were coffeehouses in London as early as 1650, and Pepys in his *Diary* wrote for September 25, 1666: "I did send for a cup of tee, a China drink of which I had never drunk before."

Coffee was first brought to America by the Dutch of New Amsterdam in 1668. As in the case of tea, the habit of drinking coffee spread slowly.

Unfamiliarity with these beverages and lack of knowledge as to how they should be prepared and served probably retarded their use in the colonies. This was particularly true as to tea. Many housewives, in their ignorance, served the tea leaves with sugar or sirup after throwing away the water in which they had been boiled.

[13] There were no dentists in the early eighteenth century, and consequently there were no false teeth, or gold crowns or dental fillings. Whenever an aching tooth became too painful for endurance it was yanked out by the family doctor. For this operation he used a pair of mechanic's pliers.

"Oh, I shall do that," said Ned Swain, laughing. "And I give you the same invitation to Belmore. It's only twenty-four miles from here, and you do visit us occasionally but you never stay long enough for Sarah to know you as I do. Come and visit us and stay a month."

Having delivered this invitation Swain turned his attention to the dish of battered eggs that the maid had placed before him. In eating he picked up food on his knife and brought it to his mouth. The eggs were slippery and hard to handle.[14]

"Stay a month!" Mary Randall exclaimed. "What with keeping house, looking after the children, and watching servants—why, if I stay abroad even overnight I'm as restless as a cow that's lost her calf."

"That's how Sarah talks, too," Swain said with a laugh. "You ladies take life too seriously."

Mary Randall sighed mournfully, "As the day runs, from sun to sun, woman's work is never done."

Her husband spoke up hastily, and changed the subject. He was sure that his wife would talk for an hour on her troubles. "That roan mare of yours, Ned," he remarked, "looks like a fine bit of horseflesh."

"She's not a mare, Harry. Only a filly. Two years old. You mean Princess, that I rode down here?"

"Aye. The roan out in the stable."

"She ain't out in the stable, now," piped up little ten year old Tommy Randall. "She's out in front." Then, raising his head from his bowl of milk, he said, "I rode her this morning, all the way down to the riverside and back."

"How did that happen?" his father asked.

"Why, Mr. Swain's man Dave was out there combing Princess and I asked him if I might ride her, and he said yes I could as soon as he had finished combing her. After he got through she was sleek as an apple——"

"Dave was getting her ready for our trip today," Swain remarked.

"—and was rearing to go," Tommy continued. "Dave put

[14] At that time—in the early decades of the eighteenth century—forks were coming into use in Virginia, but many persons still used the knife for conveying food to the mouth as a matter of preference. The Randalls had forks at the table, but Swain preferred the knife.

on the saddle and I rode her down to the river and back. Dave was right behind me on that horse of his'n, and on the way back we had a race. I won." The last two words were uttered in a boyish note of triumph.

"It seems to me that you were taking a lot of liberty with a guest's horse," was his father's comment.

"It doesn't matter," said the horse's owner. "I'm glad he rode her; gives her a little exercise."

"She's built like a racer," Randall said.

"Well, she has a right to be. Princess is out of Empress Julia, and her sire is Black Warrior."

"Yes, I know. You bought her when she was a colt."

"That's right," Swain agreed. "From Robert Fitzhugh."

"Your Princess is certainly no plow horse, if breeding counts," Harry Randall said. "Well do I remember seeing both her sire and her dame on the race track, and I've seen them win in some hot trials. Why don't you have their filly on the track?"

"Oh, I don't know. I've enough race horses as it is. Too many, to tell the truth. All eating their heads off. Little Princess makes a nice saddle horse."

"I'm sure she does."

"Come out to Belmore with me today, Harry. I'll show you the stud, and we'll call on some of the neighbors, and can have a lively time. You can get along without him, can't you, Mary, for a couple of days."

"Surely. A change will do him good," Mrs. Randall agreed.

"You hear that, Harry? Ned Swain continued. "I'll take you home with me today."

Then Henry Randall spoke up. "There you go," he exclaimed, "both of you, making plans for me. How do you know I have the time to spare? I have a great deal to do right here. Maybe I'll go and maybe I won't. Anyway, you're not leaving for a couple of hours, and I'll see if it's possible for me to go. If I have to say no to your kind invitation I want you to understand that I appreciate it."

Before he had delivered this speech he had already made up his mind to visit his friend's plantation, but he would not admit it. Why? Because he had cultivated all his life an air of reluctance to agree to anything without first disparaging it, or doubting its worth or validity. This manner had become a deep-seated habit.

By virtue of it, he had become one of the most successful traders in Virginia. In buying tobacco from small farmers to ship to England he began usually by telling the grower that the tobacco market was oversold; that only the best weed had any value, and that was not much; that prices were going down; and that he didn't know what was going to happen if things kept on as they had been going.

He would take a handful of the tobacco offered for sale, roll it between his palms until it was pulverized, and then hold it before his nose. After he had taken a couple of sniffs he would say "Whew!" with a look of disgust and throw the tobacco away. Then he would brush his hands carefully and say to the farmer, "I'm sorry. It's low grade—poor quality. How much do you want if I take it off your hands?"

In purchasing land or slaves he followed the same principle. With the exception of what he had inherited from his father everything he possessed had been acquired by taking it off somebody's hands. Through living and thinking in this manner he had built up within himself a sense of benevolence, a feeling that in taking land and goods off people's hands at low prices he was playing the part of a benefactor.

Outside of this propensity to trade he was an excellent fellow, full of good humor and hospitality. But many of those whose property had been so generously taken off their hands by Mr. Randall were unmoved by his jolly laughter and his wise sayings. They were inclined to sit in sullen, dark-browed contemplation even while he was telling his funniest stories.

When breakfast was over Swain and Randall delayed their departure to play a game of billiards and to have a long and meaningless talk with a music master who had come out from the village to tune a spinet that stood in the large hall, or living room.

They were both saturated with the spirit of leisure which was an outstanding quality of life in colonial Virginia. In this respect Puritan New England and Virginia were far apart. The Puritans were tense, nervous, industrious and so reluctant to waste time that they labored even when there was nothing to do.

The Virginians were placid, friendly, lazy and pleasure-loving. They did not mind if time were wasted, for they had learned from experience that many a thing that ought to be done today could wait until tomorrow without harm.

Their sense of hospitality was so remarkable that one may search the files of history in vain for a parallel. In the eighteenth century a stranger in Virginia, if he were decent and well-behaved, might have lived for a year without any expense for board and lodging, simply by moving from one locality to another and allowing the inhabitants of the various places to entertain him as a guest.

This desire to entertain strangers showed itself in some rather astonishing ways. There are recorded instances of Virginia gentlemen waiting on horseback on a well-traveled road for the purpose of intercepting wayfarers and inviting these travelers to come home with them as guests. The Virginia inns complained frequently that they could make no money because most of the travelers who passed through the neighborhood were entertained, without charge, at private homes.

This overflowing hospitality continued into the early decades of the nineteenth century. It is well known that Thomas Jefferson's poverty, in his old age, was caused by his habit of taking care of so many guests. They ate him out of affluence into poverty. Captain Bacon, his overseer, said of these people:

"They traveled in their own carriages and came in gangs, the whole family with carriage and riding horses and servants, sometimes three or four such gangs at a time. We had thirty-six stalls for horses and only used ten of them for stock we kept there. Very often all the rest were full, and I had to send horses off to another place. I have often sent a wagon load of hay up to the stable, and the next day there would not be enough left to make a bird's nest. I have killed a fine beef, and it would all be eaten up in a day or two."

In curious contrast to the boundless hospitality of the Virginia colonials was the attitude toward strangers in Massachusetts and other New England colonies during this period.

In those colonies all strangers who arrived in a town and appeared to be ready to stay awhile were called upon by the local sheriff, who warned the stranger that if he did not conduct himself properly he would be expelled from the community. Good conduct in the Puritan sense included industry, godliness, sobriety, besides a number of lesser virtues. This notification by the sheriff was known as a "warning out." [15]

Mrs. Earle, in one of her informative books on early New England, mentions a widow in Dorchester who was not permitted to entertain her son-in-law from another town, and there is on record an instance of a woman having been fined for keeping her own daughter as a guest for more than a week. The daughter in this case was a married woman who declared that she could not return to her husband because the weather was too bad for traveling.

If these women had lived in Virginia the town authorities, in all probability, would have urged the daughter to make a longer stay and to invite her husband to come too.

3

Edward Swain and Henry Randall did not leave Williamsburg until ten o'clock. About a dozen yards behind them rode their two servants on shaggy farm horses. Swain's man, Dave Pottle, was white, blond and Welsh by birth. He was an indentured servant who had still two years to serve before his freedom was due. Swain had bought him from a ship captain in 1708 for twenty-five hundred pounds of tobacco, which covered the cost of his passage from Bristol, the money value of which was around twelve pounds sterling. To repay this debt David had been indentured for seven years. Upon his release from service his master would give him, according to the Virginia law, fifty acres of land, two suits of clothing, a felt hat, twelve bushels of corn meal and a gun worth twenty shillings.

Randall's servant was a negro slave, a native of Africa, alert and quick and unusually intelligent. He was about twenty-five years old, and had been in America for more than ten

[15] As late as 1714 the town of Boston prohibited citizens from entertaining strangers without giving notice to the town authorities, with a description of the stranger and a statement of his reasons for coming to Boston.

years. As he had never worked in the fields, but had always been a house boy, he spoke English remarkably well. His master had acquired him in the course of a somewhat complicated financial deal with a poverty-ridden planter who was in debt to a merchant in England and could not pay what he owed. The merchant threatened to get a judgment against the Virginian and seize all his property. At this point Henry Randall, who was familiar with the state of affairs, stepped in and agreed to take the whole thing off the planter's hands. He proposed to pay the debt in full; in return for which the planter would transfer to him half his land and four slaves. The planter would then be free of debt and would have half his land left—also a number of slaves.

The debtor owed sixty thousand pounds of tobacco to the London merchant for merchandise and moneys advanced at various times. Randall, upon reading over the contract between the planter and his English creditor, noted that no money value of the tobacco was stated in the document. It specified simply that payment was to be made in sixty thousand pounds of "first grade tobacco." But when the debt was incurred first grade tobacco was selling at sixpence a pound. Some time afterward the price began to drop steadily, year after year, and when Randall paid off the obligation any quantity of first-grade tobacco could be purchased for twopence a pound.

This transaction turned out very well for Randall, though he said at the time that he expected to lose money on it, and was going into it merely to assist a worthy man. Through it he acquired three hundred acres of farming land and four able-bodied negroes for an outlay, on his part, of less than five hundred pounds sterling.

In all his business dealings Randall was meticulously careful to do everything that was required of him, and even a little more. One of his favorite sayings was, "It pays to be generous." So, in this case, he not only sent sixty thousand pounds of first-grade tobacco to the creditor in London but also two thousand pounds additional. He explained, in a letter to the merchant, that some of the shipment might possibly be damaged by sea water on the voyage, and the extra two thousand pounds was sent to cover such a possibility.

The London merchant, who seems to have been a grasping

person, mean in spirit, did not thank Randall for the gift of the two thousand pounds of tobacco. Instead, he wrote angrily that a few more transactions of that kind would ruin him.

One of the four slaves that Randall had acquired through this financial deal was Mathew, or Mat, who was now riding behind him. He took care of his master's clothes and saddle horses. The garments of a gentleman, in that period of Virginia history, required a great deal of attention, for they were expensive and made of delicate fabrics. The greater part of Mat's time was given to them. He had become a fairly competent journeyman tailor, and could make repairs in the garments.

Henry Randall's suits, like those of many Virginia gentlemen of that era, were made in London. Every Virginian of means had an English tailor who kept his measurements on file and also knew his tastes in clothing. An order for a suit took from three to five months to fill, on account of the long ocean voyage both ways. There were some tailors in Virginia, but it seems that the higher social class did not patronize them.

The usual costume of men of wealth and authority consisted of knee breeches made of broadcloth, velvet or silk; a vest of colored silk—usually green or scarlet; and a coat of broadcloth. The vest was long in front and tight fitting. The coat reached nearly to the knees and was square-cut, with large pockets. Below the waist it flared out. It was usually dark-blue or black, but other colors—such as scarlet, brown and green—were also worn. A gentleman's clothes had buttons of silver or brass; men of lower rank had wooden buttons.[16] Shirts were of white linen, with lace ruffles on the bosom and at the wrists. The well-dressed man wore silk stockings, usually red in color, and boots with wide, spreading tops. But these clumsy boots were not worn all the time. On bright, clear days the gentleman would appear in low shoes, and indoors at home he wore soft leather slippers. The head covering was a large,

[16] The ordinary horn button, so common today, was unknown until after the Civil War. In Colonial times all buttons—even those of wood—were expensive. In 1790 a metal-working concern in Waterbury, Connecticut, began to make buttons of pewter. Gradually they supplanted the buttons of silver and brass. Thirty-six years later, in 1826, Joel Hayden, of Northampton, Massachusetts, invented an ingenious machine for covering wooden buttons with cloth. Most of the outer garments worn by our great-grandfathers had these wooden buttons.

wide-brimmed felt hat which carried a plume. In cold or rainy weather a cloak was worn. There were no overcoats.

The habit of wearing wigs never became as poular in Virginia and the southern colonies as it was in New England; nevertheless wigs were common enough. Nearly all men of authority, or distinction, or wealth, wore them. But wigs were seldom seen on the heads of small farmers, or servants, or workingmen in Virginia, while it is no exaggeration to say that virtually all males in New England—from about 1710 to 1770—had wigs of some kind.[17]

Both Randall and Swain were wig-wearers. Randall had adopted the fashion because he was partly bald and he thought that a fine, bushy wig would not only conceal his baldness but give him also an air of dignity. Swain's reason was altogether different. He detested wigs, but he wore them because Governor Spotswood was a wig-wearer, and he wanted the Governor to have a good opinion of him. He owned ten wigs, of different shades of brown.

The road was merely a lane, or so it would be called today. It was not wide enough for two carriages to pass while going in opposite directions, but this was no hardship, for carriages were so few in Virginia that two of them were not likely to

[17] The wig-wearing craze, if one may so call it, lasted in the colonies for approximately one hundred years, and it came to an end almost as suddenly as it had begun. Around 1680 wigs began to appear in sufficient numbers to cause comment. The fashion was imported from England. At first—and, indeed, for many years—they were called *periwigs,* a word which comes, through some strange etymological transition, from the French word *peruke.* Common people in England, who knew no French, pronounced the word *perwyke* or *perwige,* and the next step in evolution was to call these head coverings *periwigs.* This word was the prevailing name until somewhere around the middle of the eighteenth century, when the *peri* was dropped and the word was simplified into *wig.*

The wearing of wigs met at first with tremendous opposition from the Puritan elders. Sermons were preached against the new fashion, and in 1675 the Massachusetts legislature denounced the wig-wearers. Nevertheless, the wig habit increased, and before long even the ministers were wearing them. Outside of New England there was no opposition to the fashion. Even the Quakers of Pennsylvania cut their hair and wore wigs.

It seemed as if the craze had come to stay, and wig-makers—haughty with affluence—strutted through the streets. But around the beginning of the American Revolution the fashion lost favor and declined so rapidly that, within a few years, it had practically disappeared. When men ceased to wear wigs they took to wearing their hair long in the back and tying it in a queue.

meet on this quiet road which ran from Williamsburg northwest to the Pamunkey River. It was a beautiful highway, running under a green arch of trees. Though it was still early spring the leaves were already out. They had the clean, smooth freshness of youth, as yet unspoiled by dust or decay.

The little cavalcade of two gentlemen and their servants had hardly left Williamsburg when they came to a straight stretch of road about half a mile long. It was entirely empty. Ned Swain changed the subject of conversation abruptly; they had been talking about the tobacco crop, a subject of neverfailing interest in colonial Virginia. Swain said, pointing down the straight road, "Let's run a race, Harry."

Harry Randall looked reflectively at the highway, his hand rubbing his chin. "How far?" he asked. "Oh, down to the end of this straight piece," Swain replied. "See there where that big tree leans across the road. Down to there. How about it?"

The two servants had ridden very close, and were listening.

"It seems to be about four furlongs, Ned."

"Yes, that's right—four furlongs, half a mile."

"Oh, I don't know," Randall said. "Your Princess can outrun my Caesar. You know that, so what's the use?"

"No, I don't know it," Swain argued. "If I were sure of it I wouldn't propose the race. My filly is not a sprinter. She doesn't get her speed under six furlongs. But your Caesar gets his speed at the start. This is a sprint, Harry, and I'd like to see how it turns out."

Randall sat still on his horse for a moment, looking up and down the road and patting Caesar's neck. Then he looked at Swain, and said, with a laugh, "What odds will you give me, Ned? I ought to have three to one—twenty shillings of mine against sixty of yours, considering——"

"No, no," Swain interrupted. "No odds at all. Even money."

"But I admit your horse is better'n mine. So I ought to have odds. Come on. How about two to one?" Swain shook his head.

"Well, then we'll make it even," said Randall, "with the understanding that the winner pays for the entertainment—dinner, drinks and so on—at Phillips' tavern, where we're going to stop at noon. Is that all right? Even money, with the winner paying the bill at the tavern."

"Oh yes, that'll do," said the owner of the fleet Princess.

With much chuckling and laughter, they dismounted and got ready for the race. Swain's servant—the serious, blond young man—was to be the starter. First, a heel mark was made across the road. This was the starting line. Then Dave took his place about ten yards in front. When the horses were on the line he was to say "Go" in a loud voice, and the horses were to start. The goal was an imaginary line under the tall tree that leaned across the road about a half a mile distant from the starting place.

Randall and Swain were busy adjusting their saddles and bridles, while the servants rubbed down the horses' legs. At last they were ready, and mounted. The two riders gave their plumed hats to the servants to hold. Dave and Mat were to follow behind the race and rejoin their masters at the goal.

When the signal was given both horses dashed forward at a gallop. Their owners sat straight upright on their horses' backs, as though they were hunting foxes, contrary to modern jockey practice which directs the rider to lean forward until his body is almost parallel with the track.

Dave and Mat cantered along behind the racers. "Want to bet?" said white-skinned Dave to black-skinned Mat.

"What mek you t'ink I got any money to bet, white man?"

"Yo' got a shillin', niggah. I saw it."

"Dat doan count; I'm savin' dat shillin'," Mat replied, "to buy somefin' for my gal. No suh, I doan do no bettin'."

"Yo' ain't got no sportin' blood," Dave remarked.

At the end of the first hundred yards Caesar was more than a length in the lead, and this lead was increasing. Swain felt for the first time that he would lose the race. Princess seemed to have no interest in the matter. He wondered if he ought to give her the whip and spur so early or wait until they were near the finish. When the race was more than half run, with Caesar leading, Princess began to pick up speed. Swain was ready to give her the whip, but she gained so rapidly that he decided to let her run the race her own way.

Then came the last furlong, with the tall tree that leaned across the road getting closer every second. Randall was urging Caesar with his voice and plying the whip, but Princess gained steadily. Now it was neck and neck, and next instant the filly forged ahead. She crossed the finish line—the shadow of the tall tree—two lengths ahead of her rival.

Randall leaped off his horse and ran over to shake hands with Swain, the winner. "You ought to be proud of that nag," he exclaimed.

"Ha! Yes, she's swift," Swain exclaimed. "But your Caesar's got something, too. I thought when we were coming along back there that he'd outrun Princess."

When the servants came up Randall was counting out twenty shillings from a capacious wallet which he carried in an inside pocket of his coat. Dave leaped off his horse and ran to Princess. He looked her over, rubbed her legs and pulled open her mouth. "Sound as a lump o' sugar," he said to his master. "I thought mebbe it tired her a little, but no—not a bit. She could run another one right now." The negro servant Mat had also dismounted, but he did not approach Randall's horse. He handed the plumed hat to his master and helped him get back in the saddle.

In a short time the four riders were on their way again. The road they followed would take them first to Phillips' ordinary on the Pamunkey River, then another road along the river led to Belmore, which was the name of Swain's plantation.

As they cantered over the level country side they discussed everything that was of public interest in Virginia, everything from taxes to churches, from firearms to ships, but their talk was light and trivial. They did not take it seriously; the chatted merely to make conversation.

"I have sixty-two pairs of mourning gloves," Swain remarked. "I wish I could get rid of them."

"You have a lot," said his friend. "I haven't half that many —no, not a third. I think I've got about a dozen pairs. How did you get so many?"

"I'm a member of the vestry out my way, you know, and surely I must attend every funeral," Swain explained, "and that means a new pair of gloves."

"Why not sell them? I've never sold any, but I know they can be sold to clothing merchants."

"I'm thinking of that," Swain said.[18]

In the northern colonies these mourning presents were sold or given away after many of them had accumulated, but in Virginia at the time under discussion—the early 1700's—there was a general feeling that such a manner of disposal indicated disrespect toward the dead.

"I know a man named Sparrow, or Starrow—something like that—who goes about in a little cart all over the country in this part of Virginia——"

"Oh, yes, I know him," Swain remarked. "He sells things to women, such as needles, wool for knitting, mirrors and so on."

"Well, he'll buy mourning presents," Randall continued, "if you tell him you have some to sell."

"Thanks. I'll keep him in mind."

As they approached tidewater the woods gave way to great fields of growing tobacco. Here and there they saw the huge barns to which the tobacco leaf was taken to dry, and near by were the plantation buildings—a mansion of brick or of heavy timber for the master, and behind it a little village of the cabins in which the servants and slaves lived. The huts of the slaves were always separated by a small field or vegetable garden from those occupied by the white indentured servants.

At that period of Virgina history, and for many years thereafter, tobacco was the life blood, heart and bones of the colony. It was an economic error of the most vicious kind for the colonists to turn all their attention to tobacco planting, but their motive may be readily understood. Tobacco was the only agricultural crop that could be sold immediately in Europe for cash on the spot. It was therefore looked upon as ready money. As a result the Virginians neglected every kind of manufacture.

The historian Robert Beverley, who was a native Virginian, wrote in these terms of his countrymen in 1705:

> They have their cloathing of all sorts from England, as Linnen,

[18] It was the custom in all the colonies at that time for the relatives of deceased persons to give, at the funeral, pairs of gloves to all those who were invited to attend. Sometimes rings were given in place of the gloves. These articles were known as mourning gloves or mourning rings. They were a large and useless expense. The custom died out before the American Revolution.

> Woollen, Silk, Hats and Leather. Yet Flax and Hemp grow no where in the World better than there; their Sheep yield a mighty Increase, and bear good Fleeces, but they shear them only to cool them. . . . The very Furrs that their Hats are made of, perhaps go first from thence; and most of their Hides lie and rot, or are made use of, only for covering Dry Goods, in a leaky house. Indeed some few Hides with much adoe are tann'd, and made into Servants Shoes; but at so careless a rate, that the Planters don't care to buy them, if they can get others. . . . Nay, they are such abominable Ill-husbands, that tho' their Country be overrun with Wood, yet they have all their Wooden Ware from England; their Cabinets, Chairs, Tables, Stools, Chests, Boxes, Cart-wheels, and all other things, even so much as their Bowls and Birchen Brooms, to the Eternal Reproach of their Laziness.

For several decades tobacco growing was very profitable. The crop sold at high prices, so high indeed that planters were encouraged to drop all other pursuits and give their whole attention to tobacco. So intense was their preoccupation that the colonial government made a law to the effect that every farmer had to plant a certain number of acres in corn or wheat to keep the colony from running short of bread.

Eventually more tobacco was produced than the market could take and pay for. Result: a drop in tobacco prices that brought the Virginians to the edge of ruin. For several years this state of overproduction existed, then the market widened, which means that more people in Europe began to use Virginia tobacco. The shipments from Virginia to Holland were as large as the shipments to England. Virginia tobacco went even to Spain, which was a tobacco-producing country. Prosperity returned to the Old Dominion. Then the next blow fell. The British government in 1660 forbade the Virginians to ship their tobacco anywhere except to England. It had to be sold to English merchants who resold it to the Continent. Out of twenty-five million pounds that were shipped to England in one year, seventeen million pounds were re-exported.

This measure of the British Government gave the English merchants a despotic power over the tobacco trade. They could pay as little as they pleased to the planter, then increase the price in reselling the tobacco on the Continent. The planters' shipments were paid for, usually, in manufactured goods, such as clothing, furniture and tools. The English merchant could put an exorbitant price on this merchandise, as he had no competition. The chief result of these uneconomic practices was that the tobacco planter ran deeper in debt, year after year. When the American Revolution began many a planter owed more to his London merchant than he could ever hope to pay.

With leaf tobacco occupying such a powerful position in the economic life of Virginia it is not surprising that it became a form of currency. People carried silver coins in their purses and had some more locked up in their houses, but metallic money was used only in small transactions. Substantial payments of every kind were made in tobacco.

A clergyman was paid a yearly salary of sixteen thousand pounds of tobacco; a schoolmaster received about half as much. The wages of carpenters, bricklayers and mechanics were stated in terms of tobacco. But tobacco varied greatly in value from time to time. These fluctuations gave a gambling uncertainty to business affairs.

The economic pattern of Virginia life was disastrous to the small farmer, and in the end it produced a permanent class of poverty-stricken whites. The owners of large estates grew their crops of tobacco with the labor of black slaves and indentured servants. These workers got no pay, and their living conditions were subnormal. The poor white farmer had to compete with them. With tobacco as low as twopence a pound the large-scale grower could produce it profitably, but the small farmer could not make a living. The estate owner had his own agent in London to sell his tobacco, while the small farmer had to sell his crop to the grasping merchant at the crossroads. Long before the beginning of the eighteenth century the colony had a class of landless poor whites, who were either tenants of the great estates, or mere drifting ne'er-do-wells.

Swain and Randall, with their servants, reached the Phillips' inn shortly after noon. The correct name of this ordinary was "Turkey in the Straw," and the large red, gold and black sign that swung before its door showed the picture of a turkey on a straw pile, scratching away, with the straw flying. But the name was seldom used in that neighborhood, for Robert Phillips and his wife Nan were local celebrities, and people thought of them before they thought of the sign.

The inn was at the side of a road that ran down to Phillips' ferry on the Pamunkey River. This was on the main road from Williamsburg to the northern counties, and it was fairly well-traveled. Those who came to take the flat-bottomed scow which served as a ferryboat usually had a drink or two at the inn while they waited, and those who had just alighted from the boat made their way, as by instinct, to the bar that ran along one side of the low-ceilinged, heavy-beamed room which served as office, dining room, drinking place and debating forum.

Phillips always had the midday meal served promptly at half-past twelve. According to Ned Swain's calculation they would have time to eat, bait the horses, and smoke an after-dinner pipe before leaving at two o'clock. Like most time-wasters, Swain was very particular about hours and minutes when making appointments or arranging the day's work. "We ought to leave the inn, Harry," he explained, "at two promptly. We're a long way from Belmore and I want to get home before the sun sets. Yes, let's make it two o'clock; certainly not later than a quarter-past two."

Henry Randall agreed, and the servants were told to get their dinner in the servants' room off the kitchen and have the horses out in front of the inn at two o'clock promptly.

It did not work out as planned. The Swain-Randall expedition did not leave at two, nor at half-past two, nor at three, nor at half-past three. It managed to depart a few minutes before four o'clock. The delay was probably unavoidable; at any rate it was anticipated by Mr. Swain's servant David, who—as soon as he had eaten—took off his shoes and lay down in the servants' room for a nap. Just before two o'clock his colored traveling companion tried to arouse him to help saddle the horses. "What time is it?" Dave asked dreamily, and Mat replied that it was almost two o'clock. "Then call me at three," Dave said, dropping to sleep again.

At the dining table in the large room of Phillips' ordinary there were three men and two women besides Swain and

Randall. One of the men was a professor—or teacher, as he was called—at William and Mary College in Williamsburg, and the women were his wife and daughter. He was on his way to his brother's plantation on the Potomac. Both Swain and Randall knew him and his ladies, and there was much friendly conversation.

One of the other men, who introduced himself as a trader from Philadelphia, got into an argument with Randall on the subject of holidays, especially Christmas. At that time in our history Christmas was not much different from Sunday in Virginia, and in all the colonies except those in New England—where it was not observed at all—and in New York, where it was a feast day.

The Philadelphia trader was no Quaker, although he came from William Penn's Quaker colony. His argument was emphatically in favor of everyone having a grand time on the birthday of our Lord. "I have to go to Europe sometimes; once in every three or four years, and I will never forget a Christmas that I spent in Strasburg. That's in Germany. It's a festival where everybody's joyful and happy, and it's a great day for the children—for grown people, too."

"What do they on that day?" This question came from Ned Swain.

"I'll tell you. Have you ever heard of Saint Nicholas?" He addressed the company at large.

"No, never; I have not," Randall answered. "He is some foolish and wicked pagan saint, I suppose." He mentally liked the idea of a holiday being made of Christmas but he disapproved of it verbally because that was the only way he knew of meeting a new idea.

"Oh, no," said the professor, who had been listening. "Saint Nicholas is a jolly fellow, full of good cheer. I've read of him. He is sometimes called Santa Claus."

"That's right," said the man from Philadelphia. "Saint Nicholas, or Santa Claus, is a very kind old saint. On the eve of Christmas the children hang up their stockings before the fireplace, and Saint Nicholas drops in during the night and puts presents in the stockings. That's what the children think, but the presents come from their parents. The good old saint is described as a jolly old soul with a long white beard. He wears a red suit trimmed with white fur. And he has a pocket full of sweets. He passes them out, so they say, to everybody he meets."

Randall exclaimed, "What nonsense! I'm glad we do not teach our children such lies. Even the very young children ought to be able to see through it."

The Philadelphia man was flustered by this reception of his tale of Saint Nicholas, but he managed to say, "It does nobody any harm. But that is not all. Every family that can afford it has a little fir tree brought into the house, and set up standing in their main room——"

"A tree in the house!" said the professor's wife. "How queer, and what for?"

"They put little candles on the tree, and at night they are lighted. They are pretty, seen on a snowy night through the windows. The grown people give each other presents and they are hung on the tree. Sometimes the children's presents are too. On Christmas morning the people are merry, opening their presents and drinking healths. They sing carols on Christmas eve."

"We sing carols here—in the towns, like Williamsburg," said Ned Swain.

"Everybody has a fine dinner on Christmas day," the Philadelphia traveler continued. "A great deal of laughing and singing."

"It must be a very pleasant occasion," said one of the ladies.

"We haven't enough holidays," Swain remarked. "The Queen's birthday, and——"

"The very idea of desecrating the birthday of our Lord with a false saint." This comment came from Henry Randall. "Here in Virginia we observe Christmas as Christians should. It is a holy day—sacred and holy, as it should be. We stop work, and listen to a sermon, and rest in the afternoon. That's sensible." By this time Henry Randall was getting very tired of his position in the discussion and wanted to be on the other side.

"Yes, Mr. Randall," said the younger lady, "but you know it's usually a very dull, solemn day."

"Well, have it your way," Randall said, laughing loudly

and winking at the professor. "I can't argue against everybody." [19]

The party lingered long over the meal. It was not served in courses, but all the dishes were put down on the table at once. There was a vegetable soup, fried oysters with a hot sauce, fish chowder, roast goose stuffed with boiled peanuts, sweet potatoes, carrots, preserved fruit, apple pie and the patrons had their choice of variety of drinks, such as ale, beer, cider, rum punch, flip, sherry and peach brandy. The ladies wanted coffee after the meal, and it was finally brought in cups as large as bowls. While waiting for it the professor's wife remarked that at home they had coffee every day. "Also tea, mother," said the young lady. "Yes, coffee and tea," the mother agreed, and anyone could see that the professor's wife considered the habitual use of tea and coffee a step upward in social prestige. When the coffee came the professor's wife looked at it critically, remarked that it was much too strong and declined to drink it. She told her daughter not to touch it. "Coffee cannot be prepared without some training," she remarked to the table at large. "People who are not accustomed to elegant living had better leave it alone. Just look at that"—she pointed to the coffee in the huge, ugly cup—"so heavy and bitter that a nail would float in it."

The professor paid no attention to his dame's discussion of the coffee situation; he was eager to set forth his views on an important matter. He thought, and said, that there should be a gazette in every colony—a gazette which would print and publish the news of the colony, of all the colonies, of the world. "As it is now I live in thick, African ignorance. All of us do. We depend on letters from friends, on hearsay, and most of the news we get is wrong. Now suppose we had a well-conducted gazette here in Virginia. It would have a

[19] Christmas Day, as we know it, was introduced into the American colonies in the 1740's by the Moravians who founded Bethlehem, in Pennsylvania. They brought their Christmas customs from Germany, their native land. Saint Nicholas was well-known in Germany, the Low Countries and in Scandinavia long before the Moravians and the New Amsterdam Dutch popularized him in America.

In Puritan New England there were strict laws against observance of Christmas in any manner. It was just another working day. Even as late as the first half of the nineteenth century Christmas was neglected in many New England communities.

reliable correspondent in London, in Holland, in Boston, New York and Philadelphia."

"Heartily do I agree with you, sir," said the fifth man at the table, a stranger who had not, until then, said a word to anyone. "Every colony ought to have at least one gazette—two would be better—for knowledge, and that means news and information, is one of the foundation stones of civilized life. As far as I know there is not a news sheet in any of the colonies."

"Yes, there is," Swain said. "There's one in Boston called the *News-Letter*. I've seen it."

"Do you call that flimsy little thing a public gazette?" the professor demanded. "It is just one sheet, about the size of writing paper, and——"

"The Boston postmaster gets it out," said the stranger. "All he puts in it is what he hears in taverns and nearly everything in it is a lie." [20]

"Yes, that's so," the professor agreed. "There are in this dominion of Virginia about ninety thousand people. Twenty thousand are negroes who cannot read or write, and that applies also to most of the whites, but I think one person in four can read. Well, a gazette ought to gain at least a thousand subscribers, and that would be enough, I should think, to support it."

There was some further conversation about the need of a gazette, or newspaper, in which all the company—including the contrary-minded Randall—agreed. The cost of starting a gazette would have been only a few hundred pounds which could have been raised right then and there without crippling anybody financially, but no proposal of the kind was made. Like many other topics everywhere, in all eras, the subject of gazettes in Virginia in 1713 was just something to talk about.

The first Virginia newspaper did not appear until 1736,

[20] The Boston *News-Letter,* the first issue of which appeared in 1704, was the first newspaper published in the American colonies. It was a weekly, and was printed on both sides of a single sheet—size 7 by 11½ inches. Its publisher was the Boston postmaster of that era, whose name was Campbell. It attained a circulation of three hundred copies. All the news or rumors that it contained came either from the post riders who delivered letters in New England, or from sea captains and sailors.

(*The Bettmann Archive*)

FIREPLACE IN A COLONIAL KITCHEN.

(Wood Engraving.)

(*The Bettmann Archive*)

SPINNING AND WEAVING IN A COLONIAL HOME.

The art of stocking-frame-work-knitting—a domestic industry.

when William Parks, a printer of Williamsburg, started the Virginia *Gazette*.

Some of the early governors of Virginia were greatly opposed to newspapers, and to free education. Sir William Berkeley, governor for many years, wrote home to England in 1677, "I thank God there are no free schools and printing, and I hope we shall not have them these hundred years." This openly expressed sentiment is quite different from the attitude toward education in New England. In 1644 the Massachusetts General Court ordered every community of fifty persons or more to establish a school.

After much more talk about this and that, the smoking of pipes and the drinking of toasts, the professor remarked that he must find his ladies and be on his way. His wife and daughter had excused themselves and were sitting in the garden.

Swain seem startled, not at the departure of the professor and his family, but at the flight of time. "Why, it's half-past three," Swain said hurriedly. "We should have been on our way long ago. Landlord, bring our bill."

Phillips came with the bill. It amounted to thirty shillings and some pence—including meals for four, baiting of four horses, many drinks and toasts to this person and that. Swain gave the landlord the twenty shillings he had won from Randall and ten shillings more, besides a handful of pence.

Out in front of the inn the professor and his family were leaving. They were going on horseback. Swain and his friend went out to say good-by. The horses had pillion saddles, so that a woman could sit sideways behind the rider and keep herself balanced by putting her hand on his shoulder. The professor's wife rode behind a white groom and the daughter rode behind her father. Both the ladies wore long, clinging skirts, cloaks fastened at the neck, and caps which sat tightly on their heads and were tied under the chin.

Behind them rode a black slave, with their boxes and bundles dangling from his saddle.

4

As the Swain party went on to Belmore in the late afternoon Swain and Randall made their horses cut out capers in the road, just for the fun of it, and now and then they would burst into drinking songs and old English ballads. After awhile they became weary of this horse-play and rode along sedately, in a manner that befitted men of standing in the colony.

"We are getting near to Belmore," Randall said, pointing to a long, low structure by the side of a creek. "There's your sawmill, Ned."

"Sure enough," Swain said, "and in another half mile we'll come to the brickyard."

He took more pride in these industries than he did in the long-reaching acres of the tobacco plantation. "I've never failed, even in the worst of years," he told Randall, "to make good money out of the distillery, and the brickyard, and the sawmill, and the carpenter shop. Even when everybody was losing money on tobacco I was making a profit on these workshops."

In the distillery he made peach brandy, and the carpenter shop was devoted to cabinetmaking in a rough way; it made kitchen furniture.

Groups of workers, white and black, appeared now and then at the roadside. They were Swain's laborers, going home, their day's work over. The male servants wore leather breeches, gray shirts, cloth caps and leather coats. Most of them were barefoot, but three or four wore heavy, square-toed shoes, without stockings. The negro women had gowns of linsey-woolsey that were raised up to their knees and fastened by a rope which ran around the waist. All of them were barefoot. There were no white women among the field hands.

It was not quite half-past six when they trotted through the gates of Belmore and up the circular graveled road to the mounting block before the front door. There they leaped off their horses and turned them over to Dave and Mat.

The manor house at Belmore was new; it had been built in 1710. In plan and architectural features it belonged to the latest type of Virginia plantation houses as they were in the early decades of the eighteenth century. It was built of dark red brick. The front steps led up to a terrace that ran across the front of the house. A striking feature of the façade was the imposing door frame of white marble.

The ground floor had only three rooms—a long and wide living room, a smaller reception room, and a dining room. A hallway that was fifteen feet wide ran through the house, from front to back. In the hallway rose a curving flight of stairs which ran gracefully to the second floor. There were six bedrooms on second floor of the main house, but no bathrooms. The people of that era bathed only on rare occasions, and when they did bathe it was in a wash tub brought into a bedroom for that purpose.

Above the second floor there was an attic which was used for storing things. The house, like most homes in Virginia, had no cellar. There were two chimneys, one at each end of the house, and four fireplaces—two downstairs and two upstairs.

The main building had two ells, or wings—one on each side. In one of the wings there was a huge kitchen on the lower floor. Upstairs there were rooms for some of the house servants. The wing on the other side of the house contained a library—Swain possessed about a thousand volumes—and its upstairs portion had four additional bedrooms.

The walls of the chief rooms were paneled in dark oak; the bedrooms had wall paneling of white pine or poplar. The hall was so wide, the rooms so spacious and the ceilings so high that the house gave a visitor an impression of airiness. In this sense it was quite different from the New England houses, which were built to resist cold weather.

All over the house sconces for candles were set in the walls. The job of keeping the place lighted took the whole time of one slave. The black man molded the candles, kept the sconces and candlesticks polished, and went around every day to replace the burnt candles with fresh ones. All the candles used in the house were infused, in the making, with the juice of juniper berries, and the rooms were filled with this pleasant odor.

In the kitchen the cooking was done at a huge fireplace, as in New England. Stoves were unknown. Outside, in the yard near the kitchen, was a brick baking oven. It was used chiefly to bake bread and cakes.

On the walls of the rooms downstairs were some paintings of inferior grade—most of them portraits of relatives. They had been made by English painters who came to Virginia to seek commissions for their work.

After having been greeted pleasantly by Mrs. Swain, whom he had known several years, Henry Randall was shown to his room by a young Negro girl, who brought him immediately a pitcher of water and some towels. He knew that dinner was ready, and he hurried through his ablutions. The lace ruffles on the ends of his sleeves were drooping, and altogether he seemed a little disheveled, but he did not take the time to change.

Then, with his face washed, his wig set straight, and the dust of travel brushed off his coat, Henry Randall descended leisurely the wide curving stairs. The family and guests were assembled in the large living room. Randall paid his respects to all in turn, bowing and taking their hands. First was old Mrs. Lightfoot, the mother of Sarah Swain; then in order came Mrs. Swain; Mr. and Mrs. Kirkland, who were house guests—their home was in Maryland; and the Swain grown-up children, Edward, Jr., who was twenty-one, and Frances (known as "Fanny") who was a few years younger. The smaller children were having their dinner in a room off the kitchen.

The dresses of the ladies were all voluminous, spreading around them in so many folds and frills that the shape of the wearer had to be a matter of inference rather than of observation. These garments of silk were highly colored, and the fabrics had figured designs on them. The effect was precisely the opposite of nunlike simplicity.

When dinner was announced the party went into the dining room with the pleasant gravity of attendants at a cheerful ceremony. Henry Randall could not help thinking that it would have been very different at his own home. There the children would have dashed in first, laughing and shouting, and the guests would have entered in a straggling manner, all in a bunch, and all talking at the same time.

On the dining table there was a spotless damask tablecloth—beautiful and costly. The candles, under their pink shades, lighted the table with a soft glow and left the rest of the room in a shadowy twilight. Under the candlelight the burnished silver dishes shone. The servants moved about as quietly as ghosts, speaking in low tones to one another and to the guests.

Randall had often been a guest of the Swains and had witnessed their manners and customs, yet he never failed to be impressed. How had they acquired such gentle suavity? This faint air of stateliness? His own home in Williamsburg was as large and as well-furnished as Edward Swain's, and he knew for a certainty that he possessed more property and money than his friend, but there was something else that he did not possess. He did not know what it was, not clearly, and when he reached out his hand to seize it, this unknown quality slipped away or melted into nothing. He bought a very expensive and beautiful silver service in London and sent it home, but he found that when it stood on his table it looked drab and tawdry. It would not have, he was sure, looked so shabby on a table at Belmore.

People never quarreled during a dinner party at the Swains', nor did they beat on the table with their fists or with their spoons when they engaged in argument, but the guests at his dinners did that. Why? He did not know.

Mrs. Lightfoot, the mother-in-law of Edward Swain, was an old lady, in her late sixties. She appeared to have lost most of her memory and had various mild delusions. One of them was that Henry Randall, whom she liked, was a close relative of the high-bred Randall family of Sussex County. In her youth she had visited them many times and, on her one trip to England she had stayed for a couple of days with the Duchess of Huntington, who had been Lady Isabel Randall before her marriage to the Duke. She had a fixed notion that Charles Randall, founder of the Virginia family, was Henry Randall's grandfather. "It is to people like your grandfather," she had said to Henry more than once, "that Virginia owes so much. They were gentlemen, my dear, and in those days the word *gentleman* meant something. It meant courage, honor, courtesy and loftiness of spirit. Today we are being overrun by the scum of the earth that are unloaded on our shores; the trash of the London streets."

Time and time again her son-in-law had told her that Henry Randall was not a relative of the other Virginia Randalls, but the old lady either forgot the information or disregarded it. Finally he ceased to remind her and Henry Randall, on his part, stopped telling her that he had no relatives in America, as he realized that she paid no attention to him.

Randall would have been embarrassed by Mrs. Lightfoot's eulogies of his mythical family if it had been possible for him to be embarrassed by anything or anybody, but his skin was too tough to be pierced by an old lady's yarns, so he took it all in smiling good humor.

The facts were that Henry's father had been a huckster in London, selling fresh vegetables from a donkey cart for his master, who owned the cart and the farm from which the vegetables came. His wages were so small that he never possessed more than three or four shillings of his own at any one time. He had heard people speak of Virginia as a new and rich land and he made up his mind to go there—but he had no money to pay his passage. Eventually a ship's captain agreed to take him if he would become an indentured servant for seven years. Young Randall agreed. The fare cost ten pounds, and the captain was to sell him to a master when the ship reached Virginia.

He had the good fortune to be sold to Thomas Whitaker, a planter who was kind and generous. Long before his servitude had expired Servant Randall was given a cow and a litter of pigs by Master Whitaker. In course of time the cow had a calf and the pigs increased in number. Randall sold cows' milk to customers in Williamsburg. When the pigs were grown he slaughtered them, smoked their hams and bacon in Virginia style, and sent this choice meat to England to his master's agent to be sold for him. With the shipment went more than thirty skins taken from beavers that Servant Randall had caught in traps.

He wrote to the agent in London to take the money coming from the sale and buy with it a number of articles of luxury, such as silk handkerchiefs, perfumes, finely carved pipes, mirrors and razors in their cases. These goods came just after he had finished his seven years' servitude. He sold them to plantation owners and their ladies at three times their cost in London. With this money he bought goods that Indians like from merchants in the colony and took them to the frontier, where he traded them for skins. The skins went to London, and back to Virginia came a shipment of luxuries.

This three-cornered trade continued for several years and Randall accumulated a considerable amount of money. Then he went into the business of importing men and women.

Under Virginia law anyone who brought a settler or an indentured servant or a slave into the colony received a "headright" from the colonial government. This headright entitled its owner to fifty acres of land on condition that it be occupied within two years. After he had the title to the land nothing more was to be paid by the recipient except a quit rent of a shilling annually on each fifty acres. This was a land tax which applied to every landowner in the colony.

Randall went to London and arranged with a shipping agent there to act as a procurer of emigrants. When they reached Virginia he sold them to planters on indentures that ran from five to ten years. He made a profit on the cost of their passage across the ocean, and received besides fifty acres for each person. When he died in 1700 he possessed three thousand acres of land, of which twelve hundred acres were under cultivation. He was also the owner of a mercantile business and of several slave ships that brought negroes from Africa. Soon after his servitude to Whitaker had expired he married a white maid servant, and she (now dead) was Henry Randall's mother.

Henry was not at all ashamed of his father's humble origin, but rather proud of his rise from poverty to wealth. However, when he inherited the fortune he sold the slave ships and got out of that business—not that he objected to slavery, but he thought slave-catching was too low an occupation for a gentleman.

The rise of Randall's father from the indentured servant class to a position of wealth and authority was not at all unusual. Contrary to modern opinion the indentured servants were not all criminals, not even a majority of them were. But all were poor. Among the poor adventurers there happened to be many who were clever, enterprising and able. To a large degree they must be considered the founders of modern Virginia. In 1665 nearly half the members of the House of Burgesses had come to Virginia as indentured servants.

In the course of the dinner, when the richness and flavor of the turtle soup had been discussed, and the baked fish brought in, Mrs. Lightfoot turned to Henry Randall and asked him if he had heard lately from his cousin Laura, who had married Lord Glendower. Randall smiled and replied, "No, I haven't heard from her in a long time, I'm sorry to say."

Mrs. Lightfoot then told the company in her highly pitched but pleasant voice, the story of Laura's marriage. "The family sent her to England to reside a year, so she might learn the customs of polite society over there. In letters she mentioned a young Lord Glendower, but the Randalls thought little of it until—lo and behold—one day came the news from Laura that she was now Lady Glendower and one also from her husband. You must have been quite young at the time, Henry. That was about thirty years ago."

"I was just a boy," Randall said.

"You remember her golden hair and fine blue eyes," Mrs. Lightfoot continued.

"Perfectly. And her fine complexion."

"Oh, dear," sighed Mrs. Lightfoot, putting her hand to her white hair upon which there was a cap of dark-blue silk. "It all passes in time—youth—golden hair—bright eyes. All in time. Then white hair and wrinkles."

The Kirklands, who were from Maryland and not well acquainted with anyone present, began to look upon Randall with obvious respect. Mrs. Kirkland remarked that there were some fine old families in both Virginia and Maryland, and her husband said emphatically that the best people ought never to intermarry with those of common origin, for it could only lead to a general lowering of the race. "It's all in the blood," he said. "Nothing can take the place of fine blood." He looked at Henry Randall. "Isn't that so, Mr. Randall?"

Henry replied, "It is, indeed."

Then, during the venison course, Mrs. Kirkland hinted at the family relationship of the Kirklands to the Calverts, founders of Maryland.

In the air there floated the mystic sense of exclusive possession, the aura of a superiority which would exist forever despite the talents, the wealth, the beauty and the daring of those who did not possess it. If Henry Randall had been gifted with a telescopic vision of the future he would have seen, in distant years, the constellation of F F V's—or First Families of Virginia.

When the subject of birth and blood had run its course Mr. Kirkland turned to Ned Swain and said, "Oh, I forgot, Mr. Swain, to ask you how your speech came out—the speech you were to deliver yesterday in the House of Burgesses."

Swain, who was one of the most modest of men, and also one of the frankest, flushed a little and said, "I'm afraid it was a failure. The fact is I didn't complete it. I'm not an orator."

"Oh, pish tush! That boy's fault," exclaimed Mrs. Lightfoot, nodding toward her son-in-law, "is that when he does a good thing, he'll never admit it. How did his speech go, Mr. Randall?"

Henry Randall, who was neither modest nor frank, said in reply, "It was quite a success, Mrs. Lightfoot. I was not there, you know, as I'm not a member, but those who were there said the House sat like people under a spell. You know he spoke against the bill and must have killed it, for the bill was defeated. Shirley Archer—you've heard of him—he always pokes fun at the speakers, came out on this occasion just the other way. After Ned's speech he said in his loud voice, 'The orator of the House at this session is Edward Swain, of New Kent County.' "

"I knew it would be that way," said Mrs. Lightfoot, with a radiant smile. "Blood will tell."

After the dinner the company played cards until eleven. Randall lost a pound and three shillings, and Swain won a little. The big winner of the evening was Mrs. Lightfoot, who seemed to have an uncanny skill in card playing. Her eyes glistened, her voice grew louder, and her thin hands shook with excitement. She won more than two pounds.

On his way upstairs to bed Edward Swain said to Sarah, his wife, who accompanied him, carrying a lighted candle, "My dear, I haven't done a thing all day, but I'm as tired as if I had been at hard work since dawn."

Chapter IV

WHEN NEW YORK WAS YOUNG

I

IN 1750 THE HOME of Major Daniel Lawrence, a sturdy house of Dutch pattern, stood on William Street, near the corner of Wall. New York was as quiet as a country town in those days. There were shade trees—locust or poplar—on all the streets; during the summer nights the air was full of the chirping of katydids, and the inhabitants were awakened in the morning by the piping of birds.

Behind the Lawrence house, and belonging to it, there was a garden, an orchard of pear trees, a stable and a press for making cider. A dovecote and a dozen beehives were just beyond the garden. It was a quiet place, with nothing to break the silence but the loud talk of the servants in the kitchen and the clatter of plates. Now and then Mistress Lawrence or her daughter Elizabeth played the spinet in the sitting room and its tinkling notes ran quivering through the air.[1]

The family had a part in the social life of the town, and occasionally the house was full of company. Then the chatter of soft feminine voices and loud masculine laughter ran all over the house and garden.

Though it stood almost in the center of the city of New York the Lawrence place had a rural air which flowed from the day's activities. Every day the cows were driven through the streets to a common pasture which was a short distance west of Broadway, and were milked on their return in the late afternoon. There was always work to be done in the gardens, the stables and the orchard, fruit and vegetables to be gathered, horses to be curried, pigs and chickens to be fed, and the ground cleared of weeds.

Like all other streets in this colonial town, William Street was simply a muddy or dusty road—depending on the state

[1] The spinet is often mentioned as the forerunner of the piano. That is not altogether correct. The strings of the spinet and the harpsichord were *plucked* by pressing the keys, and in that respect they resembled the harp, not in appearance but in action. On the other hand, the clavichord resembled a piano in that the strings were *struck* by hammers which were moved by pressing the keys.

of the weather—and there were no sidewalks, nor was there a street-cleaning department in the town administration. But every Friday, the year round the streets had to be cleaned by the householders and the refuse thrown into the river. Each resident cleaned only that part of the street which lay in front of his house.

The street lighting was done by the citizens. One householder in every seven hung out a lantern before his residence, and six of his nearest neighbors shared with him the expense of keeping the light burning.

The Lawrence house was nearly fifty years old. Major Lawrence's father had built it in 1705, and the Major had lived in it all his life. He said he did not like the place, and that if he could sell it he would build a more elegant and spacious residence, but he never tried to sell it, nor to acquire another place. He declared that the house was out of date, and it was, for since it was built the spacious Georgian type of residence had become the prevailing architectural pattern. The Major complained that the ceilings were too low, the halls too narrow, and that the little windows with their diamond-shaped panes did not admit enough sunlight.

The house was as rigidly rectangular as a barn, without any projecting wings, bow windows, or architectural frills of any kind. But it was well-proportioned and the bricks used in building it were of various colors, such as yellow, brown, blue and red, arranged in curious designs. This decorative brick gave the house a certain air of lightness and charm.

Following the Dutch fashion, one of the narrow ends of the house faced the street, and was right on the thoroughfare. Before the front door there was a little porch called a *stoop,* a word which comes from the Dutch *stoep.* From these stoops came the idea for porches and verandas. Strange as it may seem, the English colonials knew nothing, at first, of these open-air attachments to houses and only learned of them from the New Amsterdam Dutch.

On warm summer evenings it was the custom for everyone to sit on the stoop, and the street had a lively appearance with all the vivacious front-door parties laughing and singing, and visiting one another.

On the ground floor the house had four rooms—parlor, dining room, library and kitchen. Above, on the second floor, there were six bedrooms; and over them was an attic used by the servants. There was also a cellar for storage of household supplies. Just behind the kitchen, with a door opening into it, was the woodshed—a dark, roomy place in which a whole winter's supply of wood for heating and cooking might be kept. The use of coal was unknown, and wood was the only fuel, not only in the American colonies but throughout Europe.[2]

On the roof there was a cupola—a sort of covered balcony which could be reached by the stairs. In the summer months the family often sat on the roof balcony in the afternoon. From it the East River could be seen, and the heights of Brooklyn. Many houses on Manhattan at that time had these cupolas.

There were, of course, no running water, toilets or bathrooms, for such conveniences did not exist in the middle of the eighteenth century. Water for drinking and washing was brought to the Lawrence house in casks by a contractor who made a monthly charge for this service. Many Manhattan families had wells on their premises, but there was none on the Lawrence place, for when they had gone down forty feet the well diggers had struck solid rock instead of water.

It is one of the pleasant features of life and human nature that we never miss anything that is unknown to us nor of which we have never heard. Many of us recall the time when there was no radio. Yet there was nothing missing; people did not feel then that they had been deprived of something they wanted. The same observation is true of motion pictures. Today there are millions of movie fans who were living before a picture ever appeared on the screen, and they did not miss

[2] When Marco Polo returned from his long trip to Asia about two hundred years before Columbus discovered America he told the Italians that, in China, he had seen black stones burned to make a fire for cooking and warmth. This story about black stones burning in a fireplace spread over Europe and was one of the tales that served to give Marco Polo a reputation as a monumental liar. Of course, the black stones were pieces of coal. They existed in Europe where coal seams came to the surface of the soil and were looked upon as a nuisance. That nobody tried to burn them until England was almost denuded of her forests is a remarkable fact. Americans did not consider coal a fuel until about 1790, when a few began to use it experimentally.

the entertainment which now occupies so much of their attention. They passed their evenings in other ways.

The colonials did not miss our "modern conveniences," nor did they feel as uncomfortable in their living arrangements as we are inclined to think. In winter, Major Lawrence arose and dressed in a room that was icy cold. There was no steam heat; he had never heard of such a thing, so he did not feel deprived of it, and he was accustomed to cold weather. If anything happened to cause him to get out of bed during the night he rose in utter darkness; there was no metal switch in the room for turning on a light, nor even an oil lamp. (Many families kept a candle burning all night in some part of the house. It was usually set in a dish that floated in a bowl of water.) If he started out on a trip to Boston he expected to be from four to six days on the road; that was all right, too, for it was in the nature of things. Most of the roads were bad, but they always had been and everybody was used to them. If he wanted a picture of a member of his family he hired an artist or painter to make it. That was expensive and inconvenient. A photograph, costing very little, would have been a better likeness, but the art of photography was not yet born, so it was not missed. The out-of-town news in the New York *Gazette* or the *Journal* was from three to twenty weeks old, depending on the distance it had to travel before it reached New York. But who had a right to complain? It took that long for the news letter to make the trip.

If one of our generation could be transported in time back to the middle of the eighteenth century he would find nothing above his comprehension in the prevailing mode of living. It would all be readily understandable, but he would probably find colonial life dull and in some ways foolish.

Excessive drinking of alcoholic liquors was virtually a universal habit. This statement does not apply to New York alone, but to all the colonies. Now and then—but very seldom—our twentieth-century visitor might encounter a person who did not drink at all, and he would soon learn that the total abstainer was looked upon with suspicion by his neighbors and was generally disliked.

The hardy drinkers of colonial times thought nothing of mixing gin with beer, and rum with beer, which are combinations usually avoided by the bar flies of the present day, as such mixtures are likely to induce rather quickly a form of temporary paralysis.

A rum-and-beer drink that bore the name of flip is mentioned so frequently in the chronicles of the time that one gets an impression that it was almost as prevalent as soda water is today. Here is a recipe for it, if you would like to give it a trial. In a quart pitcher two-thirds full of strong beer add enough sugar or sirup to give the beer a sweet taste. Then put enough rum in the pitcher to fill it. About half a pint will be needed. The mixture should then be heated by stirring it with a red-hot poker.

The iron, or poker, used for this purpose in colonial days was called a loggerhead. If it is sufficiently heated it will cause the mixture to boil and to acquire a burnt, bitter taste.

A loggerhead was part of the mechanical equipment of every fireside. At times it was used in controversy to take the place of the logical syllogism. In the debates that followed the convivial absorption of flip the disputants would sometimes seize loggerheads for the purpose of bringing their opponents to a state of material, if not mental, conviction. Thus arose the expression, "to be at loggerheads."

2

It snowed heavily on the night of the fourth day of December of the year 1750. On the morning of the fifth Major Lawrence walked to his office through the snow. There was a brightly painted sleigh standing in his stable, but he preferred to walk for the exercise. He did not have to go far, as his office was at the foot of Maiden Lane and scarcely three blocks from his house.

On account of the snow he had put on cavalier boots as overshoes. His feet were not small, and to accommodate them and his shoes, too, the boots—reaching above his knees—had been made very large. Standing in them, he looked rather grotesque, like a man walking around with barrels on his legs.

He wore a plum-colored square-cut coat which reached to his knees and flared out from the waist downward. His knee breeches were of black broadcloth. His vest, or doublet, was of dark yellow silk with flowery designs on it. There were lace ruffles on his shirt front and at his wrists. He wore a three-cornered cocked hat. At his side he wore a sword, buckled around his waist, beneath his coat. As a protection from the weather he carried over his shoulders a whittle, which was a sort of cross between a shawl and a blanket. In those days whittles were worn by both men and women in place of heavy coats.

The Major was an importer; he had correspondents in the West Indies, and on the African coast. From the islands of the West Indies came molasses (to be made into rum), raw sugar, and various tropical fruits. From the coast of Africa his ship brought slaves—not to New York, but to South Carolina—for at that period black slaves had becomes so numerous in New York that their prices had collapsed and the trade in them was no longer profitable.[3]

He did not have much to do at his place of business on this snowy day, so he returned home shortly after noon and had his dinner. As soon as the meal was over he went into his library, leaving word that he was not to be disturbed by anyone, as he had much work to do. He remembered suddenly, however, that this was the fifth of the month, so he turned to Dykins, his man servant, and said, "That does not apply to Miss Fraser. If she comes bring her in at once. This is her report day, but with all the snow on the ground I hardly expect her."

"She is very prompt, sir, as a rule," Dykins remarked.

"Yes, she is; and she is the only one I intend to see, if she comes. Tell anyone else who calls that I'm too busy today to see people."

The Major had no work to do in the library and Dykins knew it. His seclusion for two or three afternoons a week on the pretence of attending to his personal affairs was one of the polite fictions of the household. He was accustomed to spend these quiet afternoons in pipe smoking and reading, or in playing solitaire. Sometimes he would take a nap on the sofa. Occasionally, just to show that he was not idle, he would make quite a fuss over some papers on his desk.

[3] In 1750 Manhattan had about 13,000 inhabitants. Twenty-five hundred of them were negro slaves. Besides the negroes held in bondage, there were many indentured white servants.

In the course of the afternoon the Major would do a good deal of solitary drinking. For his convenience a liquor cabinet had been installed in one of the closets that stood at the side of the chimney. The cocktail had not yet been invented, but there were other varieties of mixed drinks—and, of course, there was beer. Rye and bourbon did not exist, and Scotch whisky was not imported. Like most colonial drinkers the Major preferred rum in its many combinations. Applejack—called "Jersey Lightning," in the current slang—was also one of his favorite tipples. Another was arrack, an ardent spirit distilled from rice and molasses.

But he never drank any of the cheaper brands of liquor, such as gin, which was consumed chiefly by working people, by slaves and servants. It was extraordinarily cheap; a few pence would buy a quart of gin. Its popular name among the lower classes was "Strip and Go Naked."

On this wintry day a fire of cedar logs blazed in the huge fireplace. They gave forth an odor that was reminiscent of a forest in summertime. In that era grates were unknown, so the fire was laid directly on the square stones that formed the surface of the hearth. Above the fireplace there ran across the chimney a thick, heavy mantel. At each end of it stood a candle in a silver candlestick.

Displayed on the mantel and on the bookcases were curios from foreign lands which the Major had acquired from sea captains. These queer ornaments were not only in the library but all over the house. On top of a bookcase there was the shrunken head of a savage from Brazil. The bones had been removed in some manner, and the whole head had shrunk until it was not much larger than a fist, yet its features were perfect. The Major took great pride in this ghastly relic.

He possessed also some colored fabrics with intricate designs. They had come from Java, he would explain to his guests, and were called *batiks*. There were, also, in his collection several small figures of carved wood, a Japanese screen, and a chair from the West Indies made of bamboo. Equally important among his show pieces was his china ware. He had decorative plates, "paper-shell" cups, platters with festive scenes on them, and liquor bowls that shone with pictures of events on a race track, horses and jockeys in gay colors dashing round the outside of the bowl. The china dishes were seldom brought into regular use on the table until much later in our history.[4]

The Major and his wife had a handsome and valuable collection of silverware which they kept in a locked closet on the second floor. It was seldom shown to visitors, but on special occasions it was used for service, as when the British admiral dined with the Lawrences. On that memorable day the dining table gleamed and glowed with tall silver tankards, great platters of solid metal, and bowls, plates and cups of silver.

In colonial times banks did not exist in America, and the unnecessary amount of silverware in the homes of the well-to-do took the place of bank accounts. It could always be turned into money quickly.

Besides the bookcases filled with solemn-looking tomes the library contained the Major's desk, a mahogany table, a sofa covered with flowery designs, and six chairs.

The desk was so typical of the eighteenth century that it might as well be selected as the most representative piece of furniture of that era. It was the kind of desk that was used by Washington, John Adams, Benjamin Franklin, Jonathan Edwards and thousands of lawyers, doctors and men of business. It was narrow and tall. The writing surface was hardly wide enough for two sheets of paper. The upright portion rose to the height of about six feet. It had glass doors and several shelves for papers and books and drawers in the lower part of the desk which could be locked. A desk of this kind is seen occasionally even today, and it is usually called a "secretary."

The materials for writing lay in a recess on the same level as the writing surface. There was an ornate inkwell of brass, a metal holder containing three goose-quill pens, and a silver shaker of fine sand to be used in blotting the freshly written sheets. Blotters were unknown and sand was used instead.

[4] The custom of using pieces of china and porcelain only as ornaments continued until the last quarter of that century. When china ware was first imported, and for years thereafter, it was considered too fragile and too ornamental to be used for the sordid purposes of eating and drinking, so it became customary to place the pieces around the house as ornaments. For table service the well-to-do had either pewter or silver, or the two combined. Common pottery was in use, however, in kitchens and among the poorer people.

On the finely polished mahogany table in the center of the room stood a bowl of long-stemmed pipes, a silver tobacco box, and a large candelabrum with branches for six candles. Also a flint-and-steel fire-maker, which was used occasionally for lighting pipes when the candles were not yet lighted and there was no fire on the hearth. The fire-maker consisted of a piece of flint held immovably in place by metal prongs. The flint could be struck by a hammer like that belonging to a musket, by cocking the hammer and pulling a trigger. The spark, thus created, fell into a little metal box filled with cotton, or lint, or fine wood shavings. The smoker then transferred the burning lint to the bowl of his pipe.

It is an astonishing fact, but it must be recorded as a matter of history, that matches did not come into existence until the 1830's. The friction match, so common today, is a simple chemical product. It has no mysterious ingredient and is not at all difficult to manufacture. One wonders why its invention was so long delayed. The lack of matches, during the thousands of years while they were unknown, must have been a perpetual nuisance—certainly it would be to us—but, as we have remarked before, people do not miss what they have never heard of.[5]

In Major Lawrence's house a fire was kept burning in the kitchen twenty-four hours a day, in summer as in winter, for the purpose of supplying coals for lighting. This was a common practice among well-to-do families. Among the poor the constant fire often went out from neglect, or from lack of fuel. In that case the family usually borrowed fire from a neighbor rather than depend on the uncertain results of flint and steel.

3

Dykins knocked at the door, opened it a few inches and peeped. "Miss Fraser has come," he said. It was then about three o'clock.

[5] In 1827 John Walker, an English druggist, invented a match made of chlorate of potash, sugar and gum arabic. To ignite this match it had to be drawn swiftly through a piece of folded sandpaper. It did not work very well.

The phosphorus match, in use today, was invented by Alonzo D. Phillips, of Springfield, Massachusetts. He was by trade a shoemaker. On October 24, 1836, he was granted a patent on his invention.

The Major replaced the book he was reading and took another from a bookcase near at hand. He had been reading Aphra Behn's novel, *The Nun, or The Perjured Beauty,* and the book he took in its place was Bunyan's *Pilgrim's Progress.* He did not consider the gabby and flamboyant Mrs. Behn's piece of fiction immoral but it was light and amusing, and after all Miss Matilda Fraser was a teacher of young girls, so he thought it better, as a matter of policy, to have her find him engaged in a more serious occupation than the reading of a trashy novel.

"Well, well, Miss Fraser," he chuckled merrily as he stepped forward to greet her. "I'm glad to see you, as always, but I hardly expected you to come on such a cold afternoon, with the snow a foot deep."

"Oh, pshaw, pshaw," she said vivaciously in a slightly high-pitched voice. "I'm neither sugar nor salt, and I can stand a little bad weather." As she spoke they sat down on the sofa. "In any case," she went on, "the sky has cleared, the sun's shining and it's a fine day."

Miss Fraser was a slender woman of about thirty-two. Her hands were large, her features were plain and her blue eyes shone with a quick and lively intelligence. Living in an era when any woman of over twenty-five was considered an old maid, Miss Fraser was a spinster who expected to remain so.

She wore a sage green cloak that covered her from head to foot. On her head was a blue silk cap of bonnet shape. When she had it on only her face was visible. It was fastened by ribbons tied under the chin. Upon entering she took off her hat and cape, and laid aside the muff that she was carrying. Her bell-shaped skirt, made of dark linsey-woolsey, was stiffened by whalebone sewed into the skirt itself and not separately as a hoop. Her green silk bodice was plentifully supplied with lace on the collar and the sleeves. The skirt was not long; it showed about three inches of leg above the shoe tops. The short skirt was an innovation, or new fashion, that was causing much comment in New York at that time.[6]

[6] Fashion is a fickle mistress, subject to unaccountable changes. The sensible vogue for shorter skirts in the early 1750's lasted only a few years, then the ladies resumed their ground-sweeping garments. The present fashion of short skirts did not come in until well along in the present century.

"How did you come?" the Major inquired. He glanced at the delicate, high-heeled shoes, made of damask. "Didn't walk, I hope."

"Oh, dear me, no!" she replied. "With these shoes!" She held out her feet. "Ned and Fanny Humphrey took me for a sleigh ride—a lovely ride over the clean, glittering snow—and I asked them to let me down here on the way back." There was a thin trace of excitement in her voice, in everything she said. The Major had often noticed it, and wondered as to the cause. "They had quite a party," she continued. "Six people besides myself, with just room enough for me to squeeze in——"

"It's a fine day for sleighing," the Major said, interrupting her. "Maybe I ought to be out myself, driving on the snow. You can hear the bells so clearly from here"—he held up a finger for silence, and into the room came the jingle, jingle of the sleigh bells in the next street—"but I felt that I ought to renew my acquaintance with this excellent book." He held up *Pilgrim's Progress* for her to see the title.

Miss Fraser, who was a little nearsighted, peered at it closely for a moment. "Oh, *Pilgrim's Progress!* That's one of the books my second year girls are expected to read. A good book, a *very* good book. Well, as I was saying, there was just room for me in the Humphreys' sleigh, and I was squeezed almost flat between Alice Knight and Mr. Stevens—you know that bachelor—Mr. Stevens—the lawyer——"

"Yes, I know him, Miss Fraser."

"I believe there must have been at least fifty sleighs on the road between here and the Kissing Bridge, driving furiously, all of them. One turned over—nobody hurt."

"Did you cross the Kissing Bridge?" Major Lawrence asked, with a smile.

"Yes, we did, and we dined at the Two-Mile Tavern. Had turtle soup——"

"Major Lawrence raised his hand and said with a laugh, "You're leaving out something. When you crossed the Kissing Bridge who kissed you?" [7]

[7] The famous Kissing Bridge was over DeVoor's mill stream, and it crossed the creek at what is now Fifty-second Street and Second Avenue. Every lady, married, single, or widow, was supposed to be kissed upon crossing this bridge by the gentleman accompanying her.

"Oh, that," she answered slowly, and her face flushed a little. "I knew you'd ask that question. Why do men always think of such things? I try to be polite, and one is expected to kiss at that bridge. A foolish custom. Why, to answer your question, Major, I was kissed by Mr. Stevens both coming and going. After we dined we played two games of backgammon, drank some toasts and drove back. They left me here at your door."

"Do you like Richard Stevens?" The Major asked this question with a twinkle in his eye.

"Ah—why—I suppose so," Miss Fraser replied. "I hardly know him. Now, don't imagine things, Major Lawrence, you teaser. Just remember that we're living in the year 1750. In this modern time women don't fall in love with every man who looks at them."

"Or who kisses them," the Major said with a laugh. "Did you bring your monthly report with you?"

"Oh yes, I have it here."

Women did not carry handbags in those days. Instead, they had voluminous pockets in their skirts. Miss Fraser delved into a pocket and brought out a folded blue paper which she handed to the Major. He unfolded it and turned the pages while she looked around the room.

Miss Fraser was the principal of a girls' school of which Major Lawrence was the chairman of the board of trustees. The school had a small endowment that was supplemented by voluntary contributions from the six trustees.

At that time general opinion, both high and low, was opposed to the higher education of women. Miss Fraser's fount of learning certainly did not pour a college education into the minds of her little flock of girls, nor was any such pretence set up. The pupils were taught about as much in the way of book knowledge as the pupils of grammar schools are taught today, perhaps even less. Nevertheless, many New Yorkers of that period thought and said that even that much instruction was wasted on females.[8]

[8] The word *female* had, for some reason, a peculiar attraction for writers of that era, and for even a century thereafter. In case of an accident, such as the sinking of a ship, the writer of the news would refer to the bravery "of the females" aboard the vessel. Publishers advertised books as especially written for

To the eighteenth-century mind woman's place was in the home, and the inference was that she had no business dabbling in things which were not in her natural province. It was clearly understood that all the thinking of affairs outside the home and the sewing circle was to be done by the men.

In many communities the girls did not attend the regular schools; they went instead to a dame school where a little primary education was given to them. When a girl had learned to read, to spell simple words, to write fairly well, and to know arithmetic up through the multiplication table, her school days were over. But her education in the arts of homemaking went on much longer.

Every young woman of a well-to-do family was taught how to knit, how to embroider, how to do fancy sewing; and most of them were taught the art of preparing meals. Also there was music and dancing. A girl of eighteen was supposed to be able to play the spinet or the harp, and to know how to dance the intricate figures of the period.

Girls of poor families did not go to school, as a rule, for there were no free schools and all pupils had to pay partly or wholly for their instruction. The laboring classes could not afford to pay the fees; and, besides, their children were usually hired out at an early age. In New York, and in the southern colonies, a large proportion of the population was illiterate.

In spite of the prejudice against the education of women Miss Fraser's little school gained a good deal of local popularity among the higher social classes. She did not accept very young pupils. "I'm not running a nursery," she said, and she insisted that before admission a girl must have passed her twelfth birthday; moreover, she must know well how to read and write and have a good knowledge of ordinary arithmetic.

Miss Fraser's father, who died when she was twenty years of age, was a professor at Oxford in England. Nearly everything she knew had come from him. In the New York school she did most of the teaching, although she had a young assistant. The girls learned a little history, enough geography

---

"females." The woman heroine in a novel was usually called "a female of great beauty." This usage of the word continued up to the Civil War. The word "woman" was considered common and applicable only to females of low degree.

to give them a fairly good idea of the continents and countries, and a bit of grammar, rhetoric and composition. Literature and the lives of authors also had a place in the curriculum. Every pupil paid a monthly tuition fee, as the income from the endowment, with the gifts of the trustees added, did not provide sufficient income to carry on the work of the school.

"This financial report," said Major Lawrence, folding up the papers, "seems to be perfectly clear. Expenses didn't eat up quite all the income last month, I see. Excellent. How did that happen?"

"We were rather lucky, I suppose," said Miss Fraser. "Mr. Lispenard, as you'll recall, gave us our entire supply of wood for the winter, from trees cut down on his estate, so we shall not have to buy any. That's an expense we usually have in November. Then we have three new students, and their fees amount to something."

"I see. The trustees will be pleased. I must pay the school another visit this month—say about the fifteenth."

"Oh, do come, Major. We were all so pleased with your talk the last time you came. The girls thought you were jolly. The new girls were surprised. They had never heard you talk before, and when I told them you were coming they expected a tight-lipped, gloomy talk on behavior, but you talked about New York, and the strange sights that may be seen right here."

The Major laughed. "Yes, yes," he said, "I'm one of those old-fashioned fellows who believe that education should begin at home. When I was a boy at school I learned that the earth is round, that it floats through space, and is called a planet. One day our teacher said something about the surface of the earth, and I asked him, in my innocent manner, where the surface of the earth is. He astonished me by saying that the ground under my feet is the surface of the earth. Before that, geography had seemed to me to deal with something far away. All of a sudden I realized that I was living in geography. That's why I talked to the girls about New York. Learn your own neighborhood first—and then spread out. That's my way."

"It's mine, too," said Miss Fraser. "It's the only sensible way. You said something that has interested me very much. New York, you said in your talk to the girls, is the most cosmopolitan community in the world. Are you sure? This little colonial town?"

"Well, I'm not absolutely sure," the Major replied, "for I have not counted the people here or anywhere else, but I am fairly certain that this little town on Manhattan Island would stand—if not at the top, then very near the top, in the list of cosmopolitan communities. At least fifteen languages are spoken here."

"As many as that?" queried Miss Fraser, who seemed astonished.

"Quite. I see you're surprised, but you don't have to deal with all classes of people, as I do in my importing business. It's a town of many nationalities. Jews come here from all parts of Europe because they are free in this colony to live their own way and to practice their religion. Then there are the French Huguenots, and the Swedes, and the Italians. Even the Arabs. We have a group of them here."

"Arabs! I've heard of them," Miss Fraser said, "but I don't think I've ever seen one."

"Oh yes, you have. They look somewhat like light-colored Negroes."

"How did the Arabs ever get here?"

"They were brought by pirates," the Major replied. "Have you ever learned of our piratical history?"

"Why, no," Miss Fraser said, after a little hesitation. "Of course, I've heard of Captain Kidd, but that's all, I think. Were there others?"

"Many," said the Major, "but it must be said in whispers only. Don't tell your pupils, not a word. About fifty years ago piracy was a flourishing New York business. It's prosperous even now, but it is carried on under various respectable disguises. Now we call them privateers, engaged in lawful warfare. Our pirates seldom preyed on ships in the Atlantic. Their operating headquarters were in Madagascar. When they returned to this port they brought Arabs with them, sometimes—and the Arabs remained."

"How extraordinary!"

"Our part in the piratical ventures," the Major continued, "was generally to furnish the ships and take a part of the spoils. Sometimes these speculations were very profitable.

Some of our best blood in these parts has piratical streaks. That's why you had better leave out mention of pirates in your talks to the girls." [9]

Miss Fraser laughed. "You may be sure," she said, "that I shall keep it all to myself. We have no course in piracy at the school—not yet, I mean—so I'll say nothing about the industry."

Major Lawrence looked at his watch. "It's four o'clock," he said, "and my wife expects us to have tea with her. But wait a minute, I must make a note of something I want to remember." He took a lead pencil from his pocket and began to write in a small memorandum book which came from another pocket.

"I'll enjoy a drink of something warm—something hot, I'd better say, after my trip over the snow," Miss Fraser remarked.

"There now," said the Major, putting the book back in his pocket. "That'll refresh my memory." He looked at the thick lead pencil in his hand, and offered it to Miss Fraser. "Did you ever see one of these before?"

She took it and looked at it curiously.

"No, sir," she said, "I've never seen one—it's a lead pencil, isn't it? But I've heard of them."

"Yes, it's a lead pencil, the most convenient implement in the world for writing."

Miss Fraser leaned over the desk and wrote some words on a piece of paper. "It writes beautifully," she said. "A few years ago I read something about lead pencils, and I got an idea that they would always be very rare and expensive—made of some precious mineral—and could never be of daily use."

"That was all nonsense," the Major said testily. "Some

[9] The most gorgeous of the retired pirates in New York history was Giles Shelly. He retired from his long piratical career and came to Manhattan in the early part of the eighteenth century, bringing with him a number of retainers. New York, at that time, was probably the only place in the civilized world where he could have lived without molestation. He acquired a house and lived in it for years in a state of splendor. That he had been a pirate was well known at the time, but he could never be induced to speak of his past life. When he died he left what seems—from reading over the list—to have been an enormous amount of belongings. Among his goods were seventy-four pictures. In those days a picture was a rare object, and many worthy people did not possess even one.

fellow writing for the newsprint. They were expensive at first because nobody knew the best way to make them. Now, they're cheaper. That one cost me sixpence. You take it; you're welcome to it. I bought six of 'em."

"Thanks very much."

"Mark my words," the Major went on. "Within a few years everybody will have a lead pencil. Get your pupils to buy them, and stop writing their exercises with goose-quill pens."

"Can they be bought here in New York?" Miss Fraser asked.

"Oh yes, at Hugh Gaine's bookstore. There's where I bought mine. But they said they were selling only a few of them. People must have time to get used to new things, I suppose."

"It might be better to have my girls use them in writing their exercises, instead of spattering ink all over themselves," Miss Fraser remarked as she put the pencil away in her pocket.[10]

All the schools, including Miss Fraser's, were lacking in equipment, simply because the equipment did not exist. Blackboards were unheard of, there were no slates, and most of the schools had nothing in the way of desks that would be acceptable today. The ordinary school desk was a small rough table with a drawer in it. The pupils sat on stools that had no backs, and wrote their exercises in ink on all sorts of paper. There was much difficulty about ink, for in those days it could not be purchased in bottles. The stores sold ink powders. The customers would take the powder home and put it in water. The resulting fluid was often too thin, or discolored, or full of lumps. Ink was first sold in bottles about the middle of the 1820's.

[10] The pencils that Major Lawrence had were very primitive and unsatisfactory, as Miss Fraser soon learned, no doubt, by trying to put them into regular daily use. The early pencils, like those of today, were made of graphite mixed with a kind of clay, but they were not baked, and they were far too soft and made marks that were too broad. The modern pencil was evolved from them, however. Some bright person thought of mixing the graphite with clay, pressing it into pencil form and baking it. This hardening process created the modern pencil, which came into use in the early years of the nineteenth century, probably around 1810. Graphite is a form of carbon. It is not related to lead, but the name lead pencil comes from the fact that graphite resembles lead in appearance.

4

Tea was served in the dining room. It was called a tea, but in effect it was a light meal. Chocolate and coffee were served as well as tea, and there were small meat pies, cheese, delicate little cakes and sugary confections.

The Lawrences had two guests besides Miss Matilda Fraser; they were young Charles Mason and his wife, from Williamsburg, in Virginia, who were in New York on a honeymoon trip. They were house guests of the Lawrences.

Mrs. Lawrence came forward, smiling, to greet Miss Fraser. She was dressed and decorated in the latest fashion as it was interpreted by the socially elect of Manhattan. She wore a *sacque* of white silk with an elaborate design of flowers on it. Below the waist it spread out, for she wore underneath a petticoat with whalebone ribs in it, so that it resembled a hoop skirt. The stays above and below her waist were tightly laced. They were not as flexible as a modern corset, but held the figure rigid. The sleeves of the *sacque* were short and ended in a fall of lace. Over the skirt of the *sacque* she had on a beautiful apron of white muslin. The apron was very fashionable.

Mrs. Lawrence's hair dressing would have seemed nothing less that preposterous to any modern woman. Her black hair was drawn up straight for about six inches above her head, and was held in that position by some ingenious devices. Distributed through the mass were a number of little objects made of leather. They had the shape of fingers, and were stuffed with something that made them stand upright, but they were invisible when the hair dressing was completed. The hair, pulled up so high above the head, would have fallen at once if it had not been stiffened by pomatum and fastened by hair pins to these leather fingers. Above the "tower," as this structure was called, the ends of the hair were frizzed.

At that time—in 1750—there were forty-one professional hairdressers in New York, and all of them were kept busy. The elaborate piles of hair affected by the women of fashion could not remain in good order more than a week or two before they had to be taken down and rebuilt.

Mrs. Lawrence received Miss Fraser graciously, calling

her "my dear" and inquiring as to the state of her health. Then she introduced the Masons and they went to the tea table. A maid servant in a green dress and a white apron was bustling in and out of the dining room. In the fireplace a cheerful fire was burning.

Miss Fraser looked around for Mrs. Lawrence's daughter and did not see her, when the girl's mother, pouring tea, said, "You're looking for Elizabeth, Miss Fraser? Why, the dear child is skating today on the Collect Pond. I told her you were coming and she'd better stay home, but she insisted on going with her young friends; she said you see her five days a week and that is enough. How is the little darling getting on with her studies?" Miss Fraser reflected that the "little darling," though only fifteen, was nearly as tall as her mother, besides being quite as heavy, and that she probably detested her mother's habit of treating her as if she were a baby.

"Oh, Elizabeth is one of my best pupils," Miss Fraser assured her. "She is indeed so diligent that she is an example to the others."

Mrs. Lawrence came from one of the original Dutch families that had settled New York. Her maiden name was Greetje Van der Lyn. She possessed the innate Dutch qualities of order and obedience. In her management of the household she retained some of the customs of her upbringing. The sitting room of the Lawrence house was, in no sense, a lounging place. It was never opened except on momentous occasions, and these were months apart. The polished floor was covered by a thin coating of white sand which had been swept by a broom into curious patterns and curlicues. Of course, this pattern was destroyed as soon as the room was occupied, but next day it had to be restored and the room closed. On all ordinary occasions the dining room was used as the living room.

"Charles and Nellie Mason," said the Major, nodding toward his Virginia friends, "are here on what may be called a leisurely tour, just to see the place. They've been to Philadelphia for a week, and after they leave our town, they're going to Boston, and from there back to Virginia by sea. Am I right, Charles?"

"You're quite right, sir," Charles Mason replied. He was

a tall, lean, handsome man of thirty-odd. Miss Fraser soon learned that he was inclined to be talkative. Nellie, his wife, had that fond, innocent look in her eyes that one sometimes sees in the eyes of pet animals. It would baffle the imagination to conceive of her doing anything contrary to her husband's will, or of being displeasing to anyone.

"We saw some very, very interesting curiosities today," said Mr. Mason. "One was a porcupine, his back full of darts, which the man said he shoots at you if he don't like you——"

"They look like writing pens," Mrs. Mason remarked.

"Did he shoot any at you?" the Major inquired.

"Not a dart," Charles Mason replied. "He liked us, I suppose. We paid sixpence to see the porcupine, and another sixpence to look at what they call a Japanese. But I don't believe it's a Japanese."

"Oh, the showman took his solemn oath that it was." This came from Mrs. Mason.

"Ha! ha! ha!" guffawed the Major. "Of course, it's not a Japanese; it's a monkey."

"This is the advertisement in the *Gazette* that we read, and it caused us to go," Mrs. Mason asserted. She produced a newspaper clipping, and read in her soft Southern voice that Mr. Edward Willet is showing—

> A creature called a Japanese, about two feet high, his body resembling a human body in all parts except the feet and tail. He walks upright and performs various actions to admiration, such as walking upon a line, hanging and swinging under it, dances to any tune, etc.

"You must not believe what you read in the gazettes," said Mrs. Lawrence.

"Well, what difference does it make?" Charles Mason argued. "I'd never seen a monkey, nor had Nellie, so our sixpences are well spent after all."

"Have you been to the theater yet?" Miss Fraser asked.

"No, we haven't; we got here only two days ago—on Thursday," Mr. Mason replied. "Mr. and Mrs. Lawrence have asked us to go one evening next week. I understand that this company of actors—Murray and Kean, aren't they—is the first set of players you've ever had in New York. That's right?" He looked to Major Lawrence for confirmation of his statement.

"No, not quite correct," said the Major. "We've had plays here before occasionally, but nothing regular. This company looks like it will be permanent. They've rented the building on Nassau Street that belonged to Rip Van Dam. He's dead now, they got it from his estate. They have a lot of plays and are going to give them all."

"Pardon me, but the owner of the building—Rip—something?" This question from Charles Mason.

"I said the building belonged to Rip Van Dam," replied the Major.

"Is that really the name of a person?"

"It is," Major Lawrence assured him. "He was an honorable and highly respected gentleman in this colony; acted as governor at one time. Why? Have you never heard of him?"

"Not until you mentioned him, Major, but of course I'm from Virginia, and wouldn't know. It sounded to me at first like some new kind of swear word. Rip Van Dam!"

"Now, now, Charles," said his wife, shaking her head at him. "We were talking about the players."

Charles Mason said no more aloud, but under his breath he would whisper now and then: *Rip Van Dam, Rip Van Dam.*

"I've never understood," the Major continued, "why the theater and its players have been so cruelly treated in the colonies."

Miss Fraser remarked that there was more than one reason. First, the character of the players—they are roving folk, with no fixed home. The second reason is, she said, that many people believe the theater attracts the idle and the dissolute. "But I don't agree with them," she continued. "The theater is a harmless means of entertainment, and is certainly on a higher level than the taverns and drinking places."

"We don't treat 'em badly in Virginia. We've had actors and theaters and plays ever since I can remember," Charles Mason said. "They are welcomed in South Carolina, too. There's the Dock Street Theater in Charleston."

"Yes, three colonies—Virginia, South Carolina, and now New York," the Major said. "Everywhere else they're condemned at sight. Why, my dear sir, do you know what would happen to you if you gave a play in Boston? The pillory and the jail, or perhaps forty stripes on your bare back, followed by expulsion from the colony."

"The Murray and Kean company—here now—gave some performances in Philadelphia," Mr. Mason remarked.

"Yes, they did, but the authorities ordered them out of Pennsylvania, so they came here."

"I've enjoyed their performance," said Miss Fraser, "but they are best in comedies. They are really a group of comedians."

"We've tickets for the *Beggar's Opera,*" Mrs. Lawrence informed the company. She said further that she thought the *Beggar's Opera* was their best play, then as if suddenly recollecting something, she told the Masons that when they went to the theaters they must take stoves.

"Stoves!" said Mrs. Mason incredulously. "Stoves to a theater!"

"She means foot-warmers," the Major explained. "The theater is not heated; the foot stoves are little metal boxes with live coals in them. You put your feet on them."

"Thanks. We'll take them. There are so many things to be seen. I've always thought I'd like to see a show of waxworks."

"There are several here," said the Major. "The best waxworks show of the lot is called *Bateman, or The Unhappy Marriage.* I won't tell you the story, but it's a marriage mixup. Waxworks angels fly around, statues play music and there are all sorts of wonders."

"New York has many interesting things," Miss Fraser remarked, "besides waxworks and monkeys and stage plays. Go to Ranelagh Gardens and Vauxhall and take a look at them. They're beautiful, even in winter——"

"We're going to see them all," said Mrs. Mason, "before we leave. I want to go down to the tip end of the island, where the fort is, and look across the bay."

"That's called the Battery now," Major Lawrence told her. "In summer it is a beautiful place, with all the trees in leaf." He paused a moment, as if in reflection; then he turned to Mr. Mason. "Charles, if you will come with me in the morning, I'll show you a piece of New York that a traveler seldom sees." Looking at Mrs. Mason, he said, "No, Nellie, this excursion is not for you. Charles will tell you all about it when he returns."

"It sounds like something devilish," Charles Mason said. "I'm all for it."

The town of New York, in the eighteenth century, was quite different, in habit and temperament, from any other colonial community. A large number of travelers and strangers were always to be found on Manhattan Island. To accommodate them there were numerous inns, with such names as the King's Arms, the Merchant's Coffee House, the Blue Boar, the Three Pigeons, The Sign of the Spread Eagle. Anybody who had the money to pay his way could come to New York and stay indefinitely without being questioned by the authorities if he behaved himself.

Most of the coastwise vessels, carrying passengers between New England and the southern ports, put into New York, where they remained from three or four days to three or four weeks. For some reason that is psychologically difficult to analyze New York attracted counterfeiters and swindlers of one kind or another, as well as tourists whose pockets were well-lined with money.

Nevertheless there was a solid core of highly respectable citizenry—both English and Dutch—in the town. On top was the community of gentle manners, quiet homes, elegant furniture, and good taste. Under this community lay a heterogeneous horde of tavern roisterers, Negro slaves, thievish servants, underpaid workingmen, and crooked individuals of all conditions. Many of them from the other colonies were fugitives from justice.

The Dutch influence on this growing town of New York in mid-eighteenth century was small. Students of colonial history know that when the English fleet took New Amsterdam in 1664 a considerable proportion of the inhabitants of the town was already English; and that Long Island had been settled to a large extent by families that had come from New England.

Throughout the entire social fabric there was a most emphatic respect for wealth. This reverence for the ownership of money and land was not confined to the province of New

(*The Bettmann Archive*)

PRIMITIVE MODE OF BRINGING TOBACCO TO MARKET IN VIRGINIA IN 1830.

The leaf tobacco was put in hogsheads which were dragged by horses or oxen to the market towns.

(*The Bettmann Archive*)

THE COUNTRY PEDDLER.

Country peddler offering his wares to a group of housewives in a rural community. After woodcut by C. G. Bush.

York; it existed everywhere from Massachusetts to Georgia. The obvious and open distinctions between the rich and the poor were much greater than they are today. The clothing of working men and their families was quite different in appearance from the costly raiment of their betters. In our time a mechanic may buy a ready-made suit of clothes that is cut in the same fashion as the suit of a millionaire, though it may be made of cheaper material, and cost much less. That would not have been possible in colonial times. A workingman who appeared in an imitation of a rich man's suit would have been brought into court to explain his strange procedure.

Newspaper announcements of marriages among well-to-do people often gave the status of the bride's fortune. Here is a typical announcement:

> Married: At St. Thomas Church, April 5, Arthur Bredon, son of Mr. and Mrs. Christopher Bredon to Margaret Stilson, daughter of Mr. and Mrs. Joseph Stilson, of "Oak Hall," Larchmont. The wedding ceremony was performed by Reverend Louis Toomer.
>
> The bride is well-to-do in her own right. She is also due to inherit a considerable fortune from her grandparents.

The craze for curiosities, peep shows, wax figures and other things of the kind was not confined to Manhattan Island in the eighteenth century. It extended all over the colonies. People would go miles to see a strange animal or to listen to a musical clock. In 1753 a Female Samson attracted great attention in New York. She was an Indian woman who, lying down, would support the weight of six men standing on her body. Another sight to be seen in New York was a "living alligator, four feet long."

One of the most popular of the sights in the 1750's were "Optical Prospects." These seem to have been pictures of landscapes, or buildings, or streets in England; also in France and Italy. The spectator paid a small fee and then looked at one "prospect" after another through a glass. Such an exhibition could have been popular only in a century when pictures hardly existed for the average person, and not in any great number for anybody.

Twice a year on Long Island there was a racing meet, with horse races, bowling matches and target shooting every day, and cock fighting now and then. Strange to say, among these various sports there was no prize fighting or anything remotely resembling it. Among the indoor games there were cards, billiards and backgammon.

Billiard playing was extremely popular throughout colonial times. Every village, however small, had a public billiard room, and there were billiard tables in most of the homes of well-to-do families.

Eating was also a favorite amusement, for the New Yorkers, like the colonials of every colony, were prodigious trenchermen. Food was cheap: milk twopence a quart, beef sixpence a pound, a large fat chicken for one shilling sixpence, pigeons a penny apiece.

Many varieties of food were pickled and sold in glass jars. A housewife could buy pickled mushrooms, pickled onions, pickled oysters, pickled herring and pickled oranges and lemons.

5

Next morning, as Major Lawrence and Charles Mason left the house together, the Major said, "I'm going up to the debtors' prison, and I thought you might like to see it. It's nothing for any community to be proud of, and it will take your mind off the waxworks and the shooting galleries for awhile."

Mason said that he wanted to see everything, and remarked that the sunshine was pleasant. There was a path on each side of the street that was free of snow; the householders had seen to that. "The prison is not far, and I thought we might walk," said the Major, "just for the exercise." [11]

Looking keenly at the Major as they walked along, Mason said, "What's the purpose of going to the debtors' prison, if I may inquire?"

"Oh, I'm going there to get a prisoner released. A bricklayer I know, named Jason Kittle. A good man and a good workman. He's been in the jail for two months, and today I take him out."

[11] The prison stood where the Hall of Records now stands, in City Hall Park, but in 1750—and until after the Revolution—the City Hall was at the corner of Wall and Nassau Streets, where the Federal Sub-Treasury is today.

"What was his crime?" Mason seemed somewhat bewildered. "Was it nothing but owing debts?"

"That's all," was the reply. "He owed four pounds and some shillings."

"Well, it's a blessing that we haven't got that particular institution in Virginia," Mr. Mason said. "If we could put everybody in jail who owes four pounds and some shillings the entire population of the colony would be behind the bars by tomorrow night and the jailers would be in there with them." [12]

"Ah, it's a relic of barbarism," the Major said, his voice rising. "But I don't want to get started talking about it, for I'd lose my temper." He pointed to the west. "Through here you get a good view of the river and the Jersey shore. See the great blocks of ice floating. That large house there just across the Broadway with the trees around it is the King's Arms, one of our most respectable taverns."

"You know I thought before I came to New York," Mason said, "that the town was on the Hudson River, but it isn't. It's on the East River."

"Yes, that's so, when you come to think of it. The town faces Long Island and the Hudson River is at the back door. Here we are now walking up the Broadway, and we get a fine view of the Hudson, because there are so few houses over here; but we can't see the East River at all, for the town is built up between us and the water's edge."

When they had reached the Commons—the square where the city hall now stands—the Major pointed to a dark, bleak, bare building and told his companion that it was the debtors' prison. "The man I'm taking out is a good workman, as I've told you. He helped build one of my houses. A few months ago he fell from a house and injured himself so that he was laid up for weeks. When he got well at last, and was ready to go back to work, he owed some money, mostly for provisions and rent. He couldn't pay and his creditors sent him to prison.

[12] Mr. Mason was in error. There were laws for the imprisonment of debtors in Virginia as in every other colony. But the Virginia laws were seldom enforced, and many citizens did not know of their existence. The treatment of impoverished debtors was more severe in New York than in any of the other colonies. Women were not sent to prison for owing money, but it was almost impossible, under the laws and customs of the time, for a woman to run into debt without a man to be responsible for her actions.

His wife takes in washing to support himself and her little daughter."

"How could he be expected ever to pay his debts if he is kept in jail and is not allowed to work?"

"The question you ask," the Major replied, "is the essence of the whole thing. They jail a man because he is unable to pay his debts and fix it so he will never be able to pay them."

"But I should think that the government would object to feeding these prisoners," said Mr. Mason.

"The government doesn't feed them, nor does it clothe them. The creditor who has the man put in jail must pay a few pennies a day for his support while he is in prison, but it is not enough to keep him alive, so the prisoners depend on the charitable public to send them food and clothes.

"I arranged yesterday with Jason Kittle's creditors. I paid them not only all he owes them but also various charges and fees, and got a release from them. Today he'll be released and I'll see that he gets work to do. Then he can repay me a little at a time."

When they reached the bleak building the jailer recognized Major Lawrence and after reading over the release which was handed to him he asked if he should bring Kittle out to the door. "No," said the Major, "we'll go and find him."

There were no cells in the debtors' prison. It consisted of a large room with fifty or sixty men in it. All the men were shabby, unkempt and hungry-looking. A fire of logs was burning in a vast chimney at one end of the room. A few tables and rickety chairs were in the place. The pallets on which the men slept were rolled up against the wall, all except three or four. On these men were lying. The prostrate men seemed very ill, all of them. One was evidently in the last stages of consumption.

Most of the prisoners were barefoot, and the clothes of some were utterly ragged so that the men clutched them with their hands to keep from losing them altogether.

On the floor some dice games were going on amid a clamor of voices. Near the fire a man sat on a stool. He had taken off his shirt and was searching for the animal life that it contained. The stench of the place was almost overpowering.

They found Jason Kittle. He was a wan, nervous-looking

man in a shabby but decent suit of clothes—the long trousers of the workingman, the stout shoes, the checkered shirt—so soiled that it looked black, and a coat of coarse gray wool. Although he recognized Major Lawrence it was some time before he could be made to realize that he was at liberty to walk out of the place. At first he was vague and shifty in manner, and seemed to think that there was some catch, or malicious device, in the proceedings. But when he understood the situation fully his gratitude was so great that tears came into his eyes. "I wouldn't have believed that there is anybody like you in the world," he stammered, "to remember me, and come to help——"

The Major raised his hand. "Tut, tut," he said, "that'll do, my man, get your things together." When they stood outside the door, the young Virginian, the Major, and the shabby man with the bundle under his arm, the Major said, "Now, Kittle, we're saying good-bye to you here. Wait"—he drew out his pocket book, counted thirty shillings, and placed the money in the man's hands. "Take this and buy yourself some warm clothes. I'll add it to what you owe me. Go to your wife, take a good rest tomorrow, and come to me the day after, and I'll find some work for you. No, no, not another word from you. On your way now."

He waved the man away and turned to Charles Mason. "Now, my young buck," he said, "I have ten shillings here that say I can beat you at your favorite game of billiards. Want to bet? Of course you do. Well, let's go down to the Merchant's Coffeehouse and try our skill. And before we start to play I'll treat you to a rum fustian."

"Rum fustian! May I inquire what that is?"

"Oh, I forgot that you are from the benighted land of Virginia, where your favorite drink is eggnog or mint julep. A rum fustian, my dear sir, is made of beer, sherry, gin, the yolks of eggs, sugar and a little nutmeg all stirred together and heated with a red-hot loggerhead."

Mason reflected a minute. "That sounds like a strong drink," he said. "But why do they call it rum fustian when there's no rum in it?"

"That's where the fustian part comes in, my inquiring lad," said the Major. "Fustian—as you know—means an imitation.

Well, as there is no rum in it, you have rum fustian. The Puritans of New England devised this beverage, and now we New Yorkers make it. I've heard—though I'll not swear to the truth of the story—that it killed off a whole tribe of Indians who had displeased the Puritans. They gave the Indians several barrels of rum fustian; it was simpler than going to war with them."

"Well, Major, look here; I don't want to be exterminated on this trip North," said Charles Mason, laughing.

"You won't be. We have stronger constitutions than the Indians. Look at me; I was brought up on rum fustian, so to speak. Come on and we'll give it a trial."

Together they walked down the Broadway.

Chapter V

YOUNG MACKENZIE SEES THE WORLD

I

PHILADELPHIA was a lively place in the spring of 1776. The Continental Congress was then in session, and all eyes in the colonies were turned to that gathering of sedate gentlemen. Momentous events were impending; they attracted people and there was a flow of visitors to the capital of the Quaker colony.

Among those who come without any particular purpose except to look on was Philip Mackenzie, of South Carolina. He came up from Charleston on the coastwise schooner *Silver Cloud,* which arrived on March 4 after a rather swift passage of eight days.

Though he was twenty-four years old this voyage to Philadelphia was the first trip he had ever made outside the borders of South Carolina. His stay-at-home tendency came from inclination rather than from necessity, for he possessed ample means for travel and could have found sufficient leisure readily enough.

But traveling, with all its privations and makeshifts, had no attraction for him. Few people traveled far from home just for the fun of it in the eighteenth century. Virtually everyone who went abroad, or even to a neighboring colony, had some definite and practical objective in view. Traveling in those days was uncomfortable even at its best.

The ocean voyages were made in cluttered and ill-smelling little ships that pitched and tossed in any kind of rough water. During a gale, or in a strong wind, their decks were constantly wet, and water frequently poured into the cabins. Even hardened sailors were often seasick. It was not possible to keep the food for the voyage fresh, and those on board lived on beef or pork that had been preserved in brine so long that it had lost its fleshy taste. Promenade decks did not exist. The passengers could not move ten feet on deck without running into some of the ship's gear. The cabins could not be heated; in winter they had a semi-Arctic temperature. And, of course, such pleasant places as lounges, card rooms and sun galleries were unheard of.

Land travel was not much better. The roads everywhere, in Europe and America—except those in the immediate neighborhood of the cities—were mere streaks of lumpy earth and mud. As for the inns, all of them in the country villages (and most of them in the big towns) had the combined characteristics of a barn and a hovel, which means they were cold and dirty in winter and hot and dirty in summer. They sheltered swarms of flies and other insects; and the mingled odors of the kitchen, the bar and the back yard made a memorable smell that was usually associated thereafter in the minds of the guests with whatever beauties the countryside possessed. The squalid bedrooms were frequently shared by two or more people who were strangers to one another. The food in the dining room was plentiful, but the cooking was coarse and careless.

2

Philip Mackenzie had not gone to college, and his education came from private tutors. His father had planned to send him either to William and Mary in Virginia or to Oxford in England. But when Philip was fourteen his father died and his mother wanted to keep him, her only son, at home, so the tutorial instruction continued.

In the course of time he was taught by several tutors, and each of them had his own methods. As a result Philip's pattern of knowledge was like a jigsaw puzzle with some important parts missing. This was not wholly the fault of his instructors, for even in the best universities, during the eighteenth century, the curriculm had a curious, impractical trend, with the major emphasis laid on a knowledge of the dead languages. At some of the universities the students were required to speak nothing but Latin at meals and in the classrooms.

Philip could read Latin fairly well; and he could manage a page of Greek if he had plenty of time and a dictionary. French was among his accomplishments, too. He had learned it, as a lad, through his daily association with the Huguenot families of Charleston. As to mathematics, he was thoroughly at home in arithmetic, algebra and plane geometry, but he had no knowledge of the calculus. Physics was another dark continent; he knew nothing whatever about it, not even the simplest facts. He did not know what oxygen is; when he heard it mentioned he thought it a kind of medicine. Nor did he know what makes a fire burn, or the freezing and boiling temperatures of water.

His knowledge of history consisted mainly of a list of wars, their dates and who won them. Even in this field his learning was chaotic and uneven. He could give, for example, a very interesting account of the campaigns of Julius Caesar, but he knew next to nothing about the campaigns of the Duke of Marlborough. He had read some of the plays of Aristophanes, and could talk about them intelligently, but he had never read a play written by William Shakespeare. Of the economic background of history he had no knowledge whatever—in fact, he did not know that there is an economic background. Wars, he thought, were caused by disputes over religion or by the quarrels of kings.

In the field of geography he moved in a fog, perhaps because his tutors knew little or nothing of the subject, and were therefore incapable of teaching it in a sensible manner. Geographical ignorance was not unusual, however, in that age. For some reason that is not entirely clear geography was almost wholly neglected both in the common schools and the colleges until after the Revolution.[1] Few of the common schools possessed either maps or globes, and the little instruction that was given was on the order of a guidebook—a description of places. Philip had a fairly correct idea of the relative positions of the various American colonies, but Europe was just a blur in his mind, and so was South America. He thought India was a part of Africa; that the Mississippi flowed out of one of the Great Lakes; that Australia was another name for Madagascar.

In English his deficiences were especially noticeable. His tutors had been so absorbed in teaching him Latin that they almost overlooked English. It was, in fact, a widely held belief in that era among teachers of all grades that Latin was more

[1] The first American textbook of geography was *Geography Made Easy,* by Jedidiah Morse. It was published in 1784.

important than English, and that a student who had acquired a good, sound knowledge of Latin would never have any difficulty in expressing himself in English.

Philip had very little to do that belonged to the category of work, nevertheless he was busy as a bee all the time. His mother owned three large plantations in the Sea Island region of South Carolina. They all had capable overseers, but Philip oversaw the overseers. There were two hundred and fifty black slaves on the three plantations, and Philip—who had a pronounced humanitarian strain in his character—made it his business to see that the slaves received good treatment.

As the nearest of the plantations was on Edisto Island, thirty miles from Charleston where Philip and his mother lived, he was frequently away for a week at a time on these inspection trips.

He had other occupations, too, besides the plantation business. He was a game hunter by nature and training, and the hunting of deer, of wild turkeys, of foxes and bears, took up a great deal of his time. But during the last year he had hunted less, curbing the desire by force of will, for he had begun to feel that other things were of more importance.

Then there were the cocking mains. His father had left him a famous breed of game cocks, and he devoted much time to them. The "Mackenzie Fighters," as the strain was called, were well known all over South Carolina. Cockfighting was going on all the time in that province, as well as elsewhere in the South, but the Mackenzie cocks were entered only in the important mains which were dated and advertised months in advance. Philip always attended the big meetings, with his trainer Andrews and a couple of negro servants to look after the cocks and feed them.

For three or four days before one of the Mackenzie battlers entered a fight Philip had him fed on a preparation made of corn meal, whisky and gunpowder. He believed that this diet gave a gamecock courage and endurance. He always made up this gunpowder-whisky compound himself; he alone knew the right proportions.

There was heavy betting at these cock tournaments, and when a Mackenzie bird was one of the gladiators Philip placed his own money all around the ring. They usually won; in the course of a year his betting showed a handsome profit.

He was no great letter writer, and is not for a moment to be classed with Chesterfield in the art of epistolary expression. In reading his letters do not expect to witness the flowering of a personality in sentences that charm the soul and inspire the mind.

He wrote in a plain, downright, factual style. His expressions are entirely devoid of the deceptive and misleading sparkle of fancy. He was a realist and set down on paper only what he knew—or believed—to be true. This manner of writing is the most ancient of all literary accomplishments, and is perhaps the most respectable.

On March 8, 1776, he wrote the following letter from Philadelphia to his mother in Charleston.

Honored Madam: I am here at last, Sound and Well, in the reputed City of Brotherly Love, tho I must Say I haven't seen much Brotherly Love passed around since I landed. The *Silver Cloud* made a fine passage. Eight dayes only from Charleston bar to the Philadelphia warf. She came up the River, all sails set, with a spanking Breeze behine her, racing along like a House Afire. The vyage was Pleasant all the Way, and difrent from what I had expected. Not a person got Seasick not even me.

I shot a Bird from the Deck when we were Two Dayes out of Charleston some kind of Bird that was very Black. Captain Clayton said it was a Bosuns Mate, but the Sailors swore up and down that it was an Albert Ross. I know this aint the right spelling of the name, but I don't know how to spell it right, and that is how the Sailors pronounced it. They got kind of Scared for they say when you Kill an Albert Ross on a vyage you are in for a peck of Trouble. Nonsense. Nobody had any Trouble and there was fare weather all the way.

Philadelphia is a Town of Bright Colors. The Shop fronts are most of them painted Red, Blue, Green or Yellow. The big Swinging Signs are like Joseph's Coat of many colors. The Carriages—there are not Many of them—are colored too, or I should Say many of them are. And the greater part of the Men wear Red or Green Coats, and the Ladies have Dresses of all colors of the Rainbow.

Well, I hear you say What about the Quakers. Do they go round dressed in Colors and Silks and Sattins? They surely do, and that

Surprised me, for I Thought all of them wore Sober Garments. Some of them do Still. You see them comeing along the Street clothed in Gray from Head to Foot, but that is Exseptional. Most of them look as Gay as you Please. I suppose that like the rest of us they Keep their Religion for Sunday.

I am staying at a Boarding House that is on Front Street near Race. I know that means nothing to you, My Dear, I am reffering to the Location, but Front Street near Race is pretty nearly in the center of Things.

The House is Run by a Mrs. Graydon, who is the Widow of an Army Officer, and she is a Real Lady, born and bred. The way I Happened to come to her House is that Alexander Porter met me when the ship came in. I mean Porter, our Philadelphia Factor and commission man, who sells part of our Rice Crop and buys Things that we want.

He was all Smiles and Handshakings when he met me. He is a man of about Fifty, thin and bony very well Dressed in Broad-cloth and Silk. Wears a curly Dark Brown wig with a Pigtail hanging down the Back. The Wig is Powdered and he carries Two Watches one in each Pocket connected by a Chain. So you can see he is a Fop. He brought me round here to Mrs. Graydon's. Very Polite Lady she is. The House is large with big Rooms. My Room and Board cost Two Pounds Ten Shillings a week. That is High, but I have the Money and can Afford it so Why Not?

They say here that all of Mrs. Graydon's Gests are high-toned and I suppose they are. Severall members of Congress are among them. But they all seem Rather Old, I mean here at Mrs. Graydon's, and I feel like a Child sitting down with them. Dinner is always at Four O'clock. The rule is four meals a Daye. Coffee or Tea and a Roll when you Rise, say round Seven O'clock, Breakfast or Lunch, call it what you will, at Eleven, then Dinner at Four, and Supper about bedtime.

When you Drink Tea here you are looked upon as Rather Countryfied and ill bred if you put your Sugar right in the Tea. No, the Lumps of Sugar are lade in the Saucer and you take a Sip of Tea and then Nibbel at a Lump of Sugar. They call it the Fashion of Nibbel and Sip.

In a Daye or Two I am going to look up our South Carolina men in Congress. I know Edward Rutledge mighty well, and You know him too, Mother. He is that young Black-haired Rutledge that used to go to the Horse Races with me and was Always talking against Tyranny. He went to College in England and knows More than most Professors. I have not Called on Him yet, but I shall Soon.

My Room is Very Pleasant. Has a Fireplace in it and plenty of

Closets. The Walls are not Painted but Papered. I cannot see why people have such Objection to Wall Paper. I am reffering to People at Home. You know they say the Print of the Paper is poysonous and Pollutes the air Because there is Arsenick in it. I have Never heard of Anybody yet being killed by Wall Paper. The Paper in my Room is beautiful. The Pictures on it are Scenes in Flower gardens and People dancing.

Mrs. Graydon has White Servants. No Blacks. It got me sort of Flustered at first, I mean Telling a Nice-looking White Woman in a neat Gray Dress to bring me so-and-so. But, as you have Often said, we Live and Learn.

I hope this finds you well. Please Give my Regards to all our Friends. Tell them I am Learning how to be a Yankee and Talk through my Nose. If you Write to Me and I hope you will address it care of Mrs. Graydon, on Front Street near Race, Philadelphia. I dont Know how long I will be Here, but for a Month any way. If a Letter comes after I Leave it will be sent on to me at New York.

My Respects to you, Honored Madam.

Your Loving Son Philip.

3

The belief that wallpaper might be dangerous because of the chemicals used in making it lasted a long time. Small quantities of it were imported as early as 1710, but little use was found for it. Yet it gained slowly in popularity. In 1765 a printer in New York began to produce wallpaper. It was printed from huge blocks, a slow and expensive process. The product was costly and his sales were small. Wallpaper did not come into general use until after the Civil War.

Philadelphia, at the time of Mackenzie's visit, was the largest town in the American colonies. It had a population of about 40,000, which was more than New York and Boston combined. Nevertheless, it was only a big village with few of the qualities that one associates with the idea of a city.

The houses had no numbers, and strangers inquiring their way were told that the house they were seeking was "near" to this or that. There were no postmen in the town and no mailboxes. A citizen who wished to mail a letter had to carry it to the post-office, and also he had to call for his mail, and pay the postage, for in those days the postage was usually paid by the recipient and not by the sender. There was, however, very little letter writing done. Ordinary folks, who were not in business, sometimes passed a year or two without receiving a letter of any kind; and people of the laboring class might not get a letter in the course of a lifetime, and if they did get one they could not read it.

In some respects Philadelphia surpassed all other American communities in civic improvements. Public street lighting began in 1752. It supplanted the old method—which was still in use in New York and Boston—of lighting the streets by means of a lamp placed in the window of every seventh house. In 1776 many of the streets were paved in the middle for carriages, and there was a footpath of hard brick on each side next to the houses.

But the water supply system was quite simple; it was, in fact, nonexistent. Reservoirs and water mains belonged to the distant future. There were pumps in the streets, and some in the yards of the houses. The fire department, made up of volunteer firemen organized into seventeen companies, upon being called to extinguish a fire, depended on the street pumps or upon wagons that brought water in barrels to the scene of the conflagration. The burning house usually burned down before the firemen arrived unless the people in the house and their neighbors managed to extinguish it.

Sewage and household refuse was removed by carts to the river. The streets were never clean, but their dirty condition was accepted as a matter of course.

The love of bright colors, mentioned by young Mackenzie, was carried further in Philadelphia than anywhere else in the colonies, though all the colonials—as seen from the twentieth century—appear to have been more or less color mad. With the love of colors went a growing extravagance in dress and luxury in living. This, too, ran to excessive lengths in Philadelphia, which was the richest of all the colonial cities.

The women were resplendent in silks, velvets and brocades. They wore high headdresses, held up by stiffening materials and worked into extraordinary shapes. Sometimes the ladies had to sit up all night before keeping an important engagement to keep from spoiling these tall confections.

This spirit of luxury extended to eating, and gourmandizing ran into gluttony in the course of time.

John Adams, who was a delegate from Massachusetts to the Continental Congress, wrote in his diary after dining at the home of Chief Justice Chew in Philadelphia: "About four o'clock we were called to dinner. Turtle and every other thing, flummery, jellies, sweetmeats of twenty sorts, trifles, whipped sillabubs, floating islands, fools, etc., with a dessert of fruits, raisins, almonds, pears, peaches."

On another occasion he wrote of a dinner to which he had been invited by a rich Quaker, where the host and his wife, "thee'd and thou'd" each other. They had, according to Mr. Adams, "ducks, hams, chickens, beef, pig, tarts, creams, custards, jellies, fools, trifles, floating islands, beer, porter and wine." [2]

Pennsylvania, from the beginning had been the most prosperous of all the colonies. Within ten years after William Penn had made the first settlement Pennsylvania was exporting wheat to the West Indies. On the eve of the Revolution there were more rich people in Pennsylvania than in any other colony. Massachusetts probably was second, and either Virginia or New York was third.

There were few wealthy families in Pennsylvania, or in any of the colonies, until the middle of the eighteenth century. All the colonials were poor in the early years of the settlements and for a long time thereafter. Most of the personal fortunes came from the shipping industry or from buying and selling merchandise and land. The farmers constituted a poor class from the beginning to the end of the colonial period. The only exceptions to this statement were the slave-owning planters of Virginia and South Carolina.

On March 18 Philip Mackenzie wrote to his friend Robert Elliott, a rice planter of St. Helena, South Carolina:

> Dear Bob: I have your Letter of February 28th. It got Here onlie yesterday so it has been on the Way three Weeks. When you wrote it I was on the Sea, on my way Here. You sent it Care of Mr. Porter, as I told you, and he Brought it over to me At Once. I am very glad to hear from you, Bob, and to Learn that you are Well. I am

[2] No wonder this profusion astonished frugal John Adams. At his own home in Massachusetts his Sunday dinner, as described by a visitor, consisted of: first course—pudding of Indian meal, molasses and butter. Second course—veal and bacon, mutton and vegetables. Besides these viands the Adamses had beer and cider to drink.

feeling Pretty Good myself Right Now, but I had to have a Doctor in last Wednesday. Now dont Jump to conclusions. I am not fading away with Rapid Consumption, or Liver Complaint, or Yallow Jaundise. The plain Fact is that on last Tuesday evening I Drank too much, so on Wednesday morning I had a bad Headache, Sick Stomach, Weak Heart, Rumatism, Flat Feet, Parshal Blindness, and Roaring in my ears. You know how it is.

Mrs. Graydon, at whose House I am living as a Boarder, is a Kind, Gentle Lady, about sixty years old, and she Said in her motherly way that I owt to have a Doctor and she sent for Dr. Pendleton.

He came, felt my Pulse, looked at my Tongue, and said I had better Lose a Pint of blood. After he had Drawn Off that much blood I felt weaker, but the Dr. said that was All Right, that it would keep me from having a Fever. He remarked that he had already Bled two other patients that Morning.[3]

By that Evening it was all over, and I went out to Dinner with some Friends.

But I must Tell you of the Doings on Tuesday Evening when I drank too much. There is a Club here in Phillie—you call the Town Phillie after you have Lived here a week, Instead of Philadelphia—there is a Club here called the Fish House Club. That aint the full Name of it which is the Fishing Company of the State in Schuykill, but everybody calls it the Fish House Club.

There are only Thirty Members, and it is organized like a Colony —I mean the Members are called Citizens, and they have a Governor, a Sheriff and a coroner, though God Knows what these Officers do. Every Member must Learn how to Cook and wash dishes, though they have regular Cooks. Well, I ran into Francis Anderson tother Daye. You Know him he married Judge Cochran's Daughter in Charleston and I was at the Wedding and so Were you. On his Invitation I went to the Fish House Club Tuesday and Did We Have a Time. Eating, Drinking, Games, Target Shooting, Stage Plays, Singing. All men no women. Before it was Half over I did not Know whether I was on Foot or Horseback. They have a Drink there called Fish House Punch. It is most Exslent if taken in Modderation, but it is so Smoothe that One who does not know its Powers is Likely to take too much. I Suppose I must have Drunk too much of it, but it did not Seem so at the Time. Next Morning was a Difrent Story.[4]

[3] Bloodletting was one of the basic, standard remedies of old-fashioned medicine. Whenever a physician was not sure what the trouble was, he drew a pint of blood; and even if he was sure in his diagnosis he drew blood. It was looked upon by the medical profession as a part of the treatment of almost any ailment.

[4] The Fishing Company of the State in Schuylkill, better known as the Fish

Nobody knows what the Continental Congress is going to do. Their Meetings are Secret, no Spectaters allowed, and if you know a Member well enough to ask him what they Intend to Do that Member gives a good Imitation of a Clam then and there, but I Did get a Sort of an Idea from one Member.

I know all our South Carolina Members, and we Drink together and Play Billards. The other Daye I invited Edward Rutledge to dine with me at the City Tavern. When I asked him to Give me a Hint of what the Outcome would be He looked me in the Face and said I wish to God I knew. Don't talk about this, Bob, I am Writeing it to you only. Ed Rutledge went on to Say that the Delegates were at Sixes and Sevens, not in a Quarrelsome way, but just difrence of Opinion.

Some of Them think the Colonies ought to get together and Form a Dominion but still stay in the British Empire. Others say it is just a Matter of Taxation and if the British would stop their Tax Levies over here all the Trouble would come to an End. Let the Colonial Assemblies attend to the Taxes, they say. There are still others, Ed says, that think we owt to ellect Members to the British Parliament.

When I Asked him if there was a strong Movement for Independence he said No not Yet, but it is growing Fast. You see New York, Pennsylvania, Maryland, New Jersey and North Carolina all went on Record against Independence in the past Few Months. Now some of their Delegates are talking in Favor of Independence Daye and Night. I asked Ed what had Brought About that Change and he ansered that there were Severall Causes. He was Silent for a Minute, and then he said to me, Have you ever heard of Thomas Paine. Certtainly I have. You remember, Bob, a Tom Paine wrote that little Book or Pamphlet called *Common Sense* which you and I read last month. It advocated Independence of the Colonies. I told Ed. Rutledge that I had Read Paine's *Common Sense,* and he said, Well, there you have one of the Causes for the growth of the Independence Spirit. Ed himself is Opposed to Independence but will go with the Majority.

Tom Paine lives here in Philadelphia and Ed wants me to meet him, and I suppose I Shall some Daye.

Talk about meeting People who do you suppose I met one Daye last week? Why none other than the cellebrated Benjamin Franklin. I had Breakfast with Thomas Lynch and when it was getting on toward Noon we walked over to the State House for Tommie said he

---

House Club, is still in existence. It was founded in 1732, and is said to be the oldest club in America. Its membership is still limited to thirty. Once every two weeks the club meets for a dinner. The club not only invented the punch that bears its name, but is also the inventor of the dish known as planked shad.

Never liked to be Late. We were Standing before the Door and the Members were going in all the Time when a Sedan came up. I noticed it had two white liveried Servants at the Shafts. They set down the Sedan before the Door and an old gentleman stepped out. Tommie said, That's Benjamin Franklin. Come on and make his acquaintance. Then you can Tell your Children, if you ever have any, that you knew Benjamin Franklin.

I was not Prepared for that. It sort of took my Breath away, but Tommie Lynch, Bold as Brass, had me by the Sleeve, pulling me on. He bowed and said Dr. Franklin, may I present one of your Admirers, a Friend of Mine from South Carolina, His name is Philip Mackenzie. He has Read everything you ever Wrote. That is not the Truth, I thought, for I have Read only a few Things but I did not Think that was the Time or Place to Denye it, so I said nothing. Dr. Franklin smiled and said Well, in that case, I feel sorry for him. Then he turned to me, bowed a little, took my hand and said he was pleased to meet me. We talked with him for a Moment. Nothing partickluyar. Just Talk. I asked him if I might call on him Some Daye, and he Replied very cheerfully, Of course, come in any afternoon. Always at Home from Five O'clock on. Will be Glad to see you. I am going to Drop in on him in a few Dayes.

Benjamin Franklin looks difrent from what I expected. Always I have thought of him as a Tall, Stern man, Very Solemn, with Eyes that are looking Far into the Future. He is not like that at all. In Height about Five feet nine. I am Six feet one, and I am at least four inches taller. He is too Heavy for his Height. His Eyes are Gray, and they are as Keen and Sharp as Steel. His Head is quite Large, his Forehead is High, and he has a Mole on his left Cheek. No wig. He wears his Hair long. It reaches to his Shoulders. Strange to say it is not yet White but only a little Gray tho he is Seventy at least. Maybe I am Wrong, but it seems to me that he is Secretly Amused and is Keeping it to himself. There is that Sort of look in his Eyes. Tho he has Conversed with most of the Great People in the World he listened intently to my Silly Remarks as if they were Really Interesting. After he left us I said as much to Ed Rutledge and he laughed. Don't fool yourself, he said. Dr. Franklin was Interested. You don't know him. He is Interested in everybody and everything from what makes leaves Green and Negroes Black, also in who you are and what you have Done all your Life.

Do you know that about one-third of the People in Pennsylvania are Dutch? I mean German but they call them Dutch here. They do not mix in much with the English speaking Settlers. They keep their own Language and the Street Signs here in Town are in both English and Dutch.

There is Complete Religious Liberty in this Province, like it owt to be everywhere else. A Jew, or a Catholic, or a Muscleman is Allowed to practice their Religion here, and if you have no Religion, that is all right too.

The place simply Swarms with indentured Servants, for there are not many Slaves, and People here prefer the Redemptioners or Indentured Servants to Negroes. Besides there is an Abolition Society here and People are afeared to buy Slaves because they might be Freed before long. From these Regions a powerful movement to Free all Negroes everywhere is Bound to arise some Daye. We at the Southward had better prepair to meet it.

I have Arranged with a Man here—name is Richard Williams—to Ship me a Cargo of Ice this Summer, around the First of June. His Price is lower than what we have been Paying those Boston people, and I suppose his Ice is just as Good, for Ice is Ice the World over. He Cuts his Ice in the Schuylkill River when it Freezes over. I am Writing about this because I Cant use a full Cargo, and I would like you and one or two Others to go in with me in taking Some of it.[5]

Well, Bob, I have written lots more than I expected when I put Pen to Paper and this old Goose-quill is getting Blunt, so I will close. Hope that this will find you and yours in Good Health and Spirits.

My Respects to you and Your Good Lady.

Philip Mackenzie

4

The Philadelphians of the period were showy people, and their elegance impressed young Mr. Mackenzie more and

[5] In the latter part of the eighteenth century, and in the first half of the nineteenth, New England, New York and Pennsylvania shipped ice extensively to other parts of the world, even as far as Calcutta. During the winter the ice was cut in large blocks from the frozen ponds and streams. The holds of the ships that carried it were insulated in various ways and hermetically sealed after the ice was stowed away on board.

Every well-to-do resident of Charleston or any other Southern seaport had an icehouse in which this ice brought from afar was stored. The icehouse was a brick or wooden structure with its foundation laid about six feet deep in the ground, and the house was always built under a shade tree, preferably an elm. The house had double walls, and the space between the walls was stuffed with moss. There was also a double roof. Ice so carefully insulated would keep for about three months even in the summer.

But there was no practicable method of carrying the ice inland. The inhabitants of country districts usually had what were known as spring houses near their dwellings. They were built like the icehouses, but a stream of water from a spring ran through them and formed a pool inside the house. Jars of milk and butter were set on the floor of the pool.

more as he lived among them. Large silver buttons were one of the marks of wealth. Some of the men who displayed their worldly condition in this manner had their initials engraved on each button. They carried gold snuffboxes and gold-headed canes. Swanky young men of fashion wore swords too, though the sword-wearing habit had, in 1776, been abandoned by most men of substance, not only in Philadelphia, but everywhere else in the American colonies. Their cocked hats were decorated with gold lace; and similar lace appeared on their scarlet vests. Lace-trimmed ruffles at the end of the coat sleeves and hanging over the hand, were also a mark of gentility. These lace cuffs were weighted with lead to make them hang down. Broadcloth was used for winter suits; in the summer the coat and breeches were usually made of silk. Long trousers were unknown. The breeches ended at the knee. Gentlemen usually wore silk stockings; those of working men were made of wool.

The custom of wearing wigs was nearing its end, and many men had given them up. In the decade of the 1760's wigs had become ridiculous because the practice of wearing them had grown too popular. Little boys wore tousled, dirty mops of false hair. The shabby laborer, in soiled buckskin breeches, who came to clean out the pig sty, was sure to have on his head a cheap wig of huge size, with the dyed wool of which it was made sticking out in all directions. Negro slaves and white servants kept up with the fashion, too. There are accounts of negroes who adorned themselves with great red wigs which made them look as if their heads were afire. At this point fashionable folk began to send their wigs to the garret where they lay for many years among the odds and ends.

Speaking of fashions, it is rather curious that during the whole of the colonial period children of both sexes wore diminutive copies of the clothes worn by their elders. There were little girls of eight or ten in long skirts, tight bodices and stays. They looked just like their mothers and older sisters. The boys were miniature copies of their grandfathers. In the later colonial era they even wore cocked hats and long, paneled coats that reached to their knees.

In the 1776 period the women wore stays that were as

stiff and hard as iron. The hoop skirts that were universally worn by all women of social position did not extend an equal distance from the body all around, but stretched out only right and left from six inches to two feet. The effect was to give the wearer a flat, wide appearance. To enter a room she had to come sideways through the door. Women of ordinary position in life, such as the wives and daughters of mechanics or laborers, wore bonnets only, but there was a great variety of hats worn by women of the upper classes. Among them was one made of horsehair, woven into flowerlike shapes; another was a "calash" bonnet, always made of green silk. It was called by that name because it resembled the flexible top of a calash—a kind of carriage. When the wearer was outdoors she pulled the top forward to cover the head, and when she went indoors she pushed the top back. All women wore aprons as a part of a stylish toilet. The poor wore checkered linen aprons while wealthy women wore colored silk ones.

Black velvet masks were usually worn by fashionable women who ventured in the hot sun of summer or in the cold wind of winter.

During this period bold innovators who scorned the derision of the public began to use umbrellas as a protection against the rain. Before umbrellas appeared people used oiled linen capes to shed the rain. The umbrella is a simple contrivance; its invention, one thinks, would occur to almost anybody; so it is a matter of wonder that this simple rain-shedder was so late in making its appearance. Its origin is unknown, but it was not in existence in the colonies until the 1770's, and the current belief at that time was that the umbrella came from India. When umbrellas were first used in Philadelphia they were looked upon as a ridiculous effeminacy and a source of fun in and out of the public gazettes. Small boys threw stones at them. They were made of oiled linen, with rattan sticks, and were very coarse and clumsy. Such a useful contrivance could not be laughed out of existence; by 1780 everybody in Philadelphia who could afford to buy an umbrella had one.

Mr. Mackenzie remarks in his letter to Robert Elliott that he saw Dr. Franklin arrive at the State House in a sedan chair. This vehicle was simply a chair with a top over it to shelter its occupant from the weather. It was supported on two poles, or shafts, and was carried by two men, one at the front and the other at the back. There was a goodly number of sedans in Philadelphia at that time, and for some years afterward.

The number of wheeled vehicles was surprisingly small. In the year 1772 there were only eighty-four pleasure vehicles in Philadelphia. This number included coaches, chaises, chariots and landaus but no work vehicles such as carts or drays. The same scarcity existed in New York, Boston, Charleston and other colonial towns. One possible explanation for this situation is that the roads in the country generally were too primitive for pleasant trips in heavy coaches.[6] Another contributing cause may have been the pronounced dislike of the common people for those who rode in coaches.

Among the well-to-do gout was a rather common ailment, owing to the prevailing habit of eating large quantities of rich food and of drinking an excessive amount of wine. Disabled by their gout, these gentlemen went about in sedans and coaches. Surly crowds sometimes gathered about the carriages, and occasionally a stone was thrown at a luxurious vehicle. One sufferer from the gout, to forestall and prevent such an attack by the mob, had a picture painted on each of the doors of his coach. In the picture a handsome vehicle, with a span of horses and a driver, appeared at the top. Just below it there was a delineation of a wretched man on crutches, hobbling along on a road. The wording that ran across the picture above the representation of the carriage said: "It is either This"—and just above the picture of the gouty man on crutches, it said: "Or This." The faithful recorders of local events of that era have asserted that the carriage so decorated was never stoned, and that when its occupant prepared painfully to alight numerous bystanders ran up to help him.

In considering colonial affairs of all kinds we should remember that colonial society was an aristocracy based on money and land. It had none of the attributes of a democracy. Workingmen, laborers, poor farmers and common people were not

[6] The carriages of that period did not have steel springs. Leather straps supported the body of the coach, and they had little resiliency on a bad stretch of road.

allowed to vote. Some few did actually have the right of suffrage, but their number was negligible, for suffrage was based on property, and only an insignificant number of the common people possessed enough property. They were given no education worth mentioning; they were not permitted to form labor unions, or even to bargain collectively for better pay or shorter hours.

As a result of this unbalanced and unjust social system most of the colonial communities were in a state of turbulence years before the Revolution. The common people were tough, rowdy and quarrelsome—also impudent. A glittering carriage in some neighborhoods was just an invitation to throw a stone.

Even lower in the social scale were the indentured servants. It is a mistake to class them all indiscriminately as criminals or dullards. Many of them had an intelligence above the ordinary, and a large proportion of them had not been transported to the colonies on account of a criminal record, but had come voluntarily. As they lacked the means to pay their passage they agreed to become servants for a term of years. This class of immigrants was known as "redemptioners."

Some of the redemptioners were sly and tricky. There is a story in the Pennsylvania annals of one who sold his master. It appears, according to the tale, that the servant—a stalwart, good-looking fellow—was purchased from the captain of an English vessel for his passage money, which was nine pounds. He was bound over to serve his new master, a farmer, for a term of years. When his term expired he was to be released, given a few acres of land, some clothes, a little money and a rifle. This arrangement was satisfactory all around; the ship captain got his nine pounds and the farmer and his new servant left Philadelphia in a chaise, a kind of gig drawn by one horse, for the farmer's home about forty miles away. Night caught them on the road, and the farmer decided to stop over at an inn.

From their appearance the innkeeper judged that the farmer was the servant. His clothes were no better than those of the redemptioner, and he had a meek, depressed air while the real servant was jaunty and confident in manner. Next morning the servant rose early and talked about this and that with the landlord. In the course of the conversation the innkeeper said he needed a man to work around the place, and would his listener sell to him the servant lying asleep upstairs. After awhile the smiling redemptioner allowed himself to be persuaded, and sold his master for twelve pounds.

"He is a good worker," said the servant as he pocketed the twelve pounds and climbed into his master's chaise to drive away, "but he has one fault that I must warn you against. He's a most ungodly liar. When I'm not around and he is among strangers he declares that he is a rich farmer, and he boasts and brags. I've heard so many of his yarns that I don't pay any attention to them, and that is what I advise you to do."

5

On the eighteenth of March Philip Mackenzie called on Benjamin Franklin. The date (March 18) is taken from his letter written on the nineteenth to Robert Elliott. It is a long, rambling missive, not worth quoting at length. In respect to Franklin he wrote:

> The Maid who met me at the Door conducted me to the library, a very Large Room with a high Ceiling. Dr. Franklin was sitting there with a number of his friends. As it was a Cold Daye a plesant Fire was burning in the Fireplace or Franklin Stove. I mean the Stove that Franklin invented.
>
> The Dr. remembered me, Strange to Say, called me by Name and introduced me to the Company—five men. His Daughter Mrs. Bache came in soon and Sat Down among us. Three of the men present were Members of Congress: Robert Morris, of Pennsylvania, and Richard Henry Lee, from Virginia were Two. The other man's name I did not Catch. Then there was a man whose name sounded like Middelberg, and a Mr. Bartlett.
>
> Tea was served and wine too besides Cakes. Franklin drinks Madeira wine, but remarked in the Course of Conversation that he had never used Tobacco in any way.
>
> He does not Look as Olde as one would Think. His manner is so Lively. When I went in he was Talking about the Mental Habits of Savages. They never attempt to trace Facts back to Causes, he said. He told of Showing an Indian an Electric Spark flying from the end of a Wire. The Indian was astonished but never asked what caused the Spark. Also, he said, the Indians have Never taken the trouble to learn how to make Gunpowder, tho they use it all the Time. They

Interpert everything Scientifick as either a Trick or a Natural Pheenomenen.

He asked me many Questions about South Carolina, our way of Growing Rice and Indigo, the way Plantations are Run, and So On. He says we in the South ought to have Conestoga Wagons on our Roads. I suppose, Bob, you have Heard of Conestoga Wagons, but I doubt if you have ever Seen one. Well, I have seen Many of them since I got here. They are long, covered Wagons shaped in such a fashion that the Front and Back ends Rise higher than the Middle. The Body of the Wagon is rounded something like a Boat. This keeps the Freight from sliding around on a rough road, or in going up or down Hill, for everything slides to the Middle. The wheels are Six feet High, and the Iron Tires are Seven and Eight inches Wide. Compare this with our flat-bottomed Wagons which, if you are Carrying a Heavy Load, are Likely to turn over on a bad road. You would have a devil of a time turning over a Conestoga Wagon and it can carry much more than one of our Wagons. I think I will have one built by Geraty, our Wagon man, as soon as I get Back Home, to run between our Plantations and the City. I am having a Drawing and a Plan made of one.[7]

The talk got around to Education, and Dr. Franklin remarked that the Teaching of Greek and Latin is a kind of Quackery, that a Knowledge of these Dead Languages is of no value whatever to the Average Man. Someone said that the Literatures of Greece and Rome are worth knowing, and that is why the Languages are Taught. Robert Morris said Yes, That is True, but he added that the Books could always be Translated by Professional Translators. I agree with him and Dr. Franklin. I hate to think of the years I Wasted in acquiring this useless Knowledge.

There was no talk at all about the Doings in Congress, except a few Trifling Remarks concerning some of the Members who are Sick. But there was quite a lot of Conversation about Thomas Paine. Robert Morris remarked that Paine's book *Common Sense* had already sold 120,000 Copies, and it has been Published only Three Months. It sells for Two Shillings. Franklin remarked that Paine as Author declined to Accept any of the Profit from the Sale. One of

[7] The Conestoga wagon was an invention of the Pennsylvania Germans. Its name came from the Conestoga Valley. This vehicle was first produced around 1750, and it became very popular in the early 1800's. Caravans of Conestoga wagons—ten or twelve in line—were used as freight trains before the railroads were built. It was the vehicle that transported most of the adventurers to the West during the California gold rush.

The word "stogie," meaning a little, cheap cigar, is an adaptation of the word "Conestoga." The drivers of the wagons in the early days smoked these little cigars, hence the name.

the other men said that his little book seemed to be changing the Sentiment of the Country toward Independence. I am going to meet Paine, but I have Neglected doing it so far. And I think I shall read *Common Sense* again just to see what is in that Book to Create such a Stir.

While I was there I learned some Things that Surprised me. I dont know how the Matter come up but in the Conversation somebody remarked that Honey Bees are native to this Country. Dr. Franklin said no; Bees were brought over by Settlers about 1650. There was none here before that Time. The Indians called them white man's flies. The Dr. said that the Wild Bees which live in hollow trees in the Woods are not native either; they escaped from the Hives and became Wild.

Then somebody asked if Watermelons are native, and the Dr. said they came from Europe. He seems to Know, for he has been looking into such Things all his Life. He said Watermelons came in the first Place from Africa but by way of Europe. Their Seed was taken to Europe two or three hundred years ago; and was brought to Massachusetts by the Pilgrims. Watermelons dont seem to be Grown now in the North, not much anyway, but we Certainly have a pile of them in the South every year.[8]

Before leaving I asked the Dr. what inspired him to invent the Franklin Stove. Why, he said, a very Simple Reason. I saw that most of the Heat from fires in our Fireplaces went up the big Chimney. You could sit ten feet from a fire and be cold. The Heat was wasted. That Started the Dr. to Thinking of ways to Throw the heated Air back in the room. So, he said, I made a Stove or Fireplace that draws in the Cold Air, heats it and sends it out again, not up the Chimney but into the Room. Then he told me that the right name for it is Fireplace and not Stove. He did not Seem to Think it an important invention, but it Certainly is very Ingenyus to say the Least.[9]

[8] Muskmelons and cantaloupes were brought to the United States from Tripoli about 1818, and were first grown at Germantown in Pennsylvania.

[9] Franklin's stove was looked upon as a newfangled novelty for many years, and people were slow to put it to use in their homes. The cooking stove was also neglected for a long time after its invention by John Conant, of Vermont. in 1819. Cooks and housekeepers had no use for it. Millard Fillmore became President in 1850, and soon thereafter he set out to modernize the White House. One of his innovations was a bathroom, with running water, and another was a cooking stove for the kitchen. The cooks quit work. They said that the old-fashioned fireplace was good enough for them and they could not use the new contraption. President Fillmore had to send to the Patent Office for an expert in mechanical devices who came over to the White House and stayed there in the kitchen for a day or two, showing the cooks how to regulate the heat with the dampers and levers.

After the Civil War the public preference went precisely in the opposite direc-

During the time I was there Mrs. Bache—his daughter—said only a few words but was busy pouring Tea. She asked me how I like Philadelphia, and I said I liked it Very Much, all I had seen of it. Then I Asked her how she liked Philadelphia. She did not Anser that Question at all, but looked Starteled and opened her Eyes wide and said: Why I've lived here all my Life. Then she went on pouring Tea.

6

The young man seems to have fitted easily into the social life of Philadelphia. In a long letter to his mother written early in April he tells her—

This is a very Social place, more so than even our own Charleston. The Carolina members have introduced me to many People and our Mr. Porter has done Likewise. The Quakers used to Live Simply they say but that time is Past. Last Evening I was at the Wetherills for Dinner. You may Recall that I Wrote you about them. Quakers they are, and seem to be very Rich. Certainly their Home is full of Expensive things. At Dinner they had Fourteen Difrent Courses besides a lot of little Nick-Nacks. Among the meats were Hams, Chickens, Ducks, Roast Beef and Meat Pies made of Lamb, I think. Also they had Soup, Oysters and the Lord knows how many Vegetable Dishes and Desserts, such as Sillabub, Jellies, Sweet creamy dishes, Custards and Floating Island. For Beverages they served Punch, Wine, and finally Coffee.

Now, I believe, Mother, in having a plentiful Table, but I don't believe in Stuffing the Family and the Gests until they are ready to Burst. If you are a Gest you are Expected to partake of each Course. You may Take only a little Dab of each, but after you have had Seven and Eight little Dabs of difrent Kinds of Meat you feel as if you had Swallowed a Cow and a Calf.

The People here are Kindly, but among those who are Well-to-do there is a vast amount of Bad Taste, Vulgarity and Ostentashous Behavior.

One thing that Bothers me is the Various kinds of Money. There is British money—pounds and shillings—worth their Face Value, but I get into Misteries and Puzzles when I am offered paper bills printed by the various Colonies, and money put out by Merchants

---

tion. The newspapers of the 1860's and 1870's are full of advertisements of cooking stoves. They became, in a certain sense, a mark of social standing. A family that continued to cook on the old-fashioned fireplace was out of the social picture. Everybody who was anybody possessed a stove in the kitchen.

and even Tavern Keepers. Besides all Kinds of Counterfeits. I Asked Mr. Porter to advise me and he gave me a List which he has Made up of the Difrent Currencies. It helps a little but not Much. When you Buy anything at a Shop, and start to Pay for it, you get into an Argument with the Merchant over the Value of the Money.

They have a Theatre here, but it is Closed right now. They say there will be no more Performances until our Trouble with Britain is over. Well, if that is the case, I think it will Remain Closed a long time. Dr. Franklin has left for Albany, with two or three other Commissioners, to try to get the Canadians to join us against Britain. It will Probably be a useless Mission.

I am going to New York in about a Week, and will Sail Home from there. It will be the last Chance I may have in some time to see the Town founded by the Dutch.

Stage Wagons run between the Two Places—I mean New York and Philadelphia—Three times a week. I have seen one of the Stage Wagons. It is a Large Wagon with a canvass top and Sides. The Seats are Benches without any backs. They make the Trip in a little less than Two Dayes. The Stage Wagon leaves Philadelphia Monday morning at Eight o'clock and Reeches New York Tuesday afternoon late. We spend the Night at some Inn on the Road. The Fare is Twenty Shillings.

They have among their special Dishes here one called Philadelphia Scrapple. It is a meat Dish made of Pork and Corn Meal all chopped together with seasonings and boiled. Then when Cooled it is fried like Sausage. I like it, and have it every Morning for Breakfast. Mrs. Graydon wrote out the receipt for me, and I shall Bring it Home.

I almost forgot to say that I went to Take a Look at the Theatre, even if closed, as I wanted to see how it Compares with our Dock Street Theatre at Home. My Guide for the Occasion was Miss Charlotte Biddle, one of the reigning Beauties, and we went in her Father's Carriage. The playhouse, called the Southwark Theatre, is a dingy Place. At first sight it looks a Church—I saw only the outside of it—but it is Painted red all over. Miss Biddle said when it was Opened, a few years ago, there was a grand Row over it. The Quakers tried to Stop all Theatrical Performances, but failed.

Our Dock Street Theatre is Certainly much better looking. Miss Biddle says they have always had Trouble by spectators going on the Stage and standing there while the Play is Going on. Young Men about Town they are. They come in through the back door Stage Entrance and act as if they own the Place. It apperes to be a Kind of Fashion. She asked me if that is so with us in Charleston, and I said No, not in my Recollection. But it is a Common Practice in New York, too, they say. Young gallants go on the Stage, hand

Flowers to the Actresses while they are Playing, then stand at the sides of Stage, making remarks to the Players and Pointing out People in the audience with their Canes. It is said here that when the Theatre is opened again this Practice will be stopped.

Although Mackenzie had arranged with Edward Rutledge to take him to meet Thomas Paine, the meeting actually came about by accident. One afternoon Mackenzie went into the London Coffeehouse, at the corner of Front and Market Streets, for a rum toddy. As he sat at a corner table he noticed a lone gentleman, whom the waiter called "Mr. Paine" at a table near by. Then a couple of men passed through the room, and he heard one say to the other, "There's Tom Paine." Mackenzie was sure, by that time, that he was in close proximity to the author of *Common Sense,* and he studied his appearance carefully while trying to make up his mind to address him and introduce himself.

He observed that Paine's face was rather thin and his nose long and prominent. His high forehead and his sensitive mouth gave him the facial characteristics of a thinker. But Mackenzie noticed that his eyes, as he looked around the room, were his most striking feature. They were large, dark eyes which carried fire and perception even in the most casual glance. Mackenzie was not much of a physiognomist, or philosopher or reader of character, but when he saw Paine's eyes and the expression in them he felt sure that he was on solid ground when he said to himself, "That man is full of fire. He's going to do something in the world—either good or bad —that will not be forgotten for ages."

A moment later Mackenzie picked up his courage, walked over to Paine's table and introduced himself as a reader of *Common Sense.* Paine did not rise or extend his hand. He smiled, waved toward a chair and said, "Sit down; have a drink." Mackenzie murmured that he had a drink already. He went over and brought back his rum toddy, and sat down. He and Paine remained there for more than an hour, discussing life and human affairs. From that day, until he departed for New York, ten days later, Philip Mackenzie spent a part of every day in the company of Thomas Paine.

During this close though rather brief companionship Mackenzie learned very little of Paine's early life and antecedents. He seemed to live in a world of ideas, and he hardly ever spoke of himself at all, though he had a great deal to say about political and economic freedom, tyranny, scientific progress, labor and its rights and the purposes and limitations of government.

He was at that time the editor of the *Pennsylvania Magazine* which paid him a small salary. He lived alone in one room.[10]

7

The day before he left Philadelphia for New York—the date was April 12—Philip wrote to his sister, Mrs. James Verdier, who lived with her husband in Orangeburg District, in the colony of South Carolina. Orangeburg is not more than eighty miles from Charleston, a short forenoon trip in an automobile in this twentieth century. In 1776 a loaded wagon usually took four days and sometimes longer to traverse the streak of mud and sand which led to Charleston. Even a rider on horseback could not make the trip in less than two days. Mrs. Verdier's husband owned a large rice plantation on the Santee, with sixty slaves at work there. He did not believe in absentee ownership, so he and his wife lived on the plantation in a spacious and airy house of two stories which sprawled over nearly an acre with its various wide halls, parlors, and sitting rooms.

Mrs. Verdier had sent to her brother in Philadelphia a list of feminine things, such as fabrics, gloves, laces, etc., that she

[10] Thomas Paine was born at Thetford, in England, in 1737. His father, a Quaker, was by trade a staymaker (meaning a maker of women's corsets). Paine had only a limited common school education. He was trained to be a journeyman staymaker, but abandoned that trade to become an excise officer. In the course of time he was selected by the excise officers to represent them in London in an effort to obtain more pay and better working conditions.

For these activities he was discharged from the government service, but during his stay in London he met Benjamin Franklin, who was then in England as a representative of the American colonies. Franklin advised Paine to go to America and gave him a letter of introduction addressed to Richard Bache, who was Franklin's son-in-law.

In January, 1776, his pamphlet *Common Sense* was published in Philadelphia. Written in simple language, it was a powerful argument for the independence of the colonies, and it has been said by many observers of events at the time that Thomas Paine had done more to bring about the Declaration of Independence than any other single person.

desired and which could not be purchased in her neighborhood. Even in Charleston, she wrote, there would not be such a large variety of materials as in Philadelphia, and the Charleston prices would undoubtedly be much higher. Would he be a nice, lovely brother and do her buying for her? Jimmie, her husband, would pay whatever the goods cost to the Mackenzie office in Charleston.

Young Mackenzie almost had a fit when he read the items on the list; what was crepe de Chine, and paduasoy, and voile de Langres? He did not know, so he did what any sensible man would do in the circumstances. He went to Miss Charlotte Biddle and told her of his trouble. Would she assist him? He assured her that he hated to ask her, that he knew it was an imposition on her good nature. He was a very young man when he made these assertions; if he had been ten years older and married he would have known that in asking Miss Biddle to go shopping with him on an unlimited spending account he was giving her a great treat which needed no apology.

They spent three days going from one shop to another. These establishments for the sale of women's finery were very different from any shop in existence today. They were all small, for the idea of merchandising in a big, expansive way had not been developed, even if it existed, which is doubtful. The great merchants of the nineteenth century had not yet been born. A shopkeeper was considered everywhere as a person of a lower rank socially than his well-to-do customers.

Complete garments could not be purchased; the ready-made suit for men, the coat and skirt for women, were not to be found in the shops. The customer bought the cloth and the making of it into garments had to be done by tailors and dressmakers. The shops for women dealt in fabrics and such articles as gloves, laces, ribbons, muffs and stockings.

These emporiums were gloomy even on a sunny day, for the light was filtered through small windows of diamond-shaped panes. Big show windows of plate glass did not exist. In the evenings the interiors were illuminated by sperm-oil lamps set in brackets on the wall. The goods were not well displayed. The fabrics were in bolts on the shelves, and the smaller articles lay in drawers.

The clerks were usually men, even in stores devoted wholly

to women's goods. The saleslady had not yet made her appearance in the world, though in small shops owned by women the proprietor and her daughter usually waited on customers.

Mackenzie and Miss Biddle saw all sorts of lovely fabrics; sometimes they would have the obedient salesman lay out most of the stock of the store on the counter. They bought all the things mentioned on Mrs. Verdier's list as well as other articles. Miss Biddle told him, however, that the silks and brocades would be nearly useless unless his sister knew the fashions, so she could make them up intelligently. Otherwise, her dresses would be all out of style, and that would never do. "Well, let's send her some drawings, or patterns that she can follow," Philip suggested.

Miss Charlotte smiled upon his ignorance benignly and said, "You can't buy patterns. Every woman makes her own, but we can buy fashion dolls, so let's do that, and send them to her." They went into another ladies' shop and purchased three dolls, each dressed differently from the others. Their attire indicated the latest styles.[11]

The dolls were wrapped up carefully and put with the rest of the merchandise. Mackenzie arranged to have the packages sent by water to Charleston.

> Dear Sister Sally: Well, you little Bag of Tricks, I bought all the Stuff on your List and have sent it to you—or to Charleston—by the schooner *Daisy May,* Captain Chambers, which is to leave here in a few Dayes. It is going to our Office in Charleston, but I have written Mr. Robertson that it is for you and he will Forward it up Orangeburg the first Chance he may have. It did not Cost as Much as you Thought it might, maybe because Miss Charlotte Biddle, a Charming young lady, helped me make the Purchases. A bill Goes with the Merchandise. Jim may pay it whenever he Pleases to our Charleston office.
>
> I sent to you in the same Package, three Fashion Dolls carefully

[11] The use of fashion dolls to spread the new modes became obsolete around the beginning of the nineteenth century when monthly magazines with colored plates of the latest fashions were published in London and Paris and sent regularly to America. One of the earliest of these fashion books was *The Ladies European Magazine,* first brought out in London in 1798.

Patterns for ladies' dresses were first manufactured in 1863, by Ebenezer Butterick, of Massachusetts. He sold them through the stores and also by mail. Before that time dressmakers and sewing ladies usually tried to imitate the dresses shown in pictures of stylish women.

(The Bettmann Archive)

THE TRAVELING SHOEMAKER.

The traveling cobbler was well known in all sections of the country for many years. Sometimes he would remain for weeks in a country village, making and repairing shoes for the people in the neighborhood. Then he would move on to another location. (From drawing by W. L. Taylor.)

wrapped. They are not for the Children to Play with, but they show the Latest Style. In making your Clothes just pick the Doll you like best and Immitate her Dress.

I hope you got the two Letters I wrote you Telling of my Doings in the City of Brotherly Love.

Among the Silks and Fol-de-rols you will find a present from me, your loving Brother, in the shape of Five Hundred Pins—500—Count 'em.

I Remember the last Time I saw you there was a Sad Complaint about Pins—you Couldn't keep them—you Lost 'em—and there were no Good Pins to be bought in Orangeburg, and they were so Expensive in Charleston. I think you said you Paid Sevenpence apiece for them.[12] Well, I don't mind telling you that the pins I am Sending you are much Cheaper. They cost me Fourpence apiece, or a Little More than Eight Pounds for the lot of Five Hundred.

I dont Recall ever having Bought a Pin before in all my Life, and I had no idea they Cost so much, tho I Remember our Mother taught us this Rhyme:

See a Pin and Let it Lie;
You'll Want that Pin
  Before you Die.
See a Pin and Pick it Up
And you'll always have
  Good Luck.

I am leaving Phillie tomorrow for New York and will Write from there in a few Dayes. I hope this finds you well and Jim also. Tell him for me that I Think the Congress will Adjourn without Accomplishing much, though the Sentiment in Favor of Independence is Growing.

Your Loving Brother

Philip

[12] Until John Ireland Howe, of Derby, Connecticut, invented a pin-making machine in 1832 ordinary pins, so plentiful today, had to be made by hand. The workman would cut a piece of wire, fashion the pin, give it a point and put on a head, which was a most difficult operation. Pins so made were very expensive. The accounts of George Washington show that he paid from five to seven pence apiece for the pins used by his family.

Chapter VI

A GEORGIA TOWN IN 1807

I

AT EIGHT O'CLOCK every morning except Sunday Major Harvey Earle left his house on Centre Street in Augusta, Georgia, and walked to his office on Reynolds Street, facing St. Paul's Church. It was not a long walk—not even half a mile—and it was a delightful one when the weather was pleasant, which meant most of the year. On a clear day the high-arching blue sky, with its fleecy tufts of drifting white cloud, seemed so far away that one, gazing upward, felt drawn into the infinite.

But after a heavy rain this walk from house to office became a mud-spattered pilgrimage. None of the streets was paved; there were neither sidewalks nor drains, and the thick, loamy soil held the water like a sponge. On rainy days Major Earle rode on horseback to his office, with a negro man following him on another horse to take the two animals back to their stable. If the rain was still falling when he set out from home he held over himself, as he sat on the horse, an oiled silk umbrella. In color the silk was yellow, and the oil made it glisten. The umbrella, the Major and the horse could be seen approaching from afar.[1]

On a bright, sunny morning in November, 1807, Major Earle left his home at the usual hour and began the brisk walk to his office. In the air there was a touch of winter, so the Major wore a dark-blue cloak over his shoulders. He carried a gold-headed cane, which he raised frequently to salute acquaintances as he met them. Everyone in Augusta, both white and black, knew the Major by sight even if they were not personally acquainted with him. He was a tall, lean, clean-shaven man of about fifty-five in knee breeches of broadcloth, a white linen shirt with ruffles on the bosom, a long blue coat which came to his knees and stiffened below the waist, so its

[1] Rubber raincoats, boots and overshoes, were unknown in 1807. Charles Goodyear, who was the Edison or Marconi of the rubber industry, succeeded in vulcanizing rubber in 1844. Its stickiness and offensive odor were removed by vulcanizing, and it was made more durable.

skirts spread out. On his head he wore a small felt hat with the corners turned up, and on his feet were low shoes with metal buckles. His stockings were of white wool.

These garments were, more or less, out of style. They were the finery of a past generation—the men of the American Revolution. Gentlemen still wore knee breeches, lace cuffs and the rest of it in the evening, but in the daytime most of them wore long pantaloons, double-breasted coats without decoration, and tall hats of beaver.

Major Earle declared that he was too old to adopt the new fashions. "I follow some good examples," he said with his customary suavity. "I dress like the father of my country, General George Washington, and like Thomas Jefferson, President of the United States." [2]

The Revolutionary War had been over for twenty-six years, but to the Major it was all as fresh and vivid as if the surrender at Yorktown had occurred last month, and references to the war came up constantly in his conversation. Someone, describing a deer hunt on the Savannah River, said, "We got not only behind 'em, but on both sides, and there was left open only one way for the deer to do, and that was straight ahead."

"Just like the time when we drove Cornwallis down into that Yorktown hole," the Major said. "I was with Lafayette then and we suttinly did push that Britisher to the jumpin' off place." After that the Major launched into a verbal essay on Lafayette, his manners and his ability.

"I was at Brandywine," he said on another occasion, "and the British beat us. I'll say this for 'em. They've got a lot of courage."

"Why I thought the Americans showed up pretty well at

[2] The first president who wore long trousers habitually was James Madison. During the French Revolution, which began in 1789, the supporters of the Revolution adopted the practice of wearing trousers instead of knee breeches. For that reason they were called *sans-culottes,* which means "without breeches"—that is, the knee breeches worn by the royalists. Between 1790 and 1800 trousers became popular in America among the common people, but those higher up did not adopt the fashion until ten or twelve years later. For some unknown reason—maybe because of the muddy roads—the long trousers of that era were cut too short to reach the shoe tops. Between the trousers and the shoes about three inches of sock could be seen.

Brandywine," said a young law student who was listening to the conversation, "even though they had to retreat."

"Of course they showed up well. You could allus count on that. We simply got wo'n out with killin' 'em. You could shoot 'em all day, jes' pile 'em up on the ground and the rest would keep on comin'. We shot 'em down till our guns got too hot to hold, and we had to rest. They were ten to our one. Finally, we ran out of ammunition and had to retire. Some of the boys could hardly walk off the field; they were so tired. Jes' suppose you'd set out to kill people all day long, one after another. I'll bet you'd be tired in seven or eight hours." This brief account of the battle of Brandywine is not supported by history, but Major Earle, like many veterans, created his own account.

Major Earle was a private banker. He made loans on personal notes; he financed small farmers on a share-cropper basis; he arranged mortgages on real estate, live stock or slaves and he assisted merchants to meet their obligations by lending them money and taking liens on their assets.

All of these transactions were small, but the total was large and would have required far more money than Major Earle possessed if he had depended on his own funds alone. Most of the cash that he lent out came from deposits. But the word "deposit" was seldom used. When money was put in the Major's bank the depositor said he had "loaned" the Major that amount of money.

It is interesting to note that the functions of banking in commercial life were almost unknown in those early days. There were no laws concerning banks; no regulation of interest rates, nor definition of the rights of depositors.[3] The little banking that was done was carried on by individuals. Some of the money lenders were loan sharks, but Major Earle was not one of them. He was a lenient creditor, so lenient indeed that his bank made only a fraction of the profits it should have earned. He owned a cotton plantation called "Fairview" on the Waynesboro road about fifteen miles from Augusta, and he used to say that he made twice as much from "Fairview" as he did from his money lending.

[3] In 1781 Congress granted a charter to the Bank of North America, a Philadelphia institution. It was the first incorporated bank in the United States. Augusta did not have an incorporated bank until 1810, when the Bank of Augusta was organized.

These primitive banks issued no check books. Instead of writing a check the depositor wrote a note to the bank to the effect that so much money should be paid to So-and-so.

The Major's hair was turning white, and he let it grow long so that it fell down to his shoulders. This patriarchal way of wearing his hair, and his custom of patting the heads of youngsters whenever he met them, gave him an air of benevolence which was emphasized by a tendency to smile kindly at anyone who spoke to him. He never laughed, not because he did not want to but because a spell of hearty laughter might loosen his false teeth and send them flying. He wore a complete set, both upper and lower dentures, and both plates were so loose that they made clicking sounds when he ate or talked. There was nothing unusual in that, as the art of dentistry was still in its early youth; even the false teeth of George Washington, made by the most skillful dentist in the country, fell out occasionally and embarrassed our first president. So, when others were roaring gleefully at a joke or a humorous incident the Major, with twinkling eyes, smiled urbanely. This restraint, arising from a badly fitting set of false teeth, contributed in a measure to his reputation as a kindly, tolerant sage.

Cotton was the lifeblood, the mainstay, the universal provider for the whole population of Augusta at this period. In 1807 that Savannah River town was the first of the inland cotton markets. But its reliance on cotton was historically recent. Before Eli Whitney invented the cotton gin the staple crop of the region had been tobacco. The tobacco leaf was gathered, put in two-hundred-pound casks, and the casks were rolled to the busy market of Augusta. Not rolled by hand, however. An axle ran through the heads of each cask, and the axle heads were attached to a horse's harness, so the horse could pull over the rough country roads as many as ten or twelve casks of tobacco. During the fall the streets of the little village that was called Augusta were often cluttered and rendered almost impassable by the multitude of tobacco casks moving along the roadway.

The cotton gin was invented in 1793. Within ten years cotton had supplanted tobacco as the money crop of middle

Georgia. It was so high in price that almost worthless land amply repaid the labor given to it. The tobacco casks gave way to cotton bales.[4]

There were no cotton mills in the South at that time, though there were many spinning wheels and hand looms in the farmhouses. This primitive, backwoods manufacturing used only a trifling proportion of the cotton crop. The rest was sent down the river to Savannah and then, by sailing ships, most of it was forwarded to England, which was then the center of the world textile industry.

All this involved a string of transactions. The farmer brought his cotton to Augusta in the first place. It was sold there to a merchant known as a cotton factor. The factor put the bales in his warehouse and resold them, later on, to another factor in Savannah or Charleston, who sent them abroad or to New England. In Lancashire or Massachusetts the cotton reached a textile mill and was made into cloth and yarn.

This indirect method was wasteful in that several middlemen made profits on the cotton before it reached the English mills. A group of British mill owners decided, after much consideration and slow overseas correspondence, to buy their cotton direct—not from the farmers, but from the Augusta cotton merchants, thus eliminating a number of go-betweens. In carrying out this purpose they sent over to Augusta a representative with authority to purchase cotton; pay for it, and ship it to England.

Major Earle, as one of the important men of the community, met the English cotton buyer on the day of his arrival. He had landed at Savannah after a six weeks' ocean voyage, and had come up to Augusta—131 miles—in the stage wagon. The trip took forty-eight hours. The roads were nothing more than wide trails through the woods and across the fields. The stage—called a "stage wagon"—was only a covered wagon with plank seats running crosswise. These seats had no backs. Mr. Cecil Lowther, the English cotton buyer, had arrived

[4] Before the cotton gin was invented the price of middling upland cotton was about forty cents a pound. Ten years after its invention the increased production of cotton had brought the price down to twenty-one cents a pound, but even when sold at the lower price the profit was very large. Slaves (prime field hands) could be bought for five hundred dollars apiece, and a negro working in a cotton field might earn half his own cost the first year.

four days ago, the Major reflected, as he walked to his office, and had become, in that short time, the subject of more comment among the people of Augusta than anything which had occurred since the Savannah River overflowed its banks in 1796 and flooded the town.

When the English gentleman alighted from the stage he wore a coarse checkered shirt with a glaring plaid tie, heavy woolen trousers, high-top boots, a brown coat with numerous pockets and a low-crowned felt hat pulled down over his eyes. He carried a pistol in a holster attached to a leather belt. Its butt protruded, ready to be drawn instantly. The reception committee did not recognize him at all among the dozen passengers of the stage wagon and picked out, by error, a dapper-looking tinware salesman from Connecticut. After they finally got in contact with Mr. Lowther they were too courteous to ask him the reason for his strange attire. It came out, however, next day that the English cotton buyer had thought that Augusta was a wild and rowdy frontier town, where murder was of daily occurrence, and where every man was supposed to protect himself.

A curious feature of this meeting was that every man who went to meet Mr. Lowther and welcome him to Augusta also carried a pistol, though they concealed their firearms better than the Englishman. Fights and shooting affrays were frequent; and there was a duel now and then in which some member of the local aristocracy met his death. But the Englishman's mistake was in dressing like a roughneck and his astonishment was as great as that of his hosts when he saw them in their handsome broadcloth suits.

Mr. Lowther did not know a soul in the place, and he intended to stay at the inn until he could find bachelor's quarters for himself. But he did not go to the inn, for Robert Harrison invited him to his home as a guest. The house of the Harrisons was one of the most elegant in Augusta, and their English visitor, in his clumsy clothes, felt very much out of place for a couple of days. Then his baggage arrived from Savannah and that evening he appeared at dinner dressed like Beau Brummell.

The Major was greatly interested in Mr. Lowther, and took every opportunity to impress himself upon that gentleman's attention. It was he who explained humorously the reason for Lowther's uncouth appearance on the day of his arrival. He invented also, in his genial, offhand way, the myth of Cecil Lowther's noble connections, asking everyone he told to keep it confidential.

The reason for these maneuvers was that Mr. Lowther would possess and keep somewhere a very large sum of money. The Major had a bank, and could keep the money safely.

As he walked to his office he was glad that Mrs. Earle had thought of having Mr. Lowther to dinner, and the dinner was to be that very evening.

Though Augusta was only a village in 1807, it was the largest inland community in either Georgia or South Carolina and was an important distributing center for merchandise as well as a receiving depot for cotton.

In the higher social circles of Charleston and Savannah, Augusta was looked upon as a frontier town, rough and uncouth, with only a half dozen of its families entitled to social distinction. This observation was not entirely true; historical research shows that Augusta was about on the same level in civilization and social graces as Charleston and Savannah, although it was much smaller than either of them.

All the streets in old Augusta ran either north and south, or east and west, and the plan of the city was rectangular. In 1807 there were shade trees in all the streets, and they served to keep out the glowing heat of the summer months. Even now most of the streets are shady, but Broad Street, which is the principal business thoroughfare, has been denuded of its trees. This street, more than a mile long, is one hundred and seventy feet wide. With trees on both sides Augusta's Broad Street would rival in appearance the Champs Élysée of Paris. There are few city streets in America as wide, as level and as straight. But without the shade trees it is just a glaring, bare, harsh avenue where the clear sunlight brings out every ugly feature of the buildings.[5]

[5] The aversion to shade trees on the business streets of cities is one of the curious features of American psychology. In New York the crusade against trees in the city was so dynamic around 1890 and 1900 that all the trees—in virtually all the streets—were cut down and removed. The controlling idea was that trees have no place in city streets, certainly not in the business sections. Now the

Back in the early days a few of the houses were built of brick, and the brick buildings were mainly on Broad Street—two-story houses with a store or shop on the ground floor, and the home of the proprietor on the floor above. The well-to-do, as a rule, lived in frame houses of three stories with a porch in front. These dwellings were usually painted a dazzling white which shone brightly even by moonlight. In the poorer section of the town there were many log houses. Almost every house was surrounded by a garden.

2

The name of Major Earle's wife was Katherine, but no one ever used it in addressing her or in talking about her. To her friends and relatives she was Kitty, and those who did not know her so well called her Mrs. Earle in a most respectful tone.

If she were living now, in our time, there is no doubt that she would be looked upon by her acquaintances as a mild, colorless person, without ideas or outstanding traits. Moreover, she would be considered almost incredibly ignorant. But in 1807 women were not judged by the standards of today. A lady was not expected to have a flock of notions fluttering around inside her head, or to be able to discuss the differences between the Federalists and the Republicans, or the iniquities of Aaron Burr, or the doings of the upstart Napoleon. Nor was she supposed to know the distance of the earth from the sun, or who Lord Bacon was, or who invented the art of printing. The women of that day, if they were well-bred, did not have an interest in anything except husband, household, a small circle of friends, and their social activities.

There were no women's clubs. The ladies took no part in politics, nor in any public movement, even if it had a charitable object. This applies not only to Georgia, but to the country as a whole. One never encountered a woman in an office unless she were a visitor. Businessmen and statesmen had secretaries, but they were invariably male. No one had ever heard of a

---

sentiment has changed and with much expense and trouble trees are being brought back.

Fifty years ago Broad Street in Augusta was shady in summer. But at the present time it has an ovenlike heat from May to September.

woman journalist, and if one had appeared she would have been followed by a curious crowd.

Women were on the stage in that era, and some of them were celebrated for their talents, but no actress, however distinguished she might be, was ever received by the ladies of society. To the men and women of that time there seemed to be something profoundly vulgar in any woman's exhibiting herself before a crowd in a theater; not only exhibiting herself, but even pretending to be somebody else, according to the role she was playing. The ladies and gentlemen might enjoy the performance, as they frequently did, but even the best performance did not raise the social status of the actors who took part in it.

A few women in every community were in business despite the rigid verdict of custom and public opinion that woman's proper place was the home. There were woman tavern keepers, for instance, and some of these hostesses of jaded travelers attained a wide and favorable renown. And, of course, all the dressmaking establishments were carried on by women. Women owned small shops of various kinds, ranging from bakeries to shoe stores.

But all places of power and distinction in commercial life were occupied by men; and in other fields of action women were conspicuously absent. There were no women doctors, dentists, lawyers, architects or professional decorators. A few literary ladies wrote novels, but their books, saturated with an unreal and sugary sentimentalism, have failed to survive.

Marriage was the first objective of all womankind. It was generally believed that something was wrong with a girl if she never married, something wrong morally, or mentally or physically. But a young woman could do very little about it. Conduct that is considered only mildly flirtatious today would have been characterized as indecent in the early 1800's, and such practices as "necking" would have served to exclude the lady in the case from good society. All a girl could do in getting a husband was to look her best, be shy and modest in company, and meek in manner. If her conversation was highly intelligent and revealed a superior education she was termed a "blue stocking" and shunned politely by a considerable proportion of the eligible men. They did not care to marry a woman who knew so much; she might outshine her husband.

Every young lady was expected to play the piano and the guitar and much time was devoted to this form of education. Dancing was also one of the necessary items on the list of things that a well-bred girl has to learn, and it must be said that dancing required a lot of learning in those days, for some of the dances followed intricate patterns. The minuet and the country dance were popular.[6] The waltz was unknown at that time. It did not take its place among the dances until after the Civil War. The Virginia reel—another favorite exercise—was an American copy of a well-known English dance called Sir Roger de Coverley. The jig, a comparatively simple dance, was performed with much clatter and laughter by everybody who was not too old and infirm to lift a foot. Every city and town of importance contained numerous music teachers and dancing masters.

Throughout this masculine civilization there was little interest in the higher education of women. Some families that did cherish such an interest employed tutors to teach their daughters. Thomas Jefferson instructed his daughter Martha in a long list of subjects which belonged to the curriculum of a university, and she was better educated when she completed her father's home course than most university graduates. But this was an exception to the general tendency.

At the beginning of the nineteenth century there were two score and some odd colleges for young men in the country, but no college for young women, although a few girls' boarding schools were in existence. Wesleyan College, of Macon, Georgia, appears to have been the first collegiate institution for women. It was founded in 1836, and is still hale and hearty after more than a hundred years of usefulness.

The prevailing conviction among our forefathers that women should be kept out of commercial pursuits and the professions did not emanate from a desire to dominate the fair sex, or to turn them all into household drudges, or to make them dependent on their husbands and parents. No; far from it. The real reason was altogether different. This

[6] The word minuet is an adaptation of the French word *menuet,* meaning a short step. Country dance has nothing especially to do with the country or with rural pastimes; it is simply a misspelling of the French word *contre-danse.*

attitude grew out of a profound respect, approaching reverence, for women in general. They lived on a loftier plane than men—so the average man believed—and women who were well-bred were believed to have neither passions nor hates. Ladies were supposed to be without sexual desire, and in their intimate relations with their husbands they consented graciously, but with inner repugnance. Gracious beings they were, without a sordid thought, according to the chivalrous notions of the time. Their purity of mind and soul was constantly extolled in public speeches and private discourse. But this purity could be easily sullied or "soiled" (which was the current expression) by contact with any form of coarseness. Even a single obscene word, heard by chance, could soil a woman. Duels were fought now and then because some careless gentleman inflamed by liquor had, in the presence of a lady, used a vulgar expression.

When a woman was once soiled there seemed to be no known way of unsoiling her. She bore the speck of stain as long as she lived. None of this applied to the women of the poor, to the wives and daughters of laborers and small farmers. They were apparently immune, or better say, it did not make any difference if they were soiled. As for the gentlemen, they were also immune. They could rub shoulders for days, months or years, with immoral people, and listen to obscene language, and have street fights, and meet their fellow men in duels, and get dead drunk, without being soiled at all.[7]

3

Mrs. Kitty Earle was entirely satisfied with her own place in life. She had no desire to earn money, nor did she want to write poems or make speeches, or do anything to attract the attention of the public. Any woman who had a public career, even one deserving of great praise, had lost some of her womanly dignity, in Mrs. Earle's opinion, and she was not alone in holding these views. She thought too much fuss had been made over Dolly Madison, then acting as the official hostess for President Thomas Jefferson, who was a widower.

[7] These observations on the status of women in the early nineteenth century apply especially to the Southern states, but they also fit, in a lesser degree, any of the states of the North.

There had been articles about Mrs. Madison in the thin little newspapers and magazines, and people who had visited Washington and met her were voluble with praise.

"She had been talked about so much that she is like an old shoe or a shopworn dress," said Mrs. Earle. "I should think she could manage the President's household without showing off all the time."

"Oh, she's not showing off, Kitty," said Mrs. Cumming, who was drinking a cup of Mrs. Earle's tea. "The official hostess for the President is in a prominent position, and people are bound to have much to say about her."

"Well, all I have to remark is that Mrs. Madison is not the President's wife, so she ought to keep away from the front of things. When George Washington was President you never heard of his wife showing off before everybody."

In the whole course of her life Mrs. Earle had never really thought about anything whatever that did not concern herself, or her family, or her friends. A personality of that type is not unknown even in the middle of the twentieth century; in the early decades of the nineteenth century it was so common among women that it attracted no attention. Kitty was not a fool by any means; she was simply not interested in distant events or in people who were even a little remote from her own orbit.

It was the middle of the afternoon on the day of the dinner party before Kitty found any time to sit down and rest. In preparing for such an occasion every nook and cranny of the house had to be cleaned, or so she thought. Being distrustful of the interest of the house servants in their allotted tasks she followed them assiduously and pointed out dusty corners and grimy windowpanes. She was in and out of the kitchen to see if the cooking were going on according to plan. The negro butler had spent an hour or two polishing the silverware, then she had him clean all the lamps and fill them afresh with sperm oil. On the dining table she planned to have candles—pink candles with shades—in her set of silver candlesticks.

Then the finger bowls—they must not be forgotten. They were a novelty; no one had ever heard of such things until Thomas Jefferson brought home some finger bowls from

France. That was ten years ago, she thought, but even now few hostesses in Augusta used them. She remembered, with a little laugh, that one of Harvey's friends—he came from somewhere around Macon—picked up his finger bowl when it was put before him and drank off the water, thinking that was what he ought to do. Thereupon Harvey raised his finger bowl and drank its contents, just as a well-bred gesture, so his friend would not be embarrassed when he discovered his mistake.

Now, Mrs. Earle's specialty in life was good breeding; she had rather die than be lacking in courtesy and have anyone consider her ill-bred, but she thought her husband's gesture of drinking from a finger bowl to conceal his friend's embarrassment was going too far. She reflected on this incident for quite a long time as she went about the house scolding the servants, for she had that kind of mind.

At last she concluded that everything had been attended to and she sat down in an armchair by one of the parlor windows that overlooked Centre Street. With a sigh she reflected that the street, which had been just a country road when their house was built in 1790, was now the chief thoroughfare for entering the town from the south. At this season, in the fall, Centre Street was noisy nearly all day with cotton wagons bringing the season's crop to market. "Ah well!" she thought. "One must take things as they come." That philosophical reflection was, however, small consolation when she looked across the narrow street and saw the blacksmith shop just opposite the Earle house, and next door to it the rumseller's drinking place. His customers were numerous and loud; they made themselves heard in song, laughter and quarrels until late at night. The blacksmith, too; his hammer was in use most of the day, and it could be heard all over the house. She recalled that when her husband had bought the ground and built their home there was nothing across the street, or road, except a beautiful pine forest.

The Earle house, or mansion, as it was sometimes called, was a medley of architectural fashions, like the houses of many well-to-do people in that era. The chief idea of its designer was to make it look imposing, and he had succeeded in accomplishing that purpose, though it was lacking in other ways.

Across its front there was a handsome portico which occupied the whole width of the house. From its outer edge rose six tall, white columns. They ran to the top of the house and supported the lofty roof of the portico. Squeezed close to the roof were the second floor windows, so completely overshadowed that the bedrooms behind them were in semi-darkness nearly all day. Looked at from the street the house was blankly flat-faced; it did not seem to be a house at all, but merely a façade. This effect was emphasized by the dazzling whiteness of the front in contrast with the dark windows and the heavy oak door.

The body of the residence did not measure up to the Greek temple boldness of its face. The most spacious place in the house was a wide hall which ran from the front door to the back. The rooms, with high ceilings, were small and crowded with furniture. On the ground floor there were four rooms, parlor (or living room), library, dining room and a so-called "smoking room" which had a billiard table. The meals were cooked in a kitchen in the yard and brought to the dining room under a covered way.

The second floor had six bedrooms, including two rather large ones in the front. The beds were wide and massive. Each had four heavy posts with a canopy and curtains. Only the two larger rooms had built-in closets; the small bedrooms were furnished with wardrobes. There was no bathroom in the house, and of course no running water. When anyone wanted to take a bath the servants brought in a large circular wooden tub and filled it with buckets of water brought up from the well. Each bedroom had a handsome washstand equipped with a pitcher and a bowl of decorative china. At all the windows there were lace curtains, but no roller shades, as the roller with a spring in it did not come into existence until near the end of the nineteenth century. Instead of roller shades the Earles had both lace and velvet curtains. The velvet curtains were blue in color and quite handsome in a stately way. When pulled across the windows they shut out the light.

During the summer months mosquitoes were a pest, but hardly less of a nuisance were the swarming flies. Wire screens for windows did not exist, but Mrs. Earle, like many other housewives, improvised screens of muslin. At meals a negro youth stood behind Mrs. Earle's chair with a fly-sweeper (a light, long rod with cloth streamers hanging from it) and moved it continually back and forth across the table.

Each of the four rooms downstairs had a fireplace, and fires of pinewood and hickory were kept going in all of them during the winter months—from December first to the middle of March.

There were only a few pictures on the walls and most of those were paintings of Kitty Earle's relatives. In place of pictures some of the walls were covered by French tapestries, and here and there hung a strip of silk colored and flaming with Chinese embroidery. In that era this type of embroidery was a country-wide fad. Many people had their chairs upholstered with it, and bedcovers made of it.

The Earles had the wide hall downstairs carpeted, but in the rooms rugs were used as floor coverings. In this practice they did not follow the local custom. As a rule, the homes of the well-to-do had no floor coverings at all, but the floors were kept waxed and polished.

The house stood in a plot of about two acres. Between it and the street was a flower garden which, in the summer months, was full of roses and other flowering plants. A wanderer from the twentieth century would have observed, with interest, no doubt, that some tomatoes were growing among the flowers. Tomatoes were called "love apples" in those days and were considered poisonous, but they were raised in flower gardens because the red love apples were pretty. Children were warned never to eat them or even to handle them.

Back of the house stood the stables, a barn and some outhouses. To the left was a vegetable garden, a grape arbor and a small peach orchard. On the right, behind the kitchen, were the cabins of the negro house servants. These cabins, built of boards, were whitewashed. Each cabin consisted of one room, and had a brick chimney, a door and a window. The slaves who lived in the cabins were not permitted to put up window curtains, for the patrol on making its rounds of slave quarters looked through the windows to see what the negroes were doing. Before the front door of each cabin there was a small porch.

For carrying on the housework there were six servants besides two more outdoors. All the housework could have been done easily by three people if energy and briskness could have been put into slaves. But that was impossible, for the servants got no wages at all, and they had developed deliberation of movement, slowness of action, and stupidity of comprehension into an art. It should be said, however, in justice to human nature, that the temptation to practice that art must be very strong in those who are never paid for their work.

There will be twelve at the dinner, Kitty Earle reflected—twelve including ourselves. And at that the dining room will be crowded. The table, with all the leaves out, is just right for us four. With the leaves in it will take twelve, but Caesar will have a pretty tight squeeze in passing around the head and foot of the table. I must remember to tell him to be careful not to spill anything down people's necks.

Our son and daughter—Francis Marion and Elizabeth—they're two. Then there's that Englishman. They say he's Lord Somebody's son or brother, I forget which. He'll put on airs. I like my home folks better. Besides, it's well known that most of the English nobility have no morals. They're drunkards and gamblers, and even worse. And, of course, we had to invite the Hutchinsons. He is the intendant of Augusta. They'd call him a mayor anywhere else, I suppose, but here he's an intendant. He's interesting and Rosa is, too. They know every blessed thing that happens in Augusta, down to somebody's dog having puppies.

Then there are the Harrisons. Mr. Lowther is their guest. He's a bachelor and is looking for a house. I wonder if the Spender place away out on McIntosh would suit him. The Spenders have moved to the country and their house is empty. But maybe he wouldn't like to live so far out. Oh, he'll find a place. I like Robert Harrison and Martha. He's so gallant, so obliging, and he smiles so pleasantly. Martha is such a good wife for him.

The Claytons are coming, too. Now, let's see, we're four;

the Harrisons and the Claytons are four—that makes eight—and there's Mr. Lowther; he makes nine. The Hutchinsons make two more, or eleven. Well, who is the twelfth? Oh yes. It's Julia Gray.

Between me and the gate post I don't like William Clayton, and I care very little for Ella. They're so formal, kind of stiff, just as if they had never met me before, and I've known both of 'em all my life. They're pushing people, too; always wanting to get ahead of somebody. When I talk to William Clayton his cold gray eyes have a distant look. He seems to be thinking of something else. And as for Ella, she studies my clothes all the time, not looking into my face. Maybe she thinks I have no taste; I don't know. But Harvey says William Clayton is an important man here in Augusta, a big man in the cotton business, and he has a large account in our bank, so we must have them here and be gracious. Very well, I've put Mr. Clayton on my left and Mr. Lowther on my right, and Ella is to sit on the right of Harvey.

And, oh—there's Julia Gray. She is to sit on Mr. Lowther's right. I'd almost forgotten that I'd invited her. Julia's a very nice old maid; she was thirty years old this summer. We needed another lady in the party, so I invited Julia, and isn't she grateful! She wrote me such a nice note of acceptance and sent it around by her good-for-nothing maid Birdie. I'm going to talk to Julia Gray about Birdie. I won't let my negroes have anything to do with her. She puts white folks' notions into their heads, and tries to make 'em think that they're just as good as their masters. Well, she's not my negro, or I'd have her out in the country hoeing corn.

There's something queer about Julia Gray, but for the life of me I don't know what it is. I know, of my own personal knowledge, that she has had at least two good, wonderfully good, offers of marriage, and she declined 'em. One was Mr. Cartwright's son, and the other was that young Mr. D'Antignac from Savannah. Both very fine young men, but Julia wouldn't have either of 'em. Prefers to keep on being an old maid, I suppose. Well, there's no accounting for taste. I hope my Elizabeth doesn't turn out like that. She's eighteen and beginning to take notice. But I've told her she's too shy. Why, at dinner I'll be surprised if she says a word, and if a man speaks to her she blushes. Now, that ain't right for a girl of eighteen. But Francis is not a bit like her, yet they're brother and sister. His father had to speak to him sternly about interrupting and contradicting older men. Because he graduated at Princeton this summer is no sign that he's as wise as Solomon, his father told him. I should say not. In the office he——

Oh, I've forgotten something and I'm so glad I've thought of it in time. Mr. Earle won't drink warm wine, and nobody really likes it, and I forgot till this very minute to have the wine cooled.

Walking across the room to the mantel Mrs. Earle reached for a red bell rope that hung by the chimney. She gave it a pull, and from a distance there came the faint tinkle of a bell. When Caesar arrived she said, "Caesar, I've forgotten something that you should have thought of and reminded me."

"What's dat, mam?" queried Caesar, pretending to look distressed.

"Why, we haven't cooled the wine yet for the dinner, and we barely have time now."

"Yes, mam, I knowed dat, but I t'ought mebbe you wuzn't goin' to have no wine t'night."

"Well, why didn't you ask me?"

"Why, Mis' Earle, I t'ought, mam, dat you didn't want to serve none at de dinner."

"How did you get that notion?"

" 'Cause, mam, you didn't say nuffin about it," Caesar replied. "I knowed youda told me if you wanted de wine served." This was a slave's trick of throwing off responsibility. Mrs. Earle had seen it worked many times, so she sighed and said:

"Yes, it's my fault. We'll go down to the cellar now, and I'll take out the wine." Followed by the butler, she went to the cellar and took out some bottles of Madeira, port and beer. While she was doing that Caesar had brought forth a large basket and had tied a rope stoutly to its handle. When the basket was full he lugged it to the well, which stood in a little orchard of peach trees back of the house, and lowered it gently to the bottom. The rope was securely tied to the well post. An hour's submersion would be enough to cool the wine.

With the wine cooling out of the way Mrs. Earle thought it

about time for her to dress for dinner, but decided to make a last visit to the kitchen before going up to her room. As she approached the kitchen house in the backyard she heard the voices of Sarah, the cook, and her two helpers—Judie and May—raised in argument. She stopped a moment before one of the open windows of the kitchen and listened. Upon hearing a few words she realized that they were arguing about the ghosts in the White House.[8]

"Cynthy said she heard it with her own ears," came from May, the younger maid. "I ain't sayin' she did or she didn't, I'm tellin' what she tole me. Cynthy said it sounded like a passel o' cats all mewin' sorter low." [9]

"Huh! Dat's what it wuz," argued Judie, the older maid. "It wuz a passel o' cats. I doan't take no heed of talk 'bout ghosts an' dead people walkin' round."

"Now here, young gal, doan't you git too biggotty," exclaimed Sarah, the cook, a large woman, very fat and very black. "Who is you to say you doan't believe in dis and dat? The *Bible* got ghosts in it, hain't it? It says de Lord Jesus rose fum de dead an' walked 'bout the yearth."

"Have you ever seed a ghost?" Judie inquired.

"I sho have, an' I doan't want to see no mo'. When I was a young gal, out in de country, dere wuz a man without any head dat went 'round at night, I seed him, an' he said somefin, I didn't wait to hear any mo'. I took it on de run. An' up at dis here White House Mr. Morgan, dat white carpenter, you know 'im; well, he met a ghost face to face. Dey sent for him to come an' fix a closet on de second flo'. Well, when he got dere, an' took his coat off, an' picked out his tools—he tole me this hisself—a man with his throat cut from year to year come

[8] This particular subject was then, and still is today, a topic of conversation in Augusta. The White House is a two-story frame dwelling on upper Broad Street. It was erected in 1750, and is said to be the oldest house in Augusta. During the Revolution it was the headquarters of one of the Tory commanders. He caused thirteen American prisoners to be hanged in the staircase well, all at the same time. Those who believe in ghosts say the house is haunted, while those who do not believe in ghosts ridicule the idea. It is said that if one stands at the foot of the stairs and counts thirteen a deep groan will shudder through the house.

[9] The word "passel," as used here, is a mispronunciation of "parcel," and the word was used to indicate a flock, as "a parcel of young folks," meaning a group of boys and girls. It is an ancient Southernism that is still in use among the illiterate.

in de room. Mr. Morgan said he could see through de man, like glass. Look like his head wuz goin' to fall off, his throat wuz cut so, an' blood all over his cloes. His face was w'ite like chalk, an' his eyes stood outside his head. De ghost looked at Mr. Morgan an' kep' sayin' somefin dat sounded like *Plee-plee-plee*. Like he tryin' to say *Please-please*. He walked right through de room an' went in de closet dat Mr. Morgan was goin' to fix an' shet de do' behin' him.

"Mr. Morgan said he left dat room in a hurry, an' when he got downstairs an' saw de fambly he tole 'em dat somebody must go upstairs an' git his coat an' his tools. A boy run up an' got 'em, an' den Mr. Morgan tole what he'd seen an' dat he'd quit de job. Somebody else could fix de closet. Den de whole crowd went up an' took Mr. Morgan with 'em. Dey opened de closet an' dere wuz nothin' in it but a lot o' cloes. But Mr. Morgan wouldn't stay, he——"

Mrs. Earle thought it was about time to interrupt the ghostly saga, so she stepped quietly into the kitchen and Sarah stopped talking at once. All three of the servants were working at something. Sarah exclaimed, "Well, well, an' here's de missus," and each of the girls made a curtsey. Kitty Earle smiled sweetly at them all, asked how the dinner was coming on, and departed.

She intended to wear that evening her new dress of yellow silk, which had been finished only the week before by Mrs. Kate Giles, Augusta's most competent dressmaker. It was fashioned in the latest style, known as Empire, which had originated in Paris and had finally reached Augusta after two years or more. The dress of yellow silk with Chinese embroidery on it was as simple and slender as a nightgown. The wearers of Empire dresses were called humorously "half-naked" because no layers of puffy petticoats were worn under them, and the lady's form was admirably revealed. They were also said to be as "lean as beanpoles" when they happened to be slender. The waist was very high—it was just under the bosom—and the dress fell sheer to the ground without frills or flounces. It was indeed a mode of extreme and graceful simplicity, but it made stout women with hips look ridiculous, nor did it go well with those who were very tall and thin. Long stays, somewhat like the modern girdle, were worn under the dress. The sleeves of Mrs. Earle's dress were short and puffed and the bodice was low in the neck.

4

Mr. Cecil Lowther had been in Augusta only five days but he had already become a man of distinction. This was due to gossip which, as most people of mature intelligence have learned, is a powerful force in small communities—and also in large communities. Harvey Earle remarked to a group of his friends that Mr. Lowther had a remarkable resemblance to the Earl of Lonsdale. He had seen a painting of the noble lord, and, "God bless me!" he said, "this Mr. Lowther is his very spit and image."

"He couldn't be the Earl's son, could he?" This from Henry Jewell, a cattle breeder.

"I don't think so," Harvey replied. "That English lord isn't old enough for a son of that age."

"By gum! I have it!" exclaimed Nat Poole, editor of *The Chronicle*. "Why, we-all must be blind. The family name of the Earl of Lonsdale is Lowther. I read that just the other day, and this fellow must be his nephew, or some relation, if not his son."

"Related in some way, I guess," said someone else. "But why is he coming here to buy cotton? It's a good paying job, of course, but I shouldn't think he'd need it."

"He doesn't need it," chuckled Joseph Hutchinson, with a laugh. "Them young Englishmen are up to all kinds of pranks—shooting tigers in India and running little shops in distant places, and exploring, and conquering native states, just for the fun of it. I wouldn't put it beyond him."

"Then he must be—how d'you call it," said Henry Jewell, "it's incognito, ain't it? He must be here incognito."

"I wouldn't be surprised," Harvey Earle agreed, "and that explains why he arrived in the queer clothes. Incognito—and I think we ought to respect it. Don't let him know that we are on to him."

"They're great horsemen, them English gentry," said Joseph Hutchinson, "riding with the hounds and leaping ditches. I s'pose we'll see some real good riding when Lowther gets settled down."

"Well, Joe," Harvey drawled, "we're pretty good that way ourselves."

When the day of the Earles' dinner came around Mr. Lowther was considered not only a close relative of an English lord, but also a man of wealth and culture. Harvey Earle did not say that Lowther was related to Lord Lonsdale; he merely said that Lowther looked like that nobleman, whose family name was Lowther. When the Englishman overheard some of these remarks about himself he hardly knew whether he was awake or dreaming. He was just an ordinary minor official in a Lancashire cotton mill. Some of his family were cotton mill hands and he did not understand at all how he had suddenly become so much higher in rank, or why he was credited with qualities and powers which he did not possess. But he was not naturally frank enough to correct these impressions, and his impulse was to cherish his false distinction. He was a mean little soul; he put successful pretense on the same level as real achievement—and, in fact, did not realize that there is any difference between them.

Notwithstanding Kitty Earle's anxiety over the dinner, and her gnawing fear that something would go ridiculously wrong in the service, or that some dish would be burnt to a crisp or hardly cooked at all, everything was just perfect—or as nearly perfect as one might reasonably expect.

Following the custom of that epoch there was a prodigious amount of food. The dinner began with turtle soup; Augusta was too far from the coast to have oysters at any season. Then came fried trout with melted butter; and after the fish came a succession of roasts. Roast ham and baked sweet potatoes came first; then baked wild turkey with a dressing made of walnuts and corn meal, and some vegetable dishes, asparagus, beans, and boiled rice.

Following the baked turkey there came a sherbet, then a course of cold venison and cheese, with stewed corn. The desserts included huckleberry pie, sweet potato pie and corn fritters with syrup. It was not customary to serve much bread at these huge meals, but both wheat biscuits and corn pone were provided and passed around once.

Before the guests went to the table a glass of sherry was

served, and during the dinner one might have a choice of Madeira wine or beer. There was neither coffee nor tea, but milk was given to those who desired it.

A great deal of the conversation at the table related to Southern life and manners, for Mr. Lowther asked a lot of questions along that line. That was natural; he was a stranger who intended to live in Augusta. He paid little attention to Miss Julia Gray, his dinner partner, and not much more to his hostess. Mrs. Earle thought his manners were bad. William Clayton was silent as usual, but now and then he turned his cold eyes to one or another of the guests and gazed at the unfortunate being with the expression of a relentless judge who is debating in his own mind whether his sentence should be hanging or life imprisonment. But, when spoken to, he replied more courteously than anyone else at the table, including even Mr. Earle. Robert Harrison and his wife Martha laughed at everything; and the host and Joseph Hutchinson told Mr. Lowther about the invention of the cotton gin.

"D'you know old Balaam Gunter, any of you," Joseph Hutchinson asked during a lull in the conversation. "I mean Balaam from across the river in South Carolina." His glance circled around the table and rested on William Clayton. "Oh yes, William, you know him, unless my memory's wrong."

"Old Balaam," said Mr. Clayton ponderously. "Surely. I used to know him well. Bought his cotton, but I haven't seen him in several years. Has anything happened to him beyond the usual mishaps of life?"

Before Hutchinson could reply Harvey Earle chuckled and said, "I knew him, too. Queer character like all the Gunters. Queer and stubborn. I mean those over in that part of our sister state. When I was in the tobacco business I used to take Balaam's crop every year. One year the price of raw tobacco fell to some ungodly low price, as I remember it was about five cents a pound, owing to overproduction. When Balaam heard about it he did not bring his crop to market at all, but burned every leaf of it. Piled it up like a pyramid, a layer of pinewood and a layer of dry tobacco leaves until the whole pile was about thirty feet high. Then he set fire to it. They said you could smell tobacco smoke for twenty miles."

"What in the world did he do that for?" was young Francis Earle's question. "Even if the price was only five cents a pound that was better than nothing."

"Hunh! I'd think so, and so would all of us, but that's not the way Balaam Gunter's mind works. He said, when I asked him why he burned the crop, that if he'd taken five cents a pound for it he would have been ashamed of himself for the rest of his life whenever he thought of the toil and sweat of raising the tobacco. So he burnt the whole crop and—well, he kept his self-respect, I suppose. Pardon me, William; you were saying something when I interrupted you."

"That's all right," Mr. Clayton said. "Joe Hutchinson wants to tell us something about old Balaam."

"All I wanted to say is that I saw him today," said Mr. Hutchinson. "He passed through Augusta in quite a caravan. Balaam, his wife, sons, daughters, niggers, horses, cows, goats, and even some coops full of chickens. Going to Alabama. I thought maybe some of you had seen him and his folks."

"I did see them, I think," said Ella Clayton. "They came across the bridge and passed right by me on Washington Street. Were there three big covered wagons, pulled by oxen?"

"Yes, three large wagons. Conestoga wagons," Mr. Hutchinson continued. "Old Balaam and the men rode horses."

"The older man had on a leather coat and a coonskin cap with the coon's tail hanging down his back."

"That's right. Well, I was riding around the town as I do every day. to look after things, when I saw Balaam and his string of wagons ambling along, and I rode with them as far as Rocky Creek."

"There are so many Carolina people crossing that bridge every day on their way to Alabam, as they call it, that I don't pay attention to them any more," said William Clayton. "Lots of land in the middle section of South Carolina is worn out. Poor farming methods. The land is not rich in the first place, they never rotate the crops, never use fertilizer, and the rains wash the soil into gullies. Then when they can't make a living any more they start for Alabama to ruin some more land."

"That wasn't Balaam Gunter's trouble," said Joe Hutchinson. "I asked him why he was going to a wilderness to start over at his age, and he said his part of South Carolina was getting too crowded and he couldn't stand it, so he's going where there ain't any neighbors."

"Crowded!" exclaimed Robert Harrison. "Why over there in that Godforsaken backwoods the houses are miles apart. What does he expect to be? The only inhabitant?"

"Balaam said that this spring a newcomer settled down within half a mile of his place," Hutchinson said, "and there are several neighbors within two or three miles. He said he felt hemmed in, so he's on his way. He's by nature a pioneer."

"Yes, that's right," said Harvey Earle. "All our forefathers were pioneers, or we wouldn't be here today. But I think it takes a good deal of resolution for a man who has settled down to pull up everything, lock, stock and barrel and go into a new land. Were there many in Balaam's party?"

"Well, he had two of his sons and their wives—the others wouldn't come—and his two daughters and their husbands, and a man who is just going along with 'em, and Balaam's six negroes. I saw several small children. They have tents for camping, and they have tools, seed, plows, clothes, a little furniture."

"Have they decided where they are going to settle?"

"Yes, so the old man said. On the Tennessee River. It runs through northern Alabama and makes a big bend toward the south. They're planning to settle down on the most southern point of the bend.[10]

"They hope to get there before the first of February, say in eight or ten weeks, living in the tents on the way, and stopping for several days at a time, here and there, to shoot game. As soon as they get to the place they're heading for they'll put up a house or two.

"I met Balaam's wife, a chatty old 'oman. She drives the leading wagon."

Martha Harrison wanted to know how Mrs. Gunter was dressed for her journey into the wilderness.

"Well, I'm not much on fashions," Hutchinson replied, "but she wore a gray woolen dress with some little white stripes on

[10] One result of this family migration was the settlement of the town of Guntersville, on the Tennessee River, in Marshall county, Alabama. But long before Guntersville became a village old Balaam had passed into another world.

it—sewed on—like little ribbons. Well, let's see what else. Why, her shoes were big, loose and rough, and she wore on her head that milliner's creation you call a poke bonnet. In spite of her gray hair she looked brave enough to tackle a den of wild cats."

"Ah, that's the pioneer woman," said William Clayton. "These women are as strong, as fearless, as able as the men. They carry civilization on their shoulders—make homes in the wilderness. I propose a toast to the pioneer women of America."

Everyone seemed pleased, and Caesar filled the glasses of the whole company. Mr. Clayton rose and made a short speech, and the toast was drunk.

Joe Hutchinson wiped his mouth with the back of his hand and resumed his discourse. "When I saw Mrs. Gunter she was using tobacco in a double fashion, smoking and chewing at the same time. She smoked a corncob pipe while she chewed a cud of tobacco. I made a remark about it and she said that smoking made the chewing taste better."

"I've seen men do that," Robert Harrison said, "but never a woman."

Cecil Lowther listened to this dialogue with an air of astonishment. In England, he said, women never smoked pipes and certainly were not given to the habit of tobacco chewing. He had never seen a woman use tobacco in any form. Some men chewed tobacco, he asserted, and there was a great deal of pipe smoking and cigar smoking among them.[11]

"Oh, I think we ought to have all this in the *Chronicle,"* said Mrs. Hutchinson. "It's such a human story."

"Have all what?" her husband asked.

"The story about these Gunter people, and their going through Augusta. It is so picturesque."

[11] Women of the higher classes in America never chewed tobacco, but it was a common habit among the women of the backwoods. It was eventually supplanted by the habit of snuff taking. The cigarette was unknown until after the Civil War, and for many years thereafter cigarettes were smoked only by boys and young men, and the habit was frowned upon by preachers, parents, teachers and employers. Cigarette smoking was usually a secret practice. The great popularity of the cigarette dates to the first World War, when women took up the habit of smoking. In 1915 the production of cigarettes in the United States was 400 per capita (meaning 400 individual cigarettes, not packages) ; in 1934 it was 1,400 per capita, and in 1943 three hundred billion cigarettes were produced which figures out as 2,300 cigarettes for every man, woman and child in the United States.

"Don't worry about the *Chronicle,* my dear; their man went with the Gunter caravan about a mile and got all the facts," said Joseph Hutchinson. "I think we'll see it all in print next week." [12]

Mr. Lowther exhibited much curiosity about American customs and manners. Those who were present did not mind answering his questions but they did not like some of his comments. He never used the word "negro" in referring to the slaves but called them "blacks," which he pronounced as if it were spelled with two a's—bl-a-a-ck—and the result was a sort of quacking sound. Harvey Earle told him that the term "black" was unknown in referring to the negroes, thinking that he would be pleased to get this information, but for some reason he appeared to resent it.

"They're called blacks in the British colonies," he said, "and that's good enough for me." His tone implied that the Americans, by not calling them blacks, showed ignorance and boorishness.

Then he wanted to know what a Georgia cracker is, and he asked if it were a person or an animal. "Sometimes it is hard to say," Robert Harrison replied, laughing. "I've seen some that looked like animals."

"Crackers are people," said Ella Clayton. "All poor white people are called crackers."

"Hold on, Mrs. Clayton," said Joseph Hutchinson, "not all poor white people are crackers. You wouldn't call George Lowrey a cracker, would you, and he's as poor as Job's turkey? But he's a university graduate, and a gentleman who hasn't been able to get ahead in the world."

"Yes, you're right," Mrs. Clayton agreed. "I spoke before I thought."

"The true cracker is a common person," Hutchinson continued. "He is illiterate and doesn't want to be anything else. He is sometimes a small farmer, or laborer, a teamster, or a mechanic. A gentleman who gets down on his luck never becomes a cracker. The chief characteristics of the cracker are

[12] The Augusta *Chronicle,* established as a weekly in 1785, is among the oldest newspapers in the United States. It was turned into a daily in the 1830's, and is still Augusta's morning paper. It has never missed an issue.

coarseness, uncleanliness, ignorance and often drunkenness. He is also lazy. Is that right, Mr. Clayton?"

There was a grin on Clayton's usually stern face as he replied: "Yes, that's right. And if I took the trouble I could name you, right now, a dozen members, at least, of the leading families of Georgia and South Carolina, who have all the traits you have mentioned. But they are not poor, and so they are not crackers. In your definition you left out poverty."

"Sure, sure," said Hutchinson hastily. "You can't be a cracker unless you're poor."

"Are the blacks among the crackers?" Lowther asked. Hutchinson answered, "No, no," and thought, what a fool that Englishman is.

"They started to calling them crackers, Mr. Lowther," Harvey Earle said, "because of their habit of cracking the whip over horses or oxen when driving them."

"How are your fine children?" Kitty Earle asked Rosa Hutchinson when the subject of Georgia crackers had worn itself out.

"Oh, they're very well, thank you," Mrs. Hutchinson replied with a smile, "and as hearty as ever."

"You must be proud of them, their red cheeks and strong bodies," Kitty continued.

"Mrs. Hutchinson's two boys and a girl are the prize children of Augusta," Robert Harrison remarked to Cecil Lowther. "Perfect examples of health."

Mr. Lowther said something that sounded like "Ripping!" He looked with interest at Mrs. Hutchinson.

"Let us in on the secret, Mrs. Hutchinson," Robert Harrison continued. "Is it just natural, or do you have a system in bringing up children?"

"I don't know—I really don't," Mrs. Hutchinson said rather shyly. "They get lots of exercise, out in the sun—and—uh—you won't make fun of me if I tell you?"

"Of course not," Kitty assured her.

"Well, I think they owe some of their good health and sturdiness to pot liquor," Mrs. Hutchinson went on. "I give each of them a pint or more of pot liquor every day, and see that they drink it. They've got so they like it."

Cecil Lowther looked up with a start. "Oh, I say! Really now!" he snorted. "Tiny youngsters drinkin' a pint of liquor a day. Eh, what!"

Everybody laughed and Kitty Earle hastened to say, "It's not alcoholic, Mr. Lowther. It's the liquid or watery leavings left in a pot after turnip greens are boiled in it."

"The negroes drink it," said Robert Harrison, "but white folks usually throw the pot liquor away. What made you think of giving it to your children?"

Mrs. Hutchinson reflected a moment. "Why, it's this way," she said, "I noticed that the children of the negroes on our plantation were healthier than mine and grew faster, and I wondered why. I looked into what they ate and learned that the little pickaninnies drank pot liquor every day. So I began to make my three young ones drink it and I'm sure it has helped them very much." [13]

When the dinner was over the ladies rose from the table at a signal from Mrs. Earle and went into the parlor, leaving the gentlemen to their brandies and toddies. As naturally as water runs downhill the conversation flowed into the perennial, inexhaustible subject of cotton.

"We were paying only eighteen cents for middling today," William Clayton remarked.

"That's quite a comedown from last season," said Harvey Earle, "and it makes me uneasy. I'm holding over a lot of cotton that I paid twenty and twenty-one cents a pound for. Do you think the price will come back?"

"I don't know, I'm sure, but to be on the safe side we must pay the farmer less. There's no sense in buying cotton at twenty cents a pound and selling it for seventeen or eighteen. What are your ideas on this subject, Mr. Lowther?"

"My instructions," the Englishman replied, "are to pay the current price, whatever that may be, but never to go above the price of the previous year, eh, what?"

"So you see how it is," Harvey Earle said, nodding to

[13] Mrs. Hutchinson did not know it, but pot liquor (usually spelled "pot likker") is simply swarming with Vitamin A, as shown by recent medical research. Turnip greens contain more of this necessary vitamin per unit of weight than any other vegetable.

William Clayton, "pay the current price, he says, but never exceed last year's prices. The tendency is downward."

"Yes, we must expect that," was Clayton's comment. "There's a bigger crop this year than there was last year, and last year's was the biggest up to that time. Twenty years from now this region—I mean the whole South—will not only grow cotton, but will think cotton and talk cotton all the time. The whole world's supply will be raised here. How it is going to affect our future, and that of our children, God only knows. I wish we were not so dependent on a single commodity."

"I never saw the town so littered with cotton bales as it is this fall," Hutchinson remarked. "I do my best to keep the streets clear, but it's beyond me. We must build more warehouses. There isn't room enough to hold the cotton as it comes in, and the buyers leave it in the streets. There are bales lying all over Reynolds Street, and right out here in Centre Street, too." Turning to Mr. Lowther, he said, "I hope you'll persuade your English people to build some spacious warehouses. Cotton is damaged by lying out in the open, in the rain, and there's always danger of fire."

"Quite," said Mr. Lowther. "I shall take it up with them."

"And Whitney's little cotton gin did it all, did it all, did it all," said Robert Harrison huskily, thrumming the table with his fingers. He had drunk too much brandy. "I've got to put it into music, or a ballad, or something. Maybe like Cock Robin——

Who made Augusta rich?
I did, said Eli Whitney,
With my little cotton gin
I made Augusta rich.

"There's one serious mistake in your rhyme, or whatever you call it," said Mr. Clayton.

"And what is that, sir?" Harrison sat up suddenly and looked across the table with an air of resentment. "I'd have you know, sir, that I never make mistakes."

"Well, you're mistaken when you declare that Augusta is rich. On the contrary, Augusta is poor and will probably continue to be for some time to come."

The young man made no reply. His head was sunk on his chest.

"I remember the days before the cotton gin," said Harvey Earle. "It seems a long time ago, but it is really only fourteen or fifteen years. Whitney invented his gin in 1793. Nobody ever expected in those days that cotton would ever be an important crop."

"It took a negro all day to get the seed out of five pounds of cotton," Joe Hutchinson said. "Five pounds—working from morning to night. John Hartley, who has a big place on the Savannah road, produced about two thousand pounds of cotton a year, and he was looked upon then as a big cotton grower, but today a crop of that size is considered pretty small. Raised four or five bales a year, and at that he had ten or a dozen negroes sitting on a barn floor separating the seeds from the lint, and it took these darkies six or seven weeks to do the job.

"Now he raises fifty thousand pounds a year, and doesn't need a single nigger to pick out the seeds. The gin does it all."

Cecil Lowther listened with vivid interest to Hutchinson's talk, and said when it was finished, "I suppose Mr. Whitney spent years in working on his idea of the gin before perfecting it." His remark was greeted by a shout of laughter. Even the semi-comatose Robert Harrison raised his head and joined weakly in the general ha-ha without knowing the cause of it. Mr. Lowther seemed perplexed.

Joseph Hutchinson kindly explained. "We were laughing at your thought of the time it took for Eli Whitney to invent the gin, but your supposition was reasonable. Inventors usually take years and years. Whitney took fifteen minutes, or maybe half an hour."

"Well, I'll be—blessed!" said Mr. Lowther.

"Mr. Clayton can tell you all about it," Joe Hutchinson continued. "He's a friend of Eli Whitney."

Mr. Clayton cleared his throat and said, "I met Eli Whitney soon after he arrived in Georgia. Fine boy, he was. From Connecticut, graduate of Yale. He went back to his native state years ago and has done some great work there.

"Well, to get back to the gin. He was a guest of Phineas Miller and his wife, on their plantation near Savannah when

(*The Bettmann Archive*

CYRUS McCORMICK, INVENTOR,
SHOWING HIS REAPER AT WORK.

Public test of Cyrus Hall McCormick's invention. The world's first reaper. Steele's Tavern, Virginia, July, 1831. (From a painting by N. C. Wyeth.)

I made his acquaintance. Mrs. Miller, by the way, was the widow of General Nathanael Greene, one of our Revolutionary heroes, and after his death she married Miller. Congress had given General Greene the Georgia plantation as a reward for being a great soldier, so that's how they happened to be living in our state. At that time I was one of their neighbors.

"One evening Mrs. Greene—I mean Mrs. Miller—had a lot of us in for dinner. After dinner we got to talking about the difficulty of seeding the cotton. As you know the lint sticks to the seed like all get-out, and you have to use some force in pulling it off. We'd given up the idea of cotton ever being a great crop in our part of the world for this reason: one farm hand, white or black, can raise about five bales of cotton in a year on good land, besides doing some work on other crops. Five bales weigh from two thousand to twenty-five hundred pounds. To take the seeds out of that much cotton the farm hand would have to work steadily from twelve to eighteen months, every day and all day. So you see.

"Well, at Mrs. Miller's that evening the matter was discussed pro and con. We knew there'd be big money in cotton if the seed separation problem could be solved. Eli Whitney listened closely; he sent out a negro for some cotton with the seeds in it, and I remember his sitting there and pulling the lint off.

"He told me later that the idea of the gin occurred to him that evening in all its features. In a week he'd built a rough little gin, not much bigger'n a hat box. He saw that the way to handle the matter was to comb the lint cotton away from seeds. So he put a lot of wire teeth on a roller, arranged in rows so that when the roller was turned the teeth would run through slots, or through a sort of grating. The cotton was put on the other side of the slots, or grating. Then, as the roller turned the teeth would pull the cotton from the seeds. That's the general idea, but there were some other little fixings on the thing.

"He invited me, and some others, to see the gin work. Well, sir, in a few hours it had ginned twenty pounds of cotton. The machine didn't have any name at the time, so Whitney called it a gin, which is a contraction of the word engine." [14]

"He must have made a fortune, eh what?"

"He did not; he made nothing whatever. He took Phineas Miller in with him as a partner, and they had the gin patented. They wanted me to go into the enterprise, too, but I excused myself. Why? Because the gin was too simple. No patent papers could protect it, for any mechanic or blacksmith could make one, so I didn't put any money in it, and now I'm glad I didn't. Miller lost all he had in fighting infringers of the patent, and Whitney ran in debt over head and ears. Eventually the State of South Carolina gave him fifty thousand dollars—I think it was—just as a reward for his invention, and North Carolina also gave him something. But this gift money went to pay his debts." [15]

"I've often wondered why I didn't invent the gin," said Joseph Hutchinson, "or you, Harvey, or any of us. It's the simplest device in the world, and looks like the idea might occur to anybody. But it didn't. It just goes to show——"

He did not say what it goes to show, for Mrs. Earle, coming to the door, smiled at the gathering, and said, "Are you gentlemen going to remain here all night?"

Her husband said, "No, darling, we're coming right away." Then he glanced at Robert Harrison, lying asleep with his head on the table, and said to his wife, "I think you'd better ask Mrs. Harrison to come in for a moment. We'll have to lay Robert out on the sofa in here, and I want her to see that he's comfortable.

To the Earles and their guests there was nothing startling, or even unusual, in seeing one of their number stretched out comfortably to sleep off the effects of too much liquor. It was a fairly common occurrence. In the case of young Mr. Harrison on this particular occasion, it had been brought on by the drinking of too many mint juleps that afternoon. He had attended a billiard match, as a spectator, and many drinks had been passed around.

[14] The principle of the cotton gin as invented by Whitney has never been improved. The great, powerful gins that handle thousands of bales of cotton work the same way as Whitney's little model.

[15] In his later years Eli Whitney was highly successful. He invented the system of mass production and the assembly line that are in operation today in all plants that make machinery of any kind, from carpet sweepers to automobiles.

It is not easy for us, living in this age of comparatively little drinking, to realize the extent of alcoholic indulgence throughout the whole colonial period and for fifty years or more after the Revolutionary War. A thorough research into the customs and manners of that era can hardly fail to convince an open-minded observer that if liquor drinking could kill a nation, then the whole American people would have curled up and died sometime around the first decade of the nineteenth century.

Senator George F. Hoar wrote, in his *Autobiography,* this description of the prevailing intemperance among the post-Revolutionary generation:

> The habit of excessive drinking was then universal in this country. Even the clergyman staggered home from his round of pastoral calls, and the bearers partook of brandy, gin and rum at funerals. It was not uncommon to see farmers, highly respected in the town, lying drunk by the roadside on a summer afternoon, or staggering along the streets. I have heard Nathan Brooks, who delivered the first temperance lecture in Concord at the request of the selectmen, say that after it was over he and some of the principal citizens went over to the tavern and each took a drink of flip.

During the Revolution the production of whisky increased so greatly that it reduced the supply of grain needed to make flour and bread, and the authorities had to restrict the amount of wheat, rye and corn used by the distilleries. Whisky making was not done by distillers who had a national distribution for their product; it was a purely local industry. There were thousands of distilleries, some of them with no more than a dozen customers, and the distiller—whose real occupation was farming, or running a store, or a blacksmith shop—had a still in his backyard. There was no tax on liquor, none at all, and anybody who had the inclination might make it and sell it.

In 1791 the Federal Government put an internal revenue tax of nine cents a gallon on whisky. This measure was extremely unpopular. It aroused such resentment that the farmers of western Pennsylvania took up arms against it. Their resistance is called the "Whisky Rebellion" in the school textbooks. The rebellion was quite a lively affair for a few months, and Federal troops were sent to put it down.

After the soldiers had quelled the opposition to the tax Congress repealed it. Whisky was not taxed at all from 1792 to 1862, when revenue was needed for the Union Army, and a small internal revenue tax was laid on the distilleries.

5

Industry in the Southern states at this period was almost wholly agricultural. Factories did not exist, but every town the size of Augusta had many small workshops where the proprietor was assisted by a few workmen. They made a variety of articles, including beaver hats, shoes, wagons, harness, simple furniture and small household articles. The blacksmiths hammered out nails and horseshoes, and some of them made such farm implements as hoes, rakes and plows. It was an age of craftsmen instead of machines; mass production was still to come.

These skilled workers were not all free white men. Among them were many negro slaves who had been trained in craftsmanship. One of these negro artisans, not in Augusta but in Charleston, made grilled iron work of such grace and beauty that gateways made by him still sell at fancy prices.

The cotton mill era did not begin until the middle of the nineteenth century. Albert Gallatin, Secretary of the Treasury in Jefferson's cabinet, wrote that in 1807 there were only fifteen cotton factories in the whole United States, and that they worked about 8000 spindles. Tiny establishments they were, employing only a few people. Today there are more than 120,000 spindles in the cotton mills of Augusta alone.

The large slave plantations produced nearly everything that was actually needed by those who worked on them. On Harvey Earle's Fairview plantation, near Augusta, there were sixty-five slaves, including both young and old; also two white overseers with their families. Six of the negro women spent all their time in the spinning and weaving shed; they spun the cotton fiber and then wove it into cloth. As the slaves' garments were made chiefly of cotton cloth, there was little necessity to buy them clothing. In the shoe shop a veteran shoemaker—an old negro with white hair—worked steadily making the rough shoes that the negroes wore in the winter time. During the summer they went barefoot. All the rough unpainted furniture of the negro cabins was made in the plantation carpenter shop.

Besides cotton, as the chief crop, the plantation also produced tobacco, corn, sugar, peaches and variety of vegetables. The cotton crop occupied about half of the tillable soil, and tobacco was cultivated in about one-half of the remainder. Sugar cane was grown for the sole purpose of providing molasses for the negroes on the place, and corn to furnish meal. There was no equipment at Fairview for making sugar, but the molasses was produced by boiling the cane juice.

The plantation grew far more peaches than its people consumed during the fresh-peach season, and the surplus was preserved for winter use by putting the peaches in jars and pouring whiskey over them. There was no market for peaches in Augusta, for the reason that virtually every householder in the community had a few peach trees in his garden; nor could the peaches be shipped to distant places, as they would spoil on the way.

Major Earle raised pigs. They cost nothing whatever to keep, for they were fed the refuse of the kitchens. In the poultry yard there were about two hundred chickens and a few geese. To keep the negroes from stealing the chickens every slave family was permitted to raise its own poultry.

The busy periods on a cotton plantation were the spring months, when the land was plowed and the cotton was planted; the early summer, when the growing crop needed attention; and about six weeks in the fall, when the cotton was picked. During these busy seasons the working day at Fairview was long; it ran from "kin to kain't," meaning from daybreak, when one can see, to sunset, when one can't see. In the more leisurely months, or about half the year, the working pace was slower, and the working day was much shorter. When there was no work to be done in the fields the slaves were put to various other tasks, such as cutting timber, repairing fences, laying in firewood for the winter and trimming the fruit trees.

It was generally believed at that time, by plantation owners and overseers, that a negro farm hand in the course of a day's labor would accomplish about two-thirds as much as a white man put to the same task. This generalization was open to many exceptions, for there were great differences in the energy, intelligence, and willingness of the negroes.

The plantation overseers were always white men. As a class they were coarse, illiterate and entirely lacking in the courtly graces. They were slave drivers, but this does not mean that they were all cruel, or that they mistreated the negroes in their charge. The letters and records of the slavery era show that many plantation owners would not permit their negroes to be cruelly treated in any circumstances whatever.

On the other hand, there are records of sadistic slave owners and brutal overseers who drove their people to work under the lash and half-starved them, but owners of slaves who treated them cruelly, or permitted their overseers to do it, were almost invariably ostracized by their neighbors.

Overseers were never considered "gentlemen," within the old-time Southern meaning of that term. Their pay was astonishingly low in view of the great responsibility placed on their shoulders. Eight hundred dollars a year was looked upon as high wages indeed for an overseer. Besides he had his house rent free, and most of his food cost nothing. From eight hundred dollars as the top the scale of pay ran down to about three hundred. For an average good overseer the standard was four hundred dollars a year.

The large plantations were few in number as compared to the whole agricultural industry. About nine-tenths of the white cultivators of the soil consisted of poor farmers who owned no slaves. They lived on their small farms, and cultivated them with the help of their families. These poor whites occupied the least productive land; in every section of the South the wealthy plantation owners had crowded the small farmers out of the rich and fertile land near the rivers and creeks. The poor cotton growers lived chiefly among the semi-barren hills—hence the name "hillbilly"—and endeavored to make a living from soil which was unsuitable for profitable farming.

These poverty-stricken whites had to compete with slave labor, with negro farm hands who received no wages at all. As a result they were eventually pulled down to the negro's economic level. Another result was the degradation of labor in the minds of the upper classes. Gentlemen did not plow or hoe for a living, but made others work for them, so in the course of time men who worked with their hands on land or in shops or factories became the objects of a social contempt, for they were doing what slaves were forced to do.

This was the most deplorable result of the Southern slave civilization, and it was not lived down for many years.

Chapter VII

SUSAN PETTIGREW MAKES A JOURNEY

I

LATE in the afternoon of an April day of the year 1836 Mrs. Susan Pettigrew drank tea with her friend Mrs. Lane in the home of the latter on Chambers Street, in New York City.

Chambers Street, now a thoroughfare of warehouses and office buildings with soiled faces, was in 1836 one of the sedate residential neighborhoods of the city. Its inhabitants were middle-class folk. The pleasant quiet street had shade trees down its whole length. The houses were of dark-red brick, and were generally two stories in height, with a well-lighted basement under the first floor.

Susan Pettigrew and Peggy Lane had known each other for many years and were old friends. Mrs. Pettigrew lived in the country, just north of Manhattan Island, in what was then a part of Westchester County. Her spacious farm has long since been built over and obliterated by the growing city, and is now the home of thousands of people—citizens of the borough of the Bronx—who live in its tall apartment houses.

Every morning of the year the Pettigrew milk wagons delivered milk to customers in the city. The milk was carried in wooden barrels. Not long after dawn the sleepy heads who had not yet arisen, and the serving maids who were making fires in the huge kitchen fireplaces, would hear a wagon stop before the house door, and the cry of "M-i-l-k!" sound like the wail of a banshee. The girls would hurry out to the street with their pitchers and the milk would be dipped from the barrels and measured out into receptacles. In those days nobody had ever heard of germs.[1] Then, after the milk was supplied the driver called attention to the fruits and vege-

[1] The practice of selling milk in glass bottles is comparatively new, historically speaking. It was not begun until 1878, when a milkman in Brooklyn thought bottled milk would help build up his business. It was so successful, and so well advertised that all his competitors adopted the milk bottle.

tables, such as cabbage, peas, onions, carrots, apples, that he had in the back of his wagon.

Mrs. Pettigrew was only one of many providers who supplied the city with milk and vegetables. Competition was sharp, and she had to be up early and late to meet it successfully. Perhaps the most interesting thing about her is that she had built up this business herself, unaided. Her husband had been dead for years, and had left her nothing but a small farm and three young children—two sons and a daughter. Her success had been due to her initiative, her sturdy capacity for hard work, and a lifelong habit of looking after things personally instead of leaving that duty to some one else.

Life for her had had no vacations or holidays, yet she did not mind or complain. She had never been more than fifty miles from New York, but as she sat sipping tea in Mrs. Lane's parlor and looking out in quiet Chambers Street she was thinking of the great journey she was to make, beginning tomorrow.

Her daughter Caroline had married, in 1825, a young man whose name was Alexander Watson. He was a carpenter, an excellent workman, and the son of one of Susan's neighbors. Within a few months after their marriage the young couple departed for Ohio to try their fortunes in that new country. Alexander found his services in great demand in Cincinnati, a young and thriving city. In the course of time he began to put up houses of his own. He had now become a builder and real estate owner. For the past two or three years both Aleck and Caroline had urged her, in every letter, to come out and stay with them on a long visit—and, at last, she was on her way. She intended to spend the night with the Lanes and start on her journey early the next morning.

The two women had discussed the trip for an hour. It would take from seven to ten days, and to accomplish it one had to travel on railroads, steamboats, horsecars, canal boats and inclined planes that ran up and down the sides of mountains. For an unattended woman to make such a trip would be a matter of gaping astonishment to everybody who heard of it, for in those days the ladies were supposed to be extremely timid, fragile and helpless without a man to look after them. We know better now—and it is altogether probable that many people knew better then—but it was the custom of the age.

"Are you sure you're not jes' a leetle doubtful about making that long trip alone?" Peggy Lane asked for the twentieth time.

"Certainly not," Susan replied. "What is there to be afraid of?" She was a plump, rosy woman of fifty-two, who looked younger than her age.

"Why, all sorts of things may come up that a man can handle better than a woman. I'm sure my heart would be in my throat if I had to start off for Cincinnati alone tomorrow."

"Well, Peggy, you and I are different, I s'pose. You see, I've run quite a good-sized business—you can call it that—for nearly twenty years, and I think I can manage about as well as anybody that grows a beard and wears breeches."

"Oh, I know you're confident, and brave, and competent, too," said Peggy, "but most women would be scared out of their wits." She nibbled at a lump of sugar, took a sip of tea and glanced admiringly at her friend. "Since it's your last evening here let's go out after dinner and have a good time. You and me and Joe. We might go to Niblo's Garden."

"I'd love to," Susan agreed, "but you must let me pay half. Mebbe Joe won't want to go. We better wait and ask him."

"Don't worry," Peggy assured her. "He'll be for it. Here he comes now." The two women, looking through the window, saw Mr. Lane turning in at the gate. The door opened and he walked in—a tall man of middle age with a pleasant countenance. Luxuriant side whiskers ran down each side of his face, so that it seemed to be enclosed in a frame of hair. He wore a brown coat that reached to his knees and flared a little below the waist; gray trousers with straps at the bottom of the legs to pass under the shoes; a yellow waistcoat embroidered with small blue figures, and a white linen shirt with a high collar. His tall "stovepipe" hat had been left on the hat rack in the hall.

"Well, well," he said heartily in a loud voice that filled the room like a blast of wind, "so here you are, Susan, on your way to the land of milk and honey." He shook hands with her, patted his wife's head and sat down in an armchair covered with black haircloth. This piece of furniture, which weighed not less than a hundred pounds, seemed to be closely akin to the rest of the room's furnishings. It was all of black walnut, heavy-featured, gloomy and sullen.

As soon as her husband sat down Mrs. Lane ran into the kitchen and came back with a pitcher of brown ale and a yellow mug of pottery ware which had a portrait of George Washington on it.

Mr. Lane took a long drink, waved his hand at Susan, and said, "That's what I call the State of Ohio—the land of milk and honey. If I were twenty years younger I'd make it my home."

"Well," said Mrs. Pettigrew, a downright realist, "I can't get much excited over milk, seein' that I've been almost wading in it every day for the past twenty years; and, as for honey, I never could abide it. It's too sweet; I like syrup better."

Joseph Lane pushed up his spectacles, which were lying on his nose, and took a good look at Mrs. Pettigrew. It was not a nasty look, or even a critical one, for he wore a countenance that was permanently benevolent in appearance, and his stare at Susan was really one of kindly curiosity.

"Oh, my remark was not intended to be taken literally," he explained. "Not literal at all." He waved his hand in a wide sweep toward the west. "It was just a general statement. Put bacon and eggs in place of milk and honey, if that suits you better."

Mrs. Pettigrew smiled and remarked that when you're hungry nothing hits the right spot like a good dish of fried eggs and bacon—"say six fried eggs, fried on one side only and not turned over, and four or five slices of bacon."

Joseph Lane was an auctioneer. His employers had an auction salesroom on William Street, where they sold everything vendible from houses and lots down to frying pans, pictures, bolts of silks and casks of rum. In that era auctions were popular and well attended; many people went to see and hear without intending to buy, and the manners and sayings of the auctioneers were discussed at social gatherings. Mr. Lane might be observed in his auction room on any week day, declaiming the merits of merchandise and inviting bids. The tone of his voice, in and out of the auction room, had become by force of habit pleasant, wheedling and penetrating. He believed, and said in his philosophic moments, that even the worst cases of depravity could be cured and redeemed by a succession of bargains, and he cited instances to prove it.

"Joseph has been all over the country," said his wife proudly, with an admiring glance at her husband. "He knows all them places, like Cincinnati and Baltimore."

The gentleman smiled at the two ladies and entered in a general description of his travels in the days when he had peddled goods from a wagon. He declared that he had been in every state in the Union, from Maine to Florida, and westward to Missouri. His speech bubbled with curious items about faraway places. Few people, in any American community, had done any traveling at all, and those who had been in three or four states were looked upon with envy by the stay-at-homes.[2]

Cincinnati, he said, was a pretty place, with nice homes, wide, shady streets and a general air of prosperity. "Sometimes I call it the Philadelphia of the West," he remarked, "for in a way it reminds me of William Penn's town. A quiet place, and the people are prosperous, But I was never able to sell much anywhere around Cincinnati. Poor place for my kind of business. The stores are well-stocked and the prices low; that ruins peddling."

He paused to take a chew of tobacco from a plug which he carried in a coattail pocket. Besides the tobacco the capacious pockets of his coattails disgorged—while he was trying to locate the tobacco—a heavy envelope containing legal papers, some samples of cloth, a man's cap and a small bottle of whiskey. The plug was brought forth eventually; it was wrapped in a stout piece of paper. Then he found a jackknife with a large blade in a trousers pocket and proceeded to cut a quid which he put in his mouth.

[2] With the building of the railroads traveling was enormously increased, and the uncomfortable trains of the time were packed with passengers who were going nowhere in particular, but were on their way just for the excitement of making a trip. One of the early railroads was the Charleston and Hamburg, which connected Charleston, South Carolina, with Augusta, Georgia. (Hamburg is on the Savannah River, opposite Augusta.) Before the railroad was opened the passenger traffic between those towns was handled by a stagecoach which departed three times a week each way, carrying about fifty people a month. After the railroad was in operation no less than 15,959 passengers made the trip by rail during the last six months in 1835.

"It'll take more'n a week to get to Cincinnati," Susan said. "I wish it was only a day."

"Shuh, shuh," muttered Joe Lane, "you're gettin' to be just like the rest of 'em. It seems like everybody is going crazy over speed. It's hurry, hurry, hurry, here and there. Why, we had a man in the store this morning who was complainin' because it took him two days to come up from Washington on the kyars. Why, in my time, it used to take a week and nobody cared.

"In my days things was difrunt. When I was on the road, selling merchandise, we jes' jogged along, reg'ler, rain or shine, in the good old wagon. No connections to make, no machinery to get out of order.

"Now they're talking of sending the kyars whirling over the land at twenty miles an hour. Take it from me, it ain't healthy to move at that speed. It will encourage flightiness of mind. Truthful people will become outrageous liars. There will be gadding about all over the country. Here today and there tomorrow.

"I'm for using beasts of burden. God made 'em. They're in the Scriptures. And if God had thought that engines and railroads would be good for people he would have made 'em, too, and put 'em down here on the earth.

"But I may be wrong. I hope it will turn out for the best in the end, though I confess I don't see how it can.

"Give me the stagecoach and the old-fashioned wagon. I was a wagon-peddler for ten years. I was never sick a day, and I had a good time."

2

The peripatetic merchant, traveling on foot or by wagon, was one of the characteristic features of American life during the first half of the nineteenth century. These peddlers were many in numbers and were encountered on all the country roads.

The stock of the village storekeepers was often old, out of fashion, and frequently moldy and dilapidated. This was the result of distance from the source of supply, for the little merchant usually bought new goods only once a year from the city wholesaler, and then there was much difficulty in delivering them. The peddler's goods were fresher, more attractive, and usually cheaper than the wares of the crossroads merchant.

There were "trunk" peddlers as well as "wagon" peddlers. The trunk peddler went on foot and carried his merchandise in a small, light trunk or canvas bag that was strapped on his back. He sold only small articles of light weight, such as scissors, razors, pins and needles, perfumes and shoddy jewelry in the form of rings, pins and brooches.

The wagon peddler sold fabrics, laces, hats, shoes, clocks, kitchen hardware, firearms, and a great variety of odds and ends. The most popular items in his stock of merchandise were, as a rule, cheap, machine-made clocks. Until the first decade of the nineteenth century clocks were made entirely by hand; every wheel and pinion was carefully cut, filed and polished by a skilled clockmaker. Their product was so expensive that it was wholly beyond the means of the common people—meaning the poor farmers, mechanics and laborers. They went by "sun time," and many of them became so expert in noting the position of the sun that they could call the correct time with a margin of error of not more than half an hour either way. What they did as time-reckoners on cloudy days is not stated by the chronicles of the era; probably they did not bother about the hours when the sky was overcast.

Around the beginning of the century Eli Terry, a young clockmaker, conceived the idea of making clocks by machinery in wholesale fashion. In 1807 he announced that he was going to make, by one continuous operation, five hundred identical clocks that could be sold at five dollars apiece, which was about one-fifth of the prevailing price of an ordinary timepiece. The five hundred were sold so rapidly that he began to expand his production, and in a few years he was making clocks by the thousands, with the work so divided that unskilled workmen did most of it. The parts of the clocks were simply stamped out and then assembled. As the volume of production increased the selling prices went down, lower and lower.

At first it took some persuasion to get people to buy the clocks as there was a general impression that they were no good. But that wore off in time, and for years these cheap clocks were one of the wagon peddlers' staples.

Some of the peddlers specialized in chapbooks, which were issued in pamphlet form, with lurid colored pictures on the cover. The little books contained accounts of famous crimes, adventures, dangers and explorations—as well as biographies of notable persons. Reverend Mason L. Weems' *Life of George Washington* was first issued in this form. The Reverend Mr. Weems was a book-peddler as well as a preacher and author. In this early life of the Father of Our Country he drew extensively on his imagination and some of the fables he created are still extant.

There were tinware peddlers who came along the country roads in wagons that glittered and tinkled with their loads of new and shining cups, pots and plates. Drugs and nostrums were sold, also, by most of these perambulating merchants. Among the popular remedies were Turlington's Balsam, Bateman's Pectoral Drops and Ward's Anodyne Pearls. These last were worn by teething infants. The makers of Turlington's Balsam claimed that it was a cure for no less than fifty-one different ailments which were listed on the wrapper.

In the 1830's store boats came into being on the Mississippi, and thereafter until the beginning of the Civil War they were a feature of river life. The typical store boat was a small steamer, its decks equipped with counters and shelves. It carried many varieties of merchandise, and it stopped at most of the small landings, or it could be signaled from the shore.

Many of the pre-Civil War peddlers came from Connecticut, and some of them were sharp traders with a streak of dishonesty. Their nation-wide reputation gave life to the wooden nutmeg fiction, and other stories of the kind. But, on the whole, these traveling merchants sold honest goods at reasonable prices.[3]

[3] Some of the peddlers of that era became well-known business men. Collis P. Huntington, who made a great fortune in railroads, began his career as a Connecticut clock peddler.

B. T. Babbitt, whose name has appeared on countless cakes of soap, peddled Yankee notions in his early days. When he began to manufacture soap he was the first to sell it in cakes of uniform size, each cake wrapped separately in a paper. The purchasers had never seen a piece of soap with a paper around it, and at first they thought that they were paying for the wrapper. To overcome this objection, Babbitt printed the word "Coupon" on the wrappers with directions for saving them and exchanging a collection of them for a prize.

3

During the dinner, which Mrs. Lane and Mrs. Pettigrew had prepared and which was eaten at a sturdy oak table in the wide, roomy kitchen, the chief topic of conversation was the Ellen Jewett murder. It is entirely probable that it was also discussed at every other dinner table in New York City, as well as at the bars, in the restaurants and on the street corners.

Ellen Jewett, who appears to have been a young woman of unusual beauty and intelligence, though sadly deficient in morals, was found dead—and murdered—on the morning of Sunday, April 10, of that year 1836. She had a room in the house of Mrs. Rosina Townsend, and her body was lying there on her bed, when it was found. Her assailant had also attempted to set the house afire. The fire was discovered and the flames extinguished before much damage was done.

The girl had had a number of regular callers, all of them well-to-do. A few hours before the body of the slain girl was found Mrs. Townsend had admitted a caller who went to the Jewett girl's room. She said the young man was Richard P. Robinson, and Mr. Robinson was thereupon arrested. He denied having visited the girl on the night of the murder and tried to set up an alibi; which was not wholly successful, but he persisted in declaring that he had not seen the girl in several days.

Then Mrs. Townsend said she was not entirely sure that the young man was Robinson, for he wore a cloak that almost hid his face, but she insisted that the cloak was precisely like the one usually worn by Robinson, and that the caller had Robinson's voice.

Extensive public interest in the matter would have subsided, in all probability, if James Gordon Bennett and his *New York Herald* had not taken it up in a big way. To clarify this statement I may say that the other newspapers of that era would not have played up a sordid murder case in any circumstances. They would have considered such a journalistic exploit beneath their dignity, besides being vulgar.

The rival newspapers approached the subject gingerly, as if they were afraid to handle it. On the morning after the murder they printed an account in the regular, stereotyped style which said in a short paragraph that a woman named Ellen Jewett, a boarder at the home of Mrs. Rosina Townsend, had been found murdered in her bed. The perpetrator of the crime was unknown, but a young man named Robinson was suspected and was being held for questioning by the police.

But Bennett's *Herald*—a newcomer in the field of journalism—had no such scruples. The day after the murder, the occurrence with all possible embroidery of detail held first page position in the *Herald*. Thereafter, day after day, the new developments in the case were described in extravagant space. The circulation of the *Herald* leaped up by the thousands, and within a week it exceeded that of any other newspaper in New York. People stood in line to buy it, and the presses could not supply the demand.

In the *Herald* story of the crime the description of the young woman's room and the appearance of her dead body ran to nearly a column. The *Herald's* public was told what elegant clothes Ellen Jewett possessed, and of her room, with its ornaments and mirrors. She was a reader of good books, or so it appeared, and her literary collection was described in fine language. Her body, lying so white and still on the bed, was said by the *Herald* to resemble a "statue of Parian marble."

Then, on succeeding days, the *Herald* went fully into all the developments of the case. The accused young man, white-faced and frightened, was depicted as stammering his denials before the police and the district attorney. The authorities, the *Herald* charged, had connived at letting some of the possible witnesses escape questioning. Mrs. Townsend's house had, as its guests, on that fatal evening, a number of men, some of them prominent in the business and professional life of the city. When the murder was discovered these guests were permitted by the police to leave the house, the *Herald* said, but it had managed to obtain all their names, and there was an implied threat that the names would be printed in some later issue.

The *Herald's* manner of handling this case was a perfect example of yellow journalism, as we know it today. There were no photographers, for their art had not yet come into existence, but in all other respects the Jewett murder stories were typical of the sensational journalism of our own time.

Though the *Herald's* circulation grew enormously, and the paper was read by thousands who had never before taken the trouble to read any of the stodgy journals of the day, its exploit aroused intense antagonism among what is usually known as the "better element," or the "people of culture and refinement," or the "people of class and social standing," you may select the phrase that pleases you, for they all mean the same thing. There were fierce arguments over the propriety of publishing the Jewett murder story, and sermons were actually preached from the pulpits against Mr. Bennett and his newspaper. Some of the "better element" bought *Heralds* by the score and tore them up on the streets, just to show the common herd what they thought of Bennett and his doings.

On Saturday, April 16, the *Herald* printed a long interview with Mrs. Rosina Townsend. Bennett himself was the interviewer and as it appeared in the paper it was in the form of questions and answers. It is said by Bennett's biographers to have been the first newspaper interview of any kind ever published in a newspaper.[4]

Mrs. Peggy Lane thought the *Herald* was a disgraceful paper for printing the details of the Jewett murder. "We all know there's evil in the world," she said as she poured the coffee, "but why make a spectacle of it? A newspaper ought to be full of brightness and sunshine. That's what I think." Her voice rose in pitch; she seemed personally offended by the *Herald's* policy.

Neither her husband nor Susan Pettigrew agreed with her. "Now, now, it's nothing to get excited about," Susan said, "but the best way to put a stop to crime is to expose it, and the newspaper is doing just that."

"I think you're right," Joseph Lane agreed. "Besides, and

[4] There is some doubt as to the accuracy of this statement. It is well known that the newspaper interview was unknown in the early years of the republic, and that any statesman of the time would have been almost speechless with astonishment if a newspaper reporter or editor had asked him to talk for publication. But Anne Royall, a feminine editor of Washington—she ran a little scandal sheet—did interview President John Quincy Adams in the late 1820's, and she printed several interviews in her paper. It is possible that they were not authentic, that she made them up, but this does not seem likely.

moreover, Bennett's paper gets more interesting every day. People love to read it. Why, when I mount the stand in my place of business to sell a banjo clock or a writing desk, or anything else, about half the people in the place are not looking at me. They got their eyes glued on Bennett's paper. This morning I was about to offer a set of silver candlesticks, but everybody was reading about the murder. So, I said: Well, I guess I'll have to go out and kill somebody to get any attention. Then you'll all look at me instead of the newspaper. That brought 'em around. They folded up their papers and began to listen to me."

"What I don't like about it all is the moral effect," said Peggy Lane. "That dead woman, say what you please, was after all nothing but a vile hussy, living a life of shame, but the paper tries to tell how well read and how charming she was. Oh, just a lovely lady! What our young girls will think, God knows. It may cause some of them to take up that kind of wicked, shameful life."

"Oh, I don't think so, Peggy," Susan remarked. "Most girls have too much sense for that. I—well, let's not get into an argument about it."

Joe Lane had pulled out his heavy, cumbersome watch. "Well, girls," he said, "if we're going up to Niblo's it's time to start. Let's forget the murder. Young Robinson's plainly guilty, and they'll try him and hang him and it will all be over."

Mr. Lane was mistaken in his prediction. Early in June Richard P. Robinson was tried for the murder of Ellen Jewett. His defense was an alibi; he declared that he was home and in bed asleep when the murder took place. The prosecution was unable to prove without a reasonable doubt that he visited the girl on the fatal night so he was set free by the verdict of the jury. Soon after he gained his freedom he disappeared and was never heard of again. There were rumors that he had gone to Texas.

There were several other men under suspicion of having murdered the Jewett girl, but the evidence against them was insufficient to be made the basis of a murder charge, so the whole matter was dropped, and the truth has never come to light.

4

It was still broad daylight when the Lanes and Susan went over to Broadway to take a bus for Niblo's. The pigs were still in the street, rooting among the garbage for food. There was no street-cleaning department, and wandering droves of pigs were expected to consume the food scraps. The pigs' ears were marked, so they could be identified by their owners, and they were turned loose every morning to find their own sustenance. At sunset they came home.

The places of amusement known as "gardens" were popular resorts during the first half of the century. They gradually went out of existence and have no counterparts today. They were called gardens chiefly to overcome the prejudices of many people who looked upon theaters as centers of evil. Performances on the stage were given at the gardens, but one did not have to enter a theater to see them. Niblo's Garden, the most famous of these enterprises, occupied several acres of land on Broadway, almost directly east of Washington Square. This location was considered far uptown, for the city lay almost wholly below Canal Street. Niblo's was on the outskirts of the town and around the place there were many vacant lots.

The Garden was surrounded by a high wooden wall. The patrons, after paying an admission fee and entering, found themselves in a park-like space, with an open-air theater, pleasant winding walks which led one to a small restaurant, an animal exhibition, a shooting gallery, a dancing pavilion, and various refreshment booths. Benches were placed here and there along the shaded walks. Families sometimes went to the Garden and spent the whole afternoon and evening, just as they go today to Coney Island or Jones Beach. The entrance fee covered nothing but the admission; everything else had to be paid for. But the patrons were not obliged to buy anything. They might even bring their own food in a basket.

Joe and Peggy and Susan waited on the Broadway corner for an omnibus to come along. The famous thoroughfare had a very different appearance from what it has today. The houses were only three or four stories in height. Above the stores on the street floor were living quarters (we would call them apartments, but that word was not in general use until much later). They were all "walk-up" apartments, for elevators were an invention of the future. Water also had to be carried up in pails, after being drawn from wells in the street.[5]

The city had no office buildings in that era, though there were many offices of all kinds in rooms over the stores, or in basements, or in the front rooms of residences.

It was a colorful city. Colored store signs, gaudy window shades, carriages painted green, yellow, scarlet. The women, passing along the street, glittered in their colored garments, rainbow silks and pink parasols.

They did not have to wait long for the bus, for there were more than a hundred of these passenger-carrying vehicles running on the streets of the city. All of them were painted in a striking fashion, and each of them had a name which appeared in heavy letters on its side—such names as Mercy Warren, DeWitt Clinton, John Hancock and George Washington. They were very different from the buses running on our streets today. Flimsily built and mounted on high and thin buggy wheels, they seemed too light for heavy traffic. The seats did not run across but lengthwise. The driver sat on a high seat outside the bus at the level of the roof. He performed the duties of both conductor and driver. A passenger, upon entering, walked to the front end of the bus and deposited his fare in a little glass and metal receptacle which was up near the roof, and was so arranged that the driver could look down into it and see if the passengers had paid. Near this fare-box there was an opening in the roof close to the driver's seat. Through it the driver, by leaning over, could speak to the passengers or take a look at them. A passenger who wanted to get change to pay his fare would pass up the bill or coin to be changed through this aperture and the driver handed back the change in an envelope. Whenever a passenger wished to get off the bus he pulled a cord which rang a bell at the side of the driver's seat.

[5] Owing to the engineering difficulties that arose from its situation on an island New York did not acquire a municipal water system until October, 1842, when the Croton water supply came into being. Croton water was brought into the city in large pipes made of hollowed logs, which were supplanted several years later by tubes of iron.

It was all very clumsy and inconvenient, yet this type of city transportation persisted for years.[6]

The Lanes and their guest found seats in the "Charles Pinckney" and Mr. Lane dropped twelve and a half cents in the fare-box for each of them. At that period in our American history the Spanish silver dollar and its sub-divisions were considered legal tender—a situation which lasted until 1857, when the Spanish money was demonetized. The twelve and a half cent coin, mentioned above, was Spanish. It was called a "York shilling."

On that pleasant evening Susan and the Lanes stayed at Niblo's until ten o'clock. They saw a rope-walker, who cut capers on a slender rope swung from the tops of two tall masts. One of his tricks was to stagger across with a bundle in his arms, thus pretending to be a drunkard taking home the week's groceries. Some of his tricks seemed so perilous that Mrs. Lane declared she could not watch him any longer, or she would faint, so they moved over to another side of the garden and ate vanilla ice cream. They saw on the stage a farce that we moderns would call a slapstick comedy; they had cocktails, which were then a novelty; they watched a juggler mystify his audience with a pack of cards; they fired at a target in a shooting gallery—and then it was time to go home. "Don't forget that I've got to be on that boat at six in the morning," Susan reminded them.

They were in the street, watching for a bus, when Mr. Lane thought of oysters. The American people were then—in the middle of the 1830 decade—at the very peak of the great oyster craze which ran from about 1810 to 1870. No evening of pleasure was complete without oysters; no host worthy of the name failed to serve "the luscious bivalves," as they were called, to his guests. In every town there were oyster parlors, oyster cellars, oyster saloons and oyster bars.

[6] Until 1827 New York City, then a community of two hundred thousand people, had no local transportation facilities whatever. Of course, some well-to-do persons owned carriages, but the ordinary individual had to walk. The first bus, which was named "Accommodation," and had seats for twelve people, was put on the streets by Abraham Bower, in the year mentioned.

The first horsecar to be operated anywhere in the world made its appearance in New York City in 1832. The cars, which were built like stagecoaches, could not carry more than ten passengers. The line ran along Fourth Avenue from Prince Street to Fourteenth Street, on rails quite similar to the car tracks of today.

At the bars the raw oysters were sometimes dipped in whisky.

An entertaining author who wrote of American ways and manners, as he had observed them, during this period, had this to say about the oyster habit:

> The American oyster, from New York to New Orleans, is large, bland, sweet, luscious, capable of being fed and fattened, and cooked in many styles, and is eaten for breakfast, dinner, supper, and at all intermediate hours. Oysters are eaten raw, pure and simple, or with salt, pepper, oil, mustard, lemon-juice or vinegar. At breakfast they are stewed, broiled or fried. At dinner you have oyster soup, oyster sauce for the fish, fried oysters, scalloped oysters, oyster pies, and when the boiled turkey is cut into, it is found stuffed with oysters.[7]

The nonsense about oysters being unwholesome in any month that hasn't an R in it had not yet been invented; they were eaten the year round. They were sent inland as far west as Cincinnati by what was known as an "oyster express." This was a light vehicle loaded with live oysters imbedded in straw which was kept moistened by salt water. Its driver went as fast as he could over the road from Baltimore to Pittsburgh. These expresses changed horses and drivers two or three times a day and went all night without stopping. At Pittsburgh the oysters were put on a swift boat. In Cincinnati they were placed in a tank of salt water into which cornmeal was deposited every day. This would keep them alive for months. All this added to the expense and oysters west of the Alleghenies were quite beyond the means of the common people.

But in New York both the rich and the poor ate oysters. Some of the oyster marts operated on what was called the "Canal Street plan." The customer gave the proprietor a York shilling, and was thereupon permitted to eat as many oysters as his stomach could hold. To these patrons, who stood at a counter while consuming their purchases, the proprietor served the small and undesirable oysters which would have been rejected by those who ate at the tables.

The oyster cellar to which Joe Lane conducted the ladies was at the corner of Broadway and Fourth Street. It was not really a cellar but the basement of a commercial building, and was called an "oyster saloon" by its owners. To enter it one

[7] *Forty Years of American Life,* by Thomas L. Nichols.

had to go down a short flight of steps. The saloon was rather gorgeous with its tall mirrors, its paintings, its gleaming gas lights, its clean linen and its resplendent bar at the end of the room. This particular bar was locally famous for its mint juleps, a Southern drink which was rarely served in the North.

The Lanes and Susan Pettigrew remained there more than an hour, eating oysters on the half shell and drinking juleps. It was nearly midnight when they got back to the house in Chambers Street.

5

Next morning Susan came within a hair's breadth of missing the boat. The Lane household was up at five o'clock, and Peggy had breakfast ready in fifteen minutes. As the boat for South Amboy, where Susan was to take the train, did not leave the Battery until six, there seemed to be plenty of time. But they had all overlooked the fact that the buses did not run that early in the morning. Mr. Lane was going to the steamboat with Susan, and when they got up to Broadway there was not a vehicle of any kind in sight. They had two heavy carpetbags and a box to carry.[8]

The Battery was a mile from Chambers Street. They set out walking down Broadway, heavily laden and making slow progress. Passing Liberty Street Joe Lane saw a milkman delivering milk from his wagon, and he gave the man a dollar to take them to the Battery. With their baggage they crowded in among the wooden barrels in which the milkman carried his milk, and they arrived at the Battery just a moment before the boat left the wharf. Susan hurriedly gave her name, address and station in life to the ticket seller who wrote it all down in the yellow pages of a book. In the early days of railroad travel the passenger "booked" a ticket, even if he were only going twenty miles from home. The fare to Philadelphia was three dollars, and the man explained to Susan that she would change to the train at South Amboy. She told Joe Lane good-by and entered the boat, and it pulled out almost instantly.

The little craft could carry about thirty people on its lower deck, where they sat in two rows—one on each side of the

[8] The carpetbag was a large traveling bag made of carpet instead of leather.

vessel—facing each other. On the open-air upper deck there was room for perhaps thirty more. Though the upper deck was windy and subject to showers of cinders and smudge from the wood-burning fires of the boiler room, Susan decided to remain there for the sake of the view.

There was nothing countrified about her appearance. She wore a dress of sage-green brocade, with leg-of-mutton sleeves, very full above the elbow, and extending up to the ears. To keep their puffiness from collapsing the sleeves had pads of cotton which held them in shape. Susan's sleeves were as full and as puffy as even the most fashionable lady could desire.

Hoop skirts were out of fashion—to return in the 1840's—but the skirts were wide and were kept extended by underskirts of crinoline, a stiff cloth, sometimes made of horsehair. The skirts came down within an inch of the ground; for a woman to show even her ankles was considered indelicate.

Susan's iron-gray hair was caught in a Grecian knot at the back. In front she wore the false curls that were then fashionable. They were held on by hairpins which came loose occasionally so that the curls dangled by the side of her nose—an accident would have mortified anybody but Susan, but it did not affect her at all. Her hat was bonnet-shaped and made of yellow straw. It was fastened by a purple velvet ribbon which ran under her chin.

Handbags were not often carried by women of that era; instead, they deposited their belongings in the large pockets of their skirts. But Susan Pettigrew, although well equipped with pockets, carried also a handsome handbag—called a reticule—that was admired by everyone who saw it. It was covered entirely by beads of various colors, arranged in an attractive pattern and it swung from her arm by long ribbons, so that when she walked the reticule was about level with her knees. She had also a green silk parasol, which was needed on the upper deck of the boat to protect her clothes from the outpourings of the smokestack.

She glanced at the magnificent panorama of New York harbor and seated herself in a deck chair. Eagerly she turned the pages of the paper to the latest account of the Jewett murder case and read the most recent developments, then she opened her reticule and took out a partly finished piece of knitting that she intended to complete on her journey to Cincinnati.

A young man, who had in his hands a thin leather-bound folder, came up to her chair, bowed and handed her a card which contained the information that the bearer, Robert Clinchy, was a silhouette artist. Mrs. Pettigrew glanced up at the young man, who bowed and smiled. "I have two silhouettes already," she said.

"Ah!" Mr. Clinchy exclaimed, "but what a lovely picture you make in that hat. Very, very attractive. And I charge only three shillings. I've made silhouettes of three presidents, and I'm well-known." Eagerly he opened his folder and produced a silhouette of Andrew Jackson, mounted on a piece of gilt cardboard.

"That's a good likeness," Susan agreed. "If your price was reasonable, I'd have you make one—but three shillings, God help us!" (Three York shillings were equal to thirty-seven and a half cents.)

"How much would you consider reasonable?"

"Oh, about half what you ask."

"No, I couldn't do it for that, madam," Mr. Clinchy said. "But if you can go to two shillings I'll make one for you."

That was what Susan was expecting, so she told him to go ahead. While making his preparations he whistled and seemed gay. That disturbed Susan inwardly; it made her fear that she was paying too much. Perhaps he would have come down to one shilling if she had held out longer. In selling her wagon loads of vegetables and fruit to the market men in New York she always managed to appear sad and depressed over the price she was paid, even if it were much more than she had expected. As she looked back on her experience it seemed as if that were one of the reasons for her success. Yet here was this young man whistling cheerfully after making a reduction of one-third in his asking price. It made her feel like a fool.

Mr. Clinchy drew up a chair, sat on it, took out a sheet of black paper and a small pair of scissors. Cutting out the profile of Susan's face, including the hat, did not take more than five minutes. Then he pasted the likeness on a small piece of cardboard, turned it over to his client, received his twenty-five cents, thanked her and bowed good-by. Susan held the silhouette in her hand and looked at it now and then until the steamboat reached South Amboy. It was an excellent likeness. These little profile portraits on black paper originated in France. They get their name from Etienne de Silhouette who was controller-general of the French treasury around the middle of the eighteenth century. He instituted widespread economies and bought only at the lowest prices so the name "silhouette" became in time synonymous with cheapness. The silhouette cutter was the poor man's artist during the first three decades of the nineteenth century. The invention of photography and its commercial development in the 1840's almost put an end to the art of silhouette cutting, but a few silhouette artists are still in business.

6

It was not quite nine o'clock when the little steamboat pulled up to the dock in South Amboy. The train for Camden (or Philadelphia) stood on its track near the landing place, and seemed ready to depart instantly if one might judge by the noise the engine was making with its safety valve blowing off a cloud of steam.

Susan hardly knew how to get her baggage on the train without leaving part of it on the boat, and coming back to get it, when one of the men passengers came to her aid. He picked up one of the carpetbags and the box and Susan took the other bag. They entered the train and piled the bags on the floor. There were no racks overhead, and no baggage car attached to the train, for at that early day in the history of railroading nobody had thought of such conveniences. She was hardly settled in her seat when a trainman came up and said he would put some of her belongings on the roof of the car to get them out of the way if she wanted more room. But after he had explained to her that the carpetbags might be damaged by flying sparks if placed on the roof she let him take the wooden box only. He remarked that the train would not leave for half an hour, "and if ye want to git out, ma'am, and walk around it will be all right. The man up front blows the whistle loud and long before she goes."

Most of the passengers were already outside, walking up

and down and staring at all parts of the train. Susan joined them. The locomotive was the principal curiosity, but the cars also attracted much attention. The cars attached to a locomotive were called a "brigade"—a term which continued in use until after the Civil War. There was a brigade of six cars at South Amboy that morning, besides a locomotive and a small flat car used for carrying fuel and water.

The locomotive would have looked strange indeed to any reader of these pages. It was a small affair, about twelve feet long, with large and rather slender wheels, a tall smoke-stack and a bell which was rung almost continually when the firemen was not stoking the boiler.

There was no cab for the engineer; he stood behind the engine in the open air on a small platform; regardless of the weather. In a heavy rain he must have been wet to the skin, and in cold weather he had no protection. Just why the engineers of these early trains were left without shelter is a mystery. Certainly he could have done his work better within a cab furnished with large glass windows.

Just behind the engine there was a little flat car on which stood a couple of barrels of water and a pile of wood in a large box. Connection between the engine and the water barrels was made by a leather hose.[9]

The engineer, proud of the attention his locomotive was attracting, for most of the passengers were staring at it, came down from his perch and explained how it worked. Susan Pettigrew heard some of his discourse but she did not understand it, nor did she admire any kind of machinery, for she was firmly convinced that in every machine of whatever nature there was a magical and evil force; and that when its working was explained the real motive power was never mentioned but kept secret.

With some of the women passengers she went slowly along the brigade of cars to examine them from the outside. Each car had the appearance of a horse-drawn carriage set on

[9] All hose, even that used by fire engines, was made of leather. Rubber was not unknown at that time, but since the art of vulcanizing had not yet been discovered it was practically useless because of its softness and its tendency to stick to anything it touched.

wheels to fit the iron rails. They had no platforms at the ends, and the passengers entered the car through doors at the side. When the train was in motion it was not possible to pass from one coach to another. The seats ran crosswise, without aisles; each seat extended clear across the car. A coach could carry sixteen people without crowding.

These coaches were painted in brilliant colors and looked as gaudy as circus wagons. There were no toilets or lavatories, and the lighting was done—whenever necessary—by candles placed in holders with tall glass chimneys. But illumination of the coaches was seldom required, for the trains never ran after dark. Even the locomotive had no headlight.

The crossties on which the rails were laid stood about ten feet apart and not close together as in the railways of today. Between the crossties and the iron rails there were long strips of timber, running from one crosstie to another. The rails were fastened to these wooden strips.

At last the whistle blew, the passengers scrambled aboard and the train was on its way. Susan had never been in a train before and she expected some unusual experience. But nothing occurred that was much different from a trip on a stagecoach except the shower of sparks and cinders that blew in occasionally through the open windows.

There were railroad stations every few miles, and the train stopped at all of them. Even if no passengers got on or off, there was always a group of sight-seers at these stations, for a train was an object of wonder.

The railroad issued timetables but they were seldom followed with anything like precision. At every station there was a "lookout pole" with short pieces of wood nailed across it as a ladder to aid in climbing. When a train did not appear on time, and people were waiting for it, the station agent climbed the pole and looked along the track for a sight of the train or of its smoke.

The telegraph did not exist in 1836, but even though it came into practical commercial use in 1844 it was not adopted by the railroads until 1851. Until then the trains ran without control or direction from the railroad's headquarters. Seven years after the telegraph had become a public convenience, used every day by thousands of people, the superintendent of the Erie Railroad wanted to stop one of his trains that was then out on the line and have it wait for another train which was moving on the line but miles behind. He wondered how it could be done until all of a sudden he thought of sending a telegram to the conductor of the first train with instructions that it be taken over to the station and held there until the train arrived. That was done, the conductor received the telegram and the train was stopped. After that incident it occurred to the railroad management that the movement of trains might be regulated by telegraph along the whole line. So the train dispatcher came into being.

The locomotive, its brigade of cars and its sooty passengers reached Camden at three o'clock. A ferry boat was waiting for them and half an hour later they were in Philadelphia.

Joseph Lane had advised Susan to stay overnight at the Mansion House on Market Street. She went there at once on a bus, guided by a porter at the ferry landing. Inwardly she was embarrassed, but kept it to herself. She had never been a guest at a hotel or an inn before, and she was not sure what she should say or do. Many a time she had stayed overnight in New York but always at the home of one of her friends. Nevertheless, she managed the registration at the hotel and the talk about prices and conveniences so well that the clerk never suspected her complete lack of experience. Her room was rather large and faced Market Street. It was on the fourth floor, and she had to walk up. Susan did not consider that a disadvantage as there were no elevators anywhere, and nobody had ever heard of such a thing; and, anyway, she would have been afraid to ride in one.

The room was lighted by gas. Under the burner a sign had this warning in large letters: "Do not blow out the gas; turn it off." The room had running water and a tidy built-in wash basin, but no bathroom. Susan had often heard of houses with pipes of water in them that one could turn on and off, but there were none in New York. Before she went to bed that night she spent a quarter of an hour playing with the faucets and the stream of water just to see how quickly it would start to run and how big a stream came from it. It started slowly and the stream was small.[10]

After she was settled in her hotel room and the baggage had been brought up, she walked about the city for two hours but did not see anything of interest except Independence Hall and the cracked bell that was rung on July 4, 1776. She asked the caretaker how long the Liberty Bell had been cracked, and he said, "Only last year. We rung it on the death of John Marshall, Chief Justice of the Supreme Court, and lo and behold, it got that big crack. I guess that bell will never ring again."

Before going to bed Susan locked her door with the huge key that the clerk had given her; then she pushed the heavy table up against the door so that if anyone tried to break in the noise would arouse everybody on that floor. She had heard a great deal about hotel thieves and strange murders that had taken place in such hostelries, and she was resolved to take no chances.

At eight o'clock the next morning (which was Tuesday) she was on the train of the Portage railroad bound for Columbia, a village on the Susquehanna River, eighty-two miles from Philadelphia. At Columbia the passengers bound for Pittsburgh would take one of the Pennsylvania Canal boats.

The cars on the Portage road—as this stretch was called because it connected the Delaware River with the state canal—were not drawn by an engine but by horses. Their progress was slow, and the train stopped for nearly an hour for midday dinner at a way station where the restaurant was crowded, noisy, hot and greasy.

[10] The Mansion House was described by journalists of that day as a "modern hotel." In the older hotels a guest seldom had a room to himself. The rooms contained two or three beds, and each room usually had more than one occupant. A guest who went to bed alone at night was likely to find a stranger in the same wide bed with him when he awoke in the morning. In the woman's wing of the hotel the same conditions prevailed.

In 1829 the Tremont Hotel of Boston instituted some changes which made it the first modern hotel. Guests were permitted to rent a single room instead of having to double up with strangers. Other innovations were a key for each room, a wash bowl and pitcher and a free cake of soap for every guest; also gas lights and running water. The rate for all this luxury was two dollars a day, which paid the rent of the room and for four meals in addition.

The success of the Tremont was so great that its plan was soon adopted by other hotels.

Although the scenery along the route was beautiful with its pleasant green hills and valleys and its prosperous-looking farms Susan Pettigrew was limp and tired when she got to Columbia. The passengers went at once on board the canal boat which was waiting for them. It would not get to Pittsburgh until Saturday, so they would be aboard for three days and four nights.

The upper deck of the canal boat was open and flat, except for a series of skylights which ran along its center and which served to admit air and light to the living quarters on the lower deck. The passengers usually passed most of their time on the upper deck. For meals and sleeping they had to go below.

On the lower deck there was a long table with chairs all around it. It was used for meals and for card games. The berths on which the passengers slept at night were on both sides of the cabin and occupied all the wall space except that taken by the windows. They were fixed and permanent and could not be folded up in the daytime, but were concealed from view by a light green curtain.

The kitchen and quarters of the crew were in the rear of the boat. When bedtime came a curtain was drawn across the cabin, about midway of its length, and the long table was divided into two parts, so that the curtain came between them. The women's cabin was in front of the curtain and that of the men behind it. Husbands and wives never slept together, but small children were taken into the women's cabin.

The berths were in three tiers. The lower tier was only about six inches above the floor while the upper one was at the height of a tall man's head, and the passengers climbed in or out of it by means of a stepladder. The berths were chosen by lot, and when the numbers were drawn during supper Susan found that she had been lucky; her berth was in the very front of the cabin and in the middle tier. Right after supper she went to bed. When she awoke during the night she felt the boat moving.

The next day (Wednesday) was bright and clear, and cool for July. Susan sat on the upper deck all day, knitting and admiring the scenery and chatting with the passengers. That day, like every day spent on the canal boat, was so memorably pleasant that she never forgot it. The boat, drawn by horses,

(*The Bettmann Archive*)

INTERIOR OF THE FIRST PULLMAN CAR—1859.

moved at a gentle pace of about four miles an hour. There was no racket or noise of any kind, no sensation of jolting, and "Thank God," said Susan to herself, no black smoke and burning sparks. The tobacco chewers were present in numbers, as they were everywhere, but they did not soil the clean deck as much as one might expect, for it was no trouble for them to spit over the boat's side into the canal.

The boat moved so slowly that the passengers had fairly long conversations with people walking on the canal bank. Now and then the boat would pass under a bridge. If it were dangerously low the captain or helmsman would yell. "Low Bridge" and the passengers would duck their heads.

The boat reached Hollidaysburg, at the foot of the Alleghenies, before daylight on Thursday. When Susan came on deck in the early morning she was almost speechless with astonishment. There stood the mountains, tall and rugged, and the inclined railway rising like a staircase to the summit. The canal boat was to be lifted over the mountains and at that moment it was being pulled onto a wheeled carriage that lay under the surface of the water.

The distance from Hollidaysburg to Johnstown—the terminus of the canal that ran to Pittsburgh—was thirty-six miles. There were ten inclined planes on the route and also a few level spaces. The boat was pulled up the slopes by means of ropes which were wound on drums by engines at the top; then it was slowly let down on the other side in the same fashion. On the level ground the boat, on its carriage, was dragged by locomotives.

The clumsy canal boat looked absurd at the crest of a mountain pass, but the passengers thought the view was wonderful. They could see for fifty miles over forests, streams, villages and farms. The trip across the mountains took all day, for the boat had to be moved slowly and cautiously. The sun had gone down and night had fallen when they slid gently into the canal at Johnstown.

At noon on Saturday the boat arrived at Pittsburgh. Susan wanted to see the town, but there was no time. The passengers for Cincinnati were rushed from the boat to the river steamer *Bluebell* with the speed of people fleeing from a dreadful catastrophe. They were hustled aboard and their baggage, flung after them, had hardly settled on the deck before the steamer had left the pier. Every foot of the vessel was trembling with the throb of the engines and the super-heated boilers. Susan said to a deck hand, "What on earth is the matter? Are we runnin' away from something?"

"No, ma'am, we ain't runnin' away from nothin,' " the man replied, "but we're puttin' on all steam to catch that boat you see yonder." With a grimy finger he pointed to a steamboat in the distance, going downstream, with black smoke pouring from its stacks. "That's the *General Harrison* and we're racing her as fur as Liverpool, about forty-five miles. She got the start on us, 'cause we had to wait for you folks. We wuz both to start at noon, and the *Harrison* got off right on the dot. We didn't git away till ten past."

Susan had a small stateroom on the *Bluebell,* just large enough for a narrow bed and a washstand. After she had been shown to it and had taken off her hat and brushed herself a little she went to the upper deck where most of the passengers were gathered. The steamboat race was causing great excitement. The *General Harrison* seemed to her to be as far ahead as ever, but the Captain said no, and declared that the *Bluebell* was gaining. Now and then the passengers would cheer.

"Ain't these races dangerous," she said to a man who happened to be standing near by, "I've read in the papers about steamboats blowing up durin' a race."

"Yes, madam," the man replied. "They are dangerous and foolish, but you see that the people like them." He waved a hand toward the mass of eager passengers—men and women—who were crowded on the front of the deck, laughing and cheering. Some of the men were drinking whisky from flasks that they passed on to their friends. "They can't hope to win without running the steam pressure up beyond the danger point," the man explained, "and that may cause a boiler explosion. I'll bet a cookie that the pressure valve is tied down in this boat right now."

Ill at ease, Susan made her way to her stateroom. She had no interest in the race, and did not care if the *Bluebell* were the slowest boat on the river—or the swiftest. But her stateroom was a dull place, so after sitting there a short while she rose and strolled about the boat. It was handsomely furnished. When she saw the walls of the salon, done in polished mahogany, and the great mirrors and the chandeliers with their myriad lights and the attractive furniture, she recalled the descriptions of palaces which she had read and said to herself, "Now I'm in a floating palace." The servants were setting the tables for dinner in the dining salon. She was half-dazed by the display of white linen, fine china, gleaming glass and silver bowls.[11]

When the dinner gong sounded its loud, vibrating clang half an hour later, and everyone trooped into the salon, the steward at the door gave her a card with a table number and a place number on it. She found herself seated between a dignified, courteous gentleman of about forty-five and a good-looking, fluttering young woman who talked all the time to a young man across the table.

The gentleman on her right explained to her the mysteries of the vast bill of fare. It had a list of about forty meat dishes and a large number of desserts, pies and cakes. "Most of these are put on here simply for show," he said. "Now, here's roasted guinea hen. If you order it the chances are a hundred to one they'll say that they happen to be out of that dish just now, and are sorry. Same thing is true of most of them, and of at least half the desserts. But you'll be safe in ordering roast beef or baked chicken or ham in any form." She ordered fried trout and roast lamb and was promptly served.

7

Mrs. Pettigrew's daughter Caroline and her husband, Alexander Watson, were awaiting her on the wharf, among hundreds of other people, as the *Bluebell* came down the river to Cincinnati. She had not seen them in more than ten years, and as she leaned over the rail she saw no familiar face, but she heard someone call "Mo-o-other!" several times in a clear feminine voice and saw a white hand and arm raised above

[11] Steamboat owners, in the early days—and, in fact, up to the Civil War—spent fortunes in the decoration and equipment of their boats. It was a kind of senseless rivalry, like the running of races, that did nobody any good. The public rooms on the boats were often overdecorated so that the effect was vulgar and blatant. In the heyday of river travel there were dozens of so-called "floating palaces" on the Mississippi and Ohio.

the heads of the crowd. When she saw her daughter's face at last over the people's heads it seemed changed and not as she remembered it. She thought that strange until she reflected that anybody's face is likely to change a bit in ten years. Carrie's countenance was broader and harsher than it had been on that day long ago when the Watsons had departed for the West.

When the greetings and the kissing and hugging were over Aleck said he had a buggy up the street to take them home. He picked up Susan's bags and stowed them away in the back of the vehicle.

"Our house is on the edge of the town," Caroline said, as they rolled along the street. "It's about a mile from the wharf."

Her mother nodded, and said, "What a beautiful place this is!" They were going along a wide, shady street with fine, spacious residences on each side. Her son-in-law laughed. "Why, it's the Queen City of the West," he said in his loud, jovial manner. "That's what we call it. The Queen City, and it deserves the name."

The houses did not have the rusty, dingy appearance of the buildings in New York. Most of them were built of light-colored brick, and they had a look of airy cleanliness. "The town has grown so fast, Mother, that it is bewildering." This remark came from Caroline. "New people every week; new streets, new houses."

"There are more than thirty thousand people living here now," said her husband. "I dunno how many there was ten years ago, when we came, but I daresay it wasn't more than half that number."

Mrs. Pettigrew noted silently that many of the men in the streets looked rougher than those one encountered in New York. They wore high-topped boots and slouchy hats. Their trousers of coarse brown jeans were tucked into the boots, and most of them were coatless, as the weather was warm. Their faces were heavily bearded. From the back trousers pockets of many of these men the butts of revolvers projected.

But there were other people of an entirely different appearance. Men who appeared in tall silk hats and handsome tailored suits. Women, also, in fashionable wide skirts of silk with many flounces. These ladies walked daintily and some of them held above their heads parasols of colored silk.

"We'd been here a couple of years when Mrs. Trollope arrived," Caroline remarked, "and we saw her now and then in the streets, with her children. A kind of fat, sloppy-looking woman."

Susan was mystified by this reference to someone of whom she had never heard. "Mrs. Trollope," she muttered. "Trollope. Trollope. The name is not familiar. Did I know her? Is she from New York?"

Aleck laughed loudly. "No, no," he chuckled. "Carrie, you're getting your mother all mixed up. No, darling, she wasn't from New York. She came here from England about eight years ago—God knows why—and when she went home she wrote a book called *Domestic Manners of the Americans,* which made everybody around here so fightin' mad that they couldn't see straight. Jes' tell anybody in Cincinnati 'at you're a friend of Mrs. Trollope if you want to see the fur fly. Ha, ha!" [12]

Susan was going to ask for more information about the indignant lady when Aleck said, "Well, folks, here we are," and pulled the horse to a stop before a white wooden house with green shutters. It stood back from the street and there was a lawn and a flower garden in front of it.

Caroline had just time to say "Welcome to our Cincinnati home," when a boy and a girl came running out of the house with whoops of joy. "This is David, Mother," Caroline said, patting the head of the nine-year-old boy. "And this is Betty, our little golden locks," Susan, almost overcome by emotion, stooped down and took both the children in her arms. "My grandchildren," she murmured, and tears trickled down her cheeks. "My little, lovely, lovely boy and girl." The children seemed embarrassed when she kissed them, and the boy dashed off, running over the lawn and shouting, "Grandma's come; grandma's come." Susan straightened up, wiped the tears from her face, and said, "I'm so glad to see the children. The older

[12] Mrs. Trollope had some unpleasant experiences during her residence in Cincinnati. Upon her return to England she wrote *Domestic Manners of the Americans,* which had a large sale and is still read by students of American social life in the 1820's. The book is highly critical of Cincinnati and of the people who lived there at that time—also of the American nation as a whole.

you get the more you love the little ones. Where's the baby?"

"Oh, he's in the house asleep, I guess," Caroline answered. "He's only three, you know, and around this time of day he has a long nap. Well, I don't know about you folks, but I'm hungry as a bear. I hope Catherine has dinner ready."

They were met in the hall by a young white maid who wore a blue dress with a white apron. "This is Julia, Mother," said Caroline, "who will take care of your room." Julia smiled and said, "I'm glad to see you, ma'am. We've all been expecting you." The lady from New York was surprised and pleased at the good manners of this servant. She had been told that politeness was not in use anywhere west of the mountains, and if the maid had appeared in soiled garments, with her hair straggling and the smell of whisky on her breath Susan would not have been astonished.

"When you've brushed up a bit come down to dinner, Mother," Caroline said as Julia picked up the three bags and started upstairs, with Susan following her. Her room was in front of the house. It had two wide windows facing the south. Through them Susan saw the majestic panorama of the Ohio River and the green hills of Kentucky. It was a breath-taking, memorable sight, almost unreal.

The room was large, twice as large as any bedroom in her house in Westchester, and the ceiling was much higher. It had a fireplace, a table and an old-fashioned tall desk, besides the huge bed and a chest of drawers. There was also a wide and deep closet, and in a corner there was a stationary wash basin, with a faucet for supplying water, built into the wall. The windows had long curtains of flowered cloth, and shades also. Susan had never seen any shades like them and when she examined them closely she saw that they were made of wall-paper suspended from a roller. The floor was covered by a thick carpet. A loud-ticking gilt clock stood on the mantel. There were three gas burners projecting from the walls, and she thought it strange—considering the attractive furnishings of the room—that the gas burners stood out in all their primal nakedness, without chimneys, or globes, or ornamentation of any kind.

Downstairs in the sitting room she found all the members of the family, including the baby who had awakened from his nap and was running about the room and talking loudly in the language of three-year-olds. His grandmother picked him up and held him in her lap a moment or two, but he struggled so violently that she had to put him down. The older boy, a bright-faced, eager youngster, was intensely interested in the fact that his grandmother lived in New York and had come so far to visit them. A swarm of questions was on his tongue. One of them was, "From New York can you see across the ocean?" He seemed disappointed when his grandma said "No."

When Julia came in and announced that dinner was ready she interrupted a story of Cincinnati's rise to opulence which Aleck Watson was telling. He referred to that city with the depth of affectionate emotion in his voice that one usually displays in speaking of the splendid accomplishments of a beloved child.

Like the rest of the house the dining room was spacious. The walls of the sitting room were papered, but the dining room walls were of dark wood. Besides the chairs and tables there was nothing in the room but an elaborate sideboard, with silver and cut glass on it. Before sitting down Aleck went to the sideboard, took a decanter and poured out drinks of whisky for Susan, Caroline and himself. "Here's to good luck," he said and drank his liquor at a single swallow. "Drink it down, mother," he said to Susan. "We'll have wine at dinner."

About two feet over the heads of those seated at the table three great fans made of cloth stretched over light frames moved lazily back and forth. They were not fan-shaped, but rectangular, about five feet wide and two feet high. At the end of the room near the sideboard a very black negro boy stood with a cord in his hand. This cord was connected with the fans, so that the act of pulling on it set them in motion. "They're to keep off the flies," Caroline said when she saw her mother looking curiously at them. "There's no way to get rid of flies altogether in summer," she went on, "but the fans help some."

Mrs. Pettigrew sat on the left of her son-in-law and on his right was Caroline. Next to Caroline was the baby, who occupied a high chair that had been specially made for him in the carpenter shop that stood in the yard. He ate a bowl of bran mixed with milk and sugar, and after that he had some baked chicken cut into little pieces which he ate with a large spoon. Now and then he would hammer on the tablecloth with the spoon and demand ice cream.

When they entered the dining room the whole meal was on the table—a large silver tureen of soup, a heaping platter of fish, a roast chicken, a baked ham, beef tongues, a meat pie, platters of boiled corn, potatoes, beans and other vegetables. Everything was there but the coffee and dessert.

The Eastern habit of serving meals in courses, considered in the West as effete and European, had not reached Cincinnati. The huge platters held far more than those at the table could possibly eat. This was intentional, for it was considered gracious and elegant in those days to overload the table as a symbol of the host's affluence and gentility. Susan understood that very well, for she had done it herself when she had guests, but not just for the folks at home. When she saw the prodigious spread she said to her daughter, "Why, Carrie, I'm jes' one of the family, you know. Don't set such a big table for me." Caroline smiled and said, "This is just our regular dinner, Mother."

Susan did not believe that statement, but before she had lived in her son-in-law's home a week she realized that it was true. Like everybody else in Cincinnati the Watsons went in for eating with enthusiasm. It was not as extravagant as it seemed for the prices of all kinds of provisions were even lower than those of New York. A grown chicken cost only ten cents in the public market. Beef was eight cents a pound, and pork was even cheaper; it could be bought for four cents a pound. At the packing plants spareribs were actually given away to any poor person who asked for them.[13] Eggs were six cents a dozen. Apples, peaches and pears were so cheap that farmers who lived at a distance let them lie on the ground and

[13] Cincinnati was the pork-packing center of the nation in 1836, and for years afterward, until Chicago gained that distinction in the decade before the Civil War. The popular nickname for the city was Porkopolis. In the 1830's the Cincinnati plants could operate only four months a year, for there was no method of artificial refrigeration and the meat would not keep during the summer. A soap industry which used the greases and fats of the packing plants also came into being.

rot, as the fruit did not pay for the cost of taking it to market.

The same cheapness applied to liquors. Rye whisky was five cents a glass at the bars, and corn whisky was even lower in price. Beer sold for two cents a glass, but if the customer wanted to take some beer home he had to bring a pitcher, as it was not sold in bottles.

After dinner Caroline took her mother over the house. The hall which ran straight through, from the front door to the back, was about ten feet wide, and the stairs were wide enough for two people to go up side by side. Silently Susan contrasted this wide hall with the narrow one in her own house in Westchester, where a grown person standing in the center of it could touch both walls by extending his arms. Yet, she reflected, she was not poor in the usual sense. She had a paying farm, well stocked with animals, and she owed no money to anyone. Were Aleck and Caroline really well-to-do, or were they just showing off, and in debt with everything mortgaged? She did not know but she intended to find out.

There were five rooms on the ground floor besides the three rooms of an ell which were used by the servants for living quarters. On the other side of the hall, opposite the sitting room, there was a library, the first that Susan had ever seen in a private house. Its rows of shelves ran all around the room, and there must have been five hundred books on them. Susan could not suppress her astonishment. "Well, I never!" she exclaimed. "Who in the name of God reads all these books?"

"I read them," said her daughter, "and now and then Aleck reads one."

Caroline went on then to explain that she was a member of the Semi-Colon Literary Club, an organization of intellectual people. Books were discussed at its meetings, and the members were all readers of books. They also wrote essays which were read at the meetings and published.[14]

As Caroline told her mother of the Semi-Colon Literary Club, of the balls at the Assembly, of the receptions in honor

[14] The Semi-Colon had a nation-wide reputation, and its activities did much in the way of creating an intellectual atmosphere in Cincinnati. Miss Harriet Beecher was a member of the Semi-Colon in the 1830's. In later years she was Harriet Beecher Stowe and the author of *Uncle Tom's Cabin*.

of distinguished visitors, Susan began to realize that she had passed out of the world in which she had lived for fifty years, and was in another sphere of existence. She felt strange and lonely. Her gray stone house in Westchester, its narrow doors, small windows and low ceilings—all that seemed as far away as life on the moon. At home she and her boys and their friends had a jolly time, and maybe Caroline and Aleck did, too, but it was different.

Upstairs there were five bedrooms and two baths with running water. Caroline turned on the water a moment to show how the bath worked. She said that when warm water was needed it had to be brought upstairs by Julia, but the ordinary cold water was always on tap. The bathtubs were of sheet metal encased in wood.[15]

After an inspection of the second floor and the attic above it Caroline took her mother down to the kitchen. "Catherine, our cook," she said, "has been with us for ten years, and considers herself one of the family. I seldom enter the kitchen, for she hates to be bossed. I don't mind, for she knows exactly what to do without being told."

Susan was not favorably impressed by Catherine, who was a middle-aged fat woman with a bloated countenance and disordered gray hair. When the ladies entered the kitchen she was seated at a table drinking beer from a glass pitcher. With apparent difficulty she rose and said, "I've heard a lot about you, ma'am, and now I'm glad you're here." Then she stood uneasily while Caroline and her mother looked about the room. The cooking was done at the wide fireplace, where

[15] The origin of the American bathtub was the subject of a hoax conceived by H. L. Mencken in 1917. In that year he wrote an article in which he stated that the first American bathtub was installed in a Cincinnati house in 1842. The tub was of mahogany, lined with sheet lead. It was installed by Adam Thompson, who was a wealthy grain dealer, according to Mr. Mencken. At a stag party given in the Thompson home in December, 1842, the guests were invited to give the tub a trial, and several of them took baths in the new-fangled contrivance.

It is an interesting story, but not a word of it is true. Since its publication Mr. Mencken has confessed that the story was a hoax, but it still continues to appear in serious publications as a fact. Nobody really knows the history of bathtubs, but tubs made of light metal—probably tin—and shaped like the modern bathroom fixture were in use long before houses were equipped for running water. When pipes were put in dwelling houses it was, no doubt, a simple matter to set up a bathtub with a pipe and a faucet, and tubs of this modern type probably appeared in various localities at approximately the same time. There were many in use in the late 1820's.

there was a bed of glowing coals. The kitchen was in disorder, Susan thought. On a large table there were mounds of soiled dishes waiting to be washed, and scraps and peelings were scattered about.

As they left the kitchen Susan thought that Caroline would be of more use to her family and herself if she really ran the household instead of fooling with Semi-Colon Clubs and fashionable teas and discussions of people and things in distant parts of the world. But she didn't say what was in her mind, for she did not want to hurt her daughter's feelings.

Then they left the house and went over to the stables. On the way Caroline remarked that they had four servants—the cook and Julia, the maid, in the house; and, living over the stable, John the colored stableman and Simon, his fourteen-year-old boy who does the chores, such as bringing in wood for the fires in winter and working in the garden in summer.

To her own surprise Susan soon became accustomed to life in the Queen City. It was so easy and softly comfortable. For most of her life she had had a hearty contempt for idle women, but now that she had become one herself she began in the back of her mind to seek justifications for them. After all, she reflected, I deserve a holiday after having worked so many years, and after having brought up a family. That was quite true, but it was not altogether satisfying to her own critical sense. Now and then she would search rather feverishly for something useful to do. She prepared special dishes in the kitchen, knitted socks and stockings, and made a complete dress for the little girl.

Her fear that Aleck and Caroline were spending more than their income came to an end one evening. They were sitting on the terrace at sunset. In the distance was the wide Ohio, with its silvery sheen, and nearer were the white houses and green trees of the town. As the sun went down the air turned cool and refreshing after the heat of the day.

Caroline mentioned Nicholas Longworth, who was Cincinnati's richest man at that time. Aleck turned to his mother-in-law and said, "He was my first employer. I worked for him as a carpenter, helping put up houses all over town. He liked my work—anyway, he said so—and I liked him, and do yet.

"I got very good pay, and we saved as much as we could, but it's mighty hard, and generally impossible, to get ahead very far by saving part of your wages. Well, Caroline and I talked it over and when we'd been here about a year I quit the job and set out to build houses and sell 'em. It seems a pretty wild project now, when I look back at it, but it worked. I bought a building lot for about a hundred dollars and started to put up a little four-room house. Before it was half-done my money played out, and I got a loan at the bank to finish the job. While I was putting the roof on that little house I sold it for twice what it cost me in money, labor and loan to a family that had jes' come from the East—it was Billy Wescott, his wife and two children—and until they bought my house they didn't have a place to lay their heads.

"In those days people poured into Cincinnati by road and river. They do now, for that matter, but not in such droves. As soon as Wescott took over that house I bought another lot and was laying the foundations of another house. Since then I've been trying to catch up with the demand. Right now I've got five houses going up at the same time, and I'll have all of 'em sold within a week after they're finished."

"Do you still borrow from the bank?"

"No, not a dime," Aleck replied. "Don't have to. I have so much cash now that I'm a lender instead of a borrower. Then there's our farm out on the Hamilton road that I bought on mortgage five years ago. Caroline wrote you about it——"

"Yes, she did. How do you stand now on the mortgage?"

"Oh, it's all paid up—to the last dime. I own the place free and clear. We'll take you out there some day soon and show it to you. There's three hundred acres of it. We raise wheat mostly."

"My goodness!" Mrs. Pettigrew exclaimed. "How do you find time to tend to it?"

"I don't. George Carter, a friend of mine—he's a mighty good farmer—runs it for me, and we divide the income. It works out fine."

8

Among the friends of Aleck and Caroline Watson was a schoolteacher named William H. McGuffey, who taught philosophy, English and one or two other subjects in the Woodward High School, or College (as it was sometimes called). He came to supper one evening during the second week of Susan's visit.

"You're going to meet a very talented man," Aleck said to his mother-in-law. "He knows history, law, mechanics, poetry, everything—and he can take the dullest subject in the world and make it so interesting that you want to hear him talk for hours."

"Tell Mother about the books Professor McGuffey is writing," Caroline suggested.

"He's getting up a new kind of school reader—to be read by classes in schools, you know," her husband explained. "He has already written a first reader, and, I believe, a second reader. There are going to be five altogether."

"How do you mean? What sort of new reader?"

"Well, you know the kind of school reader you had when you were a child. I had the same kind—all the stories were sad, and some of them scared me half to death——"

"Yes, I remember 'em," Mrs. Pettigrew said, "one story was about a girl who went to a dance when her parents thought she was going to a prayer meeting. She caught cold on her way home, and died in a few days. She awoke in hell, where the fiends roasted her body on live coals. She screamed and begged, but the devil told her that the burning would go on forever because she lied to her mother, and then went to a dance."

"That's the way they were," Aleck said. "Well, Professor McGuffey is writing a new series of readers that are full of pleasant little tales about boys and girls, without any mention whatever of damnation, sickness, sin or sudden death. They are about home life and animals and pets and games that children play."

"I wish him well in that undertaking," Mrs. Pettigrew said emphatically. "What's the sense of teaching children all the gloomy side of life in school? God knows we see enough of it after we're grown up."

"Mother, you'll like Professor McGuffey. He's not solemn and pompous," Caroline remarked.

Susan Pettigrew thought she might, but she made up her

mind to speak no more than might be necessary while he was there for fear of making grammatical errors. When he arrived, however, she knew she was going to like him before he had been in the room five minutes. He had a jolly look in his eyes and he laughed a lot. Susan lost her timidity at once and talked as usual, regardless of her double negatives and "ain't" for "isn't," and "heap" for "much," and "bully boy" for "good fellow." The professor did not seem to notice her mistakes, and most of his conversation was about people and events instead of about books.

After a current epidemic of measles and the high-handed doings of President Andrew Jackson had been discussed at supper—with a few remarks about the large number of recent marriages—Aleck Watson said, "Well, Professor, I've bought a McCormick reaper at last for the farm. Got it this week."

"I thought you would, Aleck, in time. It's a great labor-saver. Does the work of six or eight men."

"I hesitated a long time, for I don't know a danged thing about farm machinery—neither does George Carter," said Aleck Watson, "so we thought we'd just wait until we saw how the reaper worked on Tom Byrd's place. He bought one last year. He says it's a wonder. I watched it at work, and I think he's right."

"I've never seen one," Susan Pettigrew remarked, "but I've heard tell of 'em. In my part of the country we don't raise much wheat; only garden sass for the city market, so there ain't no need for reapers."

"We need them here," said the professor, "with these big farms."

"I should say we do," Aleck agreed. "Why, every year up to now it took ten men a month to cut the wheat on our farm, with hand scythes, working from sunrise to sunset. I mean to cut it and bring it in. This year I expect to do the job with the reaper and one man in three weeks. One of our big troubles heretofore has been in getting enough workers at the right time, for of course everybody wants his grain harvested at the same time as everybody else, and there aren't enough men to go around."

Professor McGuffey said slowly, "I'm convinced that there

could never be any extensive wheat-growing farms in this country without the mechanical reaper. That's why I call it one of the world's great inventions. Without it we would have developed into a race of peasants, like those in Europe. Peasants with farms of a few acres, and one man doing all the work by hand. The reaper is certain to reduce the price of bread everywhere by making wheat cheaper to produce."

"I wonder what happened to Hussey's invention? It was going good and strong about three years ago," said Aleck Watson. "You remember, Caroline, that we went to see Obed Hussey's reaper cut a field of wheat here on the edge of town."

"Certainly, I remember the occasion," said Mrs. Watson. "That was in the fall of 1833. Mr. Hussey, you know, the man who invented that reaper, was there and we met him. He told us a lot about it and we watched it at work."

"That's right. Maybe you can tell us, Professor, what's happened to Mr. Hussey and his invention. Did McCormick buy him out?"

The professor cleared his throat and said dryly, "No, McCormick didn't buy him out; he drove him out, you better say. I'll tell you all I know about it. Obed Hussey, a Yankee from the island of Nantucket, invented a reaper and took out a patent for it in December, 1833. Sometime during the next summer Cyrus McCormick took out a patent for his reaper. The two machines were very much alike, and it isn't clear why the Patent Office gave patent papers to both of them.

"Both Hussey and McCormick claim to have worked out the idea independently, and each says he hadn't seen the other's machine. That's quite possible; it has happened before at various times in respect to inventions.

"Their case is in court now. McCormick has proved that although he did not apply for a patent until after Hussey had obtained one he had a machine that actually cut wheat in 1831, which was before Hussey had gone into the matter of reapers at all.

"In the meantime McCormick is selling his machine all over the country. He seems to be a pushing business man; anyway, he's getting hold of the reaper trade."

"Well," said Aleck Watson, "he sells his reapers on the installment plan, and that's a big thing when you're pushing sales. I'm going to pay only one-third down on the reaper I intend to buy—the rest monthly over two years." [16]

"Lack of progress in the art of the soil—I mean agriculture—is one of the outstanding facts of history," said the professor. "Men have depended on farming to produce most of their food for thousands of years, yet the business has been the most backward of sciences, or trades.

"Consider the plow. For thousands of years men plowed the soil with crooked sticks, or—instead of plowing furrows—they merely made holes in the ground and dropped the seed into them. The old-fashioned plow that our grandfathers used was made of a couple of slabs of wood. It didn't turn over the soil; that had to be done by a farm hand following the man who did the plowing, and the wooden device was soon worn out by the hardness of the soil.

"In 1797 Charles Newbold, an American, invented a plow made of iron throughout. It was cast in one piece, and in shape it was a great improvement over the crude plows then in use. It could be operated by one man, and only one yoke of oxen was needed. Newbold patented his invention and thought it would quickly supplant the old-style clumsy plow. He was sadly mistaken; he sold only a few of his plows. Farmers would have nothing to do with them."

"I remember that time," Susan Pettigrew exclaimed. "I was a young gal then, and they tried to sell my father one of them iron plows. He wouldn't have nothing to do with it; he said the iron poisoned the soil."

"That's right," the professor resumed, "and you may wonder how such an absurd idea got around. Iron, the farmers argued, is a foreign substance which has no kinship with the soil. They disregarded the fact that iron ore comes out of the ground. Furthermore, they said, it is well known that nothing will grow in the earth that comes from iron mines. That is true, but the passing of an iron plow along a furrow does not turn the field into a mining dump.

[16] Obed Hussey lost his life on August 4, 1860, while on a train bound from Boston to Portland, Maine. In those days there was often no water in the cars. The train stopped at a station where a little child asked for a drink of water and Mr. Hussey stepped out to get one for her. As he was in the act of reentering the car the train started. He was thrown beneath the wheels and instantly killed. He was sixty-eight at the time of his death.

"On the other hand, they argued that the wooden plow is a product of the soil; when it goes into the ground and makes a furrow it has returned to its mother, for wood comes from trees, and trees grow out of the earth like corn and wheat. Like to like is a good old rule. To treat the soil with iron, they declared, would have the same effect as feeding the harmful juice of pokeberries to a baby, and then expecting the baby to grow.

"The poison-plow delusion lasted more than twenty years. Newbold, who expected his invention to meet with great success, faded from sight, in disappointment and poverty.

"Among the tillers of the soil who took no stock in the theory of iron poisoning the ground was Jethro Wood, a farmer in the State of New York. He used Newbold's plows and found that they were much more effective in results, and more economical in operation, than the clumsy wooden plow. But he discovered that they had one serious defect; if the plow struck a stone or a sturdy root with such force that a piece of the share or mold was broken off, the entire plow had to be discarded.

"To remedy this fault Wood invented, and patented in 1819, an iron plow made in several parts bolted together, so that a broken part could be quickly replaced. He expected to have a lot of difficulty in selling his plows, but to his astonishment, the farmers bought them as fast as he could make them. By that time the poison-iron superstition had quietly faded away. What brought that about is a matter of conjecture; maybe it had just lived its day. A new conviction precisely contrary to the old one had taken its place. Many of the farmers maintained that iron improved the fertility of the soil. Strong iron—strong soil—fine crops. Neither this belief nor the one it supplanted has any scientific basis.

"Newbold's plow had come ahead of its proper time; the agricultural world had not been prepared for it, but Wood's plow came at the right moment."

The professor paused and grinned cheerfully at his little audience. "There's something in that we should all keep in mind. I mean that it is just as bad to be too early as it is to be too late.

"Well, Jethro Wood brought out his iron plow at the right

time, but he had his big troubles, too. How? Why, he had the plow patented as a protection of his rights as the inventor, but how on earth could anybody keep blacksmiths from making it? The demand for the iron plow was tremendous, and——"

"I bought the iron plows for my farm about fifteen years ago," said Mrs. Pettigrew, "and I had no idea they was patented. Mine was made by a blacksmith in White Plains."

"You see, there you are," the professor continued, nodding toward Susan Pettigrew. "You wouldn't think of her as a patent infringer, would you? In those days, everybody wanted an iron plow and Jethro Wood's little shop couldn't meet one-tenth of the demand. The blacksmiths copied his plows right and left without giving a thought to patent rights. Wood sued them in the courts with venom and fury, but without much success. Most of his profits were expended in lawsuits.

"This situation preyed on his mind; he became morose and irritable. Human iniquity in all its forms, especially the brazen rascality of those who steal patents, was the daily subject of his discourse. About two years later Jethro Wood died—an embittered man."

"Listen, Professor McGuffey," said Caroline Watson, "didn't Thomas Jefferson invent a plow? There was something about that in one of our discussions at the Semi-Colon Club."

"Yes," the professor answered, "but it wasn't a whole plow—just the moldboard which, as you may know, is above the plowshare. The moldboard turns over the earth and perfects the furrow. Jefferson's invention was quite successful in reducing the resistance of the plowed earth.

"The French nation, by the way, gave Jefferson a gold medal in recognition of his invention."

Just as Professor McGuffey finished his remarks the clock on the mantel struck eleven, which was a late hour for Cincinnati people in the 1830's. Aleck Wilson and the professor had a rum toddy and the ladies each drank a glass of wine before the professor took his leave.

"He's a little professorial," Caroline remarked after their guest had departed.

"Professorial? Professorial?" Susan Pettigrew silently turned over the word in her mind. She had never heard it before. Then she said aloud, "Professorial? You mean he talks like a professor?"

"That's what she means," said her son-in-law with a laugh, while he poured out a bedtime drink for himself.

"Well, he is a professor," Susan remarked. "Why shouldn't he talk like one?"

"Oh, forget it," Caroline said petulantly. "I meant that he lectures us—and everybody, for that matter—just as if we were a class of college students. You can't have any conversation when he's present. He doesn't discuss anything; he just tells you what's what, and let's it go at that."

"I don't see any objection to that," said her mother. "I want people to tell me whatever I don't know, and I can listen all day. Everything the professor said interested me."

9

Susan thought it a lot of fun to play the great lady now and then. She liked to have the family carriage brought out, and with John—the colored coachman—on the box, she would drive slowly through the streets of the busy town. Then she would stop at one of the fashionable stores where she was known and order some feminine finery sent home and charged to her account. The bowing proprietor would say, "Yes, Mrs. Pettigrew" half a dozen times and escort her to the door. With Caroline she made calls on the well-to-do in their homes, and drank tea with the ladies. But on such occasions she had little to say, for she was observant and shrewd enough to realize that her grammar and her company manners were more at home on a dairy farm than in a city mansion.

In October a showboat came down the river and tied up at a Cincinnati wharf for a week that ran into two weeks, and then three weeks, for every person in that community who was not bedridden wanted to go to one showboat performance, at least. Some of them saw every show that was put on.[17] The play that Susan and the Watsons saw was called *Wedded by Mistake*. The piece, though intended to be serious, was

[17] The first showboat on the river was owned by William Chapman, an English actor, who originated this form of theatrical entertainment in 1830. His company consisted of three sons and two daughters. The venture was such a success that he had many imitators.

really a farce or light comedy, and the audience roared with laughter at the most solemn passages. Barbara, a pretty and innocent-looking girl, was in love with Worthing Baxter, an upstanding young man who intended to propose to Barbara when he had earned a competence. The villain, whose name was Ralph Stevens, also wanted her, but he knew he did not have a chance. He was a tricky chap, however, and at a gay party where there was a mock wedding he married Barbara. She thought it was just a play, but Stevens managed to have the wedding ceremony performed by a justice of the peace who was one of the guests, by telling him that Barbara wanted to surprise her family.

After that the complications began and Susan found herself with tears running down her cheeks, not in sorrow but from too much laughter.

About twice a month she got a letter from home, written by one of her sons. She was glad to learn that they were both well, that the dairy business was fine, and that the crops were growing splendidly. All that was pleasant news, but the letters were invariably bulky, and the postage that Susan had to pay on each letter was seventy-five cents.[18]

To her thrifty mind this semi-monthly tax seemed exorbitant, as it truly was, and several times she was half-resolved to write to her sons and tell them to make their letters shorter, but this economical intention was overruled by her ardent desire to hear from her boys and learn what was going on. So frugality was conquered and the costly letters were looked upon thereafter as a sort of necessary luxury.

In November she got a letter from her eldest son who wanted to know when she was coming home. "We are all looking forward," he wrote, "to seeing you either this month

[18] Until 1847 the recipient of letters paid the postage. For a "single" letter (meaning a letter written on a single sheet of paper) the postage rate was six cents for distances under thirty miles. From that basis the rate rose, by gradual increases, to twenty-five cents for a single sheet letter sent for any distance over four hundred and fifty miles.

In the 1840's the post office system was revised, and the rates were greatly reduced. A half-ounce letter going under three hundred miles could be sent for five cents, as against twenty cents for a single sheet under the old regulations. Postage stamps came into use in 1847, and thereafter the sender of a letter paid the postage.

or before Christmas." So his letter ended. She held it in her hand a long time, thinking deeply. Then she wrote to him that the trip over the mountains would be disagreeable and perhaps dangerous in winter, and so she had decided to remain in Cincinnati until spring.

Chapter VIII

FOUR YOUNG MEN IN THE GOLD RUSH

I

THE MOVEMENT of gold-seeking adventurers toward the newly found California gold fields in 1849 and in the early fifties is quite correctly described as a "rush" rather than a migration. Whenever people migrate to a new country —or to an old country which is alien to them—they go as settlers and usually after long preparation. They are accompanied by their wives and children, for they are looking for a new home, where they expect to remain. There was nothing like that in the famous gold rush, which was dominated by a hysterical recklessness. Men by the thousands left their homes in the Eastern states and rushed pell-mell toward the setting sun.

This movement, which has no parallel in American history, was inspired by the accidental discovery of gold in the Sacramento Valley in January, 1848. Captain John A. Sutter, a prosaic-looking German-Swiss, owned a large tract of land in that region. The population of California was small, and there were great areas of forest, desert, and mountain ranges that were uninhabited. Parts of the territory had never been explored. That is probably the reason why gold had not been found much earlier.

Captain Sutter employed James W. Marshall, a mill builder, to put up a sawmill on Sutter's Creek. In the course of this job Marshall found some nuggets of gold in the bed of the shallow stream. He was not sure that the little yellow pebbles were really gold, but he thought they were, so he took them to his employer. Sutter and Marshall messed over the nuggets —treating them with acids—for a week or so, and then Sutter sent them to San Francisco for further analysis. The chemist's report that the nuggets were pure gold leaked out within a few days and there was a stampede of men of all classes and conditions toward the Sacramento Valley. For a few months this frenzy was limited to the inhabitants of California, for there was no railroad or telegraph line across the continent, and it took many weeks to send letters on their long journey around the Horn, or across the Isthmus of Panama. The news reached the East in the early summer of 1848.

It came with prodigious tales of wealth suddenly acquired, of hills heavy with gold, of the surface of the ground covered by the precious metal. Most of these stories were fanciful lies, but there was a stratum of truth in some of them. Gold was to be found, indeed, but hard, back-breaking work was necessary, and even then the finding of a fortune in the ground was mainly a matter of pure luck.

At first these yarns were skeptically received and the Eastern newspapers printed them under such farcical headings as *Aladdin and His Wonderful Lamp* and *Sindbad the Sailor Says.* One of the current fables appeared in a thin little book called *Three Weeks in the Gold Mines,* written by a hack writer who used the name of H. I. Simpson. This author had never been within two thousand miles of California, but in the book he declared that, with no other implement than a pocket knife, he had picked gold nuggets worth fifty thousand dollars off the ground in ten days. After that he traveled all over the western country, having a good time. This yarn was not believed by intelligent people, but it was read by thousands who were not intelligent and who were ready to believe anything that had a pleasant sound.

But even those who possessed a good critical sense began to take notice when they read the report of Colonel R. B. Mason, military governor of California. This document was sent by the governor to the War Department and was supposed to deal only with facts without exaggeration. He wrote that "There is more gold in the country drained by the Sacramento and the San Joaquin Rivers than would pay the cost of the late war with Mexico a hundred times over." That made even the most cynical sit up and take notice—that report of a literal-minded army officer to his superiors in Washington. It was closely followed by similar reports from geologists and others who were supposed to know what they were talking about.

The movement toward California was under way in 1848, but it did not assume great proportions until the spring of the next year. By the midsummer of 1849 it had become a senseless stampede.

Farmers left their fields untilled and went off with only a few dollars in their pockets. What did it matter if they reached California without a cent? Gold could be picked up from the ground. Workmen quit their jobs without notice and began to tramp across the continent on foot, hoping to join some wagon train in Missouri or Kansas. Small shopkeepers—not a few, but many—advertised that they were selling their goods at cost because they were leaving for the land of gold. In every town and village one might buy gold-seekers' manuals, guides and maps of the fabulous region. Among the advertisements in the newspapers one finds a "Goldometer" offered for three dollars. This instrument, it was claimed, would instantly reveal the presence of gold under ground.

But the psychological impulse behind the gold rush was deeper and more urgent than the desire to gain wealth. For a vast number of men it was a flight from reality; an escape for those who were tired of the monotony of existence, of their petty shops and trades, of their wives and families. They could not leave home without an objective that appeared to be worthy, or without an explanation that would be satisfactory to themselves. In faraway California there could be found both the objective and the explanation. It was a desperate adventure, of course; they made that clear to their families and their friends, so that waves of sympathy would flow after them on their long trail; but wouldn't it be wonderful to return in a year or two, laden with gold, to live happy ever after?

Then there was the powerful impulse of vanity, a motivation which has never had its due recognition in historical works. Vanity has probably inspired more daring adventures, more heroic exploits and more renowned accomplishments in all fields of human effort than any other human motive.

In the days of the gold rush a village blacksmith's helper, let us say, announces that he is going to California and will leave for that distant land next week. In the meantime he quits work and swaggers about the tiny community in his best clothes. He is a center of attraction; even the grave and reverend seniors of the village converse with him, as one man to another, about his trip and the coming election and the Indians on the plains and the national need for more money and the rising prices of farming land. The girls who never gave him a glance before his project was announced now look at him curiously and smile as they pass by. The solemn, black-coated minister gives him a *Bible* to take on his long journey. His coming departure is even recorded in the local newspaper, where he never expected to see his name in print. He who was a Nobody has become a Somebody for a little while.

2

"If anybody wants to drop out now's the time to do it," said Jacob Birdsall, looking at the three young men sitting around the table. "As for me," he continued, "I'm going, even if I have to go alone."

"Aw, Jake, you know we're all going, so what's the use of asking us again?" This came from Andy Gordon, who seemed annoyed by Birdsall's question. "We ought to be on our way in a week, or we'll have a late start. It would've been better if we'd left here a month ago. Here it is the middle of April, and they all say it takes four months to get out there—"

"Takes longer'n than that from here," said the youngest member of the party, whose name was Tom Plunkett. "Anyway, that's what it says in the guidebook I bought. It says there that it takes four months from Independence, Missouri, or from St. Joseph, and we're not at either one of those places, but right here in our home town of Memphis, Tennessee—so it'll be 'bout a week longer, starting from here."

"Yes, yes," Birdsall said peevishly. "I know all that. The reason I asked if any of you want to drop out is that we'll have to buy our things right away and get going. It's now or never."

The fourth man present in the back room of the grog shop where they were seated was Matthew Gordon, brother of Andrew. He raised his arms toward the ceiling in a tired gesture, yawned noisily and said, "My God! Stop talking and do something. Come on and let's lay in some supplies. As it is we can't leave under a week from now." He rose from his chair and strode toward the door with the others following him. The California gold rush had gained four new recruits.

Jake Birdsall was the oldest member of this quartet and its natural leader. He was a stalwart six-footer with a bullet-shaped head and a fist like a small ham. His heavy beard, in which he took great pride, almost covered his face and made his blue eyes look as though he were peeping from behind a bush.[1]

His home town was Memphis but he had gone up and down the Mississippi for years as a deck hand on river steamers. He was as illiterate as a nine-year-old schoolboy, but during his thirty-five years he had seen a great deal of the rough side of life and had acquired a lot of knowledge that can be gained only by experience. As a soldier of the republic of Texas he had fought the Mexicans in the Texan struggle for independence. He had hunted buffaloes on the prairies, had served as a sailor before the mast on a trading schooner, and had been employed as a bouncer in a barroom at Fort Worth until that career was cut short by a mischance; a quarrelsome patron of the bar had been bounced so hard that he bounced into the Great Beyond without regaining consciousness.

But Jake Birdsall was not as pugnacious as this brief record might lead one to believe. On the contrary, he was good-natured in his harsh way and sympathetic with people in distress. Moreover, he liked hard work and—though this may seem astonishing—he declared, on various occasions, that he had not taken a drop of strong liquor in ten years. When drinking was in order he would make a glass of beer last the whole evening.

The two Gordons, Andy and Mat, were much younger than Birdsall. Andy was twenty-four and his brother was twenty-two. Tom Plunkett was even younger; he had not reached his twentieth birthday, but his father gave his consent to the California adventure, as he thought the experience would harden the boy and develop in him the virtue of self-reliance. The elder Plunkett, who was well-to-do, gave his son fifteen hundred dollars to help pay the expenses of the venture. The

[1] In the late 1840's beards were coming into popular favor again after having been out of fashion for seventy or eighty years. All the heroes of the American Revolution were beardless, as one may see by looking at their portraits. Around the 1820 decade side whiskers began to appear as facial ornaments, but it was not until the late forties that men, in considerable numbers, were wearing beards. Lincoln was the first bearded President.

total sum raised by all the participants was only a little over three thousand dollars, so it appears that Tom Plunkett's father gave half the money required.

This Birdsall-Gordon-Plunkett party was fairly well but not extravagantly financed for the journey. Thousands of men began the long hike across the continent without any money at all. These penniless gold rushers hoped to earn their way by doing odd jobs for other pilgrims, such as repairing wagons, helping with the cooking, washing clothes, etc.

The Gordon brothers were tall, slender young men who had come originally from Georgia. An uncle in Savannah had left them a legacy of a few thousand dollars which they had brought to Memphis in 1847. They migrated to the Tennessee town because it was new and rapidly growing, and their intention was to "grow up" with the community. So they invested the legacy in general merchandise and opened a store. There seemed to be something wrong with their idea, for the store lost money from the start. Then came all the talk about gold in California. The Gordons sold the store at a loss and, with the few hundreds of dollars that it brought them, they were ready to seek new fields.

Tommy Plunkett was the only one of the four who had never done anything in the form of work during his twenty years of existence. If he lived today he would probably be called a "playboy," but in Memphis in the year 1849 he was widely known as "Judge Plunkett's no 'count son." Although he had never engaged in useful toil he was by no means an idler. He could be found at parties, at picnics, and at other joyous occasions, playing the banjo or guitar, singing songs and teaching new games to those present. His jokes and pranks evoked the laughter of even his most sedate critics.

One of his accomplishments was the organization of the Memphis baseball team among the young men of the town. On the team he played as pitcher.[2]

[2] The game was new in those days. Modern baseball owes its existence to General Abner Doubleday, a civil engineer of Cooperstown, New York. In 1839 he laid out the first baseball diamond with three bases and adapted to it the ball game known as "One old Cat," which had been played with one base only. The new game became popular all over the country during the 1840's.

The term "baseball" is, however, much older than the game as we know it. In 1762 Hugh Gaine, a printer of New York, brought out *A Little Pretty Book,*

3

That same evening the four adventurers, after a catfish dinner in a water-front restaurant, went to Jake Birdsall's room to talk over their plans. During the weeks that had passed since the idea of going west had come to them they had decided on the main features of the expedition, but not on the details. At first they thought they would go by the Panama route, for all they had to do in that case was to take passage on a ship at New Orleans for Colon, then cross the isthmus on muleback to the town of Panama. There they would have to wait until they could get passage on a ship going north to San Francisco.

Their early enthusiasm for the Panama route subsided gradually as they learned more about it. It was very expensive; the steamship companies got all they could from the eager travelers. And the reports coming back from those who had made the trip laid much emphasis on the unhealthy climate of the isthmus. Cholera, yellow fever and a variety of tropical ills had to be encountered, and many of those who set out to cross the isthmus died in the jungle and were buried there. Besides these disadvantages there were stories of the long waits at Panama for passage on steamers or sailing vessels bound for San Francisco. The town of Panama was said to be as hot as an oven and full of fleas and fevers. Sometimes travelers bound for California had to wait for two months, and when at last they got aboard a steamer they found it so crowded that there was hardly room enough to lie down. Men who had paid as much as two hundred dollars for their passage were often forced to live and sleep on deck as there was no place for them in the staterooms.[3]

Intended for the Instruction and Amusement of Little Master Tommy and Pretty Miss Polly, which contains a woodcut depicting a game called "baseball," in which boys are shown at play. Under the woodcut this verse appears:

> The Ball once struck off,
> Away flies the Boy
> To the next destined Post,
> And then Home with Joy.

[3] The overland trail across the continent was the favorite route of the gold seekers. Comparatively few went across the isthmus or around Cape Horn. It was said at the time that the sea passengers were generally merchants, or government officials, or professional gamblers.

Tom Plunkett wet a finger on his tongue and turned a page of the guidebook that lay on the table before him. "It says here," he said, "that the wagons ought to be light instead of heavy, because you'll run into deep sand, mud and mire, and a heavy wagon would sink to the hubs."

"Yeh, but it's got to carry a heavy load, and how you goin' to manage that with a light wagon?" This came from Jake Birdsall.

"Well, now, let's see what we'll have to put on the wagon," said Mat Gordon. "We'll have to carry a tent big enough for four to sleep in, and four mattresses——"

"Git out!" Jake sneered. "Four mattresses. D'you want to take all the household furniture? We'll sleep on the ground. Take along a lot of blankets. No sheets; you'd have to wash 'em."

"All right," Mat continued. "A tent—and blankets—no mattresses. Lemme write it down. Then everybody'll have to take some clothing, such as shirts and drawers and one more suit—maybe two suits—and extra boots."

"Oughta to be several pairs of boots," Jake remarked. "The way they wear out in a rough country."

"What does it say in that guidebook?" Andy Gordon asked. "Read some more, Tommy, about what we'll need on the way."

"Yeh, go on," said Jake Birdsall. "Who wrote the book?"

Tommy looked at the title page. "By J. E. Sherwood, it says. The name of the book is *Pocket Guide to California.*"

"All right, read on," Birdsall said. "I dunno if this Sherwood's ever been to California, but it don't do no harm to hear what he says."

First in the list of supplies to go in the wagon, according to the book, was a kit of carpenter's tools—a saw, an auger, an axe, a hatchet, a gimlet, a chisel, a hammer, and a lot of nails of all sizes.

"Naturally we take all of them things without being told," was Birdsall's comment. "What else?"

Tommy read aloud a long list which included coils of rope, some light chains (you never know when you may need them, the book said), half a dozen balls of twine, some tin buckets, tin plates for use at meals, a coffee pot, tin cups. Needles, thread, buttons and scissors for repairing clothes. Also a strong box or two, with locks on them. Some warm woolen clothes and a heavy overcoat for it gets very cold out there. A large quantity of soap, some towels, several wicker baskets, writing paper and pens and ink, a few blank books, pocket-knives, a lot of matches in boxes. Tommy stopped reading at his point and kept his place with a finger on the page. "The book says the matches are very important," he explained, "and be sure not to forget 'em, for you won't find a match on the way. It says to take plenty of candles and a lantern for each person."

Mat Gordon wrote each article down on his list, slowly and with painstaking care.

In the matter of arms the author advised every man to carry a good rifle, a pair of pistols, five pounds of powder and ten pounds of lead. Also a bowie knife.

"What about grub?" This from Andy Gordon. "We eat on the way, you know. Maybe we're expected to browse on grass."

"Oh, there's plenty of mention here of food supplies," Tommy said, turning the pages of the guide.

"Well, anyway, I know already about what we ought to carry," Birdsall said. "You see, we ain't the first, by any means, that have gone from Memphis to the gold fields. I've talked with a pile of 'em, and have looked over their loads. Besides, parties on their way are going up the river on the steamers right along, and I've been helping 'em. But read what this Sherwood says."

Tommy read the list of groceries: one hundred and fifty pounds of flour; bacon, one hundred and fifty pounds; coffee, twenty-five pounds; sugar, thirty pounds. "That's just for one man. For the four of us it would be four times that much."

"It's an awful lot of grub," Andy said. "Don't you think so, Jake? Twenty-five pounds of coffee for each of us. I don't believe I'd use half that much in four months. And bacon—a hundred and fifty pounds. That's nearly ten pounds a week for every man. We better talk over that list and——"

"Wait a minute," Tommy interrupted. "There's more to come. He's got down a keg of lard, fifty pounds of crackers, some cheese, salt and pepper."

"That all?" Birdsall asked.

"That's all the food mentioned here," Tommy replied.

They discussed food supplies for half an hour and decided to cut down every item to about two-thirds of the amount proposed. "To help out on the meat we may be able to shoot some buffaloes, and I guess there'll be birds that we can kill," said Andy Gordon. "We're all purty handy with guns."

The group sat in silence for a little while. "I guess that about covers it," Jake Birdsall said. "We'll start to buy the things tomorrow. Also we must find a covered wagon and six oxen. We'll take them all by steamboat from here to St. Joseph."

Mat Gordon took from his pocket a map of the United States west of the Mississippi. "This map," he explained, "was sent to me by Bob Perrin. You-all know Bob; he went out there last year by land, the way we're going, and he sent this map back by mail—around by Panama, it took three months to get here—and it shows the route his party took. He says it's the best route of all."

He spread out the map. It was large enough to cover most of the top of the table, leaving just room for the ill-smelling, smoking whale oil lamp. All of them were interested and they bunched their heads together while they leaned over the table and stared at the heavy pencil line which ran from St. Joseph in Missouri to Sacramento in California.

"There ain't light enough to get a good view of the thing," Mat complained, "but I suppose it's the best you can do, eh, Jake?"

Birdsall thought a moment. "No," he said, "I've got some candles." He opened a chest in the corner of the room and took out several tall candles which he lighted and placed on the table. The map, tinted a light pink, glowed in the illumination.[4]

[4] There were no kerosene lamps as early as 1849. Some of the cities were lighted by gas, but the inhabitants of Memphis depended on candles or lamps burning whale oil. Kerosene, as an illuminant, was unknown until late in the 1850's. The first commercial petroleum product was called Kier's Rock Oil, and was made by Samuel M. Kier, a Pittsburgh druggist. He distilled the oil (this was in 1855) in the back room of his drugstore and sold it for fifty cents a bottle. It was used externally for rubbing. About the same time (in 1855) Dr. Abraham Gesner, of Newtown Creek, Long Island, New York, made the first kerosene from raw petroleum. He invented the word "kerosene." It comes from

The penciled route shown on the map did not run straight toward California, but pointed toward the northwest until it reached Pocatello, in Idaho, then it veered sharply toward the southwest. "I wonder why we can't go straight across," someone said "By going straight—due west—we'd save several hundred miles of travel."

The letter written by Bob Perrin to accompany the map was read and it explained the peculiar wide curve made by the overland route. "If you went straight west from St. Joseph," the letter said, "you would pass through western Kansas, and if there were a drought you would not find any water, and probably no grass. You must think of the oxen and mules. Then, further on, in Colorado you would run smack up against the Rocky Mountain wall. If you got over that, then you have to cross the deserts of Nevada. Keeping this in mind, sensible travelers bear toward the northwest."

The route, as mapped out, ran from St. Joseph to Fort Laramie, in Wyoming. From there on to Pocatello, in Idaho. The trail did not touch Colorado or Utah, but ran through Kansas, a corner of Nebraska, across Wyoming into Idaho. There it turned sharply across Nevada in a southwest direction, entering California just below Lake Tahoe.

"I wonder just how far it is by this trail," Jake Birdsall inquired.

"It's figured out here," Mat replied. "Perrin says it's a little more than two thousand miles from St. Joseph to Sacramento. I've checked that up by measurements made on the map, and he's right."

"Well, we can't count on more'n fifteen miles a day with these ox teams, taking everything by and large, such as deserts, mud, mountains and so on," Jake said, as if talking to himself, "and that means only ninety miles a week if we lay off on Sunday as a rest day. Now, let's see—gimme a pencil and a piece of paper." He figured slowly, straightened up and said, "It means twenty-two weeks, fellows, so if we start on May 1 from St.

---

the Greek *keros,* meaning a wax. He did not sell much of it as there was no lamp then in existence in which it could be burned efficiently. The petroleum industry did not begin in a large way until 1859, when Edwin L. Drake bored through the rock at Titusville, Pennsylvania. His first well produced four hundred gallons a day, and was the beginning of the oil boom of the 1860's.

(*Schoenfeld, Photo from Three Lions*)

HUSKING BEE IN NEW ENGLAND.

Corn was one of the principal crops of New England farms in the early days. A farmer, when his corn was gathered and ready for husking, usually invited the neighbors to help on the job, which was made a form of merriment. The husking was done in the farmer's barn. Food and drinks were supplied in profusion, and husking bees often lasted until after midnight. Any young man who happened to run across a red ear of corn had the right, according to custom, to kiss any girl there. Judging from this picture it appears that several red ears must have been found at the same time.

Joseph we won't reach the gold fields before October—unless we can find some way of moving faster. Yet they say that lots of 'em make it in four months." He threw the pencil down on the table with a bang.

As a matter of fact, the caravans usually did better than fifteen miles a day, though some lazy and shiftless wagoners loitered by the way and took six months to make the trip. It could be done, and was done regularly, in sixteen or seventeen weeks, which meant an advance of about one hundred and twenty-five miles a week.

Oxen were used chiefly as the motive power, but mules were preferred by some of the emigrants. Mules traveled faster, and could pull as heavy a load as oxen, but they were less manageable and were frequently stolen by the Indians at night.

4

The Birdsall party, full of excitement, left Memphis April 20, on the steamer *Prairie Belle,* for St. Joseph in Missouri. Their six oxen, for which they had paid sixty-five dollars apiece—a high price—stood in the stalls on the lower deck, and there also was their covered wagon, heavily laden with supplies for the journey.

The day before their departure they had gone to Dial's Daguerreotype Studio to have what they called their "likenesses" taken. These pictures were to be left with friends and relatives as mementos of the daring adventurers. If they were alive today they would take a lot of snapshots of each other, but the quick action camera did not come into use until about 1890. Anyone who wanted his picture to be perfect, without blurs or blemishes, had to remain before a camera as immovable as a statue for at least one minute. The poser's head was usually clamped between a pair of metal prongs, so arranged that they would not show in the picture.

The four young men had a number of pictures made, and were in Dial's place about an hour. In one picture Jake Birdsall was seated while the three boys bent over him as if they were listening intently to what he had to say. All of them had their hands cupped behind their ears and all of them were laughing, which meant that they had to keep their mouths open. It was not easy to persuade "Professor" Dial to make this picture. He himself looked as queer as a brownie, with his short stature, long hair, bushy beard and myopic eyes behind their thick glasses. He had no sense of humor—not a trace—and had never been known to laugh, or even smile. He declared that such a picture as they wanted would "degrade" the art, but he was finally induced to take it.

Another picture showed Tommy Plunkett playing his banjo, while the rest appeared to be singing. Then they had a "ladder" picture—a famous pose in the early days of photography. Birdsall was seated in a chair for this grouping and the others stood on a step ladder behind him, so that each head showed above those below.[5]

On the day of their departure many of their friends went with them to the steamer and gave them a great rousing send-off, with liquor, food and songs. Tommy played his banjo and the crowd sang *Susannah* and *Nellie Was a Lady* until they were hoarse. Rum and rye were dispensed by the Birdsall outfit and by their guests, most of whom carried bottles of whisky in their pockets. The dining room steward sent around refreshments on trays carried by his white-coated negro waiters. It was not only a joyous affair but also a hilarious one, so hilarious indeed that some of the farewell party had to be led ashore gently by the deck hands when the boat's whistle blew. "It was a festive occasion though a little rough near the end," said the editor of the local paper as he went ashore with his handful of notes for the article he intended to write. "But it will be many a month before they have any more fun," he continued, "so why not send 'em off in a jolly sort of way?"

Long before the *Prairie Belle* reached its destination it was

[5] These pictures were daguerreotypes. They were different from the photographs of today in that they had no negatives but were made directly on a copper or silver-coated plate. Duplicate prints could not be made and if two pictures were needed the subject had to sit twice. The tintype that was popular after the Civil War was a cheaper form of the daguerreotype. Louis Daguerre, a Frenchman, invented this process in the 1830's, but it had many faults and was more or less impracticable until it was improved by John W. Draper, a professor in New York University. In 1840 Draper took an excellent picture of his sister Dorothy on the roof of a house on West Fourth Street, in New York City. He appears to be the first who used the term "photograph," but of this I am not certain. The words "daguerreotype" and "photograph" were used interchangeably for many years.

crowded with California-bound travelers; their equipment clutttered the boat from stem to stern. But some of them possessed no baggage at all; they had vague, undefined notions of getting there somehow, even if they had to beg their way. Some of the others had obviously too much impedimenta, more than they could possibly carry across the mountains. One man had a gold dust sifter of his own invention. It was about six feet tall and was complicated by what seemed to be a lot of useless gadgets.

Some of these passengers got off at Kansas City. They intended to make Independence, Missouri, their point of departure or their "jumping-off place," as they called it. But most of the California-bound travelers went on to St. Joseph, where the *Prairie Belle* arrived on April 28.

As the boat pulled up slowly at the wharf the Birdsalls, like the rest of the passengers, crowded to the deck railing and stared at the scene before their eyes. The settlement consisted of scattered cabins, sod houses and other primitive buildings. Beyond the houses, which stood on the river bank, there was another community of white tents and makeshift shelters.

It was a moving picture of men, animals, covered wagons, saloons, open-air cooking, muddy boots, red shirts, rifles, dirks and whisky bottles. The sounds fitted the picture—loud greetings, laughter, songs and quarrels. In the distance, on the skyline, the men on the *Prairie Belle* saw a line of covered wagons moving silently toward the west. Close to the Birdsall party on the deck stood a man about sixty in a battered, high-top beaver hat. He wore a long broadcloth coat, like a member of one of the learned professions, but his knee-high boots did not seem to go with the coat or the hat, nor did his checkered shirt. Instead of a collar and tie he had a black scarf wrapped about his neck. He had got on the boat somewhere in Illinois, and all that was known of him was his name —which was Kendall.

"So this is St. Joseph," he said to the Birdsalls. "If it was my duty to name places, I'd call it Bedlam."

"Yes, it's kind of crazy," Jake Birdsall agreed, "but we have to put up with that. We'll soon be on our way to the land of gold. All of us together."

"They'll probably have to bury me on the way," Kendall

remarked in a tired tone. "I'm too old for such adventures." He had what Birdsall called an "educated" voice. When he spoke he sounded like Judge Plunkett, Tommy's father.

"Then what made you come, sir?" Jake added the "sir" without thought or intention.

Kendall, if that was really his name, smiled grimly and said, "Well, the weather got a little too warm for me in my home town." Then, more briskly, he said, "I wonder if I can buy an outfit here in St. Joseph. I don't want to wear these clothes any longer."

"Oh, I'm sure you can, sir," Jake replied. "There must be something in the way of stores here besides saloons."

The top-hatted man moved away and Jake said to himself: I'll bet there are thousands of 'em. Done something or other—embezzling, stealing, row over women, maybe murder—they change their names and start for the gold fields. Kendall seems to have left in a hurry; didn't have time to change his clothes.

With much difficulty the Birdsalls got the covered wagon and the oxen ashore, found a place to set up their tent, and then proceeded to look around. They decided that as long as they were in St. Joseph—a day or two—one man would have to stay with the wagon; there were so many desperate-looking men prowling around the camp that they thought it unwise to leave their goods unprotected. Upon drawing lots the duty of remaining with the wagon fell upon Andy Gordon, and he was left in his shirt sleeves with a paint brush in his hand. They had observed that nearly all the wagons had names painted on them, such names as "Rough and Ready," "Gold Seeker," and "On My Way." The Memphis outfit must be in fashion, they thought, regardless of every other consideration, so they sat down solemnly and thought of names. After arguing for a long time over all sorts of words and phrases they decided to put "Now or Never" in black lettering on their white wagon cover.

They had not gone far in strolling about the camp before they realized that their clothes did not come up to the gold rush standard by any means. There was the matter of shirts, for instance. They had brought with them some excellent shirts of brown gingham, but they soon learned that a real, honest-to-god gold seeker must wear a red shirt. It had to be a vivid red with an attached collar. Without the red shirt a California-bound pilgrim was tolerated in a kindly way, but he was insignificant socially. The right kind of coat was made of rough woolen cloth. It reached nearly to the knees and was provided with a lot of capacious pockets. The trousers were invariably tucked into the heavy top boots. Slouch hats were in the prevailing mode. In the matter of arms every gold seeker was supposed to wear a leather belt with a holster for a rather heavy cavalry pistol. Besides this firearm the alert and forthcoming traveler was equipped with a dirk about twelve inches long in the blade.

Beards were in high favor, and the three younger men of the Birdsall party resolved to grow them as quickly as they could. Jake Birdsall himself was already provided for splendidly in the matter of beards, and as he went about the camp, as a total stranger, his companions observed that he was listened to with great respect.

Next day, which was April 29, the Birdsalls went shopping. They had some money left, and at a rough and ready clothing store which was sandwiched in between four saloons they purchased the red shirts, the long coats and the shapeless slouch hats.

They bought also four dozen bottles of whisky, an empty barrel for carrying water across the dry and arid stretches that they expected to encounter; and they obtained a Dutch oven which sat on four legs so that it could be put over a fire burning on the ground.

At one place, which a loud-voiced man standing in the door invited everyone to enter, they found what the proprietor called "canned meat." The meat was contained in receptacles made of tin, and were called "cans," as the proprietor explained patiently over and over. Each can was about four inches square and two inches deep. Buzzing around in his shirt sleeves, waiting on customers, and talking loudly all the time, the storekeeper declared that the canned meat would keep fresh a hundred years, and was just the food for those bound for the gold fields. "Long before you get there," he orated, "you'll be sick and tired of rancid bacon and dried pemmican as hard as nails and with so many fly specks on it that you can't tell what its color was before the flies got at it. But here we have canned meat, a new invention. It's always sweet and fresh. Why? Because it is cooked before it goes into the can and, furthermore, the can is sealed so that no air ever gets in. Here, try a piece of our wonderful canned beef."

An open can stood before him. He dipped into it deftly with a fork, removed some pieces and placed them on slices of bread which he passed around among his audience. Nearly everybody bought some of the cans at one dollar apiece. "Let's try the darned thing," said Jake Birdsall. "If what he says is true, it'll be fine to open a can now and then on the way and get the taste of bacon out of our mouths." He bought six cans.[6]

5

In company with fourteen other wagons the Birdsall outfit left St. Joseph on April 30 of the year 1849. There were sixty-one persons in this expedition—fifty-two men, three women and six children. One of the women, whose name was Anna Gowdy, boasted that she was either eighty or eighty-five years old, but she couldn't remember which, she said, and she had lost the *Bible* with her birth date set down in it. With Mrs. Gowdy was one of her grandsons, who seemed to be about forty years of age. The venerable old lady chewed tobacco and swore like a sailor. When she arose at daybreak every morning she would go outside the tent, stand in the open air and scream several times at the top of her voice. They were loud, piercing shrieks. Whenever anyone complained she replied that she did the screaming for health's sake, that it "cleared the lungs," and she thought everybody ought to do it. Her health seemed to be

[6] Cans were introduced, or invented, by Peter Durant in 1818, but many years passed before canned food became popular. One reason why it was long in making headway was due to the expensiveness of the cans. They had to be made by hand. Another reason was the distrust of the public for food sold in that fashion. During the Civil War canned food was supplied to the Northern soldiers and they liked it. The canned food industry, as we know it today, had its beginning in 1885 when a machine for making cans automatically and cheaply was put in operation at Baltimore.

The word "can" comes from canister, a shell filled with gunpowder and bullets. The cans for food, made of bright tin, resembled the canister projectiles used by the army.

excellent. She could chop down a tree with an axe, cook a meal, treat a sick ox, knit socks and undershirts, and help repair a broken-down wagon, all as part of the day's work.

The two other women were middle-aged farmers' wives who accompanied their husbands. One of them had three of the six children on the expedition and the other wife had two. The remaining child was a boy of ten who was going across with his father.

Andrew Gordon kept a diary of the trip. It is here before us, battered and soiled. Its leaves are lined for writing, its covers are of yellow pasteboard, and it resembles generally the blank books that are used for school exercises. The doings of each day are set down in very black ink, but all the pages are yellowed by age, and some of them have become illegible.

A voluminous writer was Andy Gordon; when he wrote he omitted very little, and most of his diary is extremely commonplace in the nature of its subjects. We shall quote here only some extracts.

April 30. We got off this morning, clear, cool day. We bought two mules yesterday—not to pull the wagons, for the oxen do that, but for two of us to ride. The other two ride on the wagon. My brother drove the oxen today, and Tommy sat with him. Jake and I rode the mules. I always thought the prairies were flat as a floor, but not so; they have a sort of wavy look, like the sea with billows.

Jake is to be cook the first week and me next week. Pretty good dinner tonight, and certainly plenty of it—bacon, beans, coffee, bread brought from St. Joe, dried figs, milk from St. Joe . . . all of us as tired as farm hands in the plowing season. Not going to put up the tent for one night only. . . . Will sleep under the stars. . . . Will close now, visitors coming from other wagons.

May 3rd. I wish I could have as much fun in a month as Tommy Plunkett has in one day. He thinks the whole expedition is just a great big picnic. Never seems tired. Has with him an accordion, guitar, banjo and fiddle and plays one or more of them every evening. Also about twenty copies of *John Donkey* that he bought in St. Louis when we stopped there. He reads them like a preacher reading the *Bible,* laughs at all the jokes and shows us the funny pictures.[7]

[7] *John Donkey* was the first American comic weekly. It first appeared in 1848, and was published in New York for a few years. It was a poor-looking sheet, and its funny items have little meaning to a reader of the present generation. Only a few copies are in existence.

May 6th. We elected a leader today for this expedition of fifteen wagons. John Peter Cullen was selected by vote. We all voted, including the three women and the young sprouts still under age. There was no opposition. After the election Cullen was sworn in on a *Bible.* He then gave us a talk sitting on his bay mare out on the prairie while the rest of us stood around and listened. He let us know, in no uncertain terms, that we had chosen him, of our own free will, as the boss of the outfit, and he intended to keep order in this "caravan," as he called it, and he wanted all of us to help him.

Cullen is a big man—six feet some inches—with broad shoulders. He is about forty. His beard is long and black, his eyes are blue, and his fists are hairy.

After his harangue, or speech, he sent one of his men around to us with several gallons of rum, and every man got a drink at Cullen's expense in honor of the occasion. The man filled the tumblers nearly full, and it made me kind of dizzy all the rest of the afternoon. We didn't go very far today and tomorrow's Sunday, which Leader Cullen has ordered to be a day of rest.

The selection of leaders arose from necessity. The caravans were, for most of their journey, far away from sheriffs and courts, and there was no legal method of handling these crowds of men, some of whom were desperados or fugitives from justice. The leaders were usually given authority, by the consent of those who elected them, to keep order; to regulate the progress of the westward march; to see that the sick and disabled were taken care of; to punish thieves and other transgressors; to put a stop to drunkenness and disorder of all kinds. They were supposed to call a jury to pass on serious misdemeanors. Criminals were occasionally executed after a jury trial. The juries—or the leader—sometimes expelled members of the caravan for quarreling, or for stealing, or for doing injury to the wagons and animals of others.

One of the curious features of the situation was that any member of the caravan could leave it at will and go ahead on his own. There were many instances. They arose chiefly because the leader insisted on making Sunday a day of rest and was supported in his attitude by most of the members, while one or two dissident voters were so anxious to reach the gold fields that they were willing to abandon the caravan.

An elected leader could be deposed and another put in

his place by a popular vote. The political principle of referendum and recall had its first practical application on the prairies during the gold rush.

May 7th. This is my week as cook for the party. I dread it, yet it must be done. In the first place there is no wood to be had to build a fire, and we have to depend on dried buffalo chips. That means that the cook and one other at least for every wagon must range the prairie —sometimes for miles—looking for the droppings of buffalos. And these leavings are no good unless they are thoroughly dry. If damp the least bit they will not burn. I had no idea of this before I came on this expedition, or I would have thought twice again before leaving home. Everybody values dried buffalo chips almost as highly as precious gems.

However, I got up three pretty good meals today with a generous amount of coffee. We camped by a little stream tonight, so I washed all the tin plates. Usually we just wipe them with a cloth and let it go at that. We also filled the water barrel. So far we have had no trouble in finding grass for the oxen and horses. The prairie is just one big meadow. It gets mighty tiresome in time. You can look for miles and not see a tree or a bush. It is not natural, for the eye likes to rest on something.

May 8th. Opened one of the cans of beef today, and it was just fine. I wish now we had bought more than six cans of it. All you have to do is to heat it a little. It was not enough for the four of us, so I fried some bacon.

We met two wagons coming back from the Promised Land today. The men with them looked pretty well down in the mouth. As soon as they saw us they yelled, "We've seen the elephant." [8] They stopped and we had a long powwow. We gave them some liquor and grub. They had not been to California—never got there. It seemed that the Humboldt desert had almost ruined them, and they turned back. Two of their men died of cholera; they had three left, and these survivors had hollow eyes and caved-in cheeks, and looked as if they were about done for. Three of their oxen had died—two of them of thirst, and the other one just could not walk any further. He laid down on the prairie and they had to shoot him. They had three oxen left, but they pulled the wagon easily, for it was almost empty.

[8] This expression came from Barnum's Museum on Broadway, in New York. After a visitor to the museum had thought he had seen everything he would run into a sign near the exit on which the words "Have you seen the elephant?" stood out in big letters, and an arrow pointed to the elephant's stable in an enclosure back of the museum. This phrase got into common use and meant, in the case of disappointed gold seekers, that they were on their way home.

They had painted on the white cover of the wagon the words: "Going for Gold." It was not funny, but sad.

They said the prairie is easy going, but when you get into the rough country it was just hell and high water all the time. Also beware of the Indians when we are further along.

These disappointed gold seekers gave some useful advice to Leader Cullen and his company. They said that the cattle should be provided with "leather boots" to protect their feet and legs from the sand and mud that would be encountered further on, after they had gone beyond Laramie. The sand was as sharp as quartz and it made the oxen's feet so tender that they could not walk. The boots were made of leather to fit the feet and run up the leg about six inches. They were tied around the leg. To make them waterproof they were smeared with grease and tar.

The stretch of alkali desert in Nevada was the most hazardous part of the whole journey. The alkali was in the air in the shape of fine dust, these returning pilgrims said, and it was breathed by both men and cattle. Human beings were better able to stand it than horses and oxen. When cattle were "alkalied" the best remedy, they said, was to force great draughts of vinegar down their throats.

The popular song of the gold rush was *Oh, Susannah.* The words and melody of this famous song were by Stephen Collins Foster, who has been justly described as "the troubadour of the American people." It was not only popular with the gold seekers, but also with everybody else in 1849, and is still sung by many, because of its catchy tune. The verse of the song that is reproduced here gives an idea of its general silliness. It runs in this fashion:

It rained all night the day I left;
The weather it was dry.
The sun shone so hot I froze to death;
Oh, Susannah, don't you cry.

Here is the chorus, as it was sung originally:

Oh, Susannah, don't you cry for me,
I'm off for Alabama with my banjo on my knee.

The gold seekers changed the last line to "I'm off to California with my wash bowl on my knee." The "wash bowl" mentioned was for the purpose of washing out the gold nuggets.

According to his diary Andy Gordon got so tired of hearing *Oh, Susannah* sung at all hours that he was afraid of losing his mind. On June 10 he wrote, "I have heard *Susannah* sung at least forty times today, and now it's bedtime and Tommy Plunkett is picking out the tune on his banjo and singing it loud enough to keep most of us awake. Don't he ever get tired of it? I used to like that song, but enough is enough, and I believe it will drive me crazy before we get to California."

The gold seekers adopted various phrases, some of them funny and some of them foolish, and made a fetish of them. "Have you seen the elephant?" was one of them. Another string of words, evidently without any relation to anything, ran this way:

> Chicken in the bread tray,
> Scratching up the dough.
> Granny, will your dog bite?
> No, child, no!

Besides singing *Oh, Susannah* and playing accordions and banjos the chief diversion of these pioneers was card playing. As soon as the day's journey was over the cards came out. They played seven-up, as a rule, varied now and then by a session of poker. The playing was invariably for money stakes; no gold seeker would think for a moment of playing just for amusement.

> *May 29th.* What a day this has been! We crossed the South Platte, and were in a nervous strain all day for fear that we would lose a man or a wagon. The stream is three thousand feet wide, but it is not deep; not more than three feet deep except in a few places. But the current is as swift as a mill race and there are unexpected beds of quicksand. Upon our arrival on the south side of the river about noon we found a lot of other trains or "caravans" waiting to cross. About fifty wagons in all. We went at it cautiously, a wagon at a time, with Cullen and two other men riding by the wagon, prepared to help. Our party came through all right, except for the water getting into the wagon and ruining about a third of our flour.

Another caravan, strangers to us, had the misfortune to lose a wagon but saved some of the mules, though not all. The men escaped, too. The wagon turned over in midstream and was swept downstream by the current.

On June 7 they reached Fort Laramie and stayed there resting for two days. The plain around the fort was white with tents and wagons. The epidemic of cholera that had begun along the Mississippi during the spring of that year had reached this point in Wyoming.[9] About a dozen cases were reported at Laramie when the Cullen train arrived. John Cullen set up his camp for the fifteen wagons about half a mile from the main body of emigrants. Then he visited each wagon and gave positive orders that no water was to be drunk until it had been boiled, and all food of every description was to be wrapped in cloth until people were ready to eat it.

No one in the train was sick, but Andy Gordon records the relief they all felt when they got away from Laramie. They had remained there two days to have some repairs made to three of the wagons, and also to obtain the leather to make "boots" for the cattle.

June 12th. As the trail gets rougher we encounter piles of things that people have thrown away to lighten their loads. This was a day of scenes of abandoned property; stoves, blacksmith tools, mattresses, cooking utensils, and provisions of every kind strung along the road. There was also an abandoned wagon with broken axles. We have been seeing dead animals from the first day, but today we saw three dead mules and an ox lying by the side of the road.

Out of a spirit of malice those who had to abandon provisions often rendered them useless. Sugar had turpentine poured over it; flour was scattered over the ground, and clothes were torn to pieces. Here and there, as an exception, foodstuffs were left in good order with a message fastened on the pile telling the finder to help himself.

News for the public was sometimes attached to boards

[9] During that period of our history epidemics of Asiatic cholera occurred frequently in various parts of the country. Their cause is still obscure but in all probability this dread disease developed from contaminated water, spoiled food, lack of sewage and general uncleanliness. There is no doubt that it was carried by flies alighting on food.

and set up in a prominent place. One such message read: "The water here is poison, and we have lost six cattle. Do not let your cattle drink from this creek."

6

At Pocatello in Idaho—on July 6—the trail turned to the southwest and ten days later the caravan entered Nevada. Besides the Cullen procession of fifteen wagons there were four other trains altogether, or forty-seven wagons in all.[10] In Gordon's diary we read of the death of a little girl, one of the three Jackson children who were going across with their parents. Gordon wrote, "We never knew what was the matter with her—a little four-year-old—as there was no doctor in the expedition. She had cramps, with chills. Her skin turned kind of bluish, then she became unconscious and passed away. A grave was dug by the side of the trail and Tommy Plunkett painted her name and the date of her death on a board which was set up at her grave. She was buried with no more ceremony than a prayer by Mr. Cullen. I shall never forget her mother's face as she looked back from the next rise and saw the lonely little grave on the prairie."

They saw several droves of buffalo pass from time to time during the long weeks, but they never had any luck in killing one, although they rode after them and tried to bring one down. But they did kill prairie dogs and Jake Birdsall's prairie dog broth became famous. "It tasted like the finest turtle soup," Gordon wrote, "but I supposed that was because we had not had any fresh meat in such a long time."

Occasionally they encountered bands of Indians who seemed friendly. Sometimes they exchanged small articles for Indian trinkets. Every night they took precautions, however, against an Indian attack by forming a square of all the wagons, more than forty of them, with the people in the center. In this enclosure there was not enough room for the cattle, and they were tied outside the square in a corral formed of ropes. Six men were detailed each night to guard

[10] From records kept at Fort Laramie it has been estimated that eight thousand wagons, eighty thousand draft animals and thirty thousand people passed westward over the trail in 1849.

the wagons and the cattle. The cattle were in some danger from wolves, but when they appeared the guards always drove them off by firing a few shots.

A rainy night was a time of general misery. No cooking could be done, and everything got soaking wet, including the bed-clothes. The whole outfit sat in their cluttered wagons and played cards amid the pervading gloom. Andy Gordon was not much of a card player so, with a lantern for illumination, he would write in his diary and reflect on the general stupidity of the human race.

> *July 12th.* My feet are soaking wet, and water is running down my back. It began to rain about noon, and it is still pouring at ten o'clock tonight. I am sitting in the wagon on a cracker box while Mat, Jake, Tommy and Gus Thorpe, from another outfit, are playing seven-up on the wagon floor. The rain pelting on the cloth top just over my head sounds like buck shot.
>
> I wish I could never hear the word *lousy* again. I am willing to bet that Tommy Plunkett uses it fifty times a day, but he is no worse than the others. It is "lousy" this and "lousy" that. The rain is lousy, the trail is lousy, the bacon is lousy, some of the drivers are lousy, and Gus Thorpe, losing in the card game, has just said that he has had a lousy deal.[11]
>
> Sometimes I think that I am going on a long journey with a traveling insane asylum, and that I am crazy myself. The thought of California—still far away—makes me want to puke. Every day we meet some outfit that has seen the elephant and is going home. They say almost anybody can scrape up eight or nine dollars worth of gold a day out there, but it costs more than that to live. Flour, they say, sells for a dollar a pound and everything else in proportion. And to get that little daily dab of gold you have to stand in cold water up to your knees about ten hours a day sifting sand and pebbles. What a life! There are no respectable women there and only a few of the other kind. Just men who are usually drunk or quarrelsome. A drink of whiskey costs from seventy-five cents to a dollar.
>
> But our fellows disregard all that. We are sure to have better luck, they say. Well, I am in for it and there can be no backing out now.

The rainy days were cheerless, but when the sun shone the air was like crystal and they could see the mountains a hundred miles away.

[11] The use of the word "lousy" as a slang term began during the 1849 gold rush.

Their outfit, by following the Wyoming-Idaho route, avoided most of the desert lands, but there was no way to get around the Humboldt Desert of Nevada, which runs from Winnemucca southwest nearly to Carson City. They reached the northern edge of it on August 12.

It is an alkali desert and is as forbidding a piece of barren soil as one is likely to find anywhere. On its eastern border is the Humboldt River; on the west the desert extends to the mountains. The soil is alkaline, and the alkali dust, fine as flour, is in the air. Tall grass grows along the banks of the river. It was cut by the gold seekers and used as feed for the animals.

August 20th. I hardly know whether I am alive or dead. All day in a blazing heat, with the air so hot that in moving my hand through it I feel as if I were thrusting it into the hot air over a bed of coals. The oxen stagger along, with their tongues hanging out. I mean our six oxen do, but the beasts of some of the other wagons have simply laid down to die. In such cases we cannot wait; we cut them from their traces and leave them lying there.

Our barrel of water helps. The river water can be drunk when it is flowing—in small quantities—but it is dangerous (I may say deadly) after it stands awhile. Why, I can't say. We have vinegar to pour down the throats of the cattle when they show signs of being alkalied; it does help.

Tommy and I spent several hours today cutting grass on the river bank for our oxen. It grows in water about twelve inches deep, and we were covered with mire in a short time.

Everybody is going around half-naked on account of the heat. Even old Mrs. Gowdy. She shed her outer garments and appeared in her petticoat. "I'm going around in my shimmy tail," she called out, "and it's cooler." Later on, when we stopped for nooning and to eat a little, I saw her grandson throwing buckets of river water over her. He threw it over while she wore her underclothes, so the old gal must have been soaking wet for hours.

All through the caravan there are high-tempered quarrels and threats and arguments. The weather is the reason, I suppose. But we four get along fine together. Jake Birdsall—God bless him—gets more helpful and sympathetic when trouble comes. He seems to be at his best when things are at their worst.

I heard one man threaten to kill his partner today because the partner was laughing at him trying to take off his shirt which was a tight fit and was stuck to his body by sweat.

> It is difficult to make much progress in the deep, soft sand. It is like fine dust. The cattle are in it up to their knees and we are constantly called on to put our shoulders to the wheel and help push the wagons out. But not for our own shebang, for our cattle are pulling only a light load now.

The Cullen train of fifteen wagons got through the desert all right, with the loss of only one man, six oxen and a mule. Daniel Faulkner, a thin and cadaverous gentleman, died on the way. He was about fifty years old, had been a lawyer in New Jersey for many years, and had gone on the expedition in search of health. He thought the fresh air would do him good. Andy Gordon wrote, "We buried Faulkner near the river's edge today. He had never done any work on the journey but lay all day in his wagon reading books. I think he had something the matter with his lungs, for he coughed most of the time. Maybe the alkali dust was too much for him."

The trail ran through Carson and south of Lake Tahoe. After two days' rest at Ragtown on the Carson River they began the mountainous ascent leading to the pass across the Sierra Nevada. There was a feeling of gaiety in the expedition, with a great deal of shouting and laughter. They were nearing the end of their long trail, though the road up to the pass was incredibly bad. The wagons ran right on the edge of deep chasms. Now and then boulders were found lying in the road; they had fallen from the heights. These obstructions had to be lifted out of the way before the wagons could proceed. In some places the ascent was so steep that double teams were hitched to the wagons and they were pulled up one at a time.

Eventually they reached the top of the pass, more than nine thousand feet above the level of the sea. They could see for many miles and the whole green world of California lay before them. The members of the expedition gathered and stood awhile in silence, staring across the land. Then a spontaneous cheer arose; it rang and echoed among the mountains. "California, here we come!"

John Cullen, the leader, shouted, "It's all downhill from now on, boys. No more climbing!"

As the dusty, tattered procession began to move down the pass Andy Gordon wrote in his diary, "We have been just four months and fifteen days on the way. When I look back over the trip it seems to me that we left St. Joseph four years ago instead of four months ago."

7

Most gold seekers from the East were surprised when they learned upon their arrival in California that the soil of the entire state was not gold-bearing. As a matter of fact, the gold fields altogether were less than one-fifth of the total area. To get a general idea of their location take a map of California and with a pencil begin, about seventy-five miles north of Lake Tahoe, on the state's eastern border, a line which runs westward to Red Bluff; then draw the line toward the southeast past Yuba City and Sacramento. After passing Sacramento incline the line still more toward the east and run in through Stockton to Madera. From that point draw the line straight eastward to the Nevada border. The territory enclosed within the line includes nearly all the gold-bearing region of California. The rest of the state consists of land devoted to cattle raising, agriculture, fruit growing and forestry.

All the gold in the early days—in '49 and '50—came from placer mining, which means mining on the surface or in shallow pits, or sifting gold from the beds of streams. Compared to the great amount of the precious metal underground this surface gold was almost insignificant in quantity, but the gold in the underground lodes could be reached only by sinking deep shafts, driving tunnels into the sides of mountains, and using expensive rock-crushing machinery. There was none of that in California in 1849; the machinery and the mining corporations came later.

The early gold seekers, who called themselves miners but were not miners at all within the real meaning of the word, may be compared to little boys who run after a fruit peddler's wagon and pick up from the ground the apples and plums that have fallen to the ground. If the gold production of the West had been limited to placer mining it would have come to an end in a few years.

In placer mining the gold was found in tiny nuggets of the pure metal, about the size of the grains of sand or even smaller, but an occasional find weighed two or three ounces. The most likely places for finding these morsels of gold were the beds of streams, but they existed also in dry ground.

A miner, working in a brook or creek, would go into the water barefoot, with his trousers rolled above his knees and his sleeves up to his shoulders. He would carry a wooden bucket or a similar receptacle. He would then scoop up the sand and gravel from the bed of the stream. The gold, if there were any, might be seen as tiny yellow specks or grains in the sand. The problem then was to separate the gold from its sandy environment. There were various ways of accomplishing that. One was a washing process. The sand, being lighter than the gold, could be washed away if the bucket were filled with water and shaken constantly so that the particles of gold would drop to the bottom; then the water and sand might be poured off. Another method involved the use of a cradle made for the purpose. By rocking the sand and gold were separated. There was much waste to gold in this work of separation, for some of the gold dust would always be washed away with the sand.

In quartz mining the method was altogether different. Where a lode of gold-bearing ore was found it was followed by means of shafts and tunnels which sometimes ran far underground. The ore was brought to the surface and crushed in gigantic rock-crushing machines, then the gold was separated by machinery which washed away the powdered rock and left the gold. The Forty-niners were not equipped for operations of this character. They were placer miners, merely scratching the surface.

After they had come down the pass into California the Birdsall outfit made its way to Sacramento, not for any particular reason, but because they did not know where else to go. Sacramento was then a wild and noisy village of the roughest character, filled with adventurers. There the Birdsalls sold their team. To their astonishment the oxen brought one hundred and fifty dollars apiece, and for the covered wagon, rickety and almost falling apart, they got one hundred dollars. In Memphis it would not have fetched more than fifteen dollars.

With all this money in hand they decided to see San Francisco before searching for gold, so they took passage on the river steamer that ran between San Francisco and Sacramento. They stayed in that incredible community only three days. In his diary Andy Gordon says:

September 24th. We got to S.F. yesterday, and have been on the go ever since. I wish I could describe the place, but I just can't do it, for it would take a whole book and more talent for writing than I have.

This town was built for eight hundred people, and now it has ten thousand. We stayed last night at the Parker House, which is called a hotel, but I would call it a shanty. It is small, having room for about a dozen people, if all the space is used. Last night four men slept in the small room we occupied on bunks put up one above the other. We paid ten dollars apiece. That means the proprietor got forty dollars for the rent of that room for one night. I mentioned it to one of the guests when we were washing our faces this morning, and he said the proprietor rents the hotel building from its owner and pays $15,000 a year for it—about $300 a week. That may not be the exact figures, but God knows even one-tenth of that amount would be high. I think we are all wrong on this gold-mining business. We ought to go into real estate. There's where the money lies. This hotel building could be put up for five thousand dollars; it is a wooden shanty. Are we all crazy?

The town is packed with red-shirted men, and all of them seem to be in a hurry, yet I don't think they are going anywhere. They yell at each other and laugh and shake hands. The gambling houses and saloons are the principal features of the place.

The houses are built of logs, rough slabs, and canvas. The streets are mud holes.

We wanted to have our clothes washed while we were here, but have struck a snag. Two Chinese have a laundry. They charge a dollar and a half for washing and ironing a shirt. We were willing to pay that, but they said they had so much work ahead that we would have to wait two weeks to get our shirts back. Then we heard of some Irishwomen who run laundries. We made the rounds and saw all of them—three or four. They don't call themselves washer-women, but "Clothing Refreshers." It was a dollar and a half apiece with them, too, but they said they were a month behind. So I guess we will have no laundry done here.

Some of the men who live here send their clothes to Hawaii to be washed. They get them back in eight weeks, and the cost is much less than here in S.F.

In San Francisco harbor there were at one time in that year of 1849 no less than four hundred ships that had been deserted by their crews who had gone to the gold fields. The whole community was hysterical and half-mad during that period—say from 1848 to 1853, when it began to regain its senses. Everybody expected confidently to be rich, and at any instant.

The fellow guest whom the Birdsalls had met casually at the hotel wash trough was a companionable person, and they became very friendly with him. He was a storekeeper of Marysville, a gold diggers' shanty town about fifty miles north of Sacramento, and he had come down to San Francisco to buy goods for his store. His name was Solomon Jackson Nathan, but his manner was far more cheerful than his solemn name would seem to indicate. According to Andy Gordon's diary Sol Nathan had a peculiar philosophy. He believed that the accidental was the governing principle of life; that the greater part of human effort was invariably wasted; that no man could shape his own career, no matter how intelligent he might be. To support his ideas he had many ingenious arguments, and he liked to put them in words. The Birdsall outfit was not much interested in his philosophical speculations and they managed usually to get him to talking about California. He knew more about the state, its gold fields, its people, its customs and manners, than any person they had met. Sol called himself an "old-timer," as he had been in California three years.

He had been a placer miner, which he declared to be a fool's game. "Now, don't let me persuade you fellows to drop your idea of looking for gold in the creeks, the hills, the highways and byways. That's what you came out here to do, and you'll never be satisfied until you give it a trial. Go to it—I say—until you get good and sick of it."

"Well, Sol," said Jake Birdsall over his glass of whisky, "we hear every day of fellows striking a rich vein and making a big haul. Why couldn't that happen to us?"

"It could," Sol replied, "but the chances that it won't

happen are about five hundred to one. I don't know how many men are trying to find gold in this State of California, but I'd say there are at least one hundred thousand. And how many of them actually and truly dig up a fortune? Very few, lemme tell you—maybe three or four hundred have got rich. The rest just make a living and lots can't even do that."

"We saw a man in Sacramento when we were on our way here," said Tommy Plunkett, "who was a tenderfoot, or rawheel, or whatever you call 'em, who struck a pocket of gold before he had been at work a week. It's no lie, either, for he had the gold with him—worth $12,000—and was going that very day to sell it to the mint. We saw it."

"I can well believe it," Sol Nathan agreed. "Up in Marysville where I live a sailor—he'd run away from his ship, I suppose—drifted into the camp and said he wanted to find a good place to dig for gold, but didn't know how to go about it.

"Well, some loafers in Conner's barroom, next door to my store, thought they'd play a joke on him. They pointed out a barren hillside, as dry as a bone, and told him to dig into it and he'd probably strike pay dirt. He bought a shovel and a pick from me and started in, working like a beaver. Well, believe it or not, within three weeks he had taken out $27,000 worth of nuggets, and had exhausted the vein or pocket."

"There you are," Mat Gordon exclaimed. "That's why we want to try our luck."

"I haven't finished the story," said Mr. Nathan. "When I left Marysville about a hundred men were digging into that hillside—in fact, they were tearing down the hill—and not one of them had found a pennyworth of the precious metal. So you see how it is. But go ahead and try it. Don't let me throw cold water on the project."

All four of them accompanied Mr. Nathan back to Marysville, as he had told them that the region was rich in ore. "Yet you say we won't find anything," Birdsall argued, "so what——"

"I didn't say that," Sol replied, "I said the chances are about five hundred to one against you making a big strike. It's just a matter of figures—statistics—but I'm sure all of you can make a living at it. Almost anybody who is willing to work hard can pick up enough splinters of gold to pay his living expenses."

"Well, Mr. Nathan," Mat Gordon asked, "what's the best way to make money out here? Tell us that."

"Why," Sol replied. "Sell something. Sell anything from clothes to barroom liquor. Sell houses, jewelry, tobacco—anything but books. You can put the prices way up, because your customers all believe they're going to be as rich as Midas in a couple of months, so what's the use of haggling over the prices of shopkeepers."

"I've been paying a dollar a drink for plain liquor since I've been here," Mat said. "I never thought that would ever happen to me in this world."

Marysville was a characteristic town of that period. Everybody in it appeared to be a stranger to everybody else; there was no background of solid, respectable citizens who had lived there for a generation or so. The state was still under a nominal military rule, for civil government had not yet been established, but the military government had been completely swamped by the influx of gold seekers, and every community governed itself. In Marysville the men had elected a "judge" who tried cases, summoned juries and pronounced sentences which were carried out at once. Stealing was considered a more hideous crime than murder, and a man guilty of thievery was hanged at once to a tree, but murderers often escaped even a trial. In such cases everyone said, "They had a quarrel and one of them shot the other. They're strangers to all of us. It's not our row; it was their own affair."

It was back-breaking labor—the job of standing in cold water all day and sifting pails of sand—and the Birdsall outfit was sick of it before the first week had run its course. All except Jake Birdsall himself, who seemed to love the work and sang all day. In the first six days they had altogether sifted out seventeen ounces of gold dust, worth about three hundred dollars, or seventy-five dollars apiece. About half of that came from Mat Gordon's work; he had had good luck. From talking with other men on the spot they got an idea that their seventy-five dollars apiece was about the average return.

8

Within three months the Birdsall outfit dissolved partnership and the four of them went their separate ways.

The reader may be interested in learning what became of them. The most successful among them was Matthew Gordon. He went to San Francisco, became a clerk in a law office, and applied himself diligently to study. "This territory—which will become a state before long," he wrote home, "is going to be a lawyer's paradise in a few years. There is hardly a land title in the whole section that is perfect, and even when one is all right a shrewd lawyer can stir up doubts and get somebody to sue and compromise."

With these sentiments he went on his way, and in time he became one of the most distinguished lawyers on the Pacific Coast, and the head of a renowned law firm. He had managed in the course of his lifetime to stir up an immense amount of strife concerning property. When he died, around the turn of the century, his funeral was attended by the great and the near great, the witty and the learned, all of whom mourned his passing.

His brother Andrew went into the real estate business in San Francisco. He had the vision to get control of land then lying outside the town limits, but now in the city. He died long ago, but his descendants are flourishing.

Tommy Plunkett went back home by sea (Panama) in 1850. He was well-to-do, or his father was, and he did not bother much about work. When the Civil War came on he entered the Confederate service and rose to be a colonel. He died gallantly at the battle of Gettysburg while leading his regiment in a charge.

Jake Birdsall continued his mining ventures for several years, moving from one place to another. Then he married a restaurant cook and opened an eating place in Stockton. The venture failed, and he and his wife moved to Berkeley. There he became a custodian of one of the college buildings. He was a well-known figure around the campus for years—a placid, white-bearded old fellow, full of anecdotes and quiet laughter.

Chapter IX

CHICAGO—THE YOUNG GIANT

I

FOR ABOUT four decades of the last century—from 1840 until well into the 1880's—Chicago grew more rapidly in population and in commercial importance than any other community in the world. It was like a hearty lad who outgrows his clothes before he has had time to get used to them. One strange feature of this button-bursting expansion is that the site of Chicago was about the last place along the shore of Lake Michigan where one might reasonably expect the birth of a metropolis. The town stood at the mouth of the Chicago River, which at that time was too shallow for navigation. The land was low, wet and malarial. The ground on which the city's principal business section stands—now known as the Loop—was a marsh only a few inches higher than the level of the lake.

In 1837 the Illinois legislature had incorporated the community as a city under the name of Chicago, an Anglicized Indian word supposed to mean the smell of wild onions. But there is some doubt over the meaning. In the speech of the Pottawottomies there is a word that sounds as if it might be spelled *chickagou*. It is said to mean "stench," but linguists skilled in Indian lore assert that an almost identical word in the Chippewa idiom means "apple blossoms." So you may take your choice, though it is a matter of small importance.

Its name in popular speech was Slab Town, and so it was known far and wide. It was called Slab Town because every house in the community was a hastily flung-together, boxlike structure of boards or split logs. Besides Chicago and Slab Town the place had still another name, evolved from the experiences of strangers who had unwittingly tried to dash across a street in rainy weather. By them it was called the Mud Hole of the Prairies, a descriptive term that was devised to convey a sense of opprobrium and disapproval. But it failed completely to have any effect on the inhabitants of Slab Town, for they were as accustomed to mud as a bird is to the air.

The new little city had a population of about 4,000, made up chiefly of fur traders, grain buyers, wagoners, blacksmiths, gamblers and shopkeepers—as well as a lot of idle adventurers, ready for anything except hard work. In manner or deportment its residents were like those of the other new towns of the Middle West. They drank their tumblers of raw whisky, gambled excessively, danced all night, whooped and yelled and fired guns and pistols frequently, with or without adequate incentive. Murders occurred too often to attract much attention.

But neither mud nor murders held Chicago down. In 1857, twenty years after its incorporation, the city had 93,000 inhabitants and newcomers were still arriving in an unbroken stream. It had ten first-class hotels—among them the Tremont, a four-story brick structure—besides forty-odd hostelries of lower degree. There were a dozen banks, forty newspapers and periodicals of various kinds, and fifteen hundred business establishments. It was the terminus of eleven trunk line railroads, and more than one hundred trains arrived or departed every day.

It was no longer called Slab Town but the derisive name of Mud Hole of the Prairies still remained. After every rain the black prairie soil became a vast mud puddle, with shallow ponds of muddy water standing in the streets.

In 1855 engineers and drainage experts who had studied the situation concluded that the only practicable solution was to raise the whole area twelve feet above the level of the lake by covering it with fresh soil.

It was a prodigious undertaking, and Chicago tackled it with the energy of muscular youth. Two square miles of land—streets, gardens, lawns and backyards—were eventually covered with earth sucked up from the bed of the river, for a channel-deepening job was going on at the same time. It was a task beset by extraordinary difficulties. For one thing, street traffic had to go on while the streets were being lifted. Thousands of buildings had to be brought up to the street level.

The Tremont Hotel, built of brick, was the largest building in the city. It was nearly two hundred feet long and four stories tall. Engineers thought this huge structure could be lifted, but they thought it would cause so many cracks, fissures, floors askew, tilted ceilings and doors out of line with their frames, that, after the job was over, the hotel would have to be almost wholly rebuilt. While the owners of the Tremont were wondering what to do the street in front of the hotel had been raised and when guests arrived they walked down a flight of wooden steps to the hotel office.

The proprietors of the hotel were about ready to tear down the building when a young man of twenty-seven—named George M. Pullman—appeared on the scene. He was a building contractor from the East, where he had heard of the Tremont and the problem of raising it. After looking over the structure he declared that he could lift it without disturbing a teaspoon in a coffee cup or breaking even one pane of glass. In desperation they gave him the contract. He employed twelve hundred workmen and used five thousand jackscrews placed at regular intervals in the basement of the hotel. Upon a signal every workman gave the lever of a set of jackscrews half a turn. The enormously heavy building rose, an inch at a time, to the street level. There was no damage done and none of the guests was disturbed by the operation.

George M. Pullman remained in Chicago. His name is world-famous; he was the creator of the Pullman sleeping car.

"Its streets were mud sloughs, its sidewalks a series of more or less rotten planks," wrote Charles Dudley Warner, in his remembrances of Chicago, where he had lived and practiced law until 1860. "Half the town was in process of elevation above the tadpole level and a considerable part on wheels—a moving house being about the only wheeled vehicle that could get around with any comfort to the passengers."

Nothing could stop the rushing progress of the wonder city of the Midwest. By 1870 its population had grown up to 300,000. Farms on the prairie were surrounded and swallowed by the advancing city, and poor farmers, to their own amazement, found themselves rich from the sale of their land. As a meat-packing center Chicago had passed Cincinnati. Seventeen huge grain elevators, with a capacity of twelve million bushels, raised their tall heads alongside the freight yards. Chicago wholesale houses had become the largest of their kind, and their salesmen were to be found traveling all over the Western states, selling goods to a legion of retail merchants.

Stone sidewalks had been laid in the downtown business section, but the rest of the city—even in the wealthy districts—still tripped along on planks. A huge sewage system had been established; it had only one serious fault—it wouldn't work. On the lake shore rose the palatial homes of the new-rich; some of them were marble palaces. Along the Chicago River, and north, west and south were the homes of the laboring poor; some of them were muddy hovels, made of rough boards.

The city was always full of strangers who had come to better their fortunes, or to escape the consequence of their misdeeds, or to avoid their creditors. But there were also many decent workmen who hoped to obtain work in a railroad shop or an industrial plant, for Chicago employers were said to pay higher wages than those prevailing in the East. The boisterous city of glamour and mud, easy fortunes and loose spending, also attracted a swarm of gamblers and plausible swindlers.

Young men who were just beginning their careers, or who had not been able to find a place for themselves at home, were probably the most numerous of all the newcomers.

2

One of these young men was Jeff Martin, who arrived in Chicago in the fall of 1871, having come from his home town of Annapolis, Maryland.

As he stepped out of the murky and smoke-blackened train shed into the bright sunlight he looked like a coal-heaver who had neglected to wash up at the end of the day's work. His face and hands were streaked with smoke and dust; his high-standing linen collar was wrinkled and smutty and his light-brown suit was disheveled. He had been two nights on the road, but he had not gone to bed at all, for he distrusted the new-fangled sleeping-car attached to the train.

He carried—and this was a deep secret—the sum of three thousand dollars in a money belt around his waist. The Pullman palace car, as they called the sleeper, was fixed up in a sort of luxurious fashion, with its carved and painted wood, its mirrors and its polished metal ware. Even the cuspidors by the side of each berth shone like gold. The big stove in the middle of the car, used for heating in cold weather, gleamed with the polish that had been rubbed on it. The oil lamps in the ceiling seemed to be made of silver.[1]

But there was no way of locking up anything. The passengers undressed and slept in public, so to speak, with nothing between a sleeping passenger and any Tom, Dick and Harry but a flimsy curtain. Jeff Martin was a sound sleeper, and he took that into account. What was there to prevent a thief among the passengers from pulling aside the curtain, unhooking his money belt, slipping it out gently and walking off with it?

No, he decided not to take the risk, so he told the man in the white jacket that he would ride in a day coach. After seeing the inside of a sleeper he wondered how many persons, in the course of a year, had missed watches, jewelry and pocketbooks after having spent the night in such a trap.

Jeff sat up two nights in the dingy, tobacco-smelling smoking car. Occasionally he would curl up on the seat and take a nap, but he felt that the money belt was safe, for a thief would have to take off most of his clothes to get to it. Moreover, he had in a coat pocket a six-chambered revolver, fully loaded. There was nothing exceptional about that; in those days men went armed as a matter of course. Firearms were not licensed; there was no restriction against owning them.

[1] The first two Pullman cars were remodeled Chicago and Alton day coaches. They were put into service in 1858, but sleeping cars of a primitive kind had been in use for more than twenty years before George M. Pullman entered the field. These early cars, before Pullman's time, were ordinary day coaches with the bunks built into one side of the car. The day seats were on the other side opposite the bunks. The bunks had rough mattresses and no sheets, blankets or pillows, or curtains. Passengers slept on them fully dressed.

The Pullman cars were much more comfortable than the sleepers then in use. They had larger bunks, fully equipped with bed clothes, and at each end of the car there was a washroom. The bunks could be swung out of the way in the daytime.

For several years after they were put into service the cars were poorly patronized. In 1870 less than a hundred Pullmans were in use on all the railroads. Most women of the time thought the cars promoted indecency by putting men and women in such close proximity while undressed. Ladies who used the cars in those early days slept, as a rule, with all their clothes on. It was also a prevalent notion of the 1860's and 1870's among business men that the Pullmans were snobbish devices that should be shunned by regular, red-blooded he-men.

The three thousand dollars that he had in his money belt was an unexpected inheritance from a rheumatic and querulous old maiden aunt to whom he had been kind and attentive.

He had reached the age of thirty-two and was vividly conscious that his life was a failure. He had tried hard, but for one reason or another, he had never made a success of anything. His first job was as a newspaper reporter in Baltimore. He was sent out every day to report on this and that—such happenings as street fights, burglaries, marital wrangles and political meetings. Now and then he interviewed such distinguished visitors as senators, authors and prizefighters. The stories he wrote were dull and commonplace. The editor told him, not once but many times, to "put life in the stuff" and "play them up." But how could he do it when the people he wrote about were either dull or pompous or silly, or inveterate liars? He wanted to be a reporter of facts—not of fiction.

The Civil War was then going on and Jeff Martin was drafted. When he reached the camp the medical examiner rejected him because he walked with a slight limp and his hearing was not perfect. He went back to Baltimore to resume his newspaper work but the editor told him coldly that they had taken on a new man in his place and there was nothing for him to do.

He found a job as a collector of rents. Day after day he went on his rounds, like a postman, taking in money and making out receipts. That occupation did not last long. He sympathized too deeply with tenants in hard luck and accepted too readily their excuses for not having the rent money at hand.

He was out of work for several months; then he got a place as a bartender in a hotel. He was almost a teetotaler himself; he would take a drink now and then but never enough to make him the least bit tipsy. It was this moderation that got the job for him. For a few months, while he was getting used to his duties and learning the names and faces of his regular customers he had little to say. But when he had once settled down in his post as bartender he talked a great deal about the evils of intemperance. "Liquor is all right in its place," he would say, "but a little of it goes a long way." If a customer began to talk loud, or stagger, or sing, Jeff would refuse to serve him, and now and then he would order a customer to leave the bar. Some of his stories, told in the course of an evening, were about families ruined by their breadwinners taking to drink. He discoursed also on murderers, thieves and tramps who had been led into their evil ways by the liquor habit.

The manager of the hotel seldom went into the bar, and he was startled one day when a guest said to him, "You have in this house right now one of the best temperance lecturers in the United States."

The manager was greatly pleased. "Is that so? It's strange that I haven't heard of his arrival. We'll have to show him some special attention, as we do in the case of all distinguished guests. What's his name and when does he give his lecture?"

"I don't know his name," said the guest, "but I'm sure you do. He's your bartender and he lectures on temperance several times in the course of an evening."

Within twenty-four hours Jeff Martin was fired.

After that he had a series of jobs. He was an insurance agent; a solicitor for magazine subscriptions and a clerk in the office of a Baltimore gas company. He did not make good at any of them, but he did not know exactly why.

After he had lost his position with the gas company he went back to Annapolis and got a job as salesman, handy man and general, all-around, white-collar slave in a dingy furniture store. The owner of the establishment had a local reputation for being the stingiest man in Maryland. Martin's salary barely paid for his food and clothes, both of which were of inferior quality. He lived rent free in a room over the store and cooked his own meals. On Sunday he visited his aunt, who lived three miles in the country, and always walked there and back.

His boss spent nearly all his time in a dingy little office at the back of the store. He was an usurious money lender as well as a furniture dealer, and when he was not listening to the hard-luck stories of borrowers he was making entries in a ledger or carrying on intricate calculations on a pad of paper. He seldom gave any instructions to Jeff Martin, and apparently did not care anything about the store.

By this time, as a result of his experiences, Jeff's mentality was permeated by defeat as a sponge is permeated by water. It was vanity in reverse. It is well-known that, in the case of vain people, their good opinion of themselves often runs far ahead of their accomplishments, but it is not so well-known that defeated people frequently think less of themselves and their own capacities than the facts warrant. It was so in the case of Jeff Martin. He had an excellent mind, and his bad judgment—which was the cause of all his troubles—was being slowly corrected by experience.

In the unspoken depth of his mind was an ardent, almost overpowering, desire to get away from Annapolis, from Baltimore, from Maryland altogether, and to begin a new life somewhere else, in a new world among strangers. For two or three years he had thought of going to Chicago to stay. That fast-growing, vigorous town was on everybody's tongue; it was in the news every day. But he could not go there without some money, even if it were only enough to keep him alive for a few weeks while he got his feet on the ground. As he never had enough to pay his railroad fare, to say nothing of supporting himself while he looked around, he finally gave up the idea as a foolish dream.

Then, all of a sudden, everything was changed. Auntie Charlotte's three thousand dollars, in the form of a check, was handed to him by a lawyer as casually as one gives a dime to a beggar; by a lawyer who shook hands, said "Good-by," and turned immediately to something else. When he left the lawyer's office the street seemed to look better than it had before, the sun shone brightly, the leaves of the trees seemed greener, and he thought for a moment that he heard bands playing and sweet voices in song. But they were only bands and voices of the mind. He carried the lawyer's check across the street to the bank, for he wanted cash. The thin paper check did not feel like money. He said to the teller that he wanted three hundred ten-dollar bills. The teller, a young, stuck-up sprout in a high collar, looked the check over carefully, turning it this way and that. Then he took it to an older man sitting at a desk. After they had both studied it awhile the teller came back to the window and counted out three hundred bills, shoved them at Jeff without saying a word and began to make an entry in a book.

3

A hack driver who saw Jeff lugging his valise out of the Chicago railroad shed said, "Hack, sir?" and when Jeff hesitated he seized the valise and put it in his hack, a rather battered vehicle. He was an old man with an Irish face. A fringe of white hair stood out under his tall hat. "Where do you want to go?" he inquired and Jeff told him that he was bound for the Briggs House and added, "Is it far?" He knew nothing about the Briggs hostelry except what he had read, and that was not much. It was reputed to be the largest hotel west of the Alleghenies, and it had been the headquarters of Abraham Lincoln during the Presidential campaign of 1860. The hackman said it was quite a trip from the station to the Briggs House and he would have to charge a dollar. The idea of paying a dollar for a hack seemed to Jeff to be outrageous. He said he would walk and reached inside the hack for his valise. After some argument the driver reduced his charge to seventy-five cents. Jeff climbed into the back seat and said he hoped the driver had no hard feelings because of the squabble over the fare. "Not a bit," the jolly old Irishman exclaimed. "I'd 'a done the same thing, by Jasus, if I'd 'a been in your place. But ye can be sure I wudna come down if I hadn't liked yer face."

Jeff was sadly disappointed in the appearance of Chicago, or of as much of it as he could see from the hack. The city blocks were a hodgepodge of wooden and brick buildings, huddled together without harmony or design. Most of the wooden houses were unpainted, and they had the sodden appearance that comes from long exposure to the weather. Some of them leaned crazily to one side, or over the street, and looked as if a little push would knock them down.

Modern stores with handsome show windows stood next door to disreputable-looking barrooms. A wind was blowing and the air was full of dust and whirling scraps of paper. The streets and sidewalks were littered and dirty.

It was Sunday morning and church bells were ringing. About a block from the Briggs House there was a large and hand-

(The Bettmann Archive)

A COUNTRY STORE IN THE TIME OF OUR GRANDFATHERS.

(After a woodcut from "A Day with the Country Doctor." By Frank French, 1890.)

some church, built of wood and painted gray. Many groups of people were coming along the street, on their way to the services. Nearly all the men wore tall silk hats and the long, double-breasted frock coats known as Prince Alberts.[2]

In the matter of hair on the masculine face there was much diversity in fashion, but every grown-up male wore either a beard or a mustache. Men without any sort of hairy facial decoration were so rare in the 1870's that people in general looked upon them as curiosities. Jeff Martin had no beard but his mustache stood out, straight and stiff; he waxed it daily.

Leaning over in the hack to get a good view of the people going to church he noticed that the ladies of Chicago dressed exactly like the ladies of Baltimore. The hoopskirt era was over and full skirts with bustles had come into favor. There is always a tendency, everywhere, for women's fashions to become exaggerated, and the bustle era was in that stage of development in the early 1870's. Some of the bustles that Jeff saw on that bright Sunday morning stood out twelve, fifteen or even eighteen inches behind their wearers.

Skirts were long, so long indeed that their hems collected dust and refuse from the pavement. All the ladies wore over-dresses of colored silk. These outside garments were ornamented with embroidered flowers and other decorations.

The hackman pulled up suddenly before the entrance to the hotel. Jeff gave him seventy-five cents and a bellboy took out his valise and carried it through an impressive doorway into a huge lobby. The floor was covered by a dark green carpet, which was speckled, here and there, by cuspidors or "spittoons," as they were called, of some shining metal. On the walls, around the room, were paintings of early Western scenes. Overhead there was a large, wide-spreading chandelier of many lights. The hotel, like most important buildings in Chicago, was lighted by gas. The enormous armchairs, thickly stuffed and too heavy to be moved easily, were covered with a red plush velvet. Besides these monsters there were a few

[2] This garment, a long cylindrical black coat, got its name from Prince Albert, the husband of Queen Victoria. It was very fashionable among men of the upper classes from the 1860's until the first decade of the twentieth century. It went out of style with whiskers, side-burns and beards, though it continued for sometime to be worn by men whose calling in life demands a certain definite sedateness of manner, such as undertakers, ministers, physicians and various public officials.

smaller chairs and some lounge seats placed against the walls.

The hotel office stood almost directly opposite the entrance. The clerk, a young man who wore side-whiskers, gave Jeff a professional smile and placed the hotel register before him. Jeff wrote "T. J. Martin" and paused in reflection. There was no use putting down Annapolis, Maryland, as his home town, for he had left it for good.

The clerk, just to make conversation, said, "Pleasant day, but a little rain wouldn't do any harm." Jeff wrote "Chicago, Ill." after his name and said, "Yes, the hackman that brought me up from the Union Station told me that there'd been no rain in two months. By the way, I had to call him down; the old devil wanted to charge me a dollar to bring me up here from the station. I made him come down to seventy-five cents. I may be a stranger here, but I've got my wits about me and nobody is going to swindle me."

Concealing a giggle as well as he could, the clerk said, "You paid him seventy-five cents? Why, the regular fare is only forty cents."

The gust of anger that came over Jeff kept him from speaking for a moment. All of a sudden he hated the jolly hackman, the smiling clerk behind the desk, the hotel and the city of Chicago. The clerk, looking down at the register with his pen poised, spoke first, "We have some elegant dollar rooms. Without a private bath, but there are two baths on the floor. Then we have some for two dollars—with a bath attached. Which would you prefer, sir?"

Jeff slammed his fist down on the desk. "I want the best you've got. Give me a two-dollar room. In Baltimore all the principal hotels send their buses to meet the trains, and the guests are brought back free. But I suppose you haven't got around to that in this backward neck of the woods."

"Oh, yes," said the clerk blandly, blotting a room number that he had just written in. "Our buses meet all trains. We met the train you came on. The bus got here before you did. If you had taken our bus it would have cost you nothing."

"Are you sure you ain't making up that story? All I can say is that I didn't see it at the station."

"You didn't! I don't understand why you failed to see it," the clerk remarked and stood pondering. "Oh, I know, you left the station by the front entrance. All buses are at the side door." He struck a bell on the desk with the palm of his hand. When a boy came he said, "Show this gentleman to Room 407," and Jeff followed the lad to the elevator. He was as angry as a hornet, though he did not know exactly why, but he got over it when the elevator began to move upward, for he was fascinated by the experience. A whole room moving up and down! He had heard, or read, of elevators, but there was none in Baltimore and he had never seen one before. It went up at a snail's pace, so slowly indeed that it seemed to be hardly moving.

In Room 407 there was a wooden poster bed wide enough for three people, at least. The bathroom was equipped with a large bathtub made of tin or zinc, its sides encased in wood. The gleaming white porcelain tub, so familiar to us today, was unheard of in the 1870's. It did not make its appearance until near the end of the century. The wash basin was also surrounded by a wooden frame which reached down to the floor and concealed the plumbing. The basin was of metal but it was sunk in a wide marble shelf that had plenty of room, right and left, for soap, toilet articles and razors. Just above the basin a cabinet, with a mirror in its door, was fastened to the wall.

The room was steam-heated, but it had a fireplace with a handy little pile of wood, to be used when the steam heat failed, as it was likely to do in those days. A glass chandelier hung down from the center of the ceiling. There were also a small marble-top table placed at the foot of the bed, a heavy-looking bureau with a number of drawers, and two chairs. One of them was a vast, overstuffed, fringed piece of furniture that looked as if it might weigh a ton, but Jeff gave it a shove and it rolled along easily; it was on casters.

A bell rope dangled alongside the door. A card on the wall beside it said, "The attendant on this floor will come when the bell is rung." [3]

[3] Telephones in hotel rooms began to appear late in the 1890's. Until that time the process of ordering anything from downstairs was somewhat complicated. When the guest pulled the bell rope the floor attendant came. He or she was given the order for foods or drinks, or whatever was required. Then the attendant went to a little cubbyhole at the end of one of the halls. It had a speaking

Our wanderer from Maryland took a nap for an hour, with his money belt tucked under his pillow. Then he got up, had a bath, or "washed all over," as he called it, shaved, waxed carefully the points of his mustache, put a touch of bay rum on his curly dark hair, and arrayed himself in fresh clothes from head to foot, for he had brought two suits with him. All that done, he felt like a new man. He did not have a grudge against anybody in the world, and was sorry that he had spoken so angrily to the hotel clerk. Even the petty swindle of the jolly hackman was forgiven: "It has taught me something," he said to himself.

It was about lunch time, he thought, and he made his way downstairs on the slow elevator. Instead of going direct to the dining room he went over to the clerk's desk with the idea of removing the bad impression that young man must have of him.

That was not hard to do; only a little pleasant conversation was needed, if even that, for the clerk was case-hardened to critical, bad-tempered guests and took them as a matter of course. He told Jeff how to find his way about the city and gave him a little pocket map with the streetcar and bus lines on it. Also, in the course of some light reminiscences he informed Jeff that his name was Claude Winter. Before turning away to the dining room Jeff said, "Listen, Claude, I'm looking here in Chicago for an old-time friend. Maybe you've run across him. His name is Henderson—Charlie Henderson; d'you know him?"

Claude Winter reflected a moment, his head thrown back, with his eyes fixed on the ceiling. "No," he said finally, "I can't say I do. What sort of business is he in?"

"That's what I don't know. When I was a reporter on the Baltimore *Sun*—that was twelve or thirteen years ago—Charlie Henderson was an advertising solicitor on that paper. We roomed together and went around together—chums, you know."

The hotel clerk nodded and said, "Yeah, I understand."

"Well, one day Charlie up and said he was sick and tired

---

tube, and the order was spoken to a clerk in the office who attended to such matters. When anyone called on a guest the caller waited in the lobby downstairs until a bellboy went up to the guest's room to announce him.

of Baltimore and was going to Chicago—I mean he was coming here—and when he got here he found a job on the *Tribune*. Advertising department, you know. We exchanged a few letters, back and forth, then one of my letters came back, undelivered. So, that's all. Now, I'd like to look him up."

Claude Winter reached under the desk and produced a thin and battered city directory. "This directory ain't much good," he remarked. "Three years old, and was pretty poor when it was new." He slowly turned the pages. "You see, Chicago grows so fast, and everything changes right before your eyes. New people coming in all the time, and others leaving every day. No, he's not in the book. Some Hendersons, but no Charles."

Next day Jeff went to the office of the *Tribune* and saw the advertising manager, who declared that Charles Henderson had not worked there in his time. "But," he added apologetically, "I've been in Chicago only four years. Maybe we can look him up in the records." That was also without result, for the records of employes ran back only seven years.

Jeff gave up the search temporarily and spent that day and Tuesday in going about the city. Studying his little map, he learned that the Chicago River ran straight east into Lake Michigan, and that about a mile and a quarter inland it was formed by two forks—one coming from the northwest and the other from the southwest—so these waterways had a shape somewhat like that of a capital letter Y, with wide-spreading branches.

The city was divided into three main divisions—North Side and South Side, meaning north or south of the river, and the West Side, which included everything between the two branches of the Y. To Jeff, as he strolled along the streets, the community seemed to be a conglomerate mixture of shanties, office buildings, marble residences, low and filthy dram shops and elegant stores.

The people he passed followed the same pattern. Sedate-looking gentlemen in high silk hats and properly equipped with gloves and canes were elbowed by toughs and street Arabs. Foreigners, with strange speech on their tongues, went back and forth. Almost every male chewed tobacco and spat on the sidewalk. Jeff was not a chewer, but he did not object to anyone else's chewing, which was just as well for his peace of mind, for it was a nation-wide habit, practiced everywhere by both high and low.

He was a smoker, addicted to cigars, and he was surprised at finding some excellent brands in Chicago, sold in clean, well-appointed cigar stores. In those days no store that sold cigars was properly equipped unless it had a wooden statue of an Indian chief to place on the sidewalk beside its front door. As he walked about the town Jeff saw a number of them, and made a mental note of their location, so he would know where to purchase his smokes.[4]

Along the lake front on the North Side were the houses of many wealthy families. Newly rich, having acquired their fortunes in the last twenty-odd years, they had lost the kindly manners of the poor without having acquired the accomplishments of culture and good taste. Pomp, haughtiness and a vulgar display of their possessions constituted their code of etiquette.

Some of the costly, pretentious lake front residences were architectural monstrosities cluttered with turrets, domes, bay windows, cornices, and porte-cocheres. Simplicity was a word left out of the dictionary of the architects who designed these structures. They endeavored to fill every blank space with some ornamental device that would disfigure the façade of the houses.

In that so-called "gilded age" men who had made a great deal of money, by any means whatever, or who were leading figures in an industry, were called "kings" in colloquial speech and in newspaper articles. Chicago was well supplied with kings. Marshall Field was a merchant king; Potter Palmer was a real estate king; William B. Ogden was a railroad king.

[4] These cigar store Indians have completely disappeared, not only in Chicago, but everywhere else. What happened to them? Why were they given up? No one knows exactly why. The abolition of the cigar store Indian resembles the curious changes of fashions—in women's hats, let us say. Everyone knows that, on occasions, women discard the most beautiful and fascinating hats for some misshapen and ugly head covering, and when inquiry is made the answer is that the fashion has changed. Who changes it, and why? The wooden Indian was really an admirable advertising device and there seems to be no sensible reason for getting rid of him.

The decline in tobacco-chewing is more readily explicable. Chewing gum has largely taken the place of the plug of tobacco, though today the tobacco-chewing habit still exists here and there.

George M. Pullman was not yet a king, nor was Cyrus H. McCormick, but they were destined to reach that lofty stature in a few years—Pullman as the palace car king and McCormick as lord and master of the reaper industry.

In its unbounded adoration of wealth, no matter how it might have been acquired, Chicago was not a bit different from the rest of the country. It was an age when success was worshiped, but Success was spelled M-o-n-e-y.

4

In the chief business section of the city—the Loop of today—there was no loitering, no strolling and sauntering. Everybody on the street walked at a pace that suggested search for a doctor to attend a critical case. This habit of hurry did not exist in Baltimore, and Jeff hardly knew what to make of it. But it caught him, too, and after the first twenty-four hours he found himself racing along as if he had an important appointment and was half an hour late. Now and then he would check himself to look at some peculiar building or to gaze in a show window.

On Clark Street, a couple of blocks north of the river, he came upon a three-story establishment that carried across its front a great sign—black lettering on a yellow background—which said, in letters six feet high:

BULLY BARGAIN HOUSE

Between the windows of the ground floor there were smaller signs, each in a frame, in which the current "bully" bargains were announced and described. Everything worn by men was carried by the store, it seemed—suits, shirts, underwear, shoes, hats. Nothing whatever was sold at its full price; the reduction was universal. The entire stock, from socks to overcoats, was called a "bully" bargain. Jeff Martin, standing pensively before this display, wondered how the proprietors of the store managed to eke out an existence with the prices of all their goods cut to rock bottom. "They must be very poor," he thought when he saw a sign which said, "Our loss is your gain." This statement was on a card in a window full of shirts.

In the main window there was a sort of three-panel cartoon, or artist's drawing. The first panel showed a young man and a girl. The man was just leaving a house, and the girl was standing in the door, watching him depart. Her face was troubled. His face could not be seen, but his back was slightly bent, his clothes were wrinkled and did not fit, his trousers were not long enough and his sleeves were too long. The artist had given a weird shade of black and yellow to his garments.

The second panel showed the girl and her mother in a parlor. "I like him, mother," the girl said. "He's a nice young man, but I simply can't go out with him. I can't—and I won't."

"Why not?" the mother asked.

"Because his clothes are just a joke. They don't fit, they're the wrong shade, and all my friends laugh at him."

"Next time you see him," said the old lady, according to the lettering on the drawing, "tell him to buy his suits at the Bully Bargain House, and then he'll be all right."

Third panel. The young man has just entered the front door. He looks as handsome as Apollo. He stands erect, and his new suit fits him splendidly. The girl has just come down the stairs. She sees him and rushes toward him with her arms wide open. She exclaims, "Oh, my precious Bully boy!"

Jeff remembered that he had brought with him only a few shirts and pieces of underwear, and needed more right away. He entered the Bully Bargain House and was waited upon by an excessively polite young fellow who endeavored to sell him far more than he needed at the moment. While waiting for his change Jeff got into a desultory conversation with the salesman. In those days the cash register had not been invented. The customer's money was given to a cash boy, who ran to some remote cashier's window to get the change.

After Chicago politics and the black-face minstrels—then a popular theatrical attraction—had been lightly discussed Jeff said, "Who owns this store?" The salesman answered, "Mr. Henderson is the owner."

Quick as a flash Jeff seized the startled young man by the lapel of his coat, peeered into his face, and demanded, "What's Mr. Henderson's first name?"

"His name is Charles N. Henderson."

"How can I get him? Is he in the store now?" Jeff was excited.

The salesman writhed and tried to pull himself loose. "I dunno," he whined. "His office is on the second floor. He only spoke to me once, and I dunno anything about his doings."

"Tell me this," Jeff said sternly, giving him a shake. "Did he come to Chicago from Baltimore?"

"I can't say," the salesman squealed. "I don't hardly know him, I tell you, and I want to be left out of the whole thing."

"I'm going to his office now," Jeff said, loosing his hold on the coat lapel. He started toward the stairway.

"You're leaving your change," the young man called after him.

"Oh, I'll get it when I come down."

The office on the second floor had a polished oaken door, with the words, "Charles N. Henderson, President," lettered on it. The door stood half-open. Without knocking, Jeff pushed it wide open and went in. The man at the desk, reading a letter, raised his head and stared. Then the letter dropped, the man rose and said, "Well, I'll be fried for an oyster if it ain't my old cell mate—Thomas Jefferson Martin, and I——"

The sentence was left unfinished, for Jeff, bounding into the room, seized his friend's hands, and exclaimed in a loud voice, "The long-lost child is found! Looks just the same too, but a little older. Geewhillikins, but I'm glad to see you. Look here, Charlie, why didn't you write to me?"

"I did, you rascal, wrote to you at the Baltimore *Sun,* but the letters came back," Henderson explained. "Sit down and rest your feet. Have a smoke." From a drawer he produced a box of cigars.

Jeff sat down, lighted his cigar, and said, "Same thing happened to my letters to you sent here to the *Tribune*. They were returned to me, stamped 'Address Unknown.' "

Henderson laughed loudly. "I guess neither of us held his job long enough to grow roots. Well, tell me about yourself. What brings you here to the magic city of the Middle West?"

For an hour or more these reunited friends sat quietly talking, relating their experiences. Whenever an employe of the store came to the door with a paper, or a message, Henderson directed him silently, by a wave of the hand, to his secretary, who sat in a little cubbyhole next door. This functionary, a scrubby-looking little man of about fifty, with gray side-whiskers, wrote steadily, by hand, one letter after another. He had a stenographic notebook at his elbow. In it were the notes of letters that he had taken that morning. Before him there was a pile of letterheads, a bottle of ink and an old-fashioned steel pen. Later on the letters, before insertion in their envelopes, would be put in a copying press. Carbon paper was non-existent, and copies were made by wetting the letters slightly and then pressing down upon them sheets of thin absorbent paper.

"So she left you three thousand dollars in her will," Henderson said. "Well, that was a stroke of good luck. Now what are you going to do with it?"

"Why, I don't know," said Jeff Martin with some hesitation. "I wish I could say, but I haven't decided whether I want to start some kind of business with it or put the money in a bank and look around for a job."

Henderson sat up suddenly and asked, "Put the money in a bank! Why, where is it now? Haven't you got it in a bank?"

"No, I've got it in a belt that I carry around my waist."

"Good God! Jeff, this town is full of thieves and crooks of all varieties. Your life wouldn't be worth a dime if any of them suspected that you were carrying a belt full of money. Not if you strolled around after sundown. Better put it in a bank today. I'll introduce you at my bank."

"No, Charlie, not today. I feel safe enough, and I don't go into the red-light districts after dark. I'll deposit these bills in some bank just as soon as I know what I'm going to do for a living." Jeff waved a hand vaguely around the room. "Tell me, Charlie, if it's no secret, just how you got this business started."

"Well, I wouldn't tell everybody, but it's no secret so far as you're concerned. In the first place I didn't have any money at all. You know how it is, I worked on a pretty small salary as an advertising solicitor on the paper. While I was on that job I met a clothing manufacturer from the East—from New York—a fellow who made men's suits. He had come here with two carloads of his goods without an order. Thought he'd sell 'em to some chance customer among the clothing stores.

"Well, he said that he was stuck with his big shipment of men's wear; the loaded cars were still in the freight yard, and he was paying rent on them. I got him to let me try to sell the goods on a percentage of the receipts. I told him I'd put them in a store and sell them as bargains. He didn't want to do it at first, but finally he agreed. This store here was empty and I talked the landlord into letting me have it for a month on credit. I quit my job, of course, and I had no money at all, but I managed to borrow a little cash from a friend.

"Then I hired three good-looking young men and I had a mighty hard time finding 'em. Had to search the employment agencies and flop houses. You see, the kind of fellows I wanted usually have a job, but the men I picked up were out of work and broke. Two of them lived here and the other one was a stranger who said he came from Buffalo.

"I dressed 'em up fine and dandy. Took the suits out of stock and had a tailor work for hours giving the clothes a perfect fit. Bought 'em all a new outfit from head to heel—hats, shoes, shirt, and everything. Then I sent them out to walk the streets all day, each of them in a different direction, and everyone had a placard on his back that said, 'This suit cost $15 at the Bully Bargain House,' and I put in this address. I called it the Bully Bargain House because it's easy to remember the word bully."

"Did you advertise in the newspapers, too?"

"No," Henderson replied. "The kind of men I wanted to reach never read anything in the papers but city hall politics and the latest murders, but they can't help seeing a fine-looking fellow on the street with a sign on his back. Of course, it wouldn't have been any good in an old town in the East, but Chicago was just a youngster as towns go—and is yet.

"Nothing happened the first day—a Monday—but the next day the store was full of customers. By the end of the week I'd sold the last suit, and I'd made more money than I had ever expected to earn in one week. I didn't keep the men walking the streets longer than that first week. Couldn't trust 'em. One of them ran away with the new suit and I never heard of him again; another one got so drunk that he had to be carted to the police station, sign and all. Now I use other methods of drawing trade, such as prize contests." He stopped and pulled out his watch. "Good heavens!" he exclaimed, "it's after one o'clock. Come on, let's go to dinner—no, I mean lunch." [5]

On their way out Jeff collected his change from the young salesman who had sold him the shirts, and whose astonished eyes stared at his customer and the boss walking arm in arm.

They lunched at the Tremont at a large round table reserved for members and guests of a business men's club which Charles Henderson had helped to organize.

5

On the evening of that same Wednesday Jeff dined at Henderson's home on Willow Street near Lincoln Park. It was far uptown, about twenty blocks north of the store. Henderson called at the Briggs House for his friend and, after a round of drinks in the gaudy Briggs House bar, they went uptown in a horsecar. Two horses with jingly little bells on their harness furnished the motive power. As the car went tinkling uptown Charlie Henderson pointed out the homes of people he knew. With the business district left behind the houses were not crowded together; they stood in open spaces, with lawns and flower gardens around them. The people of the North Side, to judge by their houses and surroundings, seemed more prosperous than those in other parts of the city.

"I'd invite you to stay with us," Henderson said, "I mean stay as a house guest until you get settled, but my wife's sister Ruth—she lived until a week ago in Springfield—has got a job teaching in a fashionable girls' school here on Michigan Avenue, and she's staying with us in our only spare room. Otherwise we'd be glad to have you."

"Oh, that's all right, Charlie," said Jeff Martin. "I understand and I like the hotel anyway. It's very comfortable. Does your wife know I'm coming to supper?"

[5] The ready-made clothing business did not come into existence until the 1830's. Before that time all men's suits were made to order, as needed, by tailors or by the men's wives or other womenfolk. The ready-made suit trade was created to take care of the needs of sailors in the seaport towns. It happened frequently that the sailors could not remain ashore long enough to have their clothing made, so the ready-made industry came into being. But it did not grow much in volume until after the Civil War, when the concerns that had been making uniforms for the soldiers turned their plants and energies into the ready-to-wear clothing field.

"No, she doesn't. We'll surprise her. I intended to send a messenger to let her know, but overlooked the matter." [6]

Henderson's house had a lawn and a flower garden. The house itself, of reddish brick, consisted of two stories and an attic, but it was a rather small structure. At one side a wide driveway led up to a porte-cochere, beyond which there was a large and handsome stable. Like the more palatial dwellings on the lake front Henderson's house was an architectural mess of gimcracks, projections, turrets and bay windows. The porch in front was so wide and its ceiling so low that it kept the rooms on the lower floor in gloomy dusk even when the sun shone brightly. The large weather vane on the ridge of the roof, shaped like a flying goose, creaked noisily with every little shift of the wind. The porte-cochere was much too big and stately for a house of such moderate size.

To Jeff Martin it all seemed very elegant. He thought it was just the kind of house he would build for himself if he ever had the means. Then he felt silently ashamed of his own shortcomings when he reflected that he had done so little while his friend Charlie Henderson had done so much.

"It seems like I've known you a long time, Mr. Martin," said Mrs. Henderson when he was introduced to her. "Charles

[6] The matter of quick communication in the large cities had become a problem of the first order before the telephone was invented. The Western Union Telegraph Company did what it could to meet the issue by establishing many branch offices, and business houses that had close relations with other concerns in the same general area were sometimes connected with them, or with their own branches or industrial plants, directly by means of the telegraph.

But these were only makeshift alleviations. As a general rule it was necessary to call at a man's office, or at his home, to discuss anything with him. Women could not have little social chats over the air, prospective passengers could not get the railroad station on the wire to inquire into the train schedule. If a doctor was needed in an emergency a messenger was sent for him; if a young man wanted to say pleasant words to his best girl he had to go to wherever she happened to be.

The telephone was invented by Alexander Graham Bell in the year 1876, but it was a long time coming into general use. The public did not take it seriously and even the Western Union Telegraph Company called it a "scientific toy" and refused to buy the patent for one hundred thousand dollars.

The members of the New York Stock Exchange declined to accept orders or instructions from their clients over the telephone for several years after the instrument was shown to be a practicable device.

The first telephone exchange was established in New Haven in January, 1878. It served twenty-one subscribers. Instead of saying "hello" after making connection over the telephone the subscribers were instructed to say "ahoy, ahoy."

has spoken of you so often, and it's a pleasant surprise to meet you." She smiled and nodded toward her husband. "He never said a word about your coming—the sly creature—intended to surprise me, I sup——"

"Oh, I didn't know it, Carrie. Jeff walked in all of a sudden this morning." This from her better half, who gave her plump elbow a pinch. "My suspicious wife can't get over the notion that I'm always playing tricks."

"Well, I'm very glad to be here, Mrs. Henderson," Jeff said, "and to meet my friend's wife."

"Don't call the lady Mrs. Henderson," said her husband in a falsely affected, deep bass voice, assumed in a desire to be humorous. "To you she's Caroline, or Carrie, and now, Mrs. Henderson, just forget the Mr. Martin part of it, and call this lad Jeff."

Mrs. Henderson laughed, made a little curtsy in Jeff's direction, and said "Howdy do, Jeff." The young man did not know how to be equally facetious, so he said, "That's right." Caroline Henderson was a small and plump brunette, with a pretty face and an agreeable manner. This conversation took place in the hall which ran through the house from the entrance door to a rear porch beside the kitchen. The hall was somber with its brown wallpaper and dark-hued carpet. Midway down its length there was a stairway to the second floor. On a landing where the stairs made a sharp turn a tall grandfather clock ticked loudly. A number of framed photographs, showing scenes in summer resorts, appeared on the walls. Opposite the hat rack there was a motto, "God Bless Our Home," which had been worked in green worsted yarn on a white background and framed in dark-brown wood.

"Take Jeff around, Charles, and show him over the place. I've got to see about dinner. I wish I'd known you were coming, Jeff; we'd have had something extra, but as it is the cook is getting ready just a plain, everyday meal."

"That'll suit me fine, ma'am—I mean Carrie," Jeff said with a blush.

"Ruth's out and around somewhere, dear. Take Jeff with you and find her." So saying the hostess disappeared down the hall.

"We used to call this meal supper," Henderson said, with

a chuckle and a dig into Jeff's ribs, "but since we bought this house—that was three years ago—we've got to be kind of society-like, and Carrie insists that the midday meal is not dinner, but lunch, and we have dinner at seven in the evening. I don't know where supper got to—it's probably disappeared. Come on and see the place."

They went first into the living room, which was called in that era either the parlor or the sitting room. The words "living room" had not yet come into use. "Now here's the sitting room," Henderson said, "where we spend most of our time."

"It's nice and large," was Jeff Martin's comment.

"Yes, it is. I like a room big enough to turn around in."

In the middle of the room there was a large black walnut table. A glass dish filled with wax fruit stood on it. By the side of the dish of highly colored wax peaches and plums there was a music box that could play six tunes. Three or four books lay on the table; also copies of *Harper's Weekly* and *Godey's Lady Book*. Henderson picked up a copy of the *Lady Book,* showed it to Jeff and said, laughing, "Indispensable, my boy, simply indispensable. It is worth more to every woman who wants to put on airs and bring social elegance into the home than the famous Siamese twins are worth to P. T. Barnum. We learned from this authority that it's bad manners to pick your teeth at the table, and that dinner shouldn't come at noon but at seven o'clock. My wife always keeps a copy of it lying here, so that our callers can see that we have it." [7]

[7] *Godey's Lady Book* was the leading magazine for women from about 1835 until the 1880's. It was a great success in circulation and influence. The owner of the magazine, Louis A. Godey, was an American by birth, although of French descent. *The Lady Book* was edited for about forty years by Sarah Josepha Hale, who had the distinction of being the first woman editor of a magazine in this country. Strangely enough, she did not begin her career until she was thirty-eight; until then she was just a housewife and mother. She died in 1879, at the age of ninety.

The Lady Book was loaded with Victorian sentimentality, affectation and prudery. But it had some excellent features also. Its fashion drawings were superb, and it taught good manners. It was one of the first powerful advocates of better education and more opportunities for women.

To Mrs. Hale belongs the credit of our national Thanksgiving holiday. For seventeen years she carried on a campaign for the establishment of a Thanksgiving Day, which was first proclaimed by President Lincoln in 1863. Before that time some of the states had Thanksgiving days while others had no official observance of the day.

At one end of the room there was a fireplace in a setting of white marble. Above it there was a marble mantelpiece partly covered by a silk lambrequin of many colors. A yellow cuckoo clock stood in the middle and on each side were photographs of the family. In a corner of the room there was a what-not, a piece of furniture that could be found inevitably in every well-furnished home of that generation. The what-not, made of polished black wood, was built to fit into the two sides of a corner. Its name "what-not" describes its purpose exactly. On its shelves might be found all kinds of ornaments and curios for which there was no other place. The top shelf of the Henderson what-not held a small example of Rogers statuary—a little marble group showing a boy who had caught a fish which he was holding up for a little girl to admire. On the shelves below there were such curios as a half dozen charms for watch chains, a number of sea shells of various colors, a little microscope, a book with pages only an inch long and half an inch wide, but with type that could be read under a magnifying glass. A tiny poultry yard occupied an entire shelf. The chinaware chickens were enclosed within a fence made of matchsticks.

Between the two windows of the room that faced the street there was an organ with an open book of music on it. "Carrie and her sister both play the organ," said Charlie Henderson, "and, if I do say it myself, they're first-class organists. We'll get them to play after dinner."

"I always like good organ music," Jeff remarked. "It's better than the piano. I think the piano is kinda tinkly, don't you?"

"It sure is. The organ sounds sort of sublime and solid. Now here's something I like." He went to a small cabinet near the organ, opened it and took out a stereoscope. On the shelves below it were hundreds of photographs, fitted for stereoscopic use with two identical pictures on each card. "I spend an hour many an evening just traveling around the world with these pictures."

"My aunt who died had one, too. They're mighty clever; make a photograph look as real as life."

About a dozen pictures hung on the walls of the room. There was the *Star of Bethlehem* and the *Three Wise Men;* the *Dog That Mourned at His Master's Grave;* the *Crying*

Little Girl Who Had Dropped Her Bowl of Milk; Abraham Lincoln with His Shawl Around Him, Speaking to a Crippled Soldier; Robert Fulton's Steamboat; a *Juliet Tossing a Rose from a Window to a Romeo Who Was Looking Up at Her.*

The floor was covered by a brightly colored carpet, and at the windows there were lace curtains with heavy green damask over-curtains. Before the fireplace stood a dark green, heavily padded settee that looked immovable. The chairs against the walls and before the table were all plush and velvet, with fringes and tassels. In one corner—the one farthest from the windows—there was a seat made to fit the space. Two people could sit in it and be concealed almost wholly by portières made of red silken ropes that fell nearly to the floor. "That's our cozy corner," Henderson said. In those days every well-appointed home was supposed to have such a cozy corner for young swains and maidens.

Over the back of every chair was a doily of embroidered linen or lace—called an anti-macassar. Nearly all well-dressed men, and some women, put macassar oil on their hair to make it shine. This oil came from somewhere in the East Indies. It was the basis of most of the preparations for preserving and brightening the hair. But hair saturated with it left the mark of grease on any fabric that it touched. To protect the backs of chairs and sofas antimacassars came into being. The word was created by simply tacking "anti" on to "macassar." Every careful housewife had a dozen or more of them, so she would always have some that were fresh and clean while the soiled ones were being laundered.

Charles Henderson led his friend outdoors. "Ruth is probably fooling around the croquet ground," he said. "We'll look her up." Ruth Lamb, a young woman of about twenty-four, was his sister-in-law. She taught history in Mrs. Crawford's Select Academy for Young Ladies.

They found her alone with a croquet mallet in her hand, practicing the childish game that was played—then and later—by millions of American men and women. She tapped the ball, sending it through a wicket, and looked up as she heard them approaching.

Jeff Martin was astonished when he saw her. He had seen, in his time, many ladies who taught school but he had never encountered a pretty one. He expected Miss Ruth Lamb to be a scrawny old maid whose facial expression had gone sour for life, and who had a voice full of vinegar and a face full of wrinkles. But Miss Ruth, to his amazement, would be called beautiful by anybody's standard. Her fair hair was blowing about her face when Jeff was presented to her. He was tongue-tied, more or less, for the next quarter of an hour, or until she made him feel at home.

Ruth laid aside her croquet mallet and joined them in a stroll about the place. They visited the stables and looked over the two horses kept there. One of them was Ruth's saddle horse, and she remarked that she rode every day in near-by Lincoln Park. "I used to ride a good deal, now and then, when I lived in Annapolis," Jeff remarked.

"Then you must come and join me some morning," Ruth said. From the way she gave the invitation she appeared to mean it, so Jeff agreed that as soon as he got settled he would arrange about a horse and go in for riding.

While they were in the stable they were joined by Jackie and Ethel Henderson, two romping youngsters, aged ten and eight respectively. "Now you know the whole family," their father said, "except Sarah, who is only three, and is probably asleep upstairs."

There was much cheerful conversation while the family, gathered in the sitting room, awaited the call to dinner. A mild cocktail, which Charlie called a "Eureka," was passed around. He had invented it, he said, and had named it Eureka for that very reason. He refused to say what its ingredients were. "The secret," he declaimed with a grin, "will never be revealed."

"Well, I don't know what you've put in it," said Miss Lamb, "but my guess is that the principal ingredient is water." She looked down into her empty glass with a frown and, rising suddenly, started toward the pantry. "I'll make you a cocktail," she said gleefully, "the kind they serve where I came from. It has authority and plenty of it."

Jeff Martin made no comment, but he could not help thinking that the young lady talked like bartenders he had known. When she brought back the product of her skill he drank a glass of it and soon felt its tingling almost down to his toes.

"It has authority," he remarked. "Yes, it's got muscle and power," Charlie Henderson agreed, "but you see, Ruth, I could drink my Eurekas all evening without feeling more than a slight exhilaration, while three or four of your mysterious cocktails would put the average man under the table."

"Well," Ruth replied with a look that conveyed the suavity of self-satisfaction, "nobody has to drink three or four. One's enough."

Just then the grandfather's clock, at the head of the stairs, struck seven. Its golden notes went shimmering and echoing through the house like a delicate ghost of sound. A moment later a maid in a gray dress with a white apron came to the door of the sitting room and announced that dinner was served.

When they were all seated at table Henderson, as head of the house, mumbled the formula of grace while they all bowed their heads. Jackie, the ten-year-old, sat next to his father; and Ethel, the little girl, cuddled up to her mother. Jeff and Ruth Lamb sat facing each other. As he looked across the table he was impressed by her fresh complexion, sparkling blue eyes and lovely hair, but her confident manner and general self-assertiveness puzzled him. He had met only a few well-educated ladies in his thirty-two years, but he knew that it was not the fashion for ladies to contradict or argue with men in public, nor to mix drinks for the company. Women were expected to play the role of shrinking violets, and those who broke the unwritten rules and made speeches and had political opinions were looked upon as cranks or fantastic old maids, and if they showed a knowledge of drink mixing they were likely to be looked upon as even worse. But this Miss Ruth Lamb was neither a crank nor a termagant. Nevertheless she was already engaged in a spirited argument with Charlie Henderson over President Grant's proposal to annex San Domingo. Jeff sat there, eating a huge slice of baked ham and wondering, while the argument was going on, where San Domingo was located. Then, all of a sudden, he remembered that Miss Lamb taught history in a girls' school. That accounts for it, he thought, and it occurred to him, with a pang of regret, that his own knowledge of history was poor. I'll remedy that, he reflected; tomorrow I'll go to a bookstore and buy the best American history they have, and I'll read it.

Mrs. Henderson looked as if she wanted to put a stop to the argument. In one of the slight pauses she asked Ruth if she ever saw Mr. Clark in her rides in the park.

"Oh, yes," said Miss Lamb, "I see him now and then, ambling along on his old mare."

"Is the horseback treatment doing him any good?"

"He says it is, but I must say he looks very thin and pale."

"Mr. Clark, one of our neighbors," Mrs. Henderson explained to Jeff, "has consumption of the lungs and his doctor is making him stay on a horse just as much as possible. Riding is said to be a wonderful remedy—will often cure consumption, so they say."

Her husband said, "It has cured many cases, but Tuscarora Rice is just as good, if not better."

"Oh, he takes the rice, too, so Mrs. Clark says. I do hope he'll get well; he's such a nice man." [8]

Later in the evening Jeff Martin, addressing the lovely young Minerva of the party, said, "Miss Lamb, I hear that you teach history." He had been told to call her Ruth, but he was still too much in awe of her to attempt any such familiarity.

"Yes, I teach American history to a lot of giggling girls."

"Do you like the work?"

"Yes, I like it, or I wouldn't do it, but I can mention some other occupations that I'd like better."

Charlie Henderson, passing behind her chair, patted her head. "Tell us, darling," he said, "just what you'd love to do if you had your choice."

"Well, I'd prefer to be in business. I think I'd make a good executive. But is there a chance? I should say not. Women are almost never hired for office work, even when they can do it

[8] The true nature of tuberculosis was unknown until 1882, when Dr. Koch discovered the tubercle bacilli. Dr. Benjamin Rush, one of the leading physicians in the early years of the nineteenth century, advocated horseback riding as an excellent remedy for consumption, and Dr. Fuller—another distinguished medico—wrote: "A consumptive, like a Tartar, should learn to live on horseback, by which means he will acquire in time the constitution of a Tartar." This foolish idea was accepted as medical wisdom until the 1880 decade.

Tuscarora Rice was a quack remedy, of which the principal ingredient was corn sirup.

better than men. It's pure prejudice; that's all." She paused a moment and looked around with flashing eyes. "And take the big stores," she resumed, "stores like Field's and Leiter's. Do they employ women to sell women's things? They do not. Just go in and buy a yard of lace or a pair of female stockings. Who waits on you? Not a woman—no, no. You'll be waited on by a man, or an excuse for one, a wretched little counter jumper.

"There's nothing for women to do in this busy world but to teach, or nurse, or cook, or make dresses, or work in factories for a beggar's wages."

"There's no use getting het up about it, Ruth," said her brother-in-law. "After all, woman's place is the home. The children and the husband and the home come ahead of everything else. Man should be the breadwinner. All women ought to marry and have a man to provide for them." Miss Lamb waved away this comment. She continued to discuss the subject for some time, and in the course of her remarks she made predictions. One was that women would be given the vote eventually, and that there would be female members of Congress; that women would enter all the professions and be employed in great numbers in stores and offices.

Jeff had never heard a feminist talk before and he listened intently to every word. On his way back to the Briggs House in the horsecar he reflected on her remarks, and he felt convinced that she was right.

As he said good night to the Henderson family he was given a general invitation to visit them at any time, and to come and share any meal, provided he did not mind taking a chance on pot-luck. But he had a fear of intruding and remained away for the rest of the week. On Saturday he received a written invitation, through the mail, from Caroline Henderson inviting him to come to a little party on Sunday evening. She wrote that after dinner a number of young people, friends living in the neighborhood, were coming in.

He made up his mind to accept the invitation, and he sent a messenger boy all the way out to the Henderson house with a polite and stilted acceptance written on hotel paper.

Tomorrow, he reflected, will be Sunday, October 8, and I will have been here just one week, and what have I done besides spend money and waste time? He resolved that next week would be different—and, as it turned out, next week was very different, indeed.

6

There were six or seven young men and women at the Sunday evening party besides a number of their elders. They ran all over the house as if they owned it, calling aloud to one another, in the highest of youthful spirits. Some played games, such as lotto, parchesi and checkers; others went in for riddles and tricks that one plays with words. Jeff was surprised to find himself the unbeaten checker champion of the party.

Mrs. Henderson had a supper served at nine-thirty, though she did not call it supper but a "collation." It was really a substantial meal, served in plates which one had to hold carefully on his knee to keep from spilling the contents on the floor.

After the collation the girls gathered around the organ and sang the current ballads and such old stand-bys as *Beulah Land, Old Black Joe* and:

> In the gloaming, oh my darling,
> When the lights are dim and low,
> And the quiet shadows, falling,
> Softly come and softly go.

The young girls, with their heads bent together over the organ, formed a beautiful picture; and their gentle voices made one think of life as a delightful emotion rather than as a harsh reality.

Jeff Martin had met a lot of girls in his time, but none like these. All of his female acquaintances had been ill-mannered and loudly dressed. He thought also of the soiled and shabby rooming houses in which, as a poor orphan boy, he had passed so many years. All his recollections were of poverty, failure, dirt and coarseness. That evening, at the Hendersons, which was the most pleasant he had ever spent in his life, inspired him to take hold of himself and do something worth while.

At about a quarter to ten Charles Henderson went out on the lawn to see if all the chairs had been brought in. He returned quickly to the sitting room and beckoned to Jeff Martin and another man. They wondered what was in his mind until they got outdoors and Henderson pointed southward. Over that section of the city—but far downtown—there stood a fiery glow that cast shadows of the three men standing on the Henderson lawn. "That's a big blaze," said the heavily bearded man—Mr. Pollard was his name—who had come out with Jeff and Charlie, "and it covers ground, too. Wide as a dozen sunrises."

"Where do you think it is, Pollard?" Henderson asked, rather anxiously, or so Jeff thought.

"It's hard to say, but my guess is that it's on the West Side, down below Harrison Street, among those lumber yards. It's a good three miles from here."

"It may spread across the river," Henderson said. "But that river's a pretty big gap for fire to cross. What d'you think?"

"Listen, Henderson, when a fire gets to going in a big way there's no telling on God's earth what it'll do," Pollard replied, speaking slowly, as if weighing every word.

A man who was known to Henderson came hurrying along the street, headed westward. "Hey, Crawford," Henderson called out. "Do you know where the fire is?"

"No, I don't know," Crawford replied. "That's what I'm trying to find out. It's a lallapalooza, for sure. I'm going up to the police station; they may know." So saying, he went on his way.

Silently the three men on the lawn watched the spreading glow in the southern sky. The strains of *A Girl in Every Port* —a comical song about a sailor and his sweethearts—came from the house, mingled with much laughter.

"That fire's got bigger since we've been standing here," Jeff remarked. "It's further over to the east now. D'you suppose it has crossed the river?"

"God knows." This came from Charles Henderson. "The wind is from the southwest, blowing straight in this direction." It was indeed a heavy wind that had whistled around the houses and blown like a gale in the streets all day.

"Well, gentlemen," Mr. Pollard said, "I think I'd better take my wife and daughter home. We've had a very pleasant evening, thanks to you and your charming better half. No, no, don't bother to come in with me. I'll say good night right here."

"I think we'd better go in, anyway," Henderson remarked. "We'll have to tell the people in there about the fire. It does look serious." They were then walking toward the house.

"Now see here," advised the phlegmatic Pollard. "Don't get worked up over this. Keep your shirt on. That fire must be nearly three miles from here. D'you think it will come this far? If it does there won't be much of Chicago left and we'll all be in the same boat, but the chances are a hundred to one that it will be stopped in an hour or two. Fires usually look worse than they really are. And don't forget that we have a fire department."

Henderson stopped the music and when he had obtained the silent attention of everyone he told of the fire and the view of it from the lawn. Immediately there was a stir. Some of the guests ran to take a look; others gathered up their wraps and made ready to leave. Caroline Henderson asked them not to go home so early. "The fire," she said, "is so far away, and we can read about it in the paper tomorrow morning." But everybody was intent on going home. The party had come to an end. It was then ten-thirty in the evening of October 8, 1871.

7

"Wait a little while, Jeff," Charlie Henderson said. "I'm going down with you. The Bully Bargain House is on the way to your hotel, and I'll go that far. I want to see if our building is in danger. The people going by in the street out there" —he pointed toward the front door—"say the horsecars have stopped running, so I think I'd better get out the horse and buggy. Then we'll start."

Jeff went with him to the stable and helped him get the horse in harness. They drove out to North Clark Street and turned south. The street gas lights were out but there was plenty of light from the distant conflagration to see everything clearly. The illumination was almost horizontal; people walking in the street cast long shadows. The southern fronts of the houses were clear and visible to even small details, but their northern sides were quite dark.

Clark Street was full of people and noise, which surprised the two men in the buggy, for they were still a long way from the fire. A group of intelligent-looking men, in workingmen's clothes, stood talking on a corner. Henderson pulled up close to them. "Can you fellows give us any news about the fire? How far downtown is it? Is it coming this way?"

One of the men came forward and said, "I've been down there, and have just walked back. At least twenty blocks are burning; it seems so, anyway. It's the hottest fire I've ever seen. Why, you can't get near it. When I left it hadn't got to the North Side yet, but the way red-hot sparks and burning planks were flying, I'd say it's over on this side now."

They drove on slowly. The fleeing crowds were all over the street. Hundreds of vehicles of all kinds were coming from the opposite direction. It was pandemonium—an inferno of oaths and yells and hurrying feet. Most of those who came out of the district were laden with their household goods and the street was littered with merchandise that had been dropped or thrown away.

"My God! Look at that!" This exclamation came from Jeff Martin who pointed to a column of flame that arose suddenly and stood high in the air far above the general level of fire. Henderson looked at it a moment and muttered sadly, "The Bargain House is bound to go, and I've worked so long and hard to build it up. All gone in a night."

"There's a fireman," Jeff said. "Stop him and let's find out whatever we can." The man in his blue fireman's uniform came over to the buggy. His clothes were covered with grime and ashes, and his face was dirty. "Why aren't you with your company?" Henderson demanded.

"I was," the man answered, "until about a thousand tons of brick wall fell on our engine. None of us was killed for we saw it coming. That was on La Salle Street, near Randolph. Then I went over to State, to join No. 12, but I hadn't been there half an hour before their hose went all to pieces—too much pressure, I guess. Anyway, it leaked and split, and we had to give up. There ain't nothing I can do, and I'm on my way home to get the wife and the kids and take 'em down to the beach."

"You mean that the fire's out of control?"

The fireman laughed sardonically. "Out of control! Don't make me laff. This ain't no regular fire. This is hell bust loose on earth. Jes' look at that." He pointed toward the sky. Overhead there was a great fiery cloud, covering half the heavens.

"Have the flames got over on the North Side yet?" This question from Henderson, who was thinking of his store. "Yes, sir," the fireman answered. "The fire is on this side now. What makes it worse is that you can't hardly move for the crowds. You see, it started on the West Side, and nearly everybody over there came across the bridges to this side, thinking that would be safer. We had to run our engine over some of 'em, but what good did it do, after all?"

Before they had gone a block farther Jeff Martin had to get out and lead the horse through the crowds and past drunken men who tried to seize its bridle. The barrooms stood wide open, selling liquor even while their roofs were blazing.

When they reached the Bully Bargain House the building was not burning; the fire was still about four blocks away. Henderson guided the horse to a hitching post in a wide alley that ran next to the store. "We'll be here only a few minutes," he said. "No use trying to save any of the stock now, but I want to get some papers and money out of the safe."

A strange sight met their eyes as they approached the front of the store. The doors had been broken open, smashed evidently by a sledge hammer, and not a pane of glass was left in any of the windows. The place was full of men—all of them from the slums, to judge by their appearance—and they were helping themselves to clothing. A large truck was backed up to the front door, and a number of men were filling it with men's suits, taking them from the shelves by the armsful.

Henderson stood for a moment looking on, his face pale and somber. Then he said, "Come on, Jeff, let's go up to the office." As they mounted the stairs Jeff said, "Aren't you going to speak to these thieves? They act as if the store belonged to them."

"What should I say? In half an hour the place will be burning down, and it's better for them to have the clothes. Now, here we are in the office. I want to get that safe open." It was apparent that the office had already been visited, for drawers stood open and papers lay all over the floor. "Stand with your back to that door, Jeff," Henderson said as the safe door swung open, "and, for God's sake, keep anyone from coming in. If they could see what I'm taking out of this safe I'd never get home, nor you either."

From somewhere in the safe he produced a canvas sack and stuffed it full of papers. Next, he opened a drawer full of money. "I don't know how much is here—about five thousand dollars, I think. How in the world am I going to take it with me?" Jeff thought of a money belt, but of course Henderson did not have one. Much of the money was in small bills, and it would make too big a wad to be carried in a pocket. All of a sudden an idea occurred to him. "I'll rip open the lining of your coat and it can go in there." In an instant Henderson had his coat off and Jeff, with his knife, opened the lining at the neck. When the wad of bills was thrust in it made a big hump, but they patted it down.

"Now, I've got to run over to the Briggs House and get my things," Jeff said.

"The Briggs House! Why, my dear fellow, there isn't a chance. Everything in that direction is on fire. You can see the hotel from these windows. Let's take a look." They went quickly to the window of the secretary's room. In the line of fire to the southwest the hotel could be seen. From its windows long tongues of flame were shooting upward. Jeff turned away without any coment. "Come along," Henderson said, "or we'll be roasted in this building."

The fire was close at hand when they ran downstairs and made for the door. Some men were still at the counters, loading themselves with armsful of clothing, but the truck had gone. Sparks were falling in the street like a fiery rain. On the sidewalk in front of the store a man was lying on his back and two men stood over him, looking down. "Is he dead?" Henderson asked. One of the men shook his head and said sadly, "No, he's just drunk, but he will be dead soon unless we can get him up." Henderson and Martin left them and hurried around the corner into the alley where they had left the horse and buggy. They were gone; somebody had stolen them.

"We'll have to walk," Henderson said. "Yes," Jeff agreed, "and we'll have to walk fast to beat the fire." Looking upward at that moment, he saw a burning plank sail, high overhead, through the heated air and land on the roof of a building a quarter of a mile away. In the memory of that fearful night two things stood out always in Jeff's mind. One was the roar of the fire. It rose above all the other noises, and it sounded like a gigantic waterfall, a Niagara of flame and destruction. Another unforgettable memory was that of the strange look of the approaching fire. It did not seem to be a fire at all, but a solid vivid yellow substance, reaching sky-high, that pushed against the buildings. It was like an advancing wall moving forward with irresistible force.

When Henderson and Martin left the store it was midnight, and it took them until one-thirty to cover the mile and a half to the Henderson house. They had to push their way through a multitude of men, women, and children who were trying to make their way northward. In some places the street was almost impassable by reason of the piles of merchandise and household furniture on the sidewalks and in the roadway. Overturned wagons lay on their sides here and there, and maddened horses ran loose through the crowds. Mrs. Henderson was standing on the porch, peering into the street, when the men returned. Sarah, her three-year-old daughter, stood by her mother and held her hand. "O my God," Caroline exclaimed, "how glad I am to see you. Did you go to the store?"

"Yes," her husband replied in a dull voice, "it's gone, but I got the money from the safe. Where's Ruth and the boys?"

"Packing up things we want to take with us. To Lincoln Park. That's where all our neighbors are going when the fire gets too close."

In the park a detachment of soldiers from the army post was trying to keep order, a difficult job, for people by the thousands were pouring into this refuge.

The Henderson party brought sacks of food, some pots and pans and a few dishes, Ruth Lamb's riding horse, blankets, piles of clothes loaded on the horse's back, and Jackie insisted on bringing the music box. Not one of them looked sad or afraid; they were too excited; it was an unexpected adventure for all of them.

It was early morning—just about dawn—when they found a vacant place for their things on a lawn in the park. The servants—Jane, the cook and housemaid and Thomas, her husband—proceeded to put the household goods in order out in the open air, and to cook breakfast. They had no stove, but they had brought some kindling and firewood from the house. A fire was soon blazing on the grass and a breakfast of ham, eggs and coffee was being prepared. The crowds that were milling about, their arms laden with clothes, stared curiously at the little group. "This is Camp Henderson," Jackie called out in shrill, boyish tones. "I wish we had some kind of shelter," said his mother. "If it happens to rain we'll be soaked." During the day the homeless refugees in the park were supplied with tents by the army.

Henderson asked one of the army officers if anyone knew what started the fire. "They say," the major replied, "that a Mrs. O'Leary, over on the West Side, went out to her cowshed to milk her cow. It was after dark and she carried a lamp which she put down on the ground, and the cow kicked it over. That set the shed afire. Don't take my word; I'm just telling you what I've heard and it may not be true." [9]

The fire burned itself out around midnight on Monday. The houses in more than three square miles of the city—about seventeen thousand houses in all—were completely destroyed. On the South Side everything was burned as far south as East Eighth Street. From there an unbroken area of destruction ran on the North Side up to Fullerton Parkway. The conflagration on the West Side ran from around West Twelfth Street up to Randolph Street, but not farther west than Sangamon Street. The strong wind blowing from the southwest drove the fire steadily toward the north and east. There it burned its way to the edge of the city. Late Monday afternoon

[9] It was not true; nevertheless, the legend of Mrs. O'Leary and the cow and the lamp will probably live a long time. As a matter of historical fact it may be said here that the fire did start in Mrs. O'Leary's cowshed, though she and her cow did not cause it. She milked her cow at five o'clock that day, which was the customary time. When the fire began, around nine-thirty, Mrs. O'Leary was in bed. The story about Mrs. O'Leary and her cow was fabricated by Michael Ahern, a newspaper reporter, who died in 1927. He admitted, several years before his death, that he had invented the yarn about Mrs. O'Leary's cow to make his account of the fire more interesting. The origin of the conflagration is unknown, but local historians who have studied all the ascertainable facts believe that the fire was started accidentally by a group of boys who had slipped into the upper story of the barn, or cowshed, to smoke. It is believed that one of them dropped a lighted match in the hay, and it set the place afire.

a little rain fell and that helped extinguish the fire here and there.

About one hundred thousand people, or one-third of the city's population, were rendered homeless. The number of persons who lost their lives is unknown; only two hundred and fifty bodies were found, but the heat was so intense that many others may have been burned without leaving a trace. The value of the property destroyed has been estimated at two hundred million dollars. The face value of the insurance policies on property in the burnt area was about eighty-eight millions, but many insurance companies failed, and it is believed that the amount of the losses actually recovered was under fifty millions.

8

The Hendersons had forgotten to bring chairs to the Park, so they had to sit on the grass whenever they sat down at all. They had just finished their picnic-like breakfast on Tuesday morning and were talking about the one subject which held all Chicago's attention that morning, when Charles Henderson rose to his feet, and said, "We might talk about the fire from now until judgment day, but it would get us nowhere. It's all over and belongs to history. This is going to be a busy day for me. I intend to rent a store, or a warehouse, or something of the kind over the West Side, as a temporary home for the Bully Bargain House."

"Do you think there's a future for Chicago, after this overwhelming disaster?" This came from Jeff Martin.

"Future! Why, a new Chicago was born this morning. A new Chicago, stronger, finer, richer than the old one."

"Miles and miles of houses are gone," Jeff asserted, "and they're a big loss, but you may be right. A new Chicago; it sounds wonderful."

"We've lost miles and miles of shanties," Henderson said. "Rickety wooden buildings that should have been torn down years ago. But the people are still here, and people make cities. These people are going to make a finer and better Chicago. Come on, Jeff, if you want to take a long walk through the ruins and over to the West Side."

Before they returned, late in the afternoon, Henderson had rented a store on West Lake Street, and had sent telegrams to four Eastern clothing manufacturers to forward at once by fast freight, to Chicago, duplicates of the last orders he had sent them. "These goods will get here in about ten days," he said to Jeff, "and by that time I'll have that lousy store cleaned up a bit, the windows washed and signs painted. It will keep us going until we can get into a new building. Well, what about you, Jeff? Have you decided what you're going to do?"

Jeff laughed. "You decided for me this morning, Charlie, when you said a new Chicago was born today. I'm going to stay right here and grow up with the baby. I'm going to sell furniture. I know more about furniture than anything else—I mean what it's worth, the different kinds, and where to buy it. I have only a little money, as you know, but I'll get along on it. Just think how much new furniture will be needed."

"You've got a big market before you, my boy," Henderson said encouragingly, "and if you lack capital you can borrow it. If I were you I'd try to have most of the furniture made right here in Chicago. There are lots of cabinetmakers here."

"I thought of that, and am going to look into the matter. As far as money is concerned, I can sell furniture for established Eastern manufacturers on a commission basis, but I want to build up a business of my own."

Henderson slapped him on the back. "Now you're talking. Get a business of your own as soon as you can. But let's get moving. I must rent a house—if I can find one—for the family to live in, and you with us, if you have no other plans."

"No, I'm homeless," Jeff said, "and haven't a stitch of clothes but these I'm wearing. I'll be glad to go in with you and pay my part of the expenses."

They did not find a house that day, although they traversed miles of streets in a hack hired by the hour. It looked as if the entire burnt-out population of Chicago was out in the West Side looking for living quarters. On Wednesday morning they resumed the search, and before the day was over they had rented a falling-down mansion on Chicago Avenue. It was much too large, and the roof leaked, and some of the floors were rotten, and the plumbing was out of order, and gas had not yet been put in. It had a spacious lawn, which at the time was littered with weeds and trash. "We'll fix it up," Henderson said cheerfully, and when Mrs. Henderson saw it she remarked that it was lots better than sitting out in the park.

By next June they were in their new home on Willow Street, and the Bully Bargain House was going strong in a building on East Washington Street, which was so new when the Henderson outfit moved in that the paint was hardly dry.

Jeff Martin, in his furniture venture, was astonished by his own success. He developed a time-payment business that eventually attained huge proportions and is well-remembered today, though under another name, by the older generation of Chicago.

Chapter X

A COTTON MILL VILLAGE IN THE 1880's

I

ON SATURDAY MORNINGS, school being over for the week, I helped my uncle in the post office. He was the postmaster at Graniteville in South Carolina. I helped sort the letters and hand them out; besides, I sold stamps, read all the postcards and made myself generally useful. I took up these duties when I was about thirteen—it was in 1887—and I continued to work, off and on, around the post office for about three years, or until I went to college.

Most of the letters were sorted into the general delivery pigeonholes, which were arranged alphabetically, but some of the mail was for the individual private boxes, which were rented by the year. There were only sixteen of these receptacles, and holding one of them was a sign of good social standing. If you were a box holder you were supposed to be somebody of importance, with a definite place in the community, and not a raggle-taggle factory hand, here today and somewhere else tomorrow. The boxes were simply pigeonholes with a pane of glass in front of them. They faced the public lobby of the post office, and each box had a number and the name of its owner pasted on it and showing through the glass. They could not be opened from the outside like those in use today. Whatever they contained had to be handed out through the general delivery window, so there was no practical advantage whatever in having a box.

Nevertheless, we never had the least difficulty in renting them. The box renters were the few professional people of the village, the head bosses in the mill, and the storekeepers. One dressmaker, as poor as Job's turkey, scraped together five dollars and rented a box for a year. I heard her tell my uncle, when she was renewing the rental for another year, that possession of the box in the post office had done her a lot of good. A better class of women had become her customers, and I suppose she was able to charge more for the dresses she made.

In some intangible way the possession of a box for her mail, with her name on it, made her and her work seem more important. But her box was empty most of the time; she received only one or two letters a week.

The recipient of the largest amount of mail during my service as post office assistant was not a box holder, or even the Graniteville Manufacturing Company—the owner of the factory and of almost everything else in the village—but a young mill hand whose name was Ben Marshall. He subscribed to a number of cheap and trashy mail-order magazines, but he read only the advertisements and answered every one that offered to send anything free. From far away there flowed to Ben Marshall a constant stream of catalogues, circulars, free samples and booklets.

But answering advertisements was only a part of his activities. He wrote to many persons whose names appeared in the newspapers, such as political leaders, governors, senators, reformers, actresses, lawyers and clergymen. In writing to these public characters he worded his letters in such a way that they generally brought a response.

This useless letter writing seemed to be the real aim of his life, with his work as a factory hand only secondary. There was a sort of trick in it, as he explained to us one day. "To get a letter back you've got to disagree with 'em," he said, "but in a gentlemanly way. If the man is a Democrat then I say I'm a Republican, but I've read some of his speeches, and he's got me halfway convinced that I'm wrong. That gets 'em going. If he's a Republican, then I'm a lifelong Democrat, but I hint that I might change if I knew more about the Republican doctrine.

"Suppose I'm writing to a preacher or a bishop. In that case I call myself an atheist, but I'm troubled and in doubt. I feel that there is some truth in Christianity, and will he please advise me. Just do that, and they'll send you a bushel of pamphlets. Once I got a fine letter from DeWitt Talmadge, and I've had several from Henry Ward Beecher."

"I saw one that you'd addressed to Robert Ingersoll," my uncle said. "And he's against religion, I understand. Did he answer?"

"Oh, I got a wonderful letter from old Bob. I wrote him

that I had been a devout churchgoer all my life, that I believed in every word of the Gospel, in heaven for Christians and hell for sinners, also in the Holy Ghost and the Blood of the Lamb. But his writings had unsettled me, I wrote, and I hardly knew now what I believed. Would he please write and tell me what to do. Well, sir, old Bob Ingersoll came right back and told me to stick to the Christian religion through thick and thin, and not let anyone persuade me to drop it. He wrote that it might be fatal for me to change my belief, as my mind might crack under the strain.

"I've had a long correspondence with some of 'em, 'specially the Congressmen. I get an argument started and then letters go to and fro, back and forth.

"But lots of people I write to don't answer at all, no matter what I write. I've never been able to get a word out of President Cleveland, though I've sent him three letters, the last one on my fine new letterhead. Newspaper men ain't any good either; you write your head off and they never reply."

Ben came to the post office every day during the hour at the mill. When his bundle of mail was handed to him he opened most of the letters then and there and smiled or frowned as he read them. He was a stoop-shouldered, thin, shabby young man in his mid-twenties with a vague and distant look in his eyes. His wages amounted to about one dollar and a quarter a day, or seven dollars and fifty cents a week. He paid two dollars and a half a week for his board, and of the remainder he spent at least a dollar for stamps. One day I overheard Major Sims, our local justice of the peace, ask him why he wrote to so many strangers. "They're not exactly strangers," Ben replied. "It's kinda hard to explain. I know—I mean we've never been introduced, but I know some of 'em better than I know lots of people here in Graniteville. Sho' I do. We're friends—not outside, if you know what I mean—but sort of inside. No suh; they're not strangers. They all belong to my world."

A few years ago I related the doings of Ben Marshall to a noted psychiatrist whom I met at a dinner party. This gentleman, the author of several books on abnormal mental states, listened attentively and asked a number of questions. "That young man was living in a dream world—a world of fantasy," he said. "It's a peculiar mental state. A vivid dream seems real to you, doesn't it, while you're asleep and dreaming? But when you wake you realize at once that it's not true. Suppose the dream persisted all your life; you would then be living in a world of fantasy. These conditions are not as rare as one would think. In the case you've just told me about I fancy the dream world came into being as a subconscious revolt against dullness and poverty. Sometimes it has its origin in fear, the subject having been frightened into a condition in which the emotion of fear no longer exists and an unreal world is built up in the mind.

"Your factory hand created a dream world of brightness and life, full of clever men and women with whom he lived on familiar terms—or so it seems to me."

Let us turn from this distressing subject to a romance carried on by means of the Graniteville post office and the United States mails. Joseph Mead, a humorless, matter-of-fact widower, was a section boss in the factory's weaving room. This job paid about as much as three good weavers could earn in tending looms, say twenty-five dollars a week. Joe—who liked to be called Mr. Mead—had no children, and not many friends, so he was lonely. One day in looking over the trash swept up from the weaving room floor, he saw a matrimonial agency newspaper. He took it home and spent the evening studying the advertisements. One of them attracted him. It was the love call of a widow in a small town in Indiana. He kept the paper for a few days while he was trying to make up his mind to write to her. No one knew anything about this at the time; it came out later.

Eventually he did make up his mind to write and there was a correspondence of several months between him and the widow. He said nothing about it to anyone, for he was a close-mouthed person who never revealed anything, even if his revelation would have been of no importance whatever. But he reckoned without the post office which, in small towns, is really a public information bureau concerning the letters sent and received. I helped spread the news that Mr. Mead was writing to a lady in Greensburg, Indiana, and that she wrote regularly to him in square blue envelopes.

There were some things, however, that even village postmasters keep secret. One day my uncle received a letter from Greensburg, Indiana, addressed to him by name and not just as "Postmaster." The writer of the letter, Mrs. Paula Finchley, requested information concerning Mr. Joseph Mead—and would the postmaster please say nothing about her letter. I do not know how she learned my uncle's name, but I suppose he was mentioned by Mead in his correspondence.

Among other data Mrs. Finchley wanted to know if Mr. Mead was a heavy drinker. Also what was his age? Had he any children? Was his job in the cotton mill a good one? Did he belong to a church? If so, of what denomination? There were about twenty questions in all. My uncle answered her letter and gave Mr. Mead an excellent reputation, which he well deserved. He was a teetotaler, a deacon of the church, alone in the world, had no children, was forty-two years old and his job in the factory was a good one, compared to the general level of cotton mill wages. He showed me the letter before he mailed it and admonished me not to say a word about it to anyone.

About a month later Joseph Mead bought a new suit, got a week's vacation and departed on a train bound west. When he returned he brought his new wife whom he had married in Indiana. He and Mrs. Finchley had never laid eyes on each other until the day before the wedding. She was known to us as "Polly," for Paula as a name was a little beyond the orbit of Graniteville's perception. Polly could hardly be called homely, but her features were distinctly plain. Her nose was too large, her eyes too pale, her hair too ashy, and the sinews of her scrawny neck stood out like ropes. But she was quick, energetic and intelligent. Although many of her comments on people and their doings were acidly critical she was kindly and helpful to those in distress.

Her voice had a sharp Midwestern twang which contrasted harshly with our soft Southern speech. When she said "water," for instance, the word sounded as if it were spelled "watter." In Graniteville we called it "wah-teh."

The most extraordinary thing about Mrs. Polly Mead, to my way of thinking, was the constant repetition of the word "fault" in her conversation. Anyone who listened to her discourse for three minutes, on any subject whatever, was sure to hear "fault" at least once. Usually she discussed faults without any malice in her speech, but just as if faults were a matter of course.

If the clock were ten minutes fast or slow she declared at once that somebody must have been at fault in failing to set the timepiece. The Meads had a few peach trees in their garden; small boys stole the peaches. Whose fault was it? Polly Mead asked the question and answered it. The mothers of the boys were at fault; they should have taught their children not to rob orchards. Joe Mead went to the barber for a haircut, and came home with his hair cut too short. Another fault. I was there when he arrived; I had taken a registered letter to her. She signed the receipt, gave me a piece of pie and a glass of cider, and then asked a lot of questions about people in the village. Their good points as well as their faults. I sat there in the old-fashioned Mead parlor for some time, giving her the low-down on the community. I told her that my family had no faults but I could not say as much for anybody else, though many people had fine qualities in spite of their faults. She remarked that the town authorities were at fault in permitting so much liquor drinking, and I said maybe the people who drank the liquor were even more at fault.

Just then her husband came home with his clipped haircut, and Polly began to discuss the matter. It was not the barber's fault, she said, for a barber is just a servant who does whatever you tell him to do. No, it was Mr. Mead's fault (invariably she spoke of her husband as Mister) ; he should have told the barber how to cut his hair.

"Next time you go to the barber, Mr. Mead," she said to him, "I'll go with you and see that it is done right."

Joe Mead liked that kind of woman, evidently. They lived together, as man and wife, many years until he died at the age of seventy.

Occasionally Mrs. Mead entertained groups of young people. It was at one of these parties that I unwittingly lost her good opinion for a few weeks. For a moment we were discussing some local woman who always had a slatternly appearance, and I remarked that the lady did not wear corsets. A silence fell on the group at once. Nothing more was said about the unkempt woman, and when the conversation was resumed it was on another subject altogether. When the party broke up I asked Frances Miller, a fourteen-year-old girl who lived near us, if I might walk home with her. She said "No" curtly and turned her back on me.

A few days later Polly Mead called on my mother, whom she knew very well, and told her that I had used the word "corset" in speaking to some girls at her house. Mother laughed over the incident after Mrs. Mead had left, but she took me in hand and set out to improve my verbal manners.

I learned that the word "corset" should never be mentioned in polite society; nor any other piece of feminine underwear. The masculine "shirt" was also interdicted—why I don't know to this day. Instead of saying "I went to bed at nine o'clock" I must say that I "retired" at that hour. I learned also that the word "woman" should not be used in referring to ladies. "Negro woman" was correct; also I might use the word in such expressions as "Eve was the first woman," and it was quite proper to say "a working woman," but "ladies" should be used in speaking of one's acquaintances.

No reference should ever be made to legs in social gatherings, mother said. Instead of "leg" I must say "limb." I wondered if that applied to animals. "If my dog hurts his leg," I inquired, "ought I to say he has hurt his limb?"

"No," mother replied rather testily. "It is all right to speak of dogs' legs—and you know it—but not of ladies' legs. Nor of their stockings."

"What ought I to say instead of ladies' stockings?"

"Say nothing. You're not supposed to know that ladies wear stockings." It was the era of long skirts which reached to the ground.

"How about men's socks?"

"Oh, you may speak of socks, or of your own stockings, but not ladies' stockings."

Mrs. Mead owned and used the first typewriter I had ever seen. She had brought it with her from Indiana. I learned to write on it, under her instructions, but it was stiff, crude and not easy to operate, and it wrote only in capital letters. The keys required heavy pressure, and the spacing mechanism was erratic. When it became generally known that Polly Mead had a typewriter lots of the townspeople came to look at it. This attention pleased Mrs. Mead. Obligingly she showed the machine and typed the names of callers on slips of paper together with some flowery nonsense. They carried these slips home with them as curiosities. But the typewriter was not at that time a brand-new invention. These machines had been in use several years, here and there, although there was none in Graniteville, not even in the company's offices.[1]

2

Compared with other Southern cotton mill communities in the 1880's Graniteville was a model town. The typical mill village of that period was a sun-baked collection of hovels on a hillside. In some of them the workers lived in barrack-like structures that housed eight or ten families in a common atmosphere of flies, dirt and foul odors. At election time the men, in some mill towns, were given the names of the candidates for whom they must vote and an official of the mill stood by the ballot box to inspect each vote. If a worker insisted on voting for a candidate not on the list he would bring down a lot of trouble upon himself.

One Carolina factory village was surrounded by a high wooden fence; no one was allowed to enter or leave this stockade without permission of the management. Some of the mills made employees sign a contract when they were hired that absolved the company for any blame or penalty in case of accident to the worker. This contract also contained a clause under which the company withheld two weeks' wages. These the worker would lose altogether if he quit his job without giving two weeks' notice in writing.

In Graniteville there were no hovels or human rabbit warrens. Wages were not held back, and every man might vote

[1] The typewriter was invented by Christopher Latham Sholes in 1867. He was a tinkering genius who had been a printer, publisher, editor and postmaster. He made the first typewriter in a little shop in Milwaukee. For several years after its invention it was looked upon as a toy by nearly everybody, including Sholes himself. At first he called his invention a writing machine, then he devised the word "typewriter." In 1874 the Remington Arms Company bought the patent rights from Sholes for twelve thousand dollars, most of which went to pay his debts. Sholes said philosophically, "All my life I have been trying to escape being a millionaire, and now I think I have succeeded."

as he pleased. The people were all poor, and could not afford even the simplest of luxuries, for the cotton mill scale of wages—not only in Graniteville, but also in every other factory town—was too low to permit any kind of extravagance. But the Graniteville operatives got plenty to eat, decent clothes to wear, and fairly comfortable houses to live in.

Every mill family was provided with a cottage that stood apart from the neighboring houses. These houses all had gardens that were large enough to grow most of the vegetables needed for the family larder. There was a chicken yard also where the wife kept ten or twelve hens; and in the pig sty at the far end of the garden a pair of porkers were fattened until November, which was the hog-killing month.

The mill cottages varied in size to fit the conditions. The typical cottage of four rooms—and there were many of these in the village—consisted of a sitting room, two bedrooms and a kitchen. In front of the house there was a porch and space between the house and the street for a flower garden. The cottages had no cellars or basements, but the entire house, resting on brick pillars, stood about three feet above the ground. The space underneath the house was often used in rainy weather by the children as a playground.

The houses were without running water, plumbing, gas or electric light. They were simply large boxes, covered by a plain ceiling and a shingle roof, with windows and doors. But the rooms were all light and airy and much larger than the rooms in workers' flats in the large cities. Most of the houses were painted white, but here and there one saw a brown, gray or yellow cottage.

There were hundreds of these cottages in the village when I was a boy, and some ten or twelve more elaborate houses in which the "quality" lived. Under this descriptive heading may be classed the superintendent of the factory, who was the most important person in the community. He and his wife were at the head of the village aristocracy. Next came the three or four managers of important departments of the mill, a couple of village merchants and two or three families that were not connected financially with the village in any way and they lived —apparently—on income from investments.

The factory employed about five hundred hands altogether—men, women, boys and girls—and the total population of the village was around two thousand.

There was not a wealthy person or family in the place—not one. A salary or income of as little as one hundred dollars a month put its possessor into the "quality" class. The social distinctions were sharply defined and the atmosphere of the village was quite as snobbish as that of Newport or Tuxedo. Even among the mill hands there were upper and lower classes.

The pomp and pride of the three-dollar-a-day men were among the interesting features of life in the village in that decade. About a score of these men were employed in the mill. They were not bosses, or department managers, nor did they belong to the white-collar office contingent, but they were capable and skilled mechanics, such as loom fixers, engineers and machine repair men. It is no exaggeration to say that they kept the plant going. Without them to look after the machinery the factory would have been tied up in snarls of one kind or another in forty-eight hours.

These workmen were on the pay roll for eighteen dollars a week, which was a straight salary, while most of the operatives were paid on a piecework basis. This rate of pay was more than twice as large as the earnings of the average mill hand.

Their friends and acquaintances pointed them out to strangers, and frequently they pointed themselves out by saying to new-comers "I'm a three-dollar man" by way of introduction.

They took pride in being extravagant in various ways, just to show off, on the same principle as that of a newly rich millionaire who builds a far larger house than his family needs, or puts a hundred thousand dollars' worth of diamonds on his wife.

One three-dollar man made a practice of smoking three or four ten-cent cigars in the course of an evening, and of handing out one occasionally to his poor acquaintances. "Have a cigar on me," he would say, "I buy 'em by the box." Another one always bought his clothes in Augusta, which is twelve miles from Graniteville. "They cost more," he said to a group of card-room hands, who were listening in admiration, "but they not only look better; they wear longer. My Augusta tailor won't let a suit leave his shop unless it's a perfect fit."

Among these free-handed spenders was one who hired a horse and buggy every Sunday to take his best girl out for a drive. "We usually drive over to Aiken and eat dinner there at the hotel. It don't leave much left out of a five-dollar bill, what with the meal and the buggy hire, and everything, but what's the diff?" He snapped his fingers. "We live only once anyway, and when we die we're dead a long time."

The three-dollar men stood at the top of the list of manual workers in the factory; at the bottom, in respect to earnings, were the doffers in the spinning room, who were little boys of ten or twelve—some even younger—and their daily wage was twenty-five cents. At that time there was no child labor law in South Carolina. The work done by these children was easy; it required neither strength nor skill. They took off or "doffed" the bobbins when the spinning machine had filled them with thread and in their places they put fresh empty bobbins. The doffers had to be present in the factory for the full twelve hours each day but they worked only part of the time. The doffing could be done in a few minutes and the bobbins were not full again for some time. In the meantime they could amuse themselves, or even take a nap in a sort of rest room on the spinning-room floor.

Duke Ross, a three-dollar man, owned the first bicycle I ever saw and the first one ever brought to Graniteville. This was in 1887, I think, or it may have been 1888. It was of the high front-wheel type, known as a Columbia. Everybody in the village knew that Ross had bought a bicycle, and it had been the chief subject of conversation for a week before he brought it out on a Sunday to learn to ride the contraption. About two hundred men and boys stood by to watch him, and there they remained the whole afternoon. After repeated failures, head-long falls, tumbles and breakdowns, he did actually ride the machine home just before nightfall, when supper for all the spectators was waiting and growing cold. Ross was a mass of bruises from head to foot, and his clothing was torn. I wondered then, and I still wonder why the early bicycle makers thought it necessary to make the front wheels of their machines so high.[2]

The wages and salaries were low, but the cost of all living necessities was low in proportion. A four-room cottage rented for four dollars a month. I know this sounds incredible—a four-room house and a large garden all for a little less than a dollar a week—but when we look into the matter closely it does not seem to have been such a wonderful bargain, after all.

The land on which these cottages were built had cost around three dollars an acre when it was purchased by the company back in the 1840's. A four-room, one-story house could be put up for about two hundred dollars. The material used was pine, and the company owned several square miles of pine forests. The carpenters, bricklayers and painters were paid the local scale of wages; not one of them got more than twelve dollars a week, and some were paid much less.

The most attractive features of the village were its airy spaciousness and its shade trees. Widespreading elms and oaks grew in all the streets. They made the place fairly cool and comfortable on the hottest midsummer days. We had live oak trees around our house; in very warm weather my mother used to spread a table under one of them, and there we would have our dinner.

There was plenty of food for everybody but it was lacking in variety. Nearly all meat was fried. I am sure that I never saw or tasted a piece of roast beef, or roast ham, until I left Graniteville and went to college. Occasionally—but rarely—we would have baked chicken when the fowl was too large and too old for frying, but even large and old poultry was more likely to appear on the table in the form of a stew.

At breakfast the usual fare was corn meal mush with sugar and cream, fried ham and eggs, pancakes and coffee. Dinner was the midday meal. Meat loaf or chicken giblets with flour

[2] The first bicycle factory was that of the Pope Manufacturing Company, of Hartford, Connecticut, organized in 1877 by Colonel Albert Augustus Pope. This concern made the Columbia bicycle, which had a high wheel in front and a small wheel behind. The Columbias were dangerous machines on account of their high front wheels. A fall from one of them might be—and often was—the cause of a serious injury. In a few years they were supplanted by the safety bicycle, of the type we see on the streets and roads today.

dumplings were commonly the principal part of the repast, though we often had fried chicken or sausage. Among the mill hands fried or boiled pork was a staple food. Boiled rice was a part of every midday meal, and usually there was pie for dessert. Sweet potato pie was almost always a part of the day's menu. In the summer we had watermelon every day. One could buy a twenty-pound melon for five cents.

Oysters were a prized delicacy, but they were sold only in cans, as the village was too far from the sea to get them fresh. The canned oysters came in large square tins, which were about eight inches long and six inches wide and three inches deep. On these tins there was no label of any kind.

Corn bread stood in high favor as a developer of muscle, strength, and height. I preferred then—and still prefer—bread made of flour, but my parents insisted that I eat corn bread at every meal. "It will build you up," my father said, "while that pale flour bread that you like so much has no strength in it. Look at Negroes working on a farm. They don't get wheat bread more than once or twice a year but they have corn bread every day, and they're as strong as oxen." This corn-bread fetish existed at that time all over the South. It was thought that bread made of white flour should be eaten only by delicate ladies and old people who had no particular need for muscular strength.

3

Early to bed and early to rise was the rule for the mill hands of that factory town in the 1880's. The working hours ran from six in the morning until six-thirty in the evening, with half an hour off at noon. It was a twelve-hour day for five days a week and nine hours on Saturdays—a sixty-nine-hour week.

At five o'clock every morning the "waking" bell tolled, rung by the night watchman at the mill. A powerful and deep-toned bell, its solemn notes seemed to run through the village and in and out of the houses like a living thing. It was still vibrating when lights began to shine through the windows of the houses; the wives were up and preparing breakfast for the mill hands of the family.

At six o'clock the bell rang again—three strokes—and the gates of the factory swung shut. Any worker who arrived after six in the morning—even one minute after—found himself staring at a locked gate. He could come again at noon and work the rest of the day, but he would be docked half a day's wages.

By nine o'clock in the evening, winter or summer, most of the houses were dark. People who rise at five in the morning and work twelve hours a day need sleep and they go early to bed. But homegoers might be met occasionally in the streets until midnight, young men and girls who had been to a party. Prayer meetings were popular, for these religious assemblies had a social atmosphere. Young men attended them with the hope of meeting a girl there and escorting her home, and the girls—or some of them—went to the meetings with the same general idea in mind.

The young fellows usually tiptoed out of the church before the services were over, if they went in at all, and stood lined up on each side of the entrance. The etiquette of the occasion demanded that the young man approach the girl he had selected, tip his hat, and say, "Miss So-and-so, may I have the pleasure of seeing you home?"

If the girl liked him and wished to encourage his attentions she nodded pleasantly, gave him her arm, and they went homeward together. But if she did not care for him she would turn her back on him and say coldly, "I don't require your company."

The young man so treated was said to be "kicked." Next morning everybody in the village—all the wives and young women, at any rate—would hear about it.

"Sally Brooks kicked Ed Thompson last night," a housewife would call across the garden fence to her neighbor.

"Well, I never," the neighbor would call back. "Why, I thought they wuz as thick as two peas in a pod."

"They wuz, but no more; she kicked him at the Baptist Church and Jack Andrews took her home."

"For land sakes! That Sally Brooks has done that befo' mo'n once. She'll keep on kickin' till she kicks herself into being an old maid."

If you are interested in peculiarities of speech you may note that the girl said "I don't require your company" instead of saying "I don't want" or "I don't need." The reason is that both "want" and "need" were lowly words in the estimation of factory girls who were putting on airs. You see, all sorts of common people, whining and complaining, used "want" and "need," saying, "I want this," or "I need that." Girls with a desire to appear high-toned in manner used the word "require" instead.

The word "took" was also banned by the stylish factory girls, for it was used so much by lowly folk who had no breeding or company manners. A young lady of the mill who thought well of herself said "taken" in place of that commonplace word "took." She would say "I taken supper there last Sunday." Also "The dance taken place at Missus Collins' house."

"Relish" was considered a high-toned word, and was employed in place of "like" or "want" as in "I relish fried eggs for breakfast," instead of saying "I like fried eggs." Once at a Sunday-school picnic I heard a young woman decline the offer of a piece of cake by saying, "No, thank you, I don't relish none."

The word "right" was employed as a synonym for "very." A factory hand who wanted to express the idea that So-and-so was very ill would say "He's right sick." The word "ill" was never used, and I think its meaning was unknown in factory circles.

Another curious twist of meaning was connected with the word "old," which was frequently used to express contempt or dislike. It was applied regardless of age. A mischievous child was often called a "little old devil." A store in Graniteville that sold inferior dry goods at high prices was referred to in conversation as "that old store," although it was the newest mercantile establishment in the village.

One of the most persistent misconceptions concerning the speech of the Southern poor whites has to do with the word "you-all." Northern writers, as a rule, seem to think that "you-all," in cracker speech, may mean one person. That is quite wrong. It is always used in the plural. Even when only one person is addressed the "you-all" refers to himself and his family, or to himself and his companions, though they may not be present at the time.

The company did not employ negroes in the factory, but they were hired to clean the streets, to work around the mill yard, and for other menial tasks. No negroes lived in the village, for the company, owning all the land and the houses, would not rent a house to a negro family. The colored folk lived in Madison, an incorporated hamlet which may be described as a suburb of Graniteville. Madison, which had a population of perhaps five hundred people—three-fourths of whom were negroes—was about half a mile south of Graniteville. It stood just outside the company's land.

The sale of liquor in Graniteville was banned, but in Madison there were three saloons. Like everything else in the factory community, the liquor sold in the saloons was low in price. A drink of corn liquor, rye or bourbon, cost ten cents, and a large stein of beer could be bought for a nickel. A man could get pleasantly drunk for fifty cents and dead drunk for a dollar.

Saturday was pay day, and the big drinking took place that night. For many a mill hand getting drunk on Saturday night was a regular custom. Around midnight the noisy topers could be heard coming home from Madison, screeching and singing, sometimes quarreling and fighting.

Besides the liquor sold across the bar the saloons carried on an extensive bottle trade. Each of the three liquor dealers had a messenger who went around quietly taking orders and delivering the whisky. Many women bought liquor in this manner, and among the masculine purchasers were some of the leading citizens, whose consciences were so highly moral that they would not think, even for a moment, of entering a saloon.

No doubt there would have been less drinking if the people of the village could have had some form of popular amusement within easy reach. But there was nothing, except hunting and fishing. Motion pictures did not exist in the 1880's, nor did the radio. Theatrical companies never came to Graniteville.

There was a theater in Augusta, across the Savannah River, and only twelve miles from Graniteville, but it might as well have been a hundred miles, for the only way that a Graniteville mill hand could attend a performance was to go to Augusta on the afternoon train and stay there overnight, coming back to the village on the next morning's train—unless he owned a horse and buggy. But what in the world would a mill hand do with a horse and buggy when he had to work indoors twelve hours a day? For nine-tenths of those who lived in Graniteville the attractions of Augusta were virtually non-existent.

Before the automobile era traveling for even short distances was so uncertain and expensive, and took so much time, that most people—not only in Graniteville but everywhere else—stayed at home when they were not at work.

In the little cotton mill village liquor drinking was a refuge from the utter dullness and boredom of life.

Anything new, or any harmless playful activity that promised diversion, became wondrously popular almost at once. In 1886, or 1887—I do not remember exactly when—a photographer set up his studio in Graniteville. His success was phenomenal. He took tintypes only and charged twenty-five cents a picture. On Sunday afternoons anyone who desired to "have his likeness taken," as the operation was known in popular speech, might have to wait two hours, sitting on one of the benches in the garden around the photographer's house, until his turn came.

Some of the factory girls, the good-looking ones, had their likeness taken many times, and in various poses. A new dress meant a new picture also. They took as much pride in the murky little tintypes as the movie stars of today have in their photographs.

In the absence of other diversions the people of the village went in for music, and in a big way. Every mill family that included young people had an organ if the family could afford to buy one—and most of them could, for the organs were sold on tiny monthly installments. In the afternoons and evenings, and all day on Sunday, the notes of organ music floated through the silence that always lay over the village. The few families that belonged to the "quality" had pianos, but a good many families of mill hands had what was called a "cottage organ." To learn to play an organ was part of a factory girl's domestic education.

Among the men the fiddle was the favorite musical instrument. Some of them were wonderful fiddlers. They could play *Turkey in the Straw* in a way that would start even the bearded deacons to dancing.

There were also skilled accordion players, and the young

boys all tried to learn, and many did learn, to play the harmonica. This last-named instrument was called a mouth organ in Graniteville; I never heard the word "harmonica" until I was grown and far from that village.

At the parties there was much music of accordions and fiddles. Among the favorite tunes were *Suwanee River, The Old Folks at Home, Carry Me Back to Old Virginny* and the popular *Jim Crow* song, of which the following lines are a sample:

> I came from ole Kentucky,
> Long time ago,
> Where I first larn to wheel about
> An' jump Jim Crow.
> Wheel about and turn about,
> And do jes' so,
> Every time I wheel about
> I jump Jim Crow.

The playing of that ditty was accompanied by weird contortions on the part of those present, such as twisting and kicking and whirling around.

I tried desperately to learn to play the accordion when I was fourteen and had just put on long trousers, for I had a notion that every regular man ought to know how to play something. But I was never able to play anything, or to learn a note. My instructor, who was a bookkeeper in the office of the factory company, gave me up after working with me about three months. He said I had no music in my heart or soul.

Strangely enough, in spite of my inability to play or sing, strains of music run through my head all day long, and every day. They come unbidden; they are all the music of songs I have heard. This has continued all my life, and I am as accustomed to it as I am of eating food or drinking water. When I awake without hearing inward music I give up all idea of working that day, for I could not write a page that would be fit to read without the music running along behind whatever I am doing.

The chief music maker of the village was Sam Arthur, a lean, sallow man of middle age. In that era every man wore a moustache, and hair on the face was such a common sight that nobody paid any attention to it, but even the most careless of onlookers stopped and stared at Sam Arthur's facial adornment—or disfigurement, if you prefer. His black moustache was so thick and heavy, and the face behind it so pale and thin, that at first appearance he seemed to be hiding behind a hedge of hair and peering over the top.

Sam could play any variety of musical instrument, from a mouth organ to a piano. He did not need sheets of music, or any kind of notes, but played by ear. At dances and parties and picnics his services were in demand, and his charges were moderate. On occasion he would turn himself into a one-man orchestra, playing a cornet, for instance, while he beat a drum with the aid of a foot-pedaling device.

He was not employed by the cotton mill, and had never been a factory hand. His living, and that of his wife and brood of children, was earned by an intense activity in half a dozen occupations. As the local representative of the Singer Manufacturing Company he sold sewing machines on the installment plan, and repaired them when the necessity arose. He solicited, too, for a life insurance company and wrote small policies, from one hundred dollars up. His pockets were always full of circulars and application blanks.

In addition to selling sewing machines and life insurance and providing the music for festive occasions he took orders for a trashy magazine that gave away two or three chromos with each year's subscription. These chromos were vividly colored pictures of a size large enough to be framed and hung in a room. The magazine was seldom read, even by its subscribers, but the chromos were in great demand and almost every house in Graniteville had several of them. In my own room there was a reproduction of Meissonier's *Napoleon at Friedland* and a scene in a peaceful Dutch village.

On Wednesday evenings Sam Arthur taught artistic handwriting to a class of ambitious young men and women of the mill. In the 1880's decorative chirography was in vogue and Sam was an adept in making the curlicues and ornamental capital letters which distinguished it.

There was a bitter division of sentiment in Graniteville over the moral aspect of dancing. Many of the older people and a few of the younger ones looked upon any kind of dancing as immoral, more or less, but most of the young men and women liked to dance and saw nothing wrong in doing so.

The waltz was then unknown in small towns; it did not become popular until late in the 1890's. The popular dance in our little mill town was the quadrille, and of course the jig. Almost every Saturday night there was a dance at Thorpe's Hall, which had the only floor large enough for a dozen couples. I was too young to dance but I would often go to the hall and look on. Sam Arthur, his moustache bristling and his face dripping with perspiration, always furnished the music. The tunes were usually *Money Musk, Pop Goes the Weasel, Arkansaw Traveler, Peas on a Trencher,* and *Old Dan Tucker.*

One of the young men acted as a figure-caller. I remember one whose voice could be heard at least a quarter of a mile as he sang out "Choose Partners, Sashay All, Swing and Change, Ladies Chain, Balance All." And there was the sound of clattering feet that could be heard afar, disturbing the deacons and elders as they lay in bed and causing them to have a poor opinion of the younger generation.

Twice a year the sleepy little town was stirred into a kind of frenzy by revival meetings. These campaigns for bringing Christianity back to Graniteville and thus increasing the membership of the churches lasted about two weeks. They were conducted by professional revivalists, assisted by the local pastor, who played a minor role for the time being.

These professional groups went from one town to another the year around. In the make-up of the organization one man was an organist, another played a powerful trombone that filled one's ears, the church and everything else with a reverberating din. There was also a singer whose voice, very tuneful, luscious and emotional, was strong enough to make all other human sounds sink into the class of whispers. Besides these musicians, there were usually two preachers in the outfit.

The revival crusade began always on a Sunday evening, and there was a meeting thereafter every evening for two weeks. For the first few days the revival services were subdued and wholly unemotional. The sermons were short and clear expositions of the Christian doctrine. Before and after the sermon the preachers would go about the body of the church, among the congregation, meeting people, shaking hands with them, and conversing in a rather jovial, good-natured manner. I was always patted on the back and given a word of welcome. "And you, my little man," the preacher would say, "it's fine to see you here."

The sermons and the accompanying music acquired more and more warmth as the campaign went on. These experts in revival tactics were skillful in building up the emotional basis for mass hysteria. Young as I was, I could see that their chief instrument of persuasion was not love of God but fear of Hell.

Yet, notwithstanding all the hell-fire element of their discourse, I must say that I heard one of them, a Reverend Mr. Evans, preach a sermon that he called, *How Easy It Is to Go to Heaven,* which remains in my memory today as the best sermon I have ever heard or read.

Mr. Evans declared that all you have to do to reach Heaven is just to be a decent fellow. You must believe in God, and in God's holy word, the *Bible.* You must join God's church. All that is easy to do, isn't it? Now here's the next easy step. You have heard of the Ten Commandments? Sure, you have. Many of you know them by heart. Well, to go to heaven you must follow every one of the commandments. Is that a hard task? I should say not. Well, what else? The rest is simple enough, said Mr. Evans. Just treat everybody as you would like to be treated. Don't lose vour temper, don't drink liquor, don't abuse your family. Always be kind and generous. That's easy, isn't it? Live that way and you'll go straight to heaven. I've always wondered, Mr. Evans continued, why sinners put themselves to so much trouble to go to hell. To sin you have to go out of your way, while it is perfectly natural to be decent and good at heart and in action.

Some of the hell-fire sermons were calculated to make one's hair stand on end. They described the tortures of the damned, their screams and the howling that rose from the burning lakes of hell. "Have you ever touched a red-hot iron?" I heard a preacher demand of his audience. "Have you ever held your hand, even for a second, in a live flame? Have you ever spilt a drop of molten lead on your flesh? In hell the damned live in flames, they walk on red-hot iron; the fiends give them molten lead to drink."

He paused a moment and held a handkerchief to his eyes as if he could not bear the sight of the damned. From around the altar came the sobs and groans of the mourners who had left their seats and gone forward when sinners and repentant souls had been invited to approach the altar and kneel.

"You wonder why they don't die under all that torture," the preacher continued. Then he shouted at the top of his voice, "They don't die because in hell there is no death. They must exist forever in a lake of fire. The suffering they have to endure would kill anyone here on earth in ten seconds but the damned souls in hell cannot die."

From the prostrate forms around the altar came a chorus of moans, and a woman's voice, calling loudly, "God save me, a sinner!"

"As long as you are on this earth, you can repent and be saved," the reverend gentleman declaimed, his voice filling the church as water fills a pail. "But you cannot repent when you are in hell; then it will be too late. God doesn't hear the prayers of those who are burning in eternal fire. Souls in hell do not belong to God; they belong to Satan, and he laughs at their suffering."

At the close of every meeting the mourners at the altar rose and with the rest of the assembly joined in singing a hymn. Many of them became members of the church then and there.

These revivals had a salutary effect on the morals of the community; for awhile, anyway. Perhaps they would have been wholly out of place in more cultured surroundings, but not so in Graniteville. The mill hands, with very few exceptions, were simply children in mind and temperament, and responded to suggestion in the manner of young and ignorant boys and girls. To them heaven and hell were localities, as real and material in their make-up as Georgia and Florida.

4

There was a constant flow of share croppers and poor folk from the country to the cotton mills. The long hours and low wages did not seem long and low to the hillbillies and poverty-stricken plow hands. To these people life in Graniteville was wonderful and thrilling.

"Why, where I come from, over in Lexington County," I heard one of them say to my father, "I never had as much as five dollars of my own from one year's end to the other. Now I get money every Saturday, what with me and my three gals at work in the mill."

"I suppose you were a share cropper," my father said, "and had to turn over most of the cotton you raised to the landlord. That right?"

"No, sir—only half the crop went to the owner. I'd pick the cotton, me and my gals—I got three daughters—then the owner would come and take his half, and after that the storekeeper down in Batesburg where I got my supplies would come and take the other half to go on account of the debt I owed him."

"Were you always in debt to the store?"

"Sure I was. Never out of debt, because, you see, the storekeeper could put up the prices on every blessed thing I got from him, and I couldn't stop him, for what would I do if he'd shut down on my credit? So that's the way it worked out. Sometimes I'd have from two to five dollars left over, and that's all the cash I'd see in a year."

"You like it better here in Graniteville, don't you? What about the working hours—the twelve hour day?"

"I worked jes' as long when I lived in the country," said this ex-share cropper, "and it was harder work, too. Anyway, I don't know what to do with myself when I ain't at work.

"I like it here. We live in a nice house, lots better'n than that cabin in the country. And there's always people around to talk with. Me and my gals—between the four of us we make from twenty-five to thirty dollars a week, and that ain't to be sneezed at, lemme tell you. And we get it in good, hard cash every Saturday, without any ifs and ands about it. The ol' woman stays at home and keeps house; me and the gals bring in the money.

"And when one of the gals needs a shawl or stockings or a dress she goes over to Miz Ethridge's store, buys it and pays cash."

Tight corsets were fashionable. Some of them were laced so tightly that it seemed hardly possible for the woman who wore them to live and breathe. The girls who worked in the factory did not wear these strait jackets on week days, or they would not have been able to work at the machines, but they did their best to make up for it on Sundays. Girls bound up in this fashion ate and drank very little for their bodies were so compressed that they had little or no room for food. Upon coming home Sunday afternoon the corset wearers would hasten desperately to get out of the corsets in the quickest possible time. Then they would lie on a bed or sofa and pant with relief.

Snuff using was an almost universal habit among the Graniteville women of that period, as it was everywhere else in the Southern states, except among women of the higher classes.

In using snuff a woman would take a large pinch of it, about half a teaspoonful, and deposit it between her lower lip and her teeth. Eventually, after years of constant use, the snuff caused that part of the lip to stick out permanently, so that from the outside it looked like a bump or swelling.

Every user of this form of tobacco owned a snuff brush, which was easily made of a twig of willow or of any soft wood. One end of the twig was frazzled into a brush-like form. With it the snuff could be moved around to reach all parts of the mouth. Snuff users were encouraged to continue the habit by the mistaken notion, widely circulated, that women who used snuff never had any trouble with their teeth.

Nearly all the men chewed tobacco, but smoking was a rare habit, because—one may suppose—it could not be done during working hours by the mill hands. The lighting of a match anywhere within the cotton factory was then, and is now, an offense on the order of high treason, murder and child-stealing. The match lighter would have been expelled from the premises and ordered out of town at once. But tobacco chewing was not under the ban, though the chewers were warned not to get tobacco juice on the cotton yarn or cloth. Cuspidors were provided.

Cigarette smoking in Graniteville in the 1880's was condemned right and left by everybody of authority, a term which included the preachers, the doctors, the factory managers and the schoolteachers. No grown man would have ever dreamed of smoking a cigarette, and an imputation that he did actually smoke cigarettes secretly would have been considered an insult.

It was exclusively a boys' vice. There was some little difficulty in buying cigarettes, as no storekeeper in the village sold them, but they could be bought in Madison, and that was only half a mile away. The price was five cents for a pack of ten, and with each pack the buyer got a small picture of some celebrated actress of that period. Fifty of the pictures—all different—formed a series, and many of the boys strove to accumulate the whole lot.

I remember smoking some of the cigarettes, and after all these years I recall the vileness of the tobacco with which they were made. The smoking was done in secret, of course, not only by me but by all the boys.

At that time many people in Graniteville believed implicitly that young men and boys addicted to cigarette smoking went insane eventually. The wise men of the village declared that they had heard of such cases. Neither my father nor my uncle took any stock in this theory, but they were both opposed to my smoking, and as I was opposed to it myself, I stopped after I had consumed ten cents worth of cigarettes and had pictures of two ladies in stage costumes. My father, who chewed tobacco all his life, said if I had to use tobacco, then "Why not chew it like a man instead of sipping at those filthy little cigarettes?" But I was not a chewer, so tobacco did not cut much figure in my young life.

If anyone, professing to read the future, had told the people of that time—not only in Graniteville but everywhere else in America—that before the middle of the twentieth century the despised cigarette would be smoked daily and hourly by men, women, boys and girls, young ladies and old ladies, professors and students, that prophet would have lost his reputation immediately, for no one would have taken any stock in such a preposterous prediction.

5

In Graniteville we had a local reader of the future. He told fortunes, sold charms and amulets, exorcized evil spirits, advised poor befuddled folks in the management of their lives and showed factory girls how to bring back their straying lovers. His name was Blewett Padgett. In the 1880's he was in his sixties and was called "old Blewett," which was a term of derision when used by some people, and of admiration when used by others.

He came into the post office occasionally for his mail when I was helping my uncle. His appearance was rather striking, as he was over six feet in height, and heavy in proportion. A gray-haired man with keen blue eyes. I was not afraid of him, nor was I embarrassed in his presence, as so many people were, for I did not believe in witchcraft, but I was curious about his doings, and I hoped that might know him better some day.

That time came sooner than I expected. On a hot afternoon in the summer of my fourteenth year I happened to be going by his house and saw him sitting on the porch in his shirt sleeves. He knew me, of course, as a nephew of the postmaster, and when I waved my hand to him in salutation he called out, "Come in and have a glass of lemonade. I've got a lot of it here." I went in, drank his lemonade and stayed for an hour, listening to his talk and asking questions. When I said "So long" and departed I had his cordial invitation to drop in at any time and I would be welcome.

When I look back now I realize that he must have been very lonely. The people of the village were either afraid of his mystic powers or, on the other hand, they held him and his magic in contempt. He seemed to have no intimate friends and no social life.

He was a widower and lived alone in a two-story, eight-room house which was filled with heavy oak furniture and a great many books. A fat, jet-black negro woman came in every day to cook his meals and take care of the place. One day I said to her, "Look here, Eliza, aren't you afraid to stay here with Mr. Padgett, a witch man, with spirits and demons going and coming?"

"No, Mr. Willie," Eliza declared emphatically. "I ain't afeard. When I started to work for Mr. Padgett, a long time ago, he put his charms on me, and I ain't skeered o' nothin'."

"What do you mean—put his charms on you? What'd he do?"

"Well, I dunno 'zackly. He put his hands on my head and said sumfin, I think it was Latin, and then he gimme this." She showed a little object that seemed to consist of a small clenched fist of metal inside a silver container that looked like a breastpin. "Yes, Mr. Willie, dat charm protects me, no matter what evil sperrits try to do." Eliza was ironing shirts while this conversation was going on, and she did not even look up when she spoke.

"I hope you're right, Eliza," I assured her, "but I hear there are ghosts going around between here and Madison lately, and suppose you run into them while you're on your way home at night. I'll bet you'd be scared."

"Huh, jes' let 'em try it," she said with a snort of contempt. "Jes' let 'em. I'd tell Mr. Padgett what dey'd done, and when he'd git through wid dem ghosts dey would be hollerin' and squallin'. Dey'd be sorry dey ever pestered me. Yes suh. He'd strip the hair and hide off'n 'em."

"But ghosts haven't got any hair and hide, Eliza."

"Maybe dey ain't," Eliza agreed, "but Mr. Padgett'll strip off whatever dey got in place o' hair and hide, and dey would be afeard to pester me any mo'."

The sorcerer and I became good friends and I would go to his house two or three times a week and make myself at home for an hour or two in the afternoon. Eliza always had some dainty for me to eat, and I spent many hours reading his books on witchcraft and listening to his rambling reminiscences of the Civil War and of strange, weird happenings on the slave plantations of the old South. At first I had an impression that he had been a sorcerer all his life, but when I grew to know him better I learned that he was a college graduate and before the Civil War had been at first a schoolteacher, then a lawyer. He had got himself mixed up in scandal over a woman, not in Graniteville but somewhere else in South Carolina—then he had disappeared for several years. Nobody knew where he had been, and his acquaintances thought him dead until he appeared as a sorcerer in the little factory town.

Whenever the doorbell rang and Eliza came in to tell him that a client or truth seeker was calling, old Blewett would pull open the bottom drawer of his old-fashioned desk and take from it a bleached skull. He would put the skull on a shelf just over his head as he sat at the desk; then he would nod silently to me, a gesture which meant that I must go into the next room. Eliza, meanwhile, was pulling the window shades halfway down to put the room in a semi-twilight. The old man would then pick up the half-emptied quart bottle of rye whisky standing on his desk and put it in the drawer from which he had taken the skull. From a crack in the door of the adjoining room I could watch these proceedings, and Mr. Padgett did not mind at all. He asked me not to tell anyone about his pleasant, friendly relations with me for, as he said, it would do me no good but a lot of harm.

With these preparations quickly made for receiving the client, Eliza would go out along the hall to the tiny reception room. In a moment she would return and usher in the caller. Old Blewett was always in some impressive pose when the visitor entered. One of his attitudes was to stand in the middle of the room, his eyes closed and his hand raised above his head, as if extended toward heaven. Eliza, in a loud whisper, would say to the caller, "He's been this way off and on all the morning, listenin' to Ohrab, his guardeen angel and guide. Jes' you set down, ma'am, but doan say nothin'. He'll come out of it soon and speak to you." Having given these instructions Eliza would go to her kitchen. Blewett would then walk slowly about the room, with his face turned toward the ceiling, for about a minute. Then he would come suddenly out of his supposed trancelike state, take his hands down and smile at the lady with a look of surprise. "Why, it's Mrs. Reardon," he would say. "I'm sorry I wasn't exactly myself when you came in, and I hope you haven't been here long. But when the lords of the sky speak to me"—he pointed upward—"I must listen, no matter where I am."

Mrs. Reardon—or whoever it was—greatly impressed and flustered, said that it didn't matter, and then she went on to tell her troubles and ask for magic relief.

Another pose was altogether different; it was the attitude of profound study. In this case, as he put away the bottle of rye in one drawer and took out the skull he would open the drawer above and take from it a Hebrew *Bible*—printed on parchment, if my memory of it is correct—and a large pair of glasses with horn rims. Then he would pore over the book, his finger tracing the lines on the page although he could not read a word of Hebrew. Eliza would put her finger on her lips and point to a seat which the caller would take silently. Sometimes he would remain looking at the page for ten minutes, muttering strange words. After awhile he would look up and slowly come back to the world. Smiling pleasantly at his visitor, and apologizing for his inattention, he said usually something on this order: "I've been far, far away—not in space but in time—thousands of years ago."

Most of his clients—and he had scores of them among the mill hands and the farmers around the village—were in trouble over unrequited love or erring husbands and wives, or inability to rise in the world. A smaller proportion were obsessed in various ways. One woman could not work in the factory because she could not endure having so many people around her. Padgett cured that trouble by using methods that would fit in with modern psychiatry, though he had never heard of such a word, and it may have been before psychiatry was discovered as a curative force. He gave her some sound advice in several sessions, and provided her with an amulet to wear on her necklace all the time. He said to me, with a laugh, "They don't think the treatment is any good unless they've got something they can hold in their hands."

He sold charms to fend off measles, whooping cough and chills and fever, but these ailments afflicted people regardless of the charms. Padgett declared that they had not used the charms properly; you had to have the charm always with you, but lots of people forgot and left it at home. At that moment the nasty old disease crept in.

I have often wondered, in the many years that have passed since I knew Blewett Padgett, why he told me so much or permitted me to listen to his clients' tales of misery. My best guess is that he hoped I would become his assistant eventually, though I may be wrong in that supposition. But I am sure that he had a deep affection for me; he treated me as if I were a close relative, a son or grandson.

It was extremely difficult to tell when he was playing a part and when he was being perfectly natural, for he was an actor by disposition. Since I knew him in those early days I have met many actors and actresses and I know now that old

Blewett Padgett had their temperament. Like most personalities with a profound feeling for pretense he could not always distinguish the merely dramatic from the real; in short, he was continually fooling himself as well as his clientele. Believe it or not, just as you please, I know that he had an implicit and wholehearted faith in his charms, amulets, love potions and disease preventives. Yet he was well-read. He knew the celebrated philosophies and was acquainted with many scientific works. He thought himself in advance of scientific knowledge.

His fee for telling fortunes was fifty cents. The amulets and charms cost anywhere from fifty cents to two dollars apiece, and he charged a dollar usually for a consultation in which he gave advice. His clients were factory workers, housewives, farmers and their families. He would not treat diseases or prescribe medicine; he always referred sick people to a physician. The function of his charms and incantations was to prevent disease—not to cure it.

Nor would he do anything calculated to injure a person, though hardly a day went by without some mill hand coming in to buy a curse that would bring disaster to an enemy. Old Blewett showed me, however, certain methods of causing people to lose their minds, or their eyesight, or bring on pains in various parts of their bodies. These secrets were imparted to me as his pupil, though he did not use them himself.

Also he showed me how to raise the dead. I set forth the method here so that any of my readers who desire to go in for a little resurrecting may know the formula.

First, you must obtain a rope with which a man has been hanged. Padgett had such a rope, but it would probably be difficult to get hold of one today when the electric chair is the legal form of execution in nearly all the states. Then on a night when the full moon is shining you take the hangman's rope and four stakes to the grave of the person whom you want to resurrect. Drive in the stakes at the four corners of the grave and fasten the rope to them so that the grave is entirely surrounded.

After that, wait until the exact moment of midnight, when, standing at the head of the grave, you must say, in a distinct and rather loud tone: "Hex mex, mere mex, Peter Pompex." Repeat this call three times. Then, without moving, say the

Lord's Prayer backwards. As soon as you have done that call out distinctly: "Rise from the dead, John Smith"—or whatever his name may be. If everything has been properly done you will see a white misty form rising from the grave. Just wait and it will take on a human shape, and in a moment you will be able to recognize the features of the deceased person, clothed in his usual garments.

A resurrected person may be kept out until dawn, but no longer, and he cannot leave the rope enclosure around the grave, but with these restrictions you may converse with him. I asked old Blewett if he had ever raised anyone from the dead. "Oh yes," he replied, "in my younger days, but I'll not do it any more. It's a piece of foolishness."

The old sorcerer told my fortune one day after I had known him a rather long time. I had heard him read the future for many others, and I could not help noting that his predictions were vague and full of generalities, with definite factual statements usually lacking altogether. But they were almost invariably cheerful, so the clients were pleased. His fortune-telling was done by means of a deck of playing cards, which were laid out by him in an intricate pattern on a table.

He told me that Graniteville would not be my home much longer, that I would "see distant lands and foreign faces." There was a lot more along the same line. I would be quite successful, he promised, but he could not, or would not, tell me in what way. I wanted to know to what distant lands I was to travel, and he said it did not appear distinctly. Then all of a sudden he rapped the board with his hand and said "Why, one place you're going to is Siam; there it stands right out as plain as day." Then he looked intently at the cards. "Siam is right, but it will be many years from now—a long time—but there's Siam sure and certain." He pointed to four cards on the table.

When I got home that afternoon I went racing around the house and in the garden, shouting, "I'm going to Siam! I'm going to Siam!" My mother asked me how I ever got such a notion in my head. "I had my fortune told today," I informed her.

Mother seemed annoyed. "So you're still going to see Blewett Padgett, the old fraud!" she exclaimed. "You've got to stop it or I'll tell your father, and he'll put an end to it." I had to spend the next quarter of an hour explaining to mother that Mr. Padgett was not an evil force, but a philosopher and learned man, and that he was doing much good among the common people.

The most interesting thing about his prediction is that I actually did go to Siam. It was, as he said it would be, many years after he had told my fortune.

As the big Dutch plane that I had boarded at Singapore flew over Bangkok on its way to the airport north of the city I looked down on the brown and gray towers of the royal palace, on the streets of white houses and green trees, and on the lazy Menam River, and I said to myself, "Here's Siam at last, and old Blewett was right."

I have no faith in fortunetelling by means of cards, tea leaves, reading of the stars, or by any other device, so I feel quite sure that old Blewett picked out Siam just because it was so far away from Graniteville and would sound more impressive than a prediction that I would visit Philadelphia or New York.

When I discussed the subject of ghosts with Eliza, the colored woman who kept house for Blewett Padgett, there were no public ghosts in Graniteville—not one—though the village had the usual number of private ghosts who moaned and mewed in deserted houses, or came walking downstairs in the middle of the night.[3]

The public phantom in Graniteville first appeared in the spring of 1889. On the upper road from Graniteville to Madison there stands—or stood at that time—the Lutheran Church. Just in front of the church a negro girl was slain by a white man who had hired her as a nurse for his baby. The slaying occurred long before my time, but it appears from all accounts that the girl choked the child to death because she was tired of hearing it cry. She was charged with murder and

[3] Ghosts do not seem to like large cities. I have lived for the greater part of my life in New York, Paris, Los Angeles and Chicago and I have never heard of a phantom or any kind of ghostly manifestation in those communities. That seems strange, for if it is the business of a ghost to scare people, there are certainly many more opportunities in New York than there are in a country village.

was being taken to the county jail at Aiken by two constables when the father of the baby came up behind them and blew out the girl's brains with a shotgun. Thereafter, the story runs, the girl's ghost haunted the spot—a sort of nebulous white figure in the churchyard or in the road. Colored servants who lived in Madison would never use the road after nightfall, but white folks paid no attention to the ghostly yarn and went back and forth at night.

The apparition became a negro legend at which the white people sneered and it was generally believed that it had been invented by the negroes so they would have an excuse for leaving their work and going home before dark.

A morning came, however, when a wave of excitement ran through the village. The ghost had been actually seen, not by black old Uncle Dave or by silly Mary Jane on her way home, but by a party of young white people returning from a dance. The girls had come home in hysterics and the young men were pale and disturbed. "The ghost was right before us," said one of the boys, "when we saw it. Where? Why, at the corner of the fence around the church where the negro girl was shot. We stood there, looking, and too scared to move. It was white all over, and had no shape at all—just white and fluttering—then as we looked it grew up in height until it was maybe ten feet tall. Then it reached out an arm toward our little crowd, and that arm had a big white hand on it about a foot across. Then the ghost gave a deep groan. We ran as fast as we could, helping the girls along. The moon was shining and everything was almost as bright as day. When we'd run about a hundred yards we stopped and looked back.

"Well, sir, believe it or not, but that creature was then shrinking in size, just going down, down, down. And we could hear it moaning. Then we couldn't see it any more."

After that first appearance the ghost was seen now and then in different parts of the village. It had a huge head with a ghastly looking mouth and red eyes, but there was something shadowy and vague about it. I saw it on one occasion—the only ghost I have ever seen. I was going to bed around eleven o'clock one evening and had just blown out my lamp when I looked out the window. The ghost stood before our gate. It was as weird in appearance as a nightmare. I was about to run into my father's room to tell him when the apparition floated away. I mean it seemed to float.

During all this period—the spring of 1889—people, as a rule, stayed at home in the evening. Adventurous souls who went out often came back with strange experiences. One such affair had the whole village laughing for a week. A Miss Carter lived with her parents "across the creek," a rather thinly settled part of the village. To reach it one had to cross a bridge. This young Carter girl went to church services one Sunday evening with her beau. Afterward, about ten o'clock, they started home through the dimly lighted village.

As they approached the bridge they saw, under a tree, the white figure of the phantom. As they hesitated it began to move toward them. They ran across the bridge with the ghost coming swiftly behind them and clutching at them and seizing the young man's hat.

When they reached Miss Carter's place the young man begged to be permitted to spend the night. There was no room for him and she told him he would have to go home. No, he said, he could not face that being from the other world, that wicked demon, and he was willing to sit up all night in the living room or sleep on the floor. By this time the girl's parents were aroused, and to settle the question her father agreed to take the young man home.

Mr. Carter was a Confederate veteran with a grouchy temperament. In a frightful ill temper he put on his clothes and escorted the young man to his boarding house. On the way he uttered only one sentence. Just as they reached their destination he turned to the boy and said, "Never darken my door again; I don't want my daughter to be friendly with cowards." That remark was overheard by some of the boarders and they repeated it next day. The young man never lived it down. He was "kicked" by the girls from that time on. In a few months he left the village for good.

Eventually the community was so worked up over the ghost that a group of men was formed secretly and quietly to run it down. They encountered and surrounded it after hunting around for a week. They were all armed and had made up their minds to shoot the ghost unless it surrendered. Upon the demand to surrender the apparition moaned, grew in height, and reached out its long arms. "I'll count ten," said Jim Crocker, leader of the party, "and then, Mr. Ghost, we'll shoot you unless you give up and let us see who you are."

He had counted eight when the ghost threw off the sheets that covered him, and with them a mechanical arrangement of light metal rods for raising them to twice his height. Out of his discarded disguise stepped Sam Atkinson, the young son of a storekeeper of the village. "Sam was purty scared when we caught him," a member of the searching party told my uncle in the post office. "He thought we wuz goin' to throw him in jail or give 'im a beatin'."

"What was his excuse for scaring people out of their wits?"

"Oh, he said he wanted a little excitement, and anyway he didn't do nobody no harm. He tried to laff it off, but Jim Crocker made him swear, then and there, 'at he'd behave himself from that time on, so we let 'im go."

In a larger community, or in a small one in touch with national and world events, Sam Atkinson's exploit would have been a subject of casual conversation for a few days, but in Graniteville it was discussed in all its bearings daily and almost hourly for a month at least.

The people of the village spread few tentacles of understanding, or even of curiosity, into the outer world. Their sense of perception was extremely self-centered and ingrowing. The indifference to everything that happened outside the community was largely, but not altogether, the effect of ignorance and illiteracy. A considerable number of the grown people could not read. Many others who were able to read in a fashion knew nothing whatever of geography or of history, or of anything else that might be learned from a printed page. So Sam Atkinson's impersonation of a ghost seemed to them to be far more interesting than anything going on in Congress, or in the White House, or in Wall Street—or even in the neighboring city of Augusta.

Many of the younger men envied Atkinson's notoriety and wished they could do something equally sensational. The older folks did not share these views. Some of them thought and said that he deserved a term in jail.

Mrs. Polly Mead, in placing the fault where it belonged, declared that the Graniteville Company was chiefly responsible for the whole thing, though that did not relieve Sam Atkinson of his share in the matter. He is a harum-scarum young man, said Mrs. Mead, and will come to no good end. But the fault runs deeper, she asserted, and may be laid at the company's door.

In the first place the village is not incorporated. It has no mayor, no common council, no police—not even a constable. Any night we might be murdered in our beds, Mrs. Mead said, and nobody would be the wiser. Why isn't the village incorporated, like all other decent communities of this size everywhere? Because it is the company's private property and the company will not permit its incorporation. So we have no protection against murderers, thieves, drunkards, and what not. Does anyone believe that young rascal would have ever gone around pretending to be a disembodied spirit if there had been a police force on the streets at night? Certainly not.

Then whose fault is it? The answer is perfectly plain: the company is at fault. So said Mrs. Mead, and she was probably right.

6

The founder of Graniteville was William Gregg. He built the factory in 1846 and laid out the village. For twenty-two years thereafter—until his death in 1868—he was president of the company and general manager of the mill. He was remarkably successful as an administrator.[4]

In some ways Gregg was a despot of the feudal baron type, but he believed in the value of education, and he established the Graniteville Academy. This school was far superior to those carried on by the state and county authorities. It was supported by the company and was quite independent of state supervision. The state schools, in the 1840's, were open only three or four months a year; their teachers were poorly trained and underpaid, and their pupils learned only a smattering of any subject, even of the primitive arts of reading, writing and arithmetic.

The Graniteville Academy had a regular nine-months course,

[4] There is an excellent biography of him to which the reader is referred for more information. It is *William Gregg, Factory Master of the Old South* by Broadus Mitchell.

from October to July. Its teachers were well paid and it occupied a comfortable schoolhouse. There was no charge for tuition; even the textbooks were furnished without cost. Any white child living in the village might be enrolled in the school, although it was not a matter of compulsion and, as we have seen, some of the young children who should have been in school were working in the factory as doffers for twenty-five cents a day.

During all the time that I attended the Academy—about ten years—the head of the institution was William Marchant. He lives in my memory as the most extraordinary teacher I have ever met, and I have known many instructors of youth, from university presidents down to kindergarten ladies.

Marchant had a passion for teaching—a fervid, burning passion like that which moves martyrs and heroes. His desire to impart knowledge was a living flame in his heart and soul. I feel sure that if he had taught in some cultural center where there were many intellectual people his fame would have spread. But Graniteville was not the right place for him; those who lived in that obscure little factory town had no appreciation of his talents. On the contrary many of the mill hands disliked him intensely. Why? Well, the answer is somewhat complicated. Some of them had been his pupils in their early days and they did not look with pleasure at his driving power. They had tried to get through their lessons as quickly as they could, just skimming the surface, while Professor Marchant was never satisfied unless the pupil was taught to "see all around the subject"—to use his own expression.

In teaching American history, for instance, his pupils were taught a great deal about the personalities of the presidents and other historic characters instead of a mere succession of dates. But such instruction was unpopular, for what in the world, said the mill hands, do we care about how Thomas Jefferson looked or how he lived? He's been dead and gone so many years. Now if he was a live one, that would be different.

On the walls of the schoolrooms large yellow maps were hung—a big one of the United States, among others, without a name of any kind printed on it. It showed the outlines of every state, all the principal cities, the rivers and the lakes, but no names. We learned where places were by their location in reference to their surroundings.

Occasionally, and always without previous warning, the whole school was taken off its regular round of studies, and the attention of all the pupils was concentrated for a week on some special subject. We had, now and then, an "Arithmetic Week" when every one of us worked on arithmetical problems all the time, without even a glance at anything else. There were geography and history weeks also. During those periods of concentration we learned a great deal, or some of us did.

I was not taught directly by Professor Marchant until I was about twelve years old. Until that time I was in the classes taught by his assistants. These were two women.

Soon after I got into the older classes Mr. Marchant took a few of the boys one Saturday on a visit to the paper mill at Bath, about five miles below Graniteville on Horse Creek. He wanted us to see how writing paper is made from linen rags. The management of the mill had been advised of our coming and was most courteous in showing us everything. We spent most of the day in the mill and the manager's wife had a fine lunch prepared for us at their house.

When we got back to Graniteville—we had gone down to Bath in a covered wagon—Professor Marchant told us that he expected each of us to write a composition about what we had seen in the paper mill. I spent the whole of Sunday, after Sunday school, in working on my composition.

In my little essay I had a linen rag tell its own story. "I was only a dirty little rag," it said, "though I had once seen better days." The rag told its experiences in going through the mill, of being washed "white as snow," of being turned into paper, "and now," it said, "I am a sheet of fine writing paper on a lady's desk, ready to carry her words anywhere."

On Monday I saw him read all six of the papers, sitting at his desk. He read mine carefully when he got around to it, then laid it down and picked it up again, apparently to look up something, for he merely glanced at one of the pages before putting it down. After he had read the others he took up my essay again and spent about ten minutes over it. Just before three o'clock he asked me to remain awhile after school hours.

When school was over for the day I went through the silent rooms to Mr. Marchant's office. He picked up my paper and said severely: "Did you write this?" I said, "Yes, sir. I wrote it." He looked at me steadily for a moment and said, "I want the truth now. Are you sure you didn't copy it from a book?" I told him no, it had all come out of my head.

He hesitated a moment, then said that it was remarkably well written and that he would like to send it to the manager of the Bath paper mill. That was done, and the manager, in about a week, wrote that they wanted to print my composition as a circular and would that be all right? They made a little eight-page pamphlet of it but did not mention the author's name. They sent the professor either five or ten dollars (I forget which) to give me for my work. It was the first money I ever earned by writing.

After that incident I was one of Professor Marchant's prize pupils. I passed many an evening at his home, listening to the scraps of knowledge that poured from him in conversation. During the summer months, when there was no school, he would often come to our house, and sit on the porch or in the garden for an hour or two.

One day in the early summer of 1889 he called on us after dinner and told us that there was a vacant scholarship for Aiken County in the Citadel, the state military academy. An examination of candidates for the place would be held early in September at Aiken. "You've got to win it," he said, looking at me. My parents agreed, and for weeks in July and August I pored over geography, history, arithmetic and grammar, with the professor coaching me.

At last the examination day rolled around, and I was in Aiken, as scared as a rabbit until I looked over the examination questions, which were given to us in sealed envelopes. I saw at once that a lot of trick questions were among them and I had been thoroughly trained in that particular field. Professor Marchant made a specialty of it.

There were nine candidates for the scholarship and I was the only one of the nine that answered every question correctly, 100 per cent right. It was not because I knew more, I am sure, but because I knew it all in a different way. For example, one of the geography questions was: "What is the largest state east of the Mississippi?" I was the only one who knew the correct answer.

The next question was: "What state has eight states on its border?" Besides myself, only two other fellows hit the bull's-eye. In the history examination one of the questions was: "What President of the United States served in office for a shorter time than any other president?" Four contestants, including myself, named this short-term president correctly; the other five merely guessed, evidently, and their answers were ludicrous.

Three days after the examination the inspectors or judges notified my parents that I had won the scholarship, and I spent the next few weeks having fun. My companions were boys and girls and we had a glorious time. Before leaving for Charleston in October to begin my career as a cadet I sent a good-bye note to a girl in which I quoted these lines from a song:

> I'm going to the wars, I'm going to the wars,
> Fighting for my country and you dear.
> When I'm far away, when I'm far away,
> Will you think of me and be true, dear?

I was certainly not going far away, but only to Charleston, where there was no war, and I was not planning to do any fighting for anybody. But it shows that I had reached the age of "you dear" and "will you be true, dear." The romantic circumstances are a trifle dimmed because I cannot remember (and I have tried hard) the name of the girl to whom I sent this lyric tribute.

Chapter XI

NEW YORK IN 1908

I

IN 1908 the prevailing and popular fashions in women's clothes seem to have been designed purposely to make their wearers as uncomfortable as possible without disabling them altogether.

The ridiculous bustle, which made its wearers look as if they were carrying around shelves concealed under the back of their skirts, had gone out of style in the 1890's, and the once fashionable over-long dress, with a train which collected trash, spittle, and germs from the sidewalks, was being supplanted by the ankle-length bicycle skirt in the early 1900's. According to the modes and manners of the day not even the slightest glimpse was permitted of the feminine leg above the ankle. When a woman boarded a bus or a street car a few inches of stocking were revealed, and even that necessary exhibition was considered immodest.

While the trailing skirt was on its way out, to the relief of everybody, including its wearers, a new atrocity was moving in. The "sheath gown" came from Paris in 1908 and was adopted with acclaim by American women. A sheath gown was simply a tube, made of cloth, that reached from the hips to the shoe tops. It had the charming contour of a gun barrel or an umbrella stand, and it was purposely made so tight that a lady who wore it could not take a long step. In the course of time it acquired the term "hobble skirt" as a name, and so it was generally known. Why anyone ever invented a skirt which held the legs of its wearers so tightly that they could take only six-inch steps, and why such a skirt became fashionable, are psychological problems that have never been solved.

Boned collars were also in style. They were made of lace, held upright by strips of whalebone, and they fitted closely around the neck. These boned collars were so high that they enclosed the entire throat. Women, as a rule, detested them, for much attention was needed to keep them in shape; nevertheless, they kept on wearing them. For years—on both sides of 1908—they were in great vogue, and then they went out of fashion as suddenly as the blowing out of a match.

Most of the women and girls of that period wore the "peek-a-boo" waist. That may not be the right name for the garment, but it is the word everybody used. These waists looked as if a dressmaker, after she had finished cutting out and sewing one of them, had then gone over the garment with a punch like those used in making holes in paper, and had punched holes in the fabric. The term "peek-a-boo" applied also to waists without holes but made of thin, semi-transparent material. The absurd Victorian code of modesty was still going strong in 1908; the "peek-a-boos" were considered "very daring" garments and almost indecent.

Bobbed hair as a feminine coiffure had not yet come into fashion. Women wore their hair long, frizzled, curled and puffed up by the use of "rats" or rolls. The Psyche knot was also popular. The hair dressing that carried this peculiar name was made by folding back the lady's long hair upon itself and giving it various twists until it stood out in a short clublike protuberance behind, or above, the head. Sometimes a ribbon went around it and held it in place.

The fashion in men's clothes was almost static, as usual, moving only sluggishly through the years, for the average man had rather face an earthquake than make any startling change in his clothing. Our great-grandfathers began to wear pantaloons, or long trousers, in place of short breeches, in the early years of the nineteenth century. Pantaloons were still in fashion one hundred years later, and so were the good old-fashioned coat and vest. But the high silk hat had disappeared as an article of daily wear. In 1908 the derby hat was at the height of fashion. Some men had also begun to wear wrist watches, rather timidly it must be said, for the stalwart males of this century's first decade had an absurd notion that the wearing of a watch on the wrist was an indication of effeminacy.

The bicycle craze had passed its high point, but it was still strong and vigorous. On Riverside Drive, on Sundays and holidays, one could see as many as ten thousand people—men, women and children—riding bicycles. There were innumerable bicycle clubs, organized for outings and sports. The members of these clubs wore conspicuous symbols of their organizations.

Apartments, in their advertisements, frequently announced that there were wheel rooms in the basement, or "we take care of bicycles."

The wealthy displayed their riches ostentatiously, for they wanted it generally known that they had money and power. Millionaires built mansions on Fifth Avenue that equaled or exceeded public buildings in size. These so-called palaces were too large to be homes, or to be domestic in any sense, but they gratified the vanity of their owners.

Bradley Martin and his wife gave a ball at the Waldorf which cost the almost incredible sum of $369,000. Decorators transformed the grand ballroom into what was supposed to be a replica of a hall in the palace of Versailles. Tailors and dressmakers, in Paris and New York, had worked for weeks on imitations—in silks, satins, lace and pearls—of costumes worn at the court of Louis XV. A rich Mr. Belmont appeared at the ball in a full suit of steel armor inlaid with gold that had cost $10,000.

The Bradley Martin affair led to so much unfavorable comment in and out of the newspapers, and to so many jokes among the populace, that the Martins decided to leave the country and reside in England. Before leaving they gave a farewell dinner to eighty-six persons at a cost of one hundred and sixteen dollars a plate, according to the trustworthy *New York World*. It was said further, that a dozen men at the dinner were worth at least ten millions apiece; and, among the forty men present, all but five or six were millionaires.

James Hazen Hyde, a ridiculously affected young man who had inherited from his father a fortune and a controlling interest in the Equitable Life Assurance Society, gave a ball at Sherry's in 1905 that was said to cost $100,000. Mr. Hyde denied these figures when the ball became a matter of public discussion and declared that the affair had cost only $20,000, but even that seems a lot to most people.

Among these entertainments must be included a "dog dinner" given by Harry Lehr, another ornament of the society of that period. To this famous repast he invited his friends' dogs, and they were treated—so it is said—to chicken, *pâté de foie gras* and other delicacies.

In contrast to these prodigious entertainments, palatial mansions and extravagant habits of living stood the poverty of those who dwelt in the slums. The movement to provide decent homes for working people had made hardly any headway in 1908. In this century's first decade there were tens of thousands of so-called homes or apartments in the slums that were really human kennels. They were dark at midday; thousands of rooms in which people lived had no windows at all. In these tenements there were no bathrooms, and a filthy closet at the head of each flight of stairs contained the only toilet or privy for that floor.

2

At eight in the morning of Monday, April 6 of the year 1908, Robert Mitchell and Ruth, his wife, were getting ready to go to New York in their automobile. They had spent the week end at their country house in Scarsdale, some twenty-odd miles north of the city, and had been busy getting it ready to be occupied for the summer. They expected to return by the end of the week, after closing their apartment on Washington Square, and to live at Scarsdale until November. To Scarsdale they brought two of their servants, a man and wife, who were to remain, for there was plenty for them to do during the coming week in cleaning the house, putting up the curtains, ordering supplies from the village, washing the windows, making up the beds and attending to things in general.

Robert Mitchell was the head of the advertising agency of Mitchell, Blair and Conlon, and he was facing a busy week, for the annual Auto Carnival was beginning that very day. The carnival took place in April every year, and it was a carnival of advertising as well as of autos. The Mitchell agency had the Haynes automobile account.

The Mitchells stood on the steps of their house while Jack, their serving man, cranked the engine of the car to start it running. The self-starter, which is in use on every automobile today, was not put on cars until 1910. Until that time the engine was started by using a crank to turn over the shaft by hand. The motorist stood in front of the car, attached the crank to a plug under the radiator and turned it until the engine started. This crude starting device required more muscular strength than most women possess. Until the electric self-starter was invented few women drove cars.

In preparing for the twenty-mile run to the city Robert Mitchell and his wife donned goggles and long yellow dusters. In addition to these protective devices Ruth wore a veil and her wide floppy hat was tied down close to her ears by a scarf which was passed over her head and under her chin. Motoring in those days involved a sort of ritual, like all snobbish pursuits before and since that era. Until Henry Ford began to produce cheap cars by the million the ownership and use of an automobile was a form of snobbery, for the mere possession of such an expensive mechanical contrivance put car owners in a class apart from the common run of humanity.

The automobile manufacturers of that day, in advertising their cars, laid stress on the fine and delicate workmanship embodied in them, on the expert grinding and polishing to make the cylinders and pistons fit and on the hairbreadth precision of all the little parts. They described them as one might describe an expensive watch.

So, with automobiles standing above all other mechanical devices in the revered attention of mankind in general, the owners put on goggles and dusters and gloves before they took their places behind the steering wheels, just as a priest dons a surplice before approaching the altar.

The Mitchells' automobile was a Haynes, which was a very good car for that time, but neither of them liked its looks and would have preferred a Stearns. They did not have much choice in the matter, for Mitchell's advertising agency would not have held the Haynes account very long if he had made a practice of driving around in a rival car. Their Haynes was a forty-five horsepower vehicle priced at $3,500. The Stearns, which they liked better, cost $6,000. The Haynes did not have sleek lines and its seats were set so high that the passengers got the full force of the wind. Like most of the automobiles then in use it was an open car, though it was called a touring car. It had a cloth top which could be pulled up and over the tonneau in bad weather. The top was difficult to handle, and two persons were usually needed to put it up. All the cars of that era, with a few exceptions, were similarly equipped.

One seldom saw a car with the top up, except in very wet weather. Motoring was distinctly an open-air mode of travel.

Robert Mitchell drove along the rutty, rough road toward New York at a steady pace of twenty miles an hour, which was considered the proper speed for the public roads. Occasionally they would pass a buggy or a wagon; before they came abreast of the other vehicle Robert would press the bulb of his air horn and produce some loud squawks. One fellow, alone in a Marmon and going in their direction, dashed by, leaving a cloud of dust swirling behind him. "There goes a reckless devil," Mitchell said in a tone of disgust. "Thirty miles an hour at least. May have a smash-up any minute, or kill somebody before he can stop. He ought to be ashamed of himself, tearing along at thirty miles an hour. Drivers like that are going to bring discredit on motoring, and we've got to have some laws enacted soon to deal with them."

The chief topic of conversation among their friends who rode in automobiles was the good and bad points of the car—its speed, performance on good roads and bad roads, its gadgets and motive power and the possibility of accidents—and the conversation extended into comments on other cars and their excellencies and shortcomings. Now the motorcar is accepted as a matter of course, like the electric light and the ice-making refrigerator, but in 1908 and for several years thereafter the American people were what might be called auto-conscious.

When the Mitchells had crossed the Harlem River and were on Manhattan Island they followed Broadway all the way down to Twenty-third Street. Then down Fifth Avenue to the Mitchell house on Washington Square. There were no traffic policemen, no shifting red and green lights at street corners, and no necessity to stop and wait for a stream of cars to go by on a cross street. Most of the traffic consisted of buses and delivery wagons, with here and there a horse-drawn hansom cab. Occasionally on the street there were family carriages. For motive power these stately vehicles had two sleek horses, and a uniformed footman rode beside the driver.

"It's going to be a busy week for me," Mitchell said, as they rolled down Broadway. "Mighty busy, with the Auto Carnival going on. I'm glad you and I are not going to take any part in the big parade tomorrow night. It'll be a tedious affair."

"I'll never forget last year," Ruth remarked. "I sat in this blessed machine for three hours while we crept slowly up Fifth Avenue and then down Broadway. I caught cold and sneezed my head off for about three weeks. I suppose the autos in the parade will be decorated, as usual."

"Yes—and even more so," Mitchell said, "from what I hear. Some will be rolling beds of flowers and others will have queer lighting effects and one is going to look like old Mother Hubbard."

"Well, I want to see it," Ruth remarked, "but no part in it for me."

"That's right, we'll just sit in the grandstand. Our office is putting out a lot of Haynes advertising between now and next Sunday. A big ad in every New York paper every day, and they're going to be out of the ordinary run, lemme tell you. We're going to publicize the owners of Haynes autos. Tomorrow we'll put our Mayor's picture at the top of the ad. He owns and drives a Haynes. Next day it will be some other well-known man. What d'you think of it?"

"Why, Bob, it sounds fine!" Mrs. Mitchell exclaimed. "It personalizes the advertising."

"I hope it sells machines," said her husband. "Funny thing about advertising is that now and then the most attractive, brilliant ideas turn out to be duds in bringing in the cash."

"Yes, I know, but I think this one is going to win."

"Well, we'll see what happens. By the way, we're going to the Bertons for dinner this evening, aren't we?"

"We are, indeed. You'd better come home early, for we're expected at seven-thirty away up there on Riverside Drive, and you'll have to change your clothes before we go. One of their guests will be Stella Starr—you know I buy my hats at her place—and I'd like to see what you think of her."

"I've never met the lady, but Jack Singleton of our office did his best to get her to advertise. It was no go. She told him that she doesn't need advertising. Jack says she's the snootiest dame on Manhattan Island—and that's a pretty broad statement."

"Oh, that's not true," said Mrs. Mitchell warmly. "She's

charming and pleasant to everyone. Moreover, she is brilliant, and when I say that I mean it. She has built up that big business all by herself, and that's something to be proud of. You'll like her."

3

Stella Starr, who was praised so ardently by Ruth Mitchell, was the most distinguished milliner in New York, and she had also a line of Parisian dresses which made women sigh with hope whenever they thought of them. She owned a business which she had built from the ground up by her own efforts. Though she was thirty-six years old, she looked ten years younger. A couple of beauty specialists spent from one to two hours every day working over her complexion, her hair, her hands and, in fact, every part of her body that was exposed to view. Miss Starr's appearance was what the French describe as *soignée.*

Fate, as most people of experience know, has so many curious and inexplicable traits that one is often tempted to give it a hearty slap and drive it away, just as if it were a frisky pup that is always getting underfoot. On a morning in the month of February, 1888, twenty years before the date of this chapter, Fate was busy as usual, interfering with human affairs. Stella Starr, who was then known as Johanna Starr, a name that her parents had given her, was looking for a job at anything—salesgirl, waitress, cashier or maid in household service. She was then only sixteen years old. Her father, who drove a laundry wagon for a living, had been sent to Bellevue Hospital as a tuberculosis patient, and she and her mother felt sure that he would not recover, so her school days were over and she had to get a job. Her mother's wages as a laundress were barely enough to pay for rent and food. In the *New York World* Johanna had seen a Help Wanted advertisement in which Macy's department store announced its desire to employ a few neat and bright young women. She went to the store at once, but the employment manager had already hired all the girls he needed.

Considerably downcast, she started to walk home. On Madison Avenue, just below Thirty-fourth Street, she saw in the window of a small millinery shop a sign which informed the public that a girl was wanted to serve as an apprentice. It had just been placed in the window; she saw a middle-aged woman put it there. If she had passed the shop even ten seconds earlier she would not have seen the sign and it is a thousand-to-one chance that she would never have become a creator of feminine headdress. But Fate, busy as ever in the job of directing human affairs, arranged things so that the girl saw the sign.

In those days her chief and secret ambition was to be the private secretary of some big businessman. That was merely a Utopian dream, for she was not a stenographer and her parents were too poor to pay for a course in a shorthand school. Anyway, she was such a poor speller that she never learned how to write even a passable letter. She was so ingenious in bad spelling that she knew three ways to spell the word "enterprise," and of the three not one was correct.

Johanna went into the millinery shop and got the apprentice job within five minutes. The pay was low—only $3 a week—and the hours were long. Nevertheless, the work pleased her immensely; she had never known before that she had an unused talent for perceiving the nuances of color, for arranging ribbons and fabrics in agreeable fashion. She learned more about shapes and colors in one year than an ordinary dull-minded milliner learns in a decade. Though her tiny salary had been raised considerably she left at the end of a year to work in the millinery department of a Fifth Avenue store, where she remained several years with annual raises of salary. When she went to the big store, she changed her name to Stella.

Paris was the center of the millinery world, and nearly all the designs of stylish hats originated there. Milliners imported some, but most of those sold to American women were copies. Stella Starr found that she had a knack for copying Parisian hats, and for really improving the designs.

Then she was invited by Madame Suzanne to become a member of her staff, an act which that lively Frenchwoman lived to regret, for when Miss Starr left Madame's employ, after five years of service, she took about half the customers of the house with her. Madame Suzanne boasted of having the most "select clientele" in New York, and the loss of so many customers to a former employee was a heavy blow.

While she was with Madame Suzanne she went in for self-improvement. She employed Mrs. Cameron, an elderly governess who had been for most of her life in the service of New York's social aristocrats, to improve her grammar and pronunciation, also her company manners. Mrs. Cameron taught her pupil that she should not say "boid" but "bird"; that "broke" was not pronounced "bruk"; that in speaking of a missive brought by the postman one ought to say "let-ter," pronouncing both syllables distinctly instead of mumbling "led'ah."

Miss Starr had always said "Who is he?" when she wanted to learn the name of an unknown man, but even as a young girl she had acquired a conviction that the really correct form was "Whom is he?" though she never used it, for it would have been considered an affectation by her neighbors on Third Avenue. She was astonished when she learned from Mrs. Cameron that "Who is he?" happens to be correct and proper. She knew that "I ain't sick" is slangy, but she thought, until her teacher set her right, that the right expression is "I aren't sick." The word "gentleman" was "jelman" according to her way, but she seldom used it, as her term for almost any male was "feller," so whenever she said, "He's a nice jelman," it really meant something special.

These deficiencies in education appear more remarkable when one learns that she had attended an East Side public school for seven years, and had gone laboriously through text-books on English grammar, arithmetic, geography and American history. But these studies—all of them except the simple operations of arithmetic—had seemed completely foreign to her. They were remote and unnecessary, or so she thought, and her teachers were too dull-witted themselves to put life into the subjects they taught.

Mrs. Cameron, who was silently shocked at first by her pupil's vast ignorance, was equally surprised by her capacity to learn when she put her mind seriously to the task. She was amazingly quick, intelligent, and bright, Mrs. Cameron said, but she had absolutely no interest in anything unless she could apply the knowledge immediately to her own personal affairs. "I've never, in my whole life, encountered a person with less intellectual curiosity," said the ex-governess to her tea-drinking cronies on Madison Avenue. "She seems to be absolutely self-centered, a perfect egoist."

Any effort to inform her of the size and shape of the solar system, or of the nature of the Buddhist religion, or of the Puritan settlement of New England, or of Thomas Jefferson's views on democracy would have been a waste of time and breath. But she wanted to speak correctly, for she needed correct speech in her relations with customers. And she spent weeks in the careful study of a historical treatise called *Costume in America* which contained many illustrations of the headdress of American women of long ago. Not only did she pore over the book, but she took straw and felt and made imitations of some of the hats.

She studied French also, her teacher being an indigent French widow, of good education. This Madame Du Pré was paid handsomely, and deserved all she got, for she had to come to Miss Starr's apartment at all sorts of queer hours, often late at night. Sometimes she spent whole week ends with her pupil. On such occasions not a word of English was spoken. Miss Starr learned rapidly to speak French, but never could be taught the grammar and even when she spoke it fluently she read it with extreme slowness. As for writing French, she was never able to write even a short note without misspelling every other word. Her knowledge of the language was almost purely oral, and when she made her first trip to Paris she was surprised at her own proficiency with the spoken language.

When she had reached the age of twenty-eight Stella Starr decided to go into business for herself. She had a rather long list of wealthy customers who would buy her hats, but she did not have money enough, by any means, to set up an establishment for such high-class trade. She was, however, on very friendly terms with Mrs. Charles Berton, who was one of her customers, and she told that lady of her predicament. Mrs. Berton volunteered at once to help her, and advanced most of the capital as a loan. Miss Starr repaid the loan in installments over three years. To her surprise, Mrs. Berton declined to accept any interest, saying that she had wished merely to be helpful and did not care to make a profit out of the transaction.

Miss Starr's new store and workroom were housed in a

white-faced building on the east side of Fifth Avenue, just below Forty-second Street. Facing the avenue were two windows on the street level. In small gold lettering on each window appeared the name "Stella Starr" and just under it the single word "Modes." The windows had creamy lace curtains, but only two or three hats were displayed on little stands. The hats on display were second-class; the best hats were never shown in the windows, for they might be sketched by someone outside the window and copied by other milliners. She explained to Mrs. Berton that the display was unnecessary anyway, for she did not depend on chance passers-by and really preferred not to have them as customers. During her second year in business she added a dress department to her establishment. Her dresses were imported from Paris; none made on the premises.

She lived and moved in a never-ending pose, to which she had become so accustomed that she held it without thought or conscious effort. Moreover, she was firmly convinced that everybody lived a life of pretense, everybody except lifelong failures and born fools. All successful people played their parts, she thought, and she admired those who were clever in making their pretenses appear to be genuine.

But an "attitude," which was her term for a pretence, was not successful unless it produced money, for money—in her opinion—was the final measure of all human values, though people who did not possess money sometimes had admirable qualities, she thought and said. She had an inner contempt for martyrs who die in glorious causes or to help humanity. They get nothing out of it, she reflected, and are fools; while they are suffering and dying others who have more sense are rolling in money and having a good time. Nor did she have any respect for those who strive to make a better world, nor for gifted men and women who produce works of art and literature without adequate monetary reward. But she did not openly say that she held such persons in contempt, for her own personal pretense, or attitude, required that she profess admiration for them.

For three years she was married to Robert McCutcheon, an actor of real dramatic ability, but they finally separated with mutual disdain. After they were divorced she said of her former spouse, "He's the strangest person I've ever met. He's like those little toy balloons that children have, all empty inside, enclosed in a bright and shining cover. All his traits, both good and bad, are assumed for the occasion. Even his love-making is according to stage directions, and when he falls into a rage—as he does sometimes—he isn't really angry. All it means is that, in the circumstances, whatever they may be, he thinks a display of anger is appropriate to the occasion. And when he says he admires someone—say President Teddy Roosevelt—he doesn't mean it, for he admires nobody but himself. He never really lived with me, I just happened to be on the stage, if you know what I mean, while he was there."

In making this comment, which aptly described Robert McCutcheon, it never occurred to her that she was also depicting herself, and she would have deeply resented the information if anyone had given it to her; also she would not have believed a word of it. She was well aware of her own custom of adopting "attitudes," but that was wholly different, she thought, from Robert McCutcheon's practice of carrying around a whole vaudeville performance within himself.

As one might expect, Stella Starr employed a press agent, not openly but secretly. He was a clever young man who never overpraised his clients. Whenever he wrote an item on Miss Starr's account he did not make the mistake of having her appear as the central figure. She was mentioned, for example, as a guest at a dinner given by some woman with a high rating in the *Social Register,* or as sitting in the box of a notable at the Opera. Now and then he had her make a witty remark. She read in the *Sun* of a comment she was supposed to have made about Henrik Ibsen's lack of warm-hearted emotion. It threw her into a sort of panic, for she knew nothing whatever about Ibsen, and if she had been pinned down to tell who he was, she would have guessed that he was a senator from somewhere out West. Next day her press agent had to send her three typewritten sheets containing information about Mr. Ibsen. Following that incident she made it a hard and fast rule that nothing whatever was to be sent to the newspapers about herself until the press agent had explained its purport.

Stella Starr is not presented here as a typical business woman of that time, for few women had risen then so high in the business world, but she was a forerunner. In 1908 there were perhaps half a dozen women in the whole country who carried on large enterprises of their own or who were high executives in large corporations. Today there are hundreds of such women. At that time women were a novelty in the business world except as stenographers and clerks. It may be said in a general sense, that with some few exceptions, only those who possessed hard and cold temperaments succeeded in climbing very far up the ladder of business success. But that age is past and gone. The business world is now accustomed to women in important positions, and they are, as often as men, people of human sympathy, culture and manners.

Just before noon on this Monday in April Miss Starr pressed a button on her desk to call Myra Kleppner to her office. That young woman, of excellent education, was employed by Miss Starr as a "special assistant," a flexible term which covered all sorts of duties, from the arranging of dinner parties to the reading of books and newspapers for her employer. Some of her time was occupied in looking up the antecedents of socially prominent women who were customers of the Starr establishment, or likely to become customers.

Stella Starr nodded to her special assistant, smiled, and waved a hand sparkling with diamonds to a seat on the other side of the desk. "Myra," she said, "did you get the names of the guests who are to be at the Bertons' this evening?"

"Yes, I did. Mrs. Berton says that besides yourself—and the Bertons—there'll be nine other people. A dinner of twelve altogether. Mr. and Mrs. Robert Mitchell——"

"Oh, the advertising man. Mrs. Mitchell is a pleasant person, one of our customers. I've never met him."

"—and Joseph Powell and his wife. As you know, he has mentioned you many times in his column—*Powell's Pick-Ups*—as a famous milliner, an arbiter of good taste, and all that sort of thing."

"I know it and I appreciate it," Miss Starr said. "Let's see now; as I recall it, we gave a hat to Mrs. Powell last Christmas."

"Yes, and you sent her a nice note," said Miss Kleppner.

"I think I ought to do something else, but I can't think of what to do. Would it be all right for me to send a check for a couple of hundred to Joe Powell, with my compliments?"

"It certainly would not," Miss Kleppner said emphatically, her voice rising. "You'd get the check back the next day, with a letter from Powell saying that his space is not for sale, and you can just be sure that your name would never be mentioned again in *Powell's Pick-Ups.*"

"Oh, dear! How queer people are! But, Myra, there's no use of your flying off the handle. No harm's done. I only want to show him that I appreciate his kindly paragraphs about me."

"All right. The best way to do that is to invite Mr. and Mrs. Powell to dinner. Have a number of guests—your friend Cissie Loftus and some other well-known actress, and that Russian prince—if he is a prince, which I for one doubt very much—I mean Prince Politnetzi, or whatever his name is. You ought to invite several other well-known people, too. In that way you'll not only repay your obligation to him—if it is one really—and also get another fine mention in his column."

Miss Starr sat in silent reflection a moment, then she smiled and said, "Thank you, Myra. I should've thought of that myself, but I'm so busy. Why, of course, I'll invite them to dinner."

"Next among the guests are a Mr. Sheridan Newell and his wife," Miss Kleppner said, looking at a list in her hand. "It seems they're from Idaho, and on their way to Europe—a pleasure trip—and are stopping in New York for a week or ten days. Newell, it appears, is a ranch owner and an old-time friend of Mr. Berton, who has been out there many times."

"Oh, I see. Who else?"

"Well, Professor Jason Broome. Have you ever heard of him?"

"Indeed, I have—from Peggy Berton—and Charles. He was Charles Berton's professor of history at college, years and years ago, and they've been close friends ever since. Charles often speaks of him."

"That's right," Myra said. "Now, Professor Broome is also an author of several historical works of great distinction. I know you've never read any of them, but here is a list of their titles on this slip which I'm giving to you, also a little summary of their contents. By the way, don't call him Professor Broome in speaking to him. Call him Doctor Broome."

"Is he a doctor? Oh, I know; he's one of those college doctors. I don't know why people call 'em doctors when they're as ignorant about medicine as I am, but that's none of my business. That's seven. Must be two more guests."

Myra Kleppner glanced at the list in her hand. "Well," she said, "there'll be Mr. and Mrs. Henry Burlingame——"

"She's Edith Burlingame, isn't she?"

Miss Kleppner nodded, and said, "Works for woman suffrage. Helps Mrs. O. H. P. Belmont by making speeches, writing to the papers, and so on. I suppose if we're ever given the right to vote Mrs. Burlingame will be elected to Congress or something."

"I'd like very much to meet her," Miss Starr said. "I admire women who do something in the world. Her husband's rich, isn't he?"

Miss Kleppner sighed and looked bored. "Rich as about seventeen national banks," she remarked.

Edith Burlingame was one of a group of New York women who took part in public movements of various kinds in the first decade of the century. She was not a leader but an active assistant in the woman suffrage campaign. She took part, also, in the movement against the employment of children in factories and workshops; and she was a determined advocate of prohibition, though she was never able to turn her own home into a dry area, for her husband had a wine cellar and a whisky closet, and he calmly drank wine for dinner and brandy and soda after dinner, even on occasions when Edith had her prohibition friends to dine. When the woman suffrage question had become a national issue Mrs. Burlingame helped to organize street parades and huge, vociferous rallies in favor of the cause.[1]

[1] The fight for woman suffrage was a long struggle, extending over many years. Wyoming, in 1890, was the first state to give the vote to women. Wyoming was followed by Colorado (1893), Utah (1896) and Idaho (1896). By 1916 a dozen states, all of them—except Illinois—west of the Mississippi, had given full suffrage to women. In 1919 the Nineteenth Amendment to the Constitution passed both houses of Congress. The Amendment forbade any state to deny the right of suffrage to any citizen on account of sex. The Amendment became effective in August, 1920, when it had been ratified by thirty-six states. Women all over the country voted in the Presidential election that year.

She was the wife of Henry Burlingame, president of the Burlingame Tool Company, which had a world-wide business in tools used by woodworkers, mechanics and other craftsmen. The company was founded before the Civil War by his grandfather. Henry, who had inherited the family fortune of many millions, was a gentle-spirited, mild and courteous person. That he would make a pleasant and attentive hotel clerk was the impression left on the minds of many persons after they had met him for the first time. He gave that same impression also to many persons who had known him well for a number of years. In short, he had no ability and no vices, but he possessed a fortune which was at least a hundred times larger than the average man of ability can accumulate in a lifetime, no matter how hard he strives or how efficient he is, or how prolific in creative ideas.

4

On Sunday, April 5, Sheridan Newell, ranch owner from the State of Idaho, sat down at a desk in his room in the glittering new Hotel McAlpin, New York City, to write a letter to a friend at home. Through the open door of the adjoining room he could hear his wife Emmadene buzzing around and doing the small duties which take up so much of a woman's time.

About once every five minutes the roar of an elevated railroad train rose from the near-by tracks and went quivering through the rooms. Herald Square was so close that Newell could look almost directly down on it and on the roof of the New York Herald building, an exact copy of a palazzo of Venice which looked as much out of place in New York as a fawn would look amid a herd of elephants.

The Newells were on their way to Europe, where they intended to remain until September, traveling around and seeing the sights. Emmadene, born and brought up in Idaho, had never been to Europe, or even farther East than Chicago, before she came on this trip. Sheridan Newell came into the world in the year 1864, when General Philip Sheridan was driving the Confederates before him in the Shenandoah Valley; hence the name Sheridan, which was usually shortened to Sherrie by his friends. His last visit to New York had been in 1901, but he had some friends in the city, such as college classmates, and men who had been guests at his ranch.

After it was filled and wiped the faithful fountain pen began to form words, as follows:

> Dear Jack:
>
> We got here last Wednesday after a pleasant trip. Since then I have been busy looking over the city and renewing acquaintances. New York seems to be pretty much the same as it was seven years ago. The buildings are higher, the stores are bigger and brighter, the hotels finer and more expensive, and the women more sensibly dressed; otherwise there is not much change. Oh yes, there is, when I come to think of it. The big retail district, as you will remember, used to be around Sixth Avenue and Twenty-third street. Well, it has moved uptown, and now you find the big stores here at Broadway and 34th, and up Fifth Avenue from 34th to 42nd. Twenty-third street looks dead.
>
> Another notable change is in the number of automobiles in the streets. There must be hundreds of them. They dash along like mad on Fifth Avenue. I wonder that a lot of people are not killed every month.

Newell had got that far in writing his letter when his wife came in from her room and said, "Sherrie, tell Jack to tell Louise that I've bought her a Paris dress, as she asked me to. Bought it Saturday—I mean yesterday—but I haven't had a chance to write her yet. I'll write tomorrow, tell her, as soon as I go up and look it over again to see if they've made the alterations I told 'em to make."

"You've bought her a dress?" said her husband. "How in the world d'you know that it will fit her?"

"Because I had it put on a model, silly."

"A model? You mean one of those wooden show window dummies? I wouldn't be so sure that——"

"No, no, Sherrie. Now get this straight. I had the dress put on a living model, a young woman that I selected from several because she's the size, appearance and build of Louise."

"Where did you find such a person?"

"Why, at the store where I got the dress. At Stella Starr's. When we called at the Bertons' home on Friday Mrs. Berton told me about the place and telephoned to Miss Starr herself to see that I was shown everything. They have some wonderful dresses and hats, but I'll buy mine in Paris where they cost less. Louise didn't want to wait till we reached Paris, so I bought hers here in New York. She's going to wear it on her twentieth wedding anniversary, when they're giving a big party. I didn't pay for it. The store is sending it out by express C.O.D."

"How much did it cost?"

"Two hundred dollars," Emmadene said in a casual tone.

Sherrie Newell almost jumped out of his chair. "Two hundred dollars!" he exclaimed. "Why, Jack'll never pay it. That much money for one dress! I can't believe it."

Emmadene smiled. "Louise will pay the two hundred. She has money of her own."

"I thought when you were talking about it that the dress had cost about thirty or forty dollars," her husband said. "There isn't any cloth in the world so precious that a dress made of it is worth two hundred dollars."

"Well now, dear, all I ask is that you don't mention the price in that letter to Jack."

Newell reflected a moment, and then wrote:

> Emmadene has been dragging me around to some of the fashionable stores with her to buy a dress for your wife which Louise asked her to get. The one she bought and is being sent to Louise by express is a knock-out. I saw it on a living model, who walked around in it and, believe me Jack, no such a beautiful, fascinating garment has ever been seen yet in the state of Idaho.
>
> We are going to dinner this evening at the home of Charles Berton. You met him two years ago when he was spending a month at my ranch. I like him very much; he's every inch a gentleman and a fine guy. Nothing sneaky or underhanded about him. I remember you said, after we had been galloping over the range together, that he rode as if he had been born in the saddle.
>
> Although I have known Charles very well for ten years I didn't know much about his personal history until I got to talking with Bill French—a newspaper man—in the Waldorf-Astoria bar Friday afternoon. French is a veteran journalist, has knocked around a lot, and was a pal of my father's in Cleveland years ago.
>
> I'll tell you about Charlie Berton in a telegraphic way here in this letter—leaving out a lot, naturally—for you are a student of human nature, and Charlie is an interesting character.
>
> His father was Carlo Bertolotti, who came to this country when he was about twenty—an Italian lad, coming in the steerage. Ran away from home. Didn't have a dollar. Couldn't speak English. Got a job as a dishwasher in a restaurant—one occupation for which you

don't have to know any language at all. That was about ten years before the Civil War. Learned English, shined shoes for a living, became a bartender. Developed eventually into a wagon peddler—that is, he went around in the country districts with a wagon-load of goods.

When the Civil War broke out any drafted man might get out of service by paying the government three hundred dollars. Most of them didn't have the money. Bertolotti got some rich people to back him and he made a business of lending the three hundred for exemption to men who wanted to keep out. Charged about thirty per cent interest. Got rich fast.

Then he changed his name legally to Charles Berton and married an Irish-American school-teacher. You may recall that Charlie has light blue eyes, though his skin is dark, and his hair is very black. My guess is that the blue eyes are Irish.

After the Civil War Bertolotti (or Berton) continued his usurious loan business. From a number of offices—he called them banks—he lent money on household furniture, salaries, wages or whatever came along. The business spread to other cities, and made profits running into the millions, which he invested in New York City real estate.

In the meanwhile he acquired a reputation as a miser and skinflint, and there were innumerable stories of his greed floating around thirty years ago, according to Bill French. When he was worth millions he lived in a wretched little house near the waterfront. His wife died when his son was a little boy. Bill French says old Berton never had a suit that cost over twenty-five dollars, that he never owned a horse and carriage, and that his lunches—even when he was worth millions—were eaten at a lunch counter and cost only fifteen cents, and no tip. He wouldn't buy a newspaper, but usually picked up one that somebody had thrown away in a street car.

That is, as you know, the conventional portrait of a miser, but here comes the funny part. Charles was his only child, and the old man sent him to Harvard, then to Oxford for a year or two. From the time young Charles was eighteen he was given ten thousand dollars a year to spend. When I heard of that big sum of money for a college youth I suggested maybe the figure is wrong; that an extra nought had got hung on to it somehow. No, Bill French said, ten thousand is right. I asked how he spent all that money—on gals, dissipation, gambling, or what? Bill said Charles was as temperate then as he is today, and that much of the allowance was given to poor college boys to help them out. Around that time he began to collect rare stamps and he has now one of the finest and most valuable stamp collections in the world. Also he collects famous autographs.

It all seems very strange to me, and I asked Bill French if he knew why the penny-pinching old devil gave his young son such a huge wad of spending money every year. Bill said, "No, I don't know why, but I can guess. Old Berton recalled his own poverty-cursed youth and was re-living that period of his life in the person of his son, with the curse of poverty removed." That seems to me a good guess. French says that when the elder Berton died he left fifteen million dollars. All of it went to Charles.

Charles spends or gives away his entire big income every year, French says, though his name never appears in any list of contributions to charity or any other cause. His contribution is always put down under the heading "Anonymous." Right now he is paying the expenses of about a dozen poor young men and women who are going through college, most of whom he has never seen.

Well, Jack, we think we know a person and then find out all of a sudden that we haven't more than a glimpse of what the person really is. I thought I knew Charlie Berton pretty well, from many days spent with him in hunting and camping, but I didn't really know him at all, and my guess is that most of this is news to you, too.

Emmadene and I are going to his house—or apartment—to dinner tomorrow evening. I think there will be a lot of other people there, and it will surely be interesting to see Charles at home and among his friends.

I will write to you again before we sail. You have my London address. Be sure to write often and give me the news.

Our affectionate greeting to you and Louise.

S. Newell.

P.S. I forgot to write that Charles has a son and a daughter, both nearly grown. The girl's at Wellesley and the boy is at the University of Michigan. Bill French says Charles gives them only moderate spending allowances.

Just as Sherrie Newell was finishing his letter Emmadene came in again and picked up the written sheets. "Oh," she said, glancing over the pages, "you say that you saw Louise's dress on a model. What a fib! You say it's a knock-out." Laughing, she read on. "Fine," she exclaimed. "Sherrie, you ought to edit a fashion page. You say that no such a beautiful, fascinating garment has ever been seen in Idaho."

"I've used your own words," said her husband. "Any objection?"

"Not the least, darling. But what makes you say that you

saw the dress? I believe in lying, too, on proper occasions, but is it necessary in this case?"

"Listen, my dear," said Mr. Newell. "There's going to be a domestic row out there in Twin Falls about the two hundred simoleons that the dress cost. My fainting spells over the beauty of the garment will help a lot to restore tranquillity. If I am so impressed Jack will think it is probably worth the money after all."

That afternoon the Newells spent an hour and a half in a nickelodeon on Sixth Avenue near Twenty-eighth Street, and saw their first motion picture. In those days motion pictures were exhibited in vacant stores; there were no motion picture theaters. The admission fee was usually five cents—hence the name nickelodeon—though in some of the better places ten cents was charged.

The motion picture was then in its grubby stage, and not more than one person in a thousand ever dreamed that it would become the basis of a great industry, paying enormous salaries and creating world-wide reputations, and that Hollywood would shine all over the world.

There was not even one distinguished actor at that time in the motion picture field, and those who were employed in exploits before the camera were the subjects of innumerable comments of derision by the actors on Broadway. "He's nobody," they would say, "just a motion picture actor." But within ten years thereafter nearly every actor in the United States was hoping for the good fortune of being called to Hollywood.

The store in which the Newells saw their first motion picture seated about one hundred and fifty people. A white sheet was stretched across the wall in the back of the store and the picture was thrown on that. A girl, at a piano placed in front of the screen, tinkled bars of music while the picture was running. This was many years before the talking picture became a reality, and the conversation among the characters appeared in printed captions.

The Newells saw *Rip Van Winkle* as a screen play. It was poorly done, but to Mr. and Mrs. Newell it seemed marvelous. It was followed by a farce in which the chief source of amusement was the throwing of custard pies into the face of a young man who was supposed to be a comedian.

In those early days the reputation of the motion picture theaters was not first-class. They were popular among working people and boys and girls, but many families of dignity and good repute stayed away from them.

5

The apartment in which the Bertons lived was called a triplex, meaning that it was on three floors. It had sixteen rooms on the twelfth, thirteenth and fourteenth floors of a sixteen-story apartment house on Riverside Drive, near Eighty-sixth Street, which was owned by Charles Berton. On the twelfth floor there was a reception room, a huge living room, a dining room and a kitchen and pantry. On the thirteenth there was a library, a sun parlor, a study fitted up like an office and the bedrooms of Mr. and Mrs. Berton. The fourteenth floor had a number of guest rooms in front and servants' rooms in the rear.

The living room, the sun parlor, the library—and, in fact, all the rooms—reminded Sheridan Newell, when he walked through them, of rooms that he had seen in museums. The fragile Chippendale chairs and the beautiful Duncan Phyfe sofas looked as if they had never been made for actual use; and he would not have been greatly surprised if the curio cabinets, with their graceful specimens of ancient silverware and cloisonné, of rings and delicate watches fashioned by Parisian artisans, had borne a sign saying "Do Not Touch."

The ceilings were of dark wood, carved in flowery patterns. The walls of the dining room were covered with tapestry on which appeared a hunting scene of the Middle Ages. In the background there was a range of hills under a blue sky and silvery clouds and in the middle distance stood a castle which looked so majestic that it could only be the home of a great lord or a king. Across the fields and forests of the foreground came streaming a cavalcade of horsemen in the colorful garb of the seventeenth century. They were accompanied by hounds and buglers. A deer, standing on the edge of a forest, looked back at them.

The living room walls were inlaid with panels of polished wood. There were too many paintings on the walls—so many that their effect was weakened and the first impression of them was simply a blur of color. The room was lighted by a chandelier hanging from the ceiling and by frosted electric light globes set into the paneled wall. A fireplace at one end of the room was chiefly ornamental, as the house was steam-heated.

A piano, seldom used, stood in one corner, and between two of the windows facing Riverside Drive there was a magnificent phonograph with a cabinet for records next to it. A similar phonograph—or gramophone, as the Bertons called it—was in the library upstairs.

A suit of armor, as rigid and erect as if a warrior were enclosed in it, stood by the wall just inside the door of the living room. It was complete with helmet, visor and gauntlets. Another suit of armor was in the library, and a third one, in the reception hall, faced any visitor who entered. Whenever he was asked, by some curious guest, why he liked armor as a decoration, Mr. Berton would smile in a slightly embarrassed manner and say that there was no particular reason; that it merely looked attractive. The curtains of all the windows were made of a specially designed fabric—a blue velvet with white and red tracings on it. Silver boxes, containing cigars, cigarettes, sweets and odds and ends, were always lying around on the tables and bookcases. On the cover of each was a Bertonesque emblem or device, a circle in which the sun was shown—either rising or setting—behind a range of hills. The rays of the sun fell on a sheet of water—apparently the sea—in the foreground, on which there was a small sailing vessel. In the middle of the design, across its face, were the initials C. B. This device might be seen on most of the belongings of the Bertons, on trays, pitchers, dishes and on the bookplates pasted in the volumes on the library shelves.

All the books in the library were bound in leather. Whenever the Bertons bought a book they read it and then decided if it should be added to their library. If they wanted to keep it the book was sent to a binder and bound in leather. The bindings were not all of one style; they were of various colors —red, white, green, blue, black—and many of the bindings were covered with intricate golden designs. If a book was not worth keeping it was put in a box reserved for contributions to some charity. The library, with its golden Persian rug, its long shelves of colorful bindings, its delicate odor of leather, and its easy armchairs and tables, was the most comfortable room in the Berton residence, and the only one that seemed, from its appearance, to be really lived in. The huge living room—or salon, as Peggy Berton liked to call it—was, in effect, a show piece that was seldom entered except to receive callers or to entertain a party.

On the thirteenth floor—or second floor of the triplex apartment—there was a small room, without a window, which could be entered only through the library. It was a room made of steel; it was, in fact, a huge fireproof safe, ten feet square, in which Charles Berton kept his valuable rare stamp and autograph collections.

He accumulated rare stamps and faded old letters with the feverish intensity that characterized his father in the accumulation of money. He called his interest in stamps a hobby, but Peggy, his wife, called it a mania.

He possessed one of the famous Mauritius blues of 1847 for which he had paid six thousand dollars. He had also a Baltimore stamp issued in 1845, and an almost priceless New Haven stamp of 1842. These were local stamps issued by a few postmasters; Congress did not authorize the issue of national stamps until 1847. Also, among his cherished possessions was a Brazilian "bull's-eye" of 1843. The stamps issued in Brazil at that time were called "bull's-eyes" because of their oval shape and general appearance. He had a complete collection of Dutch stamps, including those issued only in Java.

The estimated value of the stamp collection, taken as a whole, was a little less than a quarter of a million dollars.

In his autograph collection might be found the signatures of all the signers of the Declaration of Independence, including one of Button Gwinnett, which is the most highly valued of all the names signed to the Declaration, owing to its rarity.

Among his cherished possessions there was an autograph letter written by Marie Antoinette, a letter from Frederick the Great to Voltaire, a letter from Thomas Paine to Benjamin Franklin, a misspelled and ungrammatical letter to one of her lovers from Lola Montez, who almost became queen of Bavaria, and missives of one kind or another from almost every leader of the French Revolution.

6

"Maybe we're too early," said Sheridan Newell, when he arrived at seven o'clock with his wife. "But the invitation gave seven as the time." As he shook hands with Charles and Peggy Berton he looked around the salon and saw that it was empty, though several decanters and a dozen glasses stood on a silver platter placed on a table at one side of the room, in expectation of guests. "No, no, you're just right," Charles Berton laughed. "You haven't yet learned our New York ways, Sherrie. When you invite people for seven o'clock you expect them to blow in sometime between seven-twenty and half-past. I wish everyone came as promptly as you." Then he shook hands with Emmadene Newell and passed her on to Peggy. "Have a glass of sherry, you two," he said and went over to the table.

"Not now, Charlie," Newell shook his head. "I'll take it later. I've been drinking gin rickeys at the Waldorf bar, and I'll let 'em settle before going in for your rare wines. How d'you like my suit?" He wore a tuxedo, which he had bought ready-made, that afternoon.

"It's fine, my lad," Berton said, "just fine. Turn around and let Peggy see it."

Newell turned around slowly, exhibiting his dinner clothes. "You know, Peggy, we never wear such clothes out in the wild and woolly West," he said, "out where men are men." He laughed loudly and fumbled at his tie to be sure that it was on straight. "Out there they wouldn't know what to think of a feller who turned up in a dress suit. I tried to get Emmadene to buy a new dress, but she showed a lot of self-restraint. She's waiting till we get to Paris."

"I'll make this one do," said Emmadene, looking down at her skirt.

"Why, it's a lovely dress," Peggy Berton remarked.

"Made by the best dressmaker in Idaho," Emmadene said with a laugh. "Oh, I mean modiste, not dressmaker, though I must say I don't know the difference."

"There isn't any," said Mrs. Berton. "If the dress is expensive you say it comes from a modiste. If not expensive, then you say a dressmaker made it."

"Peggy," Berton said, "before the others come let's show them the library. Sherrie said they'd like to see it."

"All right," Peggy agreed, "but let's all four of us go, unless you and Sherrie want to have a secret conference. Would you like to look over the place, Emmadene?"

"Sure I would," said that lady. "I've never seen one of these big city apartments."

They walked upstairs, though the triplex apartment had a private elevator of its own, and inspected half a dozen rooms, chatting rather facetiously all the time. The two Westerners were especially charmed with the sun parlor. From it they could look across the Hudson and over miles of the New Jersey landscape in the face of the setting sun. It's fine, Sheridan Newell thought, but it doesn't compare for a moment with the great sweeping views we can get from any one of a half dozen mountains around our place in Idaho. That was a comment which he left unsaid.

When they got back to the living room, or salon, Joseph Powell and Belle, his wife, had arrived. Berton introduced them to his Western friends. "Joe Powell here," he said, "produces every day a column called *Powell's Pick-Ups*. Mostly about people, but it has also bits of verse, jokes and miscellaneous items."

"I've seen it, it's very clever," Newell remarked. "I don't see how you manage to produce it every day. I'd have to work a month on one column, and then it wouldn't be any good."

Greatly pleased at this comment, Powell grinned and said, "Well, it isn't easy, I must say, but I'm used to the work. They say you can get accustomed to anything." Then he laughed loudly without any particular reason. He was short, blond and round-faced, a smiling little man who seemed to be always amused at something. Sheridan Newell, with his height of six foot three, was nearly a foot taller than the columnist, and they were a strange-looking pair when they stood close together; the lean, tall, sunburned rancher and rolypoly, pale city man who had to look up to see Newell's face.

Powell, a good-natured person, was inclined to think the best of everybody and everything. No hints of scandal ever appeared in the personal notes in his column, nor any half-veiled innuendoes. Sometimes he criticized people, but only mildly, and always accompanied the criticism with a note of praise about some other aspect of the person's character or accomplishments. To some of his readers—to Charles Berton, for instance—Powell's faith in the deep, underlying goodness of human nature seemed somewhat overdone. Most people, however, liked that quality of his column.

By seven-thirty all the guests had arrived and their high-pitched voices resounded in the paneled living room. Professor Broome, standing by the mantel and chatting with his host, wondered why people speak louder at social gatherings than they usually do at home, but he did not say anything about that to Charles Berton; their talk concerned the weather and the probability of its remaining cool and fair during the coming week. James the butler, who was the gravest and most dignified person in the room, went here and there with glasses of sherry on a tray.

It was not customary to serve cocktails as an apéritif at homes, for the cocktail had not yet attained its present high standing as a social accessory, although it was popular in theatrical and sporting circles. While the guests were waiting for dinner to be announced the host, as a rule, had glasses of sherry, or some other wine, passed around, though in some homes the apéritif was a rye or bourbon highball.

Everybody in the Bertons' living room took a glass of sherry except Edith Burlingame. She wanted the wine, for she was tired and low-spirited, but she thought that it might reflect on the sincerity of her prohibition work in the minds of those present. Moreover, she hoped that someone would make a remark concerning her refusal of the sherry, and that would give her a legitimate excuse to say a few words about the curse of liquor drinking and the benefits of prohibition. But apparently nobody noticed her abstention or cared anything about it, so her remarks remained unspoken.

Joseph Powell went with the Newells around the room as they were introduced to the guests. He hoped that they might say something that he could print in his column. Already a paragraph was forming itself in his mind. It ran in this fashion: "Sheridan Newell, jovial cattle king from Idaho, is in New York with his charming wife. They intend to sail next week for Europe where they will spend the summer. Last Monday evening Mr. Newell, who is called Sherrie by his friends, was a guest at a dinner given by the Charles Bertons, and he held the company spell-bound with his stories of the wild West. One of his anecdotes concerned—" Right there Joe Powell stopped. He hoped that before the evening was over Newell would tell a humorous story or relate an interesting experience. But if nothing worth while was said by the gentleman from Idaho or his charming wife Mr. Powell would not be at much of a loss, for he knew plenty of stories and jokes that he could, and often did, put in the mouths of people mentioned in his column.

This practice was usually—but not always—gratifying to those who were mentioned as storytellers. Some of the reputed raconteurs were really as solemn as owls, and purposely so, for they wanted to be looked upon as leaders of the thought and philosophy of the age, and a reputation as a joker and funny fellow hardly fitted in with their conception of the career they had in mind.

Now and then the dignified subject of a pleasing but laughable anecdote, or the supposed teller of one, threatened to sue Powell and the *Evening Star,* but nothing ever came of these threats, for how in the world would the courts handle a suit for libel in a case where the misrepresentation consisted of nothing but too much praise?

While the guests were standing in chattering groups Stella Starr glided across the room to where Dr. Jason Broome stood talking to Charles Berton. She stood at the tall, white-haired professor's side, glancing up at him and sipping her glass of sherry. In a moment Berton walked away, then Miss Starr said, "Doctor Broome, I must thank you for some very interesting hours that I spent with your *Colonial Men and Women.* I finished reading it last week."

She had never read it at any time, as she did not read books at all. When Myra Kleppner had given her a list of Dr. Broome's works that morning she picked out the book on colonial people because the title sounded interesting, then she told Miss Kleppner to get the book at once from the Society

Library and make a digest of it and turn the book and the résumé of it over to her by five o'clock. Myra Kleppner was already familiar with the contents of the volume and had no difficulty in making a digest. While Miss Starr lay in her bath that afternoon she read the three-page digest several times and memorized all its leading points, then she picked up the volume and turned its pages, looking long at the many illustrations and chapter headings.

"I feel greatly complimented, Miss Starr," said Dr. Broome, bowing. How do you find time to read, with all your social and business engagements?"

"I make time, but even so, my reading is scrappy—a half hour now and then. *Colonial Men and Women* is the first book of yours that I've read. I am so excited by it that now I intend to read them all." She laughed and said, "May I ask how you find time to write such wonderful books?"

"Oh, it's my business; it's my trade. I go to it every day just as you go to your business of beautiful garments. I'd like very much to know what interested you most in my book?"

"Oh, I was interested in all of it, every chapter, every page. I learned so much from it. Until I read *Colonial Men and Women* I thought they burned the witches at Salem, but I know now that they hanged the poor old women. Why do people speak of witch burning?"

"Well, they were burned in England, and all over Europe," said Dr. Broome. "Many people here in America think, as you did, that the colonials went in for roasting them."

"What I like most about the book," Miss Starr continued, "is that you make the people live. They're not just dummies or patterns cut out of paper; they're live, red-blooded, three-dimensional." (Miss Starr had memorized these expressions from Myra's comments on the book.) "I feel that I know them, and I wouldn't feel much surprised to meet Roger Williams or Jonathan Edwards in the street."

"I'm glad to hear that, for the sense of life is what I try at all times to put into my histories. What colonial is your favorite, if you have any preference?"

"Why, Anne Hutchinson, above all others. Maybe that's just because I'm a woman. I'd read of her before, but you've made her live and breathe for me."

"Anne was an extraordinary character," the professor said. "If she were living now she'd be a leader in the woman suffrage movement."

"Indeed she would," Miss Starr agreed. She spoke then to Mrs. Burlingame, who was standing near and looking over some magazines lying on a table. "I've just been reading *Colonial Men and Women,* Mrs. Burlingame," she said, "and I've been much impressed by Anne Hutchinson. What do you think of her?"

"Splendid woman!" Mrs. Burlingame said with feeling. "A real leader, a woman of spirit, and unafraid. But she lived two hundred years before her time. I wish she were here in this land today. With her courage, her wisdom and her help we'd make the old mossbacks down in Washington realize that the right to vote belongs to women as well as to men."

She laid down the magazine which she had been holding in her hands and came over to Miss Starr and Dr. Broome. For a few minutes she talked about woman suffrage.

Within those two or three moments Stella Starr became a suffragist. She had heard the suffrage movement discussed, pro and con, for several years, but she had never taken a definite "attitude" toward it. It was not close enough to her own affairs to be worthy of her attention, she thought. But her general impression had been unfavorable. "Why, in the world, do they want to vote?" she had said to some of her close friends. "I'm neither for 'em or against 'em, but I do think that women have enough troubles without going out of their way to look for more. The movement is run by a lot of lonely, idle women who can't get a man."

Her conversion to the cause came about not because of anything Edith Burlingame said, for Miss Starr hardly listened to her remarks, but because of the circumstances in which they were made. In the first place, Mrs. Burlingame held herself straight, her head erect, and she spoke with such a clear and pleasant enunciation that the mere sound of her voice was charming. In the second place, Mrs. Burlingame wore in her earrings a pair of the most beautiful diamonds that Stella Starr had ever seen. They must have cost a fortune. And last, but not least, she was greatly impressed by the deference shown by Professor Broome to Mrs. Burlingame and her arguments. The learned professor was a man of much distinction, and surely he would not be so attentive to an inferior person, or to one who stood for an unworthy cause.

While the suffragist advocate was talking, dinner was announced. Charles Berton bowed gracefully to Mrs. Newell, offered her his arm and conducted her through the wide door of the dining room. She was to sit at his right. The rest of the company followed and seated themselves according to the place cards at the plates. The table was lighted by candles in silver candlesticks that had shades of pierced silver lined with pink silk. On the table was a great centerpiece of pink sweet peas and lilies of the valley.

The dinner was not elaborate, but it had six courses, beginning with oysters on the half-shell and ending with ice cream (served in fancy shapes) for dessert. Between the oysters and the ice cream there were soup, a fish, guinea hen and salad, besides various vegetables, and such side dishes as salted almonds and celery stuffed with cheese. It was served by a butler and two footmen.

A French white wine was served with the first two courses, and with the third course burgundy or champagne, according to the diner's preference.

7

Robert Mitchell was full to bursting with the topic of the Auto Carnival. "It's by far the most attractive one we've ever had. Even if you can't spare the time to watch the various stunts, such as the hill climbing and maneuvers—and they'll be well worth seeing, let me tell you—I advise you by all means to go down to Madison Square and look over the show. I mean the new models on exhibition. The auto makers are abandoning the old freight-car type that weighs a ton or more and are developing light cars that run fifteen miles on a gallon of gasoline."

"That so?" This from Henry Burlingame who spoke as if he doubted the information. "I've had several autos in my time, and the most economical one I ever owned could make only nine miles to the gallon."

"Well, you can take it from me," Mitchell asserted, "that the new cars do very much better. There's the Haynes, for instance. I rode in one about twenty miles today over country roads. Fifteen miles to the gallon—and as for easy riding—it's like riding on a cushion. The new Ford uses even less gas, but otherwise it's just a rattletrap—a car for farmers and plumbers and so on, not for people who value comfort and appearance. If you buy a new car just give the Haynes a trial. It has many points of superiority and its cost has been cut down to $3,000."

"Who does the advertising for the Haynes?" This question came from Miss Starr.

Robert Mitchell looked a bit flustered, and paused a moment before he said, "I do their advertising, but wait, hold on. I was speaking just now as a mere bystander. I wouldn't let the advertising account influence me in conversation with friends."

Everyone present, except Robert Mitchell, burst into laughter. Charles Berton shook his finger at Mitchell when the laughter had subsided and said gravely, "Never work after office hours, Bob." Mitchell looked rather sour and said grouchily, "I'll say no more; have it your own way."

"I wonder if the automobile is here to stay, or is it just a fad," said Edith Burlingame. "I mean, will it be a factor in our national life in the future, or will it continue to be a rich man's toy, for that is certainly what it is today."

Dr. Broome said he thought it would be a permanent feature of American life. "The price will be reduced in the course of time. There's that fellow Ford; he's selling his cars right now at about $600 apiece, I believe. I think the auto has a big future."

"But I doubt if Henry Ford will get anywhere with his cheap contraption," said Robert Mitchell. "Automobiles are luxuries—naturally—and I don't believe there'll ever be a large demand for them among the common people."

Charles Berton said, "I ran into Duncan Curry today at the club. He's the automobile editor of the Hearst newspapers and is considered an authority on the subject. Well, he says the automobile age is just beginning and that by the time the demand for cars is filled there'll be a million automobiles running around in this country."

"A million!" This exclamation of Henry Burlingame was

reflected by a look of astonishment on the faces of others at the table. "How many are there now?"

"Curry said he wasn't sure, but he thought that about two hundred thousand machines were in use today."

"Well, let's do a little figuring," said Jason Broome. "A million autos. There are about ninety million people in this country. That means one car to ninety people. No, I don't agree with his estimate. It's far too high. The people can't afford a million autos."

"I think you're right," said Robert Mitchell, coming back into the conversation. "The saturation point, I think, will be reached when half a million cars are in use. After that the new cars will be needed only for replacements." [2]

"This talk of automobiles and their future," said Edith Burlingame, "reminds me of something that has often occurred to me. We're so close to the nineteenth century that we haven't yet got the achievements of that century into their proper perspective, but I've often thought that in the century that ended eight years ago more progress was made than in all the centuries that came before." She turned toward Professor Broome and said, "Am I right?"

"Well, it depends on what you mean by progress," the professor replied.

"I mean inventions that save labor, make life easier, make work more productive."

"Yes, you're right; most decidedly. More was accomplished in that direction during the nineteenth century than in all the previous history of the human race," said Doctor Broome. "The facts are startling. In histories that may be written in the future—say three or four hundred years from now—I have no doubt that the nineteenth century will be given some fanciful name, such as the Glittering Age, the Century of Achievement, the Century of Awakening, or something of that kind."

"I never, never thought of that before," said Peggy Berton, rather breathlessly. "The nineteenth century always seemed to

[2] Both estimates were miles away from the truth. In 1941 the number of passenger cars registered in the United States was 32,557,954; and the production of passenger cars during that single year amounted to 3,744,300.

me just about like the ones that came before, except there was more exploration and the world was getting more civilized. Tell us about it, Professor."

Jason Broome laughed. "The story of the nineteenth century is rather too long to be told at a dinner party, but—well, let's see—here are a few high spots.

"Let's go back one hundred years ago—to the year 1808. This house would have been lighted by candles. The houses were never well lighted, and the streets were all dim or completely dark after nightfall. The nineteenth century brought illumination into the world, and most of the great improvements in lighting came after the middle of the century. They did not exist in 1808—a hundred years ago."

"How about gaslight? Didn't it come in use about that time?" This question came from Ruth Mitchell, who was interested in inventions and the origin of things, and who had read much on that subject.

"No," said Doctor Broome, "the first use of illuminating gas was in the 1820's, and I think it was first used here in New York, though I'm not sure. There were whale-oil lamps, too, in 1808, as well as candles, but the candles were much preferred, for the whale oil had a bad smell and was very smoky. I forgot to say that matches were unheard of; you struck a flint to set fire to tinder or cotton, and from that flame you lighted your candle."

"Must have been hard on pipe smokers," Sheridan Newell remarked.

"It was. If the pipe happened to go out while the smoker was taking a walk in the country he just had to make the best of it unless he had brought the flint and tinder with him.

"When I spoke of houses being lighted by candles," the professor continued, "I mentioned this house, but it happens to have sixteen stories, and of course there were no buildings of this kind a hundred years ago. Elevators were not in use until the 1850's and one could hardly expect tenants to walk up sixteen floors. Besides, it would have been impossible to build a house of this kind until steel girders were made. I don't know when they came into use, but it was, I think, about thirty years ago."

"A sixteen-story building would have been one of the wonders of the world a hundred years ago," said Charles Berton. "Like the pyramids or the Sphinx."

"That's so," said Doctor Broome, "and I think one of the most interesting things about human nature is that we get accustomed so quickly to wonderful things. Just think of what a mystery the telegraph is, and the telephone—yet we handle them as if we knew all about them.

"If you wanted to send a message in 1808 to someone in—well, let's say Savannah, Georgia—the quickest way would have been to send it by sea, by a sailing vessel, which would take about a week to make the trip from New York to Savannah. A messenger on horseback couldn't do it under ten days. There were no railroads, no steamers, no automobiles; and the telegraph and telephone were far in the future.

"Plumbing was unheard of. Whenever you took a bath, which would not be daily, but one a week if you were fussy, the tub was filled by water brought in buckets. Bedrooms had washstands with basins that were filled from water pitchers. There was no central heating, in the winter the hallways and bedrooms were freezing cold."

"I don't think there's anything exceptional about that," Sheridan Newell remarked. "Most of the houses in this country have no steam-heating or plumbing today. These conveniences are common enough in the cities, but not in the country, unless I'm greatly mistaken. I had plumbing and running water put in our house on the ranch out in Idaho only four years ago——"

"And it's always getting out of order," said his wife.

"Yes, we pump the water from a deep well and the engine gets stuck, or the pipes clog, or something. On the whole, however, it's an improvement over the old water-bucket method. But still we have no central heating—just the good old fireplace and logs of wood."

When the dinner was over Mrs. Berton rose and led the way into the living room where coffee was served and delicate glasses of brandy and Benedictine were passed around to those who desired them.

The professor, seated comfortably on a sofa, took a pony of brandy from the butler and said, "One of the most curious facts in history is that for two thousand years, or more, the human race went on living in pretty much the same way, then all of a sudden it began to invent this and that."

"Typesetting and printing goes back to Gutenberg," said Joseph Powell, "away back to 1400 and something."

"Yes, that's right," Professor Broome agreed. "A few inventions came into use during the early centuries, but on the whole the homes of the people who lived in 1808 differed only slightly from the homes of the fifteenth century. If we could bring a man or woman of the year 1808 into this house right now that person would be too bewildered to speak, and would probably go mad with terror after someone pressed a switch and turned on the electric lights and spoke over the telephone and took the stranger from the last century down in the elevator to the ground and then took him or her on a trip around the city in a carriage that had no horses or, apparently, anything else to pull it.

"But that person from the year 1808 could be taken back into time—not forward, but backward—to, let us say, the year 1508, and he would feel pretty much at home."

"What do you consider the most important invention of the last century, Doctor Broome?" Ruth Mitchell asked the question, and eagerly awaited the professor's reply.

"That's a difficult question to answer," he said after some quiet reflection, "because there are several inventions of almost equal importance."

"Maybe it's the telephone," Joseph Powell remarked. "One of the vice-presidents of the telephone company told me that if we had no telephones in New York no less than fifty thousand messenger boys would be needed to carry messages here and there."

"Nonsense," Professor Broome exclaimed. "If the telephone had not been invented every one of us here this evening —and virtually everybody else in the city—would be trained in telegraphing. I venture to say that telegraph instruments would be installed in most houses and apartments, and in business offices and in booths at the corner drugstores.

"Telegraphing is easy to learn; probably it would be taught in the public schools. Then instead of talking to our friends over the phone we'd tap out a message.

"Coming back to the question you asked, Mrs. Mitchell, my opinion is one that may seem strange, but I have reasons for it.

"I think that the invention of the sewing machine by Elias Howe was the most important invention of the nineteenth century from the standpoint of social progress; also it was one of the most ingenious inventions.

"Its great importance comes from the fact that it liberated women from the drudgery of sewing by hand. I think the women of the world ought to put up a monument to Elias Howe as tall as the Statue of Liberty."

"I agree with you completely," Edith Burlingame exclaimed. "Before Howe women were the slaves of the needle."

"Howe was a New England mechanic," the professor continued, "and after many ups and downs he made a machine that would sew. Before his time many others had tackled the problem, but most of them went the wrong way about it. They tried to imitate, by mechanism, the motions of a woman in the act of sewing—that is, passing the needle through the cloth, then turning the needle around and bringing it back the other way.

"Howe didn't try to imitate a seamstress. His conception of the matter was original; he approached the problem in a new way. He put the eye of the needle close to its point instead of at the other end. Then, he invented a shuttle, or lockstitch device, to catch the thread after it had passed through the cloth. The sewing machine is a most ingenious piece of mechanism."

"When was it invented?" Mrs. Newell wanted to know.

"In the early 1840's. Howe was granted a patent in 1846," the professor answered, "though he had made a machine four or five years before that. He almost starved while he was working on the invention, but the machine became so popular and was sold in such numbers when it was offered to the people that Howe made a lot of money, and before he died he was a rich man."

Later in the evening, some of the guests played lotto and parchesi but most of them merely talked. Card playing was not then fashionable as an after-dinner diversion. The women surrounded Stella Starr and asked her many questions about the coming fashions.

The guests went home around eleven o'clock. Before parting Miss Starr said to Mrs. Burlingame, "I want to ask one favor of you, Mrs. Burlingame, and I hope you'll not consider me presumptuous. I'm in favor of woman suffrage, and I've thought of writing you a letter to tell you what splendid work you're doing for the cause. But I didn't know you, and I hesitated.

"Now, here is what I want to ask you. In my business I employ about seventy-five girls and women. I wonder if it would be too much trouble, or interfere with your plans, to come in some day, have tea with all of us and then give the girls a talk—for, say half an hour—on the suffrage cause. I'm sure it would do a lot of good."

"Why, yes, I'd love to do just that, but how about your business, customers coming in and so on?"

"Oh, my dear, that's easily arranged. We'll keep only a skeleton staff at work that day after you arrive. Will four o'clock be convenient to you?"

"Yes, four's all right," said Mrs. Burlingame. "When? Will next Thursday do?"

"Thursday will be excellent," said Miss Starr

"Thank you, Stella," Mrs. Burlingame said. "May I call you Stella?"

"Yes, Edith; why not?" said Stella Starr as they parted.

BIBLIOGRAPHY

Adams, Grace: *The Mad Forties*. New York. 1942.

American Social History, as Recorded by British Travellers, compiled by Allan Nevins. New York. 1923.

Anburey, Thomas: *Travels Through the Interior Parts of America.* London. 1789.

Asbury, Herbert: *Gem of the Prairie*. New York. 1940.

Avary, Myrta Lockett: *Dixie After the War*. New York. 1906.

Bayard, Martha: *Her Journal—1794–1797*. New York. 1894.

Beard, Mary R.: *America Through Women's Eyes*. New York. 1934.

Blackwell, Alice Stone: *Lucy Stone, Pioneer of Woman's Rights.* Boston. 1930.

Brooks, Geraldine: *Dames and Daughters of Colonial Days*. New York. 1900.

Brown, Henry Collins: *The Story of Old New York*. New York. 1934.

Brown, Harriet C.: *Grandmother Brown's Hundred Years—1827–1927*. Boston. 1929.

Bruce, Philip Alexander: *Economic History of Virginia in the Seventeenth Century*. (2 vols.) New York. 1896.

Buck, Franklin A.: *A Yankee Trader in the Gold Rush*. Boston. 1930.

Burlingame, Roger: *March of the Iron Men*. New York. 1938.

Engines of Democracy. New York. 1940.

Byrd, William: *Secret Diary of William Byrd of Westover*. Richmond. 1941.

Carlson, Oliver: *This Man Made News*. (A life of James Gordon Bennett.) New York. 1942.

Casson, Herbert N.: *Cyrus Hall McCormick*. Chicago. 1909.

Cobb, Sanford H.: *The Rise of Religious Liberty in America*. London. 1902.

Commons, J. R., and others: *History of Labor in the United States.* (2 vols.) New York. 1918.

Cotton Mather's Diary. 1681–1708. Massachusetts Historical Society, Series 7.

Dewey, Davis R.: *Financial History of the United States*. New York. 1928.

Dexter, Elizabeth Anthony: *Colonial Women of Affairs*. Boston. 1924.

Diary of Sarah Eve in Pennsylvania Magazine of History and Biography. Vol. V.

Dickens, Charles: *American Notes*. Boston. 1867.

Dictionary of National Biography. New York. 1939.
Drinker, Cecil K.: *Not So Long Ago*. (A Chronicle of Medicine and Doctors in Early Philadelphia.) New York. 1937.
Dunbar, Seymour: *A History of Travel in America*. Indianapolis. 1915.
Earle, Alice Morse: *Home Life in Colonial Days*. New York. 1898.
Stage Coach and Tavern Days. New York. 1900.
Finley, Ruth E.: *The Lady of Godey's—Sara Josepha Hale*. New York. 1931.
Fish, Charles R.: *The Rise of the Common Man*. New York. 1927.
Fisher, Sydney George: *Men, Women and Manners of Colonial Times*. (2 vols.) Philadelphia. 1898.
Fiske, John: *Old Virginia and Her Neighbors*. (2 vols.) Boston. 1897.
The Dutch and Quaker Colonies in America. Boston. 1899.
Frink, Margaret A.: *Original Journal of an Adventurous Trip to California in 1850*. Privately printed. n.d.
Gilder, Rodman: *The Battery*. New York. 1936.
Goodwin, Maude Wilder: *Historic New York During Two Centuries*. New York. 1898.
Goodyear, Charles: *The Application and Uses of Vulcanized Gum Elastic*. Published by the Author. New Haven. 1855.
Greene, Follett L.: *Obed Hussey Who, of all Inventors, Made Bread Cheap*. Privately Printed. 1912.
Hone, Philip: *Diary*. New York. 1910.
Hornblow, Arthur: *History of the Theatre in America*. (2 vols.) Philadelphia. 1919.
Hudson, Frederic: *Journalism in the United States from 1690 to 1872*. New York. 1872.
Hulbert, Archer Butler: *Forty-niners*. Boston. 1931.
Iles, George: *Leading American Inventors*. New York. 1912.
Jackson, Emily: *Toys of Other Days*. New York. 1908.
Jackson, Joseph Henry: *Anybody's Gold*. New York. 1941.
Johnson, Clifton: *Old Time Schools and School Books*. New York. 1904.
Kaempffert, Waldemar: *Popular History of American Inventions*. New York. 1924.
Kimball, Fiske: *Domestic Architecture of the American Colonies and of the Early Republic*. New York. 1922.
Kirkland, Edward C.: *A History of American Economic Life*. New York. 1933.
Knight, Sarah: *The Private Journal of a Journey from Boston to New York in the Year 1704*. Albany. 1865.
Langdon, William Chauncey: *Everyday Things in American Life, 1607–1776*. New York. 1939.

LaWall, Charles H.: *Four Thousand Years of Pharmacy.* Philadelphia. 1927.

Lawrence, Henry W.: *The Not-Quite Puritans.* Boston. 1928.

Lee, James Melvin: *A History of American Journalism.* Boston. 1927.

Mabee, Carleton: *American Leonardo. A Life of Samuel F. B. Morse.* New York. 1943.

Martineau, Harriet: *Society in America.* (3 vols.) London. 1837.

McClellan, Elizabeth: *History of American Costume—1607–1870.* New York. 1937.

Ornsbee, Thomas H.: *The Story of American Furniture.* New York. 1934.

Osgood, Herbert L.: *The American Colonies in the Eighteenth Century.* (4 vols.) New York. 1924.

Parkes, Henry Bamford: *Jonathan Edwards, the Fiery Puritan.* New York. 1930.

Parton, James: *The History of the Sewing Machine.* Atlantic Monthly, May, 1867.

Paxson, Frederic L.: *History of the American Frontier, 1776–1893.* Boston. 1924.

Phillips, Ulrich B.: *Life and Labor in the Old South.* Boston. 1929.

Samuel Sewall's Diary. 1674–1729. Massachusetts Historical Society, Series V.

Shortleff, Harold R.: *The Log Cabin Myth.* Harvard University Press. 1939.

Singleton, Esther: *Social New York Under the Georges, 1714–1776.* New York. 1902.

Stannard, Mary N.: *Colonial Virginia; its People and its Customs.* Philadelphia. 1929.

Stevens, William Oliver: *Pistols at Ten Paces.* Boston. 1940.

Stillman, Louis J.: *Mother Lode.* San Francisco. 1934.

Sullivan, Mark: *Our Times,* vols. II and III. New York. 1930.

Train, Arthur, Jr.: *The Story of Everyday Things.* New York. 1941.

Trollope, Frances M.: *Domestic Manners of the Americans.* London. 1832.

Tryon, Rolla M.: *Household Manufactures in the United States, 1640–1860.* Chicago. 1917.

Wecter, Dixon: *The Saga of American Society—1607–1937.* New York. 1937.

Weeden, William B.: *Economic and Social History of New England, 1620–1789.* (2 vols.) Boston. 1890.

Wertenbaker, T. J.: *First Americans, 1607–1690.* New York. 1927.

Wharton, Anne H.: *Social Life in the Early Republic.* Philadelphia. 1902.

White, Stewart Edward: *The Forty-Niners.* New Haven. 1938.

Winsor, Justin: *Narrative and Critical History of America.* Boston. 1884–1889.

Wright, Richardson: *Grandfather Was Queer.* Philadelphia. 1939.
Hawkers and Walkers in Early America. Philadelphia. 1927.
Forgotten Ladies. Philadelphia. 1928.

INDEX